Hollywood At Your Feet

November 25, 1930: The world premiere of Morocco (1930), starring Gary Cooper and Marlene Dietrich.

Hollywood At Your Feet

The Story of the World-Famous Chinese Theatre

by

Stacey Endres and Robert Cushman

POMEGRANATE PRESS, LTD.

LOS ANGELES   LONDON

This is a Pomegranate Press, Ltd. Book.

Hollywood At Your Feet

The Story of the World-Famous Chinese Theatre
By Stacey Endres and Robert Cushman

Copyright 1992 by Stacey Endres and Robert Cushman

First published September 1992 by
Pomegranate Press, Ltd., Post Office Box 8261, Universal City, California 91608
Manufactured in the United States of America

Library of Congress Catalog Card Number: 92-60798
ISBN: 0-938817-08-6

10 9 8 7 6 5 4 3 2 1

For Rudy,
Judith,
and
my parents,
with love, gratitude, and respect.
S.E.

To the memory of Mrs. Evelyn Spray, my extraordinary English teacher at Fort Wayne, Indiana South Side High School, who provided me with a solid foundation in the basics of writing, grammar, and composition;

And to the memory of Mary Pickford, a great star, a great actress, and a great human being, without whose inspiration, enthusiasm, and encouragement, I never would have become professionally involved with the world of film history in the first place.

R.C.

Acknowledgments

We can only thank modern technology for the computer, as well as Patrick Stockstill of the Academy of Motion Picture Arts and Sciences and Lucia Schultz of that organization's Margaret Herrick Library, who trained Stacey on same, without which this book would probably not have seen the light of day until the turn of the century.

We wish to convey a special thank you to film historian Marc Wanamaker of the Bison Archives and photographer Frans Offermans of the Herrick Library who, along with Robert, produced many of the photographic prints contained in these pages, and to Rudy Behlmer who gave us the benefit of his experience as a respected film historian and writer by making helpful suggestions along the way.

Professional services above and beyond the call of duty were cheerfully rendered by attorney Stephen D. Ashley, Ned Comstock of the University of Southern California, Raymond Daum of the University of Texas at Austin, Samuel Gill, Howard Prouty, and Warren Sherk, of the Herrick Library, and Linda Harris Mehr, Library Director. The skills of two other Herrick Library staffers—graphics artist Tina McKenzie, who constructed our Forecourt of the Stars map, and Kathryn Reesman, whose calligraphy enhanced the title page of our presentation manuscript, proved invaluable. And a special acknowledgment to Daniel Sublett of the Ray M. Johnson Studio. Thanks to his computer enhancement of the only known surviving photograph of the four original squares along Hollywood Boulevard, you can better view the imprints and signatures.

Also, Eddie Brandt, Bill Chapman, Bill Gleason, John Kobal, and Lou Valentino made extensive materials available from their personal collections, as did historians Terry Helgesen, Bruce Torrence (Hollywood Historical Collection), and, once again, Marc Wanamaker. Thanks are due these gentlemen, not only for their kindness to us, but for the care they have taken in preserving artifacts of film and theatre history.

And finally, the following Chinese Theatre celebrities and their family members contributed invaluable reminiscences and materials to this book. Without their generous assistance this volume would not be as complete as it is, nor would it have been as much fun to write and research:

Julie Andrews, Gene Autry, Fred C. Bartholomew, Natalie Cantor Clary (daughter of Eddie Cantor), Jackie Cooper, Chris Costello and Paddy Costello Humphreys (daughters of Lou Costello), Deanna Durbin David, Olivia de Havilland, Irene Dunne, Douglas Fairbanks, Jr., Ava Gardner, Charlton Heston and his wife Lydia Clarke Heston, Bob Hope and his sister-in-law Wyn Hope, Van Johnson, Sylvia Fine Kaye (Mrs. Danny Kaye), DeForest Kelley, Deborah Kerr, Walter Koenig, David Ladd (son of Alan Ladd), Jack Lemmon, Mervyn LeRoy, Keye Luke, Arthur Marx (son of Groucho Marx), Ib Melchior (son of Lauritz Melchior) and his wife Cleo Baldon, Hayley Mills, Nichelle Nichols, Victoria Horne Oakie (Mrs. Jack Oakie), Margaret O'Brien, Donald O'Connor, Gregory Peck, Romina Power (daughter of Tyrone Power), Charles "Buddy" Rogers (husband of Mary Pickford), Ginger Rogers, Roy Rogers, Mickey Rooney, Ann Rutherford, George Stevens, Jr., James Stewart, George Takei, Elizabeth Taylor, Lana Turner, Rudy Vallée, Dick Van Dyke, Jane Withers, and Loretta Young.

For their various courtesies and generous cooperation, we wish to thank the following organizations and individuals (in alphabetical order) who helped to make this book a reality:

Academy of Motion Picture Arts and Sciences' Center for Motion Picture Study, Margaret Herrick Library:
The staff, especially Val Almendarez, Sandra Archer, Craig Campbell, James A. Davis, Don Dumas, Carol Epstein, Barbara Hall, Marlene Laskey, Tom McCown, Adrienne Parks, Tim Stansbury, Eve Sullivan, Therese Trujillo, and Daniel Woodruff.
Architectural Digest:
Catherine Richardson
Archive Photos Stock Photo Library:
Eric Rachlis
Alan Berliner Photography:
Alan Berliner, Alex Berliner, and Silvia Mautner
Bettmann Archive:
Peter Dervis and Liz Orr
Beverly Hills Public Library
Eddie Brandt's Saturday Matinee
Leo Burnett Company:
Don Keller and Al Lira
CBS, Inc.
Chapman's Picture Palace

Chen Sam and Associates, Inc.:
    Chen Sam
Cinema Collectors
Collector's Bookstore
Color Media Co. and Hecht Custom Photo/Graphics Lab:
    Leslie Hecht
The Walt Disney Company
Larry Edmunds Bookshop
FPG International:
    Marci Gershel
Globe Photos, Inc.:
    Ray Whelan, Jr.
Ray M. Johnson Studio
Kellogg Company:
    Celeste Clark
KUSC-FM:
    Jim Svejda
Los Angeles County Museum of Art, Film Department:
    Ronald Haver
Los Angeles Public Library:
    Betty Ellison and Tom Owens
Los Angeles *Times*:
    Joan Stern
Lucasfilm, Ltd.:
    Halina Krukowski
Mann Theatre Corporation:
    William F. Hertz, Mary Lyday, and Ted Mann
McNaughton and Gunn, Inc.
    Frank Gaynor and Norma Keller
William Morris Agency:
    Julie Forkert and Jerry Martin
Motion Picture and Television Photo Archive:
    Sid Avery
Museum of Modern Art/Film Stills Archive:
    Mary Corliss
Paramount Pictures, Inc.:
    Alison Jackson
Photofest:
    Howard Mandelbaum
Producers Photographic Laboratory, Inc.:
    Nancy Kennedy and Lee Lawrence
Quartet Films:
    Michael Lah
Sharp & Associates Public Relations:
    Jeff Abraham
Sony Pictures Entertainment:
    Lisa Krohn and Terrance McCluskey
Southwest Color, Inc.
Stone/Hallinan Public Relations:
    Vicki Crawford
Theatre Historical Society of America:
    William T. Benedict
Timic Productions:
    Cindy Smith
Turner Entertainment Co.:
    Richard May

UNICEF (United Nations Children's Fund):
    Adriana Vink
Union of Tao and Man:
    Daoshing Ni
University of California, Los Angeles, Department of Special Collections:
    Hilda Boehm
University of California, Los Angeles, Theater Arts Library:
    Brigitte J. Kueppers and Audrée Malkin
University of Southern California, Cinema-Television Library and Archives of Performing Arts:
    Stephen L. Hanson, Robert Knutson, and Anne Schlosser
University of Texas at Austin, Harry R. Ransom Humanities Research Center:
    Charles Bell
University of Wisconsin, Wisconsin Center for Film and Theater Research:
    Maxine Fleckner Ducey and Reg Shrader
Warner Research Collection:
    Susan Hurlbert and Joan Michaels
World Graphics
and:
    Joe Adamson, Bayard H. Brattstrom, Richard Brian, Joan Cohen, James R. Curtis, Joan Diaz, Terry Diggs, Clarence and Eleanore Endres, Robert Epstein, Lena and Larry Evaristo, Jim Farber, Howard Frank, John Fricke, Robert Furmanek, Bruce Henstell, George Hocutt, Abe Hoffmann, Richard Hudson, Marty Kearns, Troxey Kemper, Richard Lamparski, Clifford McCarty, Leonard Maltin, Sheldon Mehr, Andy Meisler, Dottie Morey, Donald Lee Nelson, Judith Orloff, Darra Romick, Dan Rothschild, Daniel Mayer Selznick, Anthony Slide, Luke Starnes, Mel and Ali Tormé, Rusty Vail, Peter Vieira, Vince Waldron, Marcia Wall, Paul G. Wesolowski, and Betty White.

Photo credits:
    Academy of Motion Picture Arts and Sciences' Center for Motion Picture Study, Margaret Herrick Library; *Architectural Digest*; Archive Photos Stock Photo Library; Authors' Collection; Rudy Behlmer; Alan Berliner Photography; Eddie Brandt's Saturday Matinee; Richard Brian; Chapman's Picture Palace; Lena and Larry Evaristo; Howard Frank; Bill Gleason; Globe Photos, Inc.; Ronald Haver; Terry Helgesen; Bruce Henstell; Cathy and Eric King/Photoking Lab; John Kobal; Michael Lah; Los Angeles *Times*; Mann Theatre Corporation; Ben Martin; Ib Melchior and Cleo Baldon; Museum of Modern Art/Film Stills Archive; Mrs. Jack Oakie; Ginger Rogers; Bruce Torrence Hollywood Historical Collection; UPI/Bettmann Newsphotos; University of California, Los Angeles, Theater Arts Library; University of Southern California, Cinema-Television Library and Archives of Performing Arts; University of Wisconsin Center for Film and Theater Research; Marc Wanamaker/Bison Archives; Lou Valentino; and Rudy Vallée.

1927: Mary Pickford christened a long-winged Alexander Eagle Rock aircraft, which advertised the Grauman prologues in the Chinese Theatre forecourt, with a bottle of milk, as Prohibition was still in effect. Sid Grauman was the owner of the plane (it was delivered to him that July), which was camouflaged to resemble an oriental flying dragon.

Table of Contents

1927: The auditorium featured "a gigantic chandelier of bronze in the form of a colossal round lantern; its only ornaments being rows of incandescent bulbs giving the effect of huge crystal strands."

Ginger Rogers.

Foreword

When I was invited by Sid Grauman to place my hand and footprints in the forecourt of his beautiful Chinese Theatre on September 5, 1939, I couldn't have been more thrilled. I had just returned from a much needed vacation in Hawaii about three weeks before, and was finishing up some retakes at the studio.

I thought about how my prints would look in cement, for all time!—and wanted them to be smaller if I could manage it. I could do nothing about the size of my hands, but my footprints—those I could make smaller. My shoe size was about 5-1/2 and my mother Lela had a smaller size shoe than I: 4-1/2. So, I borrowed a pair of my mother's shoes and slipped my toes into them and stepped into the cement and made my prints!

I sure was glad when I could take off the "cement shoes" and put on my regular walking shoes again.

I am pleased to have this opportunity to share my memories of Hollywood's Chinese Theatre, and in these pages you'll read about the many celebrities represented in the forecourt throughout the theatre's glamorous sixty-five year history.

Ginger Rogers

Sid Grauman felt that having Cecil B. DeMille's production of The King of Kings *open his Chinese Theatre with the film's Los Angeles premiere on May 18, 1927 "was a great break." The film ran at the theatre for 5-1/2 months.*

Preface

The Story Behind the Book

Sometime during 1980, it occurred to us that among the thousands of books on the subject of film history and all related topics no one had ever produced a book exclusively devoted to the history of the Chinese Theatre, Hollywood's most celebrated and visited landmark. We had known each another since 1975 as fellow staff members of the Academy of Motion Picture Arts and Sciences' Margaret Herrick Library (this book is an independent project and not affiliated with the Academy), and felt it would be wonderful to collaborate outside the business office in creating a book that would not only tell the story of the background of the theatre and its founder, Sid Grauman, but also, for the first time, reproduce a photograph of every single person who has ever placed his or her prints in its famous Forecourt of the Stars cement—in the act of performing said ritual.

Sid Grauman, founder of the Chinese Theatre. He said in 1918: "If the show is good and the audience likes it—don't drag it out. Cut it short. Make the audience want more." It was reported that the showman was the originator of the souvenir program as well as the first person to use searchlights in front of a theatre to light up the skies on premiere nights. Sid felt his theatregoers should have a "Theatrical dinner, not just popcorn."

Ted Mann. In 1973 the exhibitor/producer became the first and only individual to be the 100% sole owner of the Chinese Theatre. Several days prior to the 1979 openings of the Chinese II and III Theatres, which were added to the east side of the main structure, he called the Chinese Theatre the "flagship" of the Mann Theatre chain and said, "The Chinese is second to Disneyland in number of Hollywood tourists, and it is to be preserved."

Why, we wondered, had this never been done? Since these ceremonies were so well covered by the news media, and based on our more than twenty years of experience in conducting photographic research, we initially assumed that coming up with the photos would be the proverbial "piece of cake." Wrong! As an exploratory project we began an attempt to locate such photos and soon discovered that, surprisingly, photographs of the celebrities placing their prints at the Chinese are extremely difficult to find.

Deciding to take the plunge and turn our idea into

ing we finally assembled the collection of photographs that appears on the pages of this book.

The research on the theatre itself, the ceremonies, Sid Grauman, and the biographical research on all the celebrities profiled herein was easier, but the work was still time-consuming.

We were greatly encouraged by the immediate enthusiasm for the project by the Mann Theatre Corporation, which had purchased the Chinese Theatre in 1973. The cooperation of Ted Mann, Chairman and Chief Executive Officer, plus the generous

Cecil B. DeMille (left) and Sid Grauman pose in DeMille's office with the contract agreeing that the producer/director's production, The King of Kings *(1927), will be the opening attraction at the Chinese Theatre.*

a reality, we next conducted an all-out campaign to unearth every possible photo of all the Chinese Theatre hand and footprinting ceremonies. Over the next several years, we contacted every conceivable source throughout the world: libraries, museums, archives, newspaper morgues, magazines, commercial stock photo sources, private collectors, fans, friends, and even the celebrities themselves and their families, many of whom graciously contributed memories of the ceremonies. After more than a decade of sleuth-

assistance of his Director of Marketing and Public Relations, William F. Hertz, and his administrative assistant, Mary Lyday, was always enthusiastic and whole-hearted.

On the recommendation of our friend and colleague, Michael Hawks of the Larry Edmunds Bookshop, we contacted Pomegranate Press, whose owners, Kathryn Leigh Scott and Ben Martin, immediately accepted our project.

So, three years following the acceptance, here is our book. We extend our heartfelt thanks to Kathryn and Ben for their belief in this project.

Release dates of films cited are the years in which the films were initially released in their country of origin. The term "debut" means the first picture released, which is not always the same as the first picture produced. In the case of foreign films, the original release title is given first, followed by the English-language title (if any). For celebrities still living, the final film cited is their most recently released credit up to December 31, 1991. The Academy Award nominations and wins for every celebrity are cited, as are the recipients of the American Film Institute's Life Achievement Award and the Kennedy Center Honors. The physical descriptions of each cement square have been carefully checked for accuracy.

This book has been a true collaboration. We freely admit that neither of us could have done this book without the abilities and dedication of the other.

It is our sincere and fervent hope that this volume will stand as an appropriate tribute to all the people who have worked on the creation and operation of the Chinese Theatre over the past sixty-five years, all of the celebrities who are immortalized in the forecourt, and, most importantly, to the memory of the genius who made it all happen, Sid Grauman.

Stacey Endres and Robert Cushman
June 1992

A scene from Cecil B. DeMille's religious spectacle The King of Kings *(Producers Distributing Corp., 1927), starring H.B. Warner as Jesus.*

1927: "Welcome to Hollywood's Chinese Theatre!" An usherette beckons ticket buyers to enter through the theatre's ornate portals. The theatre's official stationery (not shown) was illustrated on the left side with a column of fourteen Chinese ideographs. They told the legend of a beautiful island unlike any other place on the earth where tranquility and longevity could be found. A visit to this island was a trip to Paradise itself. Thus, the tale symbolizes that "the portals of the theatre are the long sought for portals to Paradise."

Hollywood's Chinese Theatre

"Without going out of doors one may know the whole world."
—*Old Chinese Proverb*
printed in the opening night program of
Grauman's Chinese Theatre (May 18, 1927)

Towering majestically above the 6900 block of Hollywood Boulevard is the wondrously impressive Chinese Theatre, the most famous motion picture palace in the world. Completed in 1927, it was the last theatre constructed under the auspices of Sid Grauman, probably the best-known exhibitor in film history, who was alternately (and appropriately) called "Hollywood's Master Showman," "Mr. Hollywood," "The P.T. Barnum of the Movies," "The Ziegfeld of Hollywood," and "The Little Giant of Show Biz."

Throughout its history and up to the present day, the theatre has served as a magnet to the literally thousands of fans and tourists who flock daily to the site to view the fascinating architecture and the cement squares in the theatre's forecourt. Here have been placed the footprints, handprints, and signatures of 176 of Hollywood's most famous celebrities, plus those of three comedy teams, one group of quintuplets, two robots and a villainous sci-fi character, one public official, a contest winner, three horses, one ventriloquist's dummy, a radio character, one U.S. military serviceman, two mothers, and the world's best known duck. There are also two time capsules and nine commemorative plaques honoring three individuals, a beloved fictional British heroine, the "family" of one of filmdom's most popular series, the CinemaScope wide-screen process and the first motion picture to be shot in same, and three anniversaries celebrating the theatre itself, the city of Hollywood, and a television/theatrical film series and its creator that became an international cult phenomenon.

Grauman was a daring showman who rightfully won fame as a "glorifier" of the motion picture as Florenz Ziegfeld had for the American girl. Grauman claimed that "showmanship is like any other merchandising. You must buy desirable material, present it to advantage and price it right. And above all, you must let the world know what you have to sell."

Los Angeles *Times* columnist Lee Shippey wrote in 1933, "When we visited theatres in New York and London and Paris we never knew nor cared who managed them. No one ever visited a Grauman house without knowing it was a Grauman house. We have seen theatres which looked like office buildings or hotels, but when you enter a Grauman house you know you are leaving the world of reality behind and entering the world of make-believe. Sid may go in for barbaric splendor, but, anyway, it's splendor."

To gain an insight into the creative forces that culminated in the Chinese Theatre, one needs to explore the background of the man who conceived it. Sidney Grauman was born in Indianapolis, Indiana, of Jewish parents (David J.—professionally known as D.J.—and Rosa Grauman) on St. Patrick's Day, March 17, 1879. That D.J. and Rosa therefore chose "Patrick" as Sid's middle name seems to indicate that they had a delightful, if unorthodox, sense of humor. In his later years, Sid, who was a religious man, said, "I owe my tremendous success to the Man Upstairs," and then added impishly, "But having a name that got both [the] Jews and [the] Irish behind me was what cinched things."

Sid's father was a minstrel man, and his family followed the small-time show circuits that peppered America during Sid's boyhood. They managed to eke out a subsistence-level living, often going hungry. When the Alaskan gold rush hit the newspapers, Sid and D.J. headed for the Klondike, where they arrived sometime during 1898. The Graumans failed to find gold but managed to make ends meet by putting on shows in Dawson. During the leanest times in Dawson, Sid supplemented the family income by selling newspapers on the street.

Finally, around 1900, the Graumans managed to show a profit and put enough money aside to leave Alaska and migrate to San Francisco, where they opened a small vaudeville theatre, the Unique, which prospered and would ultimately boast such attractions as Sophie Tucker, Al Jolson, and Roscoe "Fatty" Arbuckle, who started out as one of the theatre's ticket takers. The Unique was converted from an old store front on Market Street near Mason. The seating consisted of 800 kitchen chairs, and the only music was provided by a piano.

Sid saw his first motion picture around 1902—a very early primitive which actually showed a train rushing directly at the audience— and was immediately enthralled. He also took note of the tremendous audience response to

Many persons wondered how Sid Grauman's Chinese Theatre could surpass his lavish Egyptian Theatre located nearby at 6712 Hollywood Boulevard. The Egyptian opened in 1922; and its interior featured hieroglyphic murals, a sunburst ceiling, and a giant scarab above the proscenium.

the film and quickly convinced his father to add motion pictures to their programming at the Unique. Even greater success resulted—until the cataclysmic earthquake and fire of 1906. The Unique, and the several other theatres the Graumans owned, were destroyed by the fire. Ever resourceful and quick to act, Sid managed to salvage one projector from the rubble. Then he went across the Bay to Oakland, scouting the area and ultimately renting a huge tent from a traveling preacher called "Cowboy Jack." From an Oakland film exchange he managed to procure some reels of film. He then borrowed a wagon from a local junk dealer, loaded up his tent and film,

and boarded a ferry back to San Francisco. Next he managed to appropriate some pews from a ruined church for seating and had them installed in his tent, which was quickly set up on the vacant lot where the Unique had stood. For the makeshift Grauman's Tent Theatre—the new house was officially called "Grauman's National Theatre"—Sid hand-lettered a sign himself: "NOTHING TO FALL ON YOU BUT CANVAS IF THERE IS ANOTHER QUAKE."

According to some accounts, Sid managed all this within a few days of the quake and fire; and the tent theatre is said to have been the first commercial business to resume operation in the devastated city. The Graumans later received official commendation from the city of San Francisco for contributing to the public morale during this tragic and trying time.

The Graumans expanded their San Francisco holdings over the next few years into several movie theatres and vaudeville houses. A man who remembered those early days recalled that Sid and his father were often spotted standing by the box offices of one of their theatres, shaking hands with everyone who purchased a ticket. This period culminated with their first all-concrete structure in downtown San Francisco on Market Street, the Empress, which had a seating capacity of 1,800. With such success in the Bay Area, by 1917 Sid set his sights on Los Angeles, which had by then emerged as the true center of the motion picture industry. Sid therefore decided that his greatest potential for future expansion and increased success lay there.

Having built a solid reputation as brilliant showmen and promoters in San Francisco, the Graumans

not known for his sense of humor, nevertheless struck a deal with the Graumans, as he was much impressed with Sid's skill, creativity, and track record for filling his theatres with patrons on a regular basis.

As a result of their agreement, Paramount would

January 5, 1926: Sid Grauman (left) with actors Norma Talmadge, Conrad Nagel, and Anna May Wong at the Chinese Theatre ground breaking.

decided to build a huge theatre in Los Angeles. Through film producer Jesse L. Lasky, with whom he had done business (and who once appeared in a Grauman vaudeville house as an unknown, struggling trumpet player), Sid arranged a meeting with Adolph Zukor, who was the head of Paramount Pictures and had come to believe that producers needed to assume control of the exhibition of their films by acquiring theatres, thus maximizing profits, securing future stability, and guaranteeing an outlet for their product. Sid, whose elaborate practical jokes later became legendary in Hollywood, was already an incurable prankster. At this crucial "make-or-break" meeting with the most powerful man in the film industry at that time, Sid switched the sugar with the salt, thereby ruining Zukor's coffee. Zukor, who was

purchase the Grauman theatrical interests in San Francisco and also obtain the financing to construct a colossal movie palace in Los Angeles which Sid would manage and in which he would own an interest. Thus began Sid's entry into the film exhibition scene in Los Angeles. The Grauman debut in the City of Angels could hardly have been more prestigious, as the theatre resulting from the Zukor deal became the lavish Grauman's Million Dollar, the most elaborate motion picture theatre in the Western United States up to that time. It opened in downtown Los Angeles at Third and Broadway on February 1, 1918, and had a seating capacity of 2,345. The premiere was a resounding success, and several thousand patrons were turned away on opening day. The Million Dollar had initially been called "The Rialto" in its planning stages; but Sid ordered the name changed, declaring, "When I spend that much on a house, I want everybody to know it!"

It was during the first few months of the operation of the Million Dollar that the stage presentations which preceded the actual films were first presented. These soon became world famous as the "Grauman Prologues" and were produced at all of Grauman's subsequent theatres, reaching their zenith nine years

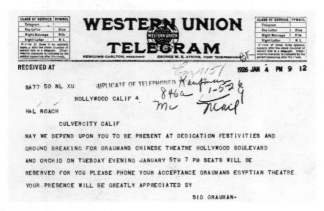

later at the Chinese. The first known mention of the term "prologue" with regard to Grauman occurred in the Los Angeles *Examiner* after the April 1, 1918, premiere of Maurice Tourneur's Famous Players-Lasky production of *The Blue Bird*, based on the Maeterlinck play: "Sid Grauman is preceding the screen drama with a delightful prologue that includes fairies, child dancers, and a musical program of much interest."

In a few years, the Grauman prologues had evolved into extraordinarily lavish theatre pieces, with full-size symphony orchestras, huge casts, and magnificent sets and costumes. Personally produced and supervised by Sid, these prologues were created and designed to fit in thematically with the main feature film that was to follow. They were performed before each screening of the feature throughout its run, and their like has never been seen before or since in the annals of motion picture exhibition. Many theatregoers claimed to have come to see the prologue as much as the feature film, so entertaining were these presentations.

Grauman followed the Million Dollar Theatre opening with an announcement in September 1918 that plans were under way for the construction of a theatre that would seat 3,500 people, thus making it the largest house west of Chicago. The location was to be in downtown Los Angeles on the Sixth and Hill streets corner of Pershing Square, opposite the Biltmore Hotel. The theatre became the mammoth

Grauman's Metropolitan Theatre, which finally opened its doors on January 26, 1923. According to the January 21 Los Angeles *Examiner*, the theatre cost approximately $4,000,000 to construct. It had a seating capacity of 3,485 and the longest concrete girder and truss system yet built in any theatre on earth, in order to support the gargantuan balcony and roof. The Metropolitan still holds the record as the largest motion picture theatre ever built in the city of Los Angeles. (The name was changed to the Los Angeles Paramount Theatre in 1929.)

Conceived, completed, and opened during the years of construction of the Metropolitan was Sid's next massive undertaking: Grauman's Egyptian Theatre in Hollywood. The first public announcement of what was to become the Egyptian appeared in the real estate section of the Los Angeles *Times* on September 26, 1920, which stated, "Sid Grauman plans to build a Class A theatre on Hollywood Boulevard at McCadden Place." One noteworthy curiosity contained in this article is that it mentions the design and motif were to be "of Spanish style." Grauman must have made the radical change to the Egyptian design in the very early stages of planning. Also, since no balcony was ever built, the seating capacity was reduced from the initially planned 2,000 to 1,770. The discovery of King Tut's tomb in November 1922

Ads inviting the public to the event appeared in the local newspapers.

sparked world-wide interest in all things Egyptian and was certainly a wonderful stroke of luck for Sid, as it gave his theatre much free publicity and kindled even greater than normal public interest in it.

Designed by the architectural firm of Meyer & Holler and completed at a reported cost of $800,000, the Egyptian opened with the premiere of Douglas Fairbanks' epic production of *Robin Hood*, complete with lavish Grauman prologue, on October 18, 1922. Sid even supplied the lyric to "Just an Old Love Song," a piece of sheet music based partially on a small portion of the film's score, which was composed by Victor Schertzinger. Today, much of the Egyptian's

purchased], Metropolitan, and Egyptian...be run as smoothly as they were. One marvels at the inexhaustible vitality that Grauman brought to the managing directorship of these four Los Angeles movie houses."

In the midst of this frenzy of activity, Grauman

In early 1926 the construction is about to begin at the site of the future Chinese Theatre. Once an orange grove, the property was the home of actor Francis X. Bushman between 1913 and 1915.

distinctive architectural features have been either dismantled or covered over by numerous remodelings, but at least it still stands and functions as a movie theatre.

In *Hollywood's Master Showman: The Legendary Sid Grauman*, Charles Beardsley points out:

"The year 1923 was one of Sid's busiest and most productive. Only with staffs who were completely willing to assume enormous burdens of responsibility in management, operation, and maintenance could the shows at the Million Dollar, Rialto [which Sid had

launched the beginnings of the project that was to culminate in the construction of the greatest—if greatness is to be measured by fame—achievement of his entire career: Grauman's Chinese Theatre in Hollywood. Toward this end, Grauman first sold his interest in the three downtown theatres to the Paramount/Famous Players-Lasky combine, controlled by Adolph Zukor. He then turned his concentration to running only the Egyptian in Hollywood and initiating the planning for the Chinese. Preliminary announcements in March 1925 proclaimed that

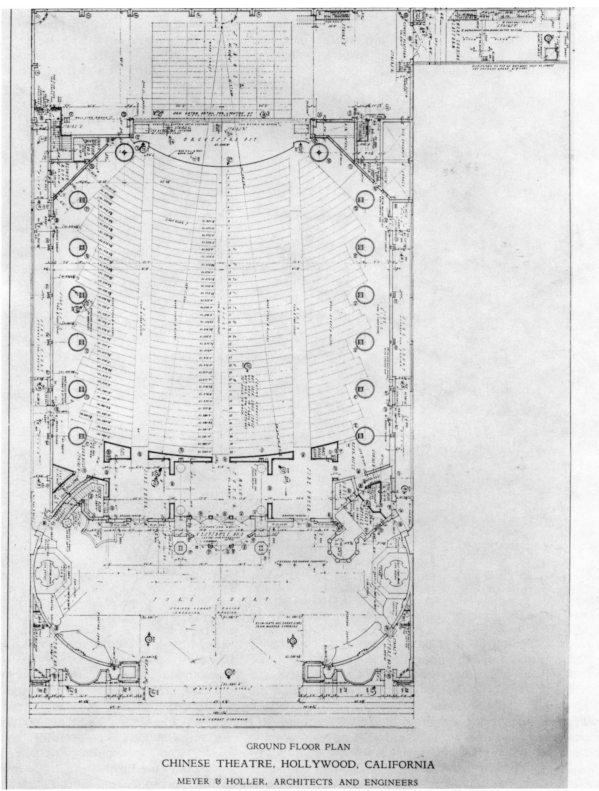

GROUND FLOOR PLAN

CHINESE THEATRE, HOLLYWOOD, CALIFORNIA

MEYER & HOLLER, ARCHITECTS AND ENGINEERS

December 15, 1925: The ground floor blueprint of the Chinese Theatre. Meyer & Holler, Architects and Engineers.

a chain of first-run houses would be built across the country by Grauman and Joseph M. Schenck.

The chain of theatres was never built, but from this initial planning emerged the seeds of the Chinese

iety invested in the project. The architectural firm of Meyer & Holler, which had previously designed the Egyptian, was contracted to construct the theatre. The individuals in the firm who were most directly respon-

The Chinese Theatre shortly before its opening on May 18, 1927. A 1984 Mann Theatres press release states, "An old Chinese Proverb says: 'To visit Los Angeles and not see the Chinese is like visiting China and not seeing the Great Wall.' "

Theatre when Grauman and Schenck narrowed the plans to build only one theatre in Hollywood—a theatre they decided would be the apex of all theatres in terms of originality, design, beauty, luxury, and showmanship. Grauman decided that his new theatre would emerge as his supreme achievement and he fixed his sights on a motion picture palace whose design motif would be ancient Chinese.

The financing was ultimately provided by Sid, Schenck, and C.E. Toberman, a prominent realtor who had many film industry connections. It was also said that Mary Pickford and Douglas Fairbanks qu-

sible for the design (color scheme, furnishings, wall hangings and murals) and construction of the Chinese were architects Raymond Kennedy and D.R. Wilkinson and designer John Beckman. Kennedy, when interviewed by theatre historian Terry Helgesen in 1969 for a pamphlet entitled "Grauman's Chinese Theatre," said the style chosen was not an authentic representation of traditional Chinese architecture, which would have given a heavier feeling, but was taken from the more delicate period of Chippendale. Kennedy followed suggestions made by Grauman and his employers Meyer & Holler and drew on his own architectural training and background in design in drawing plans for the theatre. He also clipped various ads from *Connoisseur* magazine in which Chinese-influenced Chippendale objects were featured.

The ground breaking ceremony for the Chinese Theatre took place on January 5, 1926, at 7:00 p.m. The streets for several blocks near the scene were decorated with banners and Chinese emblems. The

Chinese actress Anna May Wong, and later operated a steam shovel. Conrad Nagel was the master of ceremonies. Celebrities attending the event included Roscoe "Fatty" Arbuckle, Lon Chaney, Charles Chaplin, Lloyd Hamilton, Louis B. Mayer, and Joseph M. Schenck.

Construction went on for slightly over a year, and the final cost was given at approximately $2,000,000.

1927: Chinese Theatre ushers and usherettes wore elaborate outfits copied from ancient Chinese theatrical costumes. They were made from fine fabrics, detailed in gold embroidery, and covered in tiny framed mirrors. The spot girl (bottom center), who examined tickets in order to send patrons to the proper aisle, wore an unusual pheasant headdress.

entire cast of 150 from Grauman's prologue to *The Big Parade* (1925), playing down the street at his Egyptian Theatre, along with the theatre's usherettes, were on hand. Shortly before the ground breaking, forty-some young women walked out on to a platform, each carrying a piece of cardboard with a large letter printed on it, and formed a sign that read: "Grauman's Chinese Theatre, completion December 28, 1926." Norma Talmadge turned the first spadeful of earth with a gold-plated shovel, assisted by

As Charles Beardsley has written:

"The Chinese Theatre [was] the ultimate realization [of Sid's goal], which went beyond even Grauman's most expensive dreams....

"Tirelessly insistent on absolute top quality throughout during the construction of the Chinese, Grauman not only passed on all the major aspects of the house but on just about every single small detail—down to the light switches and the laying of tiles. He personally designed the stage, the largest used by any motion picture house anywhere."

The Chinese originally seated 2,258 spectators. (Numerous alterations over the years and respacing of the seats have diminished the seating capacity to its current 1,400.) The theatre's facade is ninety feet high, and its jade green pagoda roof is fashioned from bronze. It is underlaid by two immense octagonal

of a huge gate or entrance to a great oriental garden, which opens to the view as a gigantic elliptical forecourt with forty-foot walls, planted with full grown cocoa palms and rare tropical trees....

"Chinese vines and verdure droop from the summit of the towering walls and hang from bronze baskets, while beneath on opposite sides of the forecourt, two colossal fountain bowls, ten feet high...catch the spray

In the mid-1930s the original box-office—a dainty Chinese pagoda that still stands in the forecourt's northeast corner—was replaced with one fronting Hollywood Boulevard, which is covered by a Chinese-style walk way leading to the theatre's entrance doors. For many years this box-office sat atop the Wallace Beery/Marie Dressler square until their block was relocated.

piers of coral red topped by huge wrought iron masks. Set between the piers is an immense stone dragon modeled in relief on a slab thirty feet square. The towering minarets on either side of the forecourt are of burnished copper. The opening night program also described the following features:

"A solid facade of masonry, forty feet high, surmounted by four ornate obelisks, presents the effect

from bronze gargoyles above, illuminated at night by gorgeous jeweled lamps casting iridescent rays....

"The center doily of the [auditorium] ceiling, sixty feet in diameter, is entwined with immense silver dragons in relief bordered with a circle of giant gold medallions....

"From the center is suspended a gigantic chandelier of bronze in the form of a colossal round lantern....The interior of the chandelier is a solid mass of light bulbs making possible a thousand different color combinations....

"The stage is flanked by two gigantic gold lanterns, thirty feet high, cleverly wrought to suggest the eva-

"The stage is one of the largest in the world....Its dimensions are 150 feet wide, seventy-one feet high and forty-six feet deep....

"The stage floor is ingeniously built in sections, making it possible to drop a portion or the entire stage

Usherettes stand beside projection booth equipment for a 1927 publicity pose. (They were not the actual projectionists!)

nescent shimmering sunlight upon waterfalls.

"The entire decorative scheme of the theatre is a color symphony, based on the one dominating color of Chinese art, red, interpreted in ruby, crimson, pale scarlet and coral lacquer, with complementary hues to provide contrasting values and accents, and bronze, gold, stone, and silver in their natural hues as principal embellishments....

"The carpets and rugs of the foyers were woven in China after designs prepared to harmonize with the theatre itself....

"The main auditorium...gives the impression of entering a gigantic shrine at the time of the Five Emperors or the Dynasty of Hsia....The massive effect is created through two rows of colossal stone columns on each side of the auditorium, octagonal in shape and seven feet in diameter, reaching the lofty ceiling....

to a twenty-foot pit beneath for disappearing or appearing sets of any magnitude....

"All the power and lighting used on the stage is developed by its own power plant and an auxiliary dynamo system makes the entire theatre independent of outside electricity....

"The retiring rooms are models of their kind, the ladies' room being solidly paneled with full length wall mirrors, each with a gold receptacle for powder and toilet articles....

"When you have visited Grauman's Chinese Theatre, Hollywood, you have seen the most wonderful playhouse in the entire world."

Most people found all of this most impressive and very beautiful indeed, but the theatre was not without its detractors. It was reported that Harry K. Thaw, the assailant of Stanford White in the infamous murder case of 1906, was visiting Hollywood shortly after the completion of the Chinese. On seeing the startling new

The auditorium in 1927: Sid Grauman's private box—The Cathay Lounge—was to the left of the projection booth (above center). The seats in the auditorium were made of red leatherette with fanciful flower designs in black, and boasted black and gold seat cushions. The jade green carpet was woven with images of clouds and dragons.

The auditorium in 1927: Huge octagonal marble pillars are on both sides of the auditorium. Behind them are brick walls painted in Chinese red lacquer, with delicate designs of trees and birds done in silver that create an outdoor feeling. Note the pagoda balcony with imperial yellow tile roof at left.

Stone-carved "Heaven Dogs" flank the main entrance to the Chinese Theatre. These ferocious-looking animals were first sculpted in China in 177 B.C. This pair is an authentic creation, dating from the Ming Dynasty (1368-1644) and was imported from China by Sid Grauman in 1927.

According to the theatre management, "'Heaven Dogs' were believed by the Chinese to ward off evil spirits and were widely used to guard the sacred Ming tombs in the interior of China." These creatures, surnamed the "Dogs of Foo" and/or "Dogs of Buddha," are half lion/half dog and "combined leonine ferocity with dog-like devotion and served to terrify the transgressors and inspire the righteous."

(Above) May 27, 1930: The world premiere of Howard Hughes' Hell's Angels was the most spectacular event of its kind ever staged in Hollywood history. Searchlights were planted throughout nearby hills, and the souvenir programs were made of hand-tooled leather and embossed with gold. A genuine World War I German Fokker D VII aircraft complete with spinning propeller hung in the forecourt during the run of the picture. The cost of an ordinary premiere in the 1930s ran from $5,500 to $10,000, while a real extravaganza could often cost up to $50,000 or more.

(Right) A poster advertising Howard Hughes' "Thrilling Multi-Million Dollar Air Spectacle" Hell's Angels. Released by United Artists (1930).

edifice, he stopped in his tracks, clasped his hand to his head, and exclaimed, "My God! I shot the wrong architect!"

And designer John Beckman recalled shortly before his death in 1989, "We had to turn the main roof

"A Shrine to Art" points out, "a king's ransom in rich art treasures" was imported from China for installation in the theatre. Foremost among those surviving are the massive stone-carved "Heaven Dogs," placed on both sides of the main entrance. These ferocious-

The auditorium in the early 1930s: A life-size figure of an unnamed "Chinese ambassador of dramatic philosophy" stands above the proscenium. Behind him is a gigantic bronze medallion of the "six immortal philosophers of dramatic genius." The original curtain was a pale gold silk velvet painted with silver trees.

over the entrance into a proper green, but it was hard to hold the chemicals on that vertical slant. So when the sun beat down, every so often the copper would pop off like snowflakes and burn holes into the clothes of the people below. We bought quite a few suits and dresses and took quite a lot of criticism." Also, while the delicate scent of perfume that wafted through the theatre made some members of the audience imagine they were inside a Chinese palace, others complained of simply feeling ill.

In the planning and design of the furnishings of the Chinese, researchers pored over more than 20,000 photographs of Chinese art, architecture, costuming, and furniture. As the 1938 Chinese Theatre brochure

looking animals were first sculpted in China in 177 B.C. This pair is an authentic creation, dating from the Ming Dynasty (1368-1644) and was imported from China by Grauman in 1927.

Many of the theatre's original features, furnishings, and fixtures have been altered or removed over the years. The huge metal and crystal pagodas that flanked each side of the stage were reluctantly removed in 1929 when the talkies arrived because sound vibrations from the new speakers caused the pagodas to shake and give off an audible tinkling sound which disturbed the audience. Many other ornamental features were eliminated in subsequent remodelings. The most noticeable one was in 1958 when a considerable portion of the stage was removed and the projection booth was relocated from its position in the upper mezzanine level and rebuilt at the rear center of the main floor, thereby eradicating the central auditorium doors. The lantern in the chandelier and the Wurlitzer pipe organ also disappeared at this time. Over the years, when the carpets wore out, copies were substituted; and when the copies wore out, other floor coverings were installed. And the original seats, with their beautifully carved wood backs, have long since vanished. Additional exterior "face-lifts" and remodeling projects took place in 1953 (to accommodate CinemaScope), 1969, and 1979. The installation of the "Sensurround" process for the 1974 release *Earthquake* actually caused pieces of ceiling plaster to crack and fall; so nets were installed to catch any falling particles lest they injure anyone in the audience.

However, the basic structure, character, and much of the original architectural detail and design still survive. A good deal of the intricate detailing and furnishings may be gone, but the initial and primary impact of the Chinese Theatre remains, and the structure still commands the attention of the many visitors per year who marvel at its uniqueness. To protect the Chinese from any future inappropriate alterations, the City of Los Angeles Cultural Heritage Board recognized its importance by declaring it Los Angeles Historic-Cultural Monument No. 55, on June 5, 1968, stating, "Grauman's Chinese Theatre is an example of an era in Hollywood that will never be surpassed. It is the zenith of exotic architecture, familiar to millions the world over."

When Ted Mann became the owner of the theatre in 1973, he did everything possible to preserve what survives of the original theatre. Mann showed a keen sense of awareness of and appreciation for the building's historical importance, and his actions with regard to this issue were exemplary. Rather than further alter the main auditorium by cutting it into separate theatres, he opted to build two additional adjacent smaller houses in 1979—the Chinese II and the Chinese III—thereby saving the original configuration of the auditorium. Mann estimated that he could have saved half of the $3,000,000 the additional theatres cost to build "by chopping up the original Chinese into three theatres. But there was never any real question of that." Also, Mann installed the Lucasfilm THX Sound System in 1984, thereby greatly enhancing the theatre's sound quality.

Mann received some criticism from the news media when in 1973 he officially changed the name of the theatre from "Grauman's Chinese Theatre" to

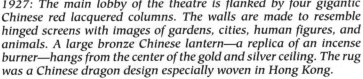

1927: The main lobby of the theatre is flanked by four gigantic Chinese red lacquered columns. The walls are made to resemble hinged screens with images of gardens, cities, human figures, and animals. A large bronze Chinese lantern—a replica of an incense burner—hangs from the center of the gold and silver ceiling. The rug was a Chinese dragon design especially woven in Hong Kong.

"Mann's Chinese Theatre." However, he did not physically *remove* "Grauman's" from the actual theatre exterior. That deed had been accomplished during the 1957-1958 remodeling by the then owners, Fox West Coast Theatres, when the huge vertical signs spelling out the name "Grauman's" were removed from the extreme east and west front corners of the building. (Fox West Coast had paid for the privilege of keeping them up to that time.) Los Angeles *Times* writer Charles Champlin expressed the opinion of many when he wrote in his December 5, 1975 column that the Mann name change "...seemed a reasonable move, on the grounds that when you have laid out $67,000,000 in cash for a chain of theatres, you buy the right to hang your shingle and let folks know you are in town."

Back to 1927: The opening night of the Chinese Theatre occurred on May 18, with the Los Angeles premiere of Cecil B. DeMille's epic production *The King of Kings*, which had opened in New York the previous month. (The film originally was to have had its world premiere at the Chinese. Various delays in the completion of the theatre caused Grauman to set back its official opening date, and he announced the May 18 date on April 25.) An estimated 50,000 people jammed the area in front of the theatre on Hollywood Boulevard and crowded the nearby streets between La Brea and Highland avenues in

Actor Keye Luke, best remembered for his portrayal of the Number One Son of detective Charlie Chan in several films during the mid-1930s, was also a talented artist. He grew up in Seattle, Washington, and showed a remarkable aptitude for drawing and painting as a boy. Coming to Los Angeles in the late 1920s, Luke began to look for work as an artist in the motion picture industry. Fox West Coast Theatre chain executive Harold B. Franklin was impressed with Luke's portfolio and hired him on the spot. Luke, whose work for the Chinese Theatre included some of the interior paintings, told the authors, "The association with Sid Grauman was most pleasant, and his mother was most sweet." Luke soon found himself a successful performer on film (The Good Earth [1937]), stage (Flower Drum Song [1958]), and television ("Kung Fu" [1972-1975]). Examples of his art work in film include murals in The Shanghai Gesture (1941) and Macao (1952). He died in 1991.

hopes of catching a glimpse of some of the celebrities who paid $11 per ticket to attend the opening. That section along Hollywood Boulevard had been made into a one-way street for the occasion, and over 300 police were on hand to preserve order. Such an impressive array of guests had probably never before been assembled for a motion picture premiere. As the program pointed out, without exaggeration, "Governors, mayors, generals, admirals, judges, millionaires, screen and stage stars of the first magnitude, city, county, state, and federal executives, producers, directors, authors—they have come—one and all—many crossing the continent just for tonight's festivities."

Sid's line-up for the preliminary speeches and introductions was certainly a knock-out: Fred Niblo (distinguished director of *Ben-Hur* [1925]) walked on the stage and introduced D.W. Griffith as master of ceremonies, who in turn introduced Will H. Hays, who next presented Mary Pickford, certainly the most prominent woman in the entire film industry at that time. Pickford formally began the evening's performance by pressing a jade button to introduce the extravagant prologue, entitled "Glories of the Scriptures."

What followed was a spectacularly entertaining, but very *long* production depicting various Biblical episodes set in five different locales, containing six different "Tableaux," and featuring a cast of about 200 actors, singers, and dancers. As one critic remarked, the show was "the damndest thing this side of Oberammergau." By the time the opening credits of *The King of Kings* lit up the screen it was after 11:00 p.m.; and the exhausted, but thoroughly satisfied audience finally trudged out of the theatre about 2:00 a.m., when the epic concluded. DeMille was initially furious at the late starting time, but when it became clear that he had one of the biggest successes of his career on his hands he later patched up his friendship with Sid. An interesting inflation note: the original program lists the post-premiere admission prices for *The King of Kings* engagement. Bottom price for matinees was fifty cents, up to a top evening price of $1.50. All performances included the complete prologue presentation.

The Los Angeles movie critics who devoted their next-day columns exclusively to this event included Louella O. Parsons, who wrote in the Los Angeles *Examiner*:

"...I had thought there was no chance to equal the Grauman first nights in the old Egyptian Theatre, but these were ordinary affairs compared with last night's festivities....

"When the final curtain fell, those who had the honor to be present at this dedication felt they had seen what is probably the most important motion picture premiere the world has ever seen. Sid Grauman should be a proud and happy man."

Sadie Mossler declared in the Los Angeles *Record*:

"...Although he has been responsible for a group of Los Angeles' most artistic theatres, Sid Grauman has achieved his greatest triumph in the Chinese Theatre, for so true is its architecture, so subtle and

The 1943, 1944, and 1945 annual Academy Award Presentations were held at the Chinese Theatre. Best Actress winner Jennifer Jones holds her Oscar (for The Song of Bernadette *[1943]) on the evening of March 2, 1944. Ingrid Bergman is at left. (Photograph © Academy of Motion Picture Arts and Sciences.)*

glowingly exotic its scheme of decoration, that the house, alone, holds the audience in its spell."

Edwin Schallert, critic for the Los Angeles *Times*, wrote:

"...No prophet is needed to foretell the future of this picturesque establishment....The house is a dream of beauty both in lighting and decorative effects—an Aladdin's wonder palace that will be visited by all who visit Southern California, or dwell here, as an institution."

Shortly over one year after the opening of the Chinese, Grauman began to speculate to the press (in a Los Angeles *Examiner* article printed on July 4, 1928) about the possibility of his leaving the exhibition business and becoming a film producer. Then in April 1929 he announced that he was in negotiation to sell his interest in the Chinese to Paramount Publix. Other bidders jumping into the fray were Warner Bros.-First National and Fox West Coast Theatres. In May, a sale to Fox West Coast was culminated, with Sid to remain in "an advisory capacity in the conduct of the theatre." But on June 17, Sid proclaimed his departure from the exhibition field and announced plans to establish his own company to produce talking pictures and atmospheric prologues. It was widely assumed that his future productions would be distributed through United Artists, by virtue of his close business ties with Pickford, Fairbanks, Chaplin, and Schenck.

However, before he got his new plans off the ground, a cataclysmic event occurred that put Grauman's production plans forever on hold—the stock market crash of October 1929. Overnight, Sid lost the bulk of his fortune—approximately $6,000,000. When informed of the dreadful news the

Janet Gaynor filming A Star Is Born *(United Artists, 1937) at the Chinese Theatre. From the time its doors first swung open to admit an eager ticket-buying public in 1927, the mystique and appeal of the Chinese Theatre has remained universal throughout its sixty-five year existence. It has been used as a location site, duplicated in detail, and/or referred to in countless motion pictures, animated cartoons, television programs and commercials. David O. Selznick's original production of* A Star Is Born *shows the theatre in early three-strip Technicolor and has Gaynor delivering the well-known line, "Hello, everybody—This is Mrs. Norman Maine," in the Forecourt of the Stars.*

Lucille Ball (left) and Vivian Vance in "I Love Lucy" (CBS-TV, 1955). Two of the most famous episodes of this television series are "Lucy Visits Grauman's" and "Lucy and John Wayne." Lucy Ricardo (Ball) convinces apprehensive neighbor Ethel Mertz (Vance) that their trip to Hollywood won't be complete without a little souvenir to take back home to New York—John Wayne's footprints at the Chinese Theatre! (Photograph © CBS, Inc.)

July 15, 1932: A crowd awaits the world premiere of Strange Interlude. *When the stars appeared that evening a riot ensued. The woman in glasses and black-and-white hat (seated left center, front row) was crushed by the mob, sustained a broken leg, and lost her glasses.*

August 3, 1977: Over 8,000 persons set an all-time ceremony attendance record as they jammed into the forecourt and the surrounding area along Hollywood Boulevard hoping to catch a glimpse of the Star Wars *(1977) characters making their imprints.*

next morning, he reacted stoically and straight-faced, saying simply, "Well, let's just chalk this up to experience." Sid was then living in a suite at the Ambassador Hotel. Because he often stayed up all night, he had made a rule that he was not to be called in his suite until noon. When the market crashed, he could have salvaged some of his fortune, but early morning

Nathanael West's movie premiere episode in his landmark novel *The Day of the Locust* (1939).

Next, when *Hell's Angels* closed in September, it was reported that Sid was again parting company with the Chinese. Grauman had an on-again, off-again relationship with the Chinese management during the next year but made an official return on Christmas

Tony the Tiger in "Grauman's" (Leo Burnett Agency, 1970), a Kellogg's Frosted Flakes cereal commercial, combining live-action with animation, in which ever-popular Kellogg's spokesman Tony is shown placing his paw prints in the forecourt while telling the world that Frosted Flakes are "Gr-r-reat!" (Photograph © Kellogg Company).

calls couldn't get to him through the switchboard.

At the time of the premiere of Metro-Goldwyn-Mayer's *The Hollywood Revue of 1929* in June of the same year, Fox West Coast Theatres announced that the Chinese would have a new general manager, Rusty White; and the famous Grauman prologues were terminated. But the following May, an article appeared in the Los Angeles *Examiner* to the effect that Sid would return to manage the Chinese and revive the prologues. Grauman's return had reportedly been arranged by Howard Hughes, who wanted Sid to produce the world premiere of his long-anticipated *Hell's Angels*, which took place at the theatre on May 27, 1930. The spectacular opening caused a near-riot. The events are said to have inspired

Day of 1931, for the premiere of MGM's *Hell Divers*, complete with Grauman prologue. He continued to operate the Chinese and by November 1932 was named general manager of all Fox West Coast theatres in Los Angeles.

Terry Helgesen recounted a fascinating sidelight of the famous Grauman prologues:

"One of the reasons that Mr. Grauman's prologues had such enormous casts was his use of extras (just as in a motion picture). They were paid the magnificent sum of one dollar a performance, which meant only two dollars a day if they appeared at both matinee and evening shows.

"Crowds of men and women used to gather at the stage door before each performance and were engaged according to size and shape that would fit the extra costumes. If you were picked, the stage manager would show you your costume in Wardrobe and tell you where and when to go on the set. The regulars would guide you about so as not to cause confusion when the prologue was being presented.

"Odd as this procedure would seem today, it worked out very well. Of course, dancers, singers and specialty people were properly rehearsed and had

viewed by film historian Ronald Haver in 1971, had been the theatre's chief projectionist for over thirty years; and he described the last stage show, in which two nude chorus girls stood absolutely motionless, spotlighted on each side of the stage, for the entire forty-minute program. Mills recalled:

"They did that every day, three times a day, for almost a month. Everything was all right as long as they didn't move. The police department had a man

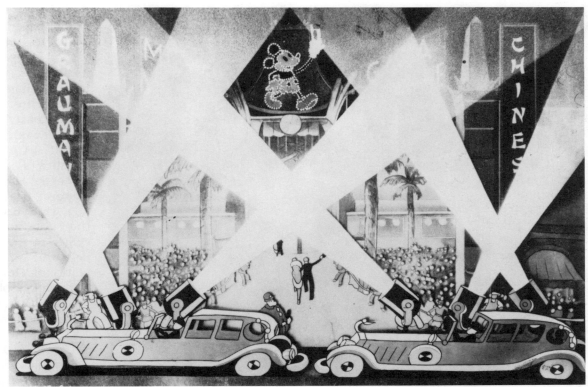

"Mickey's Gala Premiere" (1933) is a Walt Disney cartoon short subject in which Mickey Mouse, accompanied by his girlfriend, Minnie, and his faithful dog, Pluto, attend the premiere of Mickey's latest movie. Members of the audience who prove to be delighted with Mickey's most recent screen antics include animated caricatures of many of the leading screen personalities of the time. (Photograph © Walt Disney Company.)

run-of-the-play contracts."

During the first years of the Great Depression, the Chinese Theatre itself underwent a series of grave financial difficulties. Total closures of varying lengths occurred in 1931, 1932, and 1934. Sid stayed on, and somehow reopenings were always managed. Reserved seating was eliminated, and many more screenings per day were added. Although the Chinese survived as one of the finest show-places in the country, the glory days of the grandiose and ubiquitous Grauman prologues were slowly phased out. Presented sporadically with increasing infrequency, the last was produced in 1938. Harry Mills, inter-

here to make sure they didn't. Even if one eyelash moved, they would have closed the show as an obscene performance. We all waited, but those girls were amazing. Not a single flicker. Grauman was nervous. Hell, we were all nervous. But nothing happened."

In 1932 Sid had been approached with an offer to take over the management of the Roxy Theatre in New York while continuing to operate the Chinese Theatre in Hollywood. Had he accepted, it would have meant a commute back and forth across the country every five or six weeks. Grauman felt life was too short for that and said:

"After all, I have lived here on the Coast thirty years. Many of my friends are here....

"Taking over the Roxy would have meant more money for me, but I have learned money is not the only thing in life.

"It is right and proper for a man to be prosperous and successful, but greed for more money and greater power does nothing but wreck a man spiritually, mentally and physically.

"The Chinese Theatre has become an institution. People from all over the world come here to see it....I find happiness in that."

Sid Grauman continued to be directly involved with the Chinese Theatre until his death in 1950. There were other "general managers;" but Sid, as "managing director," always stepped in to officiate at the footprinting ceremonies in the forecourt and was instrumental in their planning.

What is largely unknown is the fact that from 1929 Sid Grauman owned no interest in the Chinese whatsoever. The theatre's history of corporate and individual ownership is as follows: When built in 1927, Sid owned one-third; and West Coast Theatres, Inc. owned two-thirds. West Coast sold its two-thirds to United Artists a few months after the theatre opened. In 1929, Sid sold his one-third to Fox West Coast Theatres, a subsidiary of

the Fox Film Corporation (which became 20th Century-Fox in 1935). Ownership remained unchanged until 1950. By that time, the original United Artists ownership had evolved to Joseph M. Schenck's United Artists Theatre Circuit. United Artists sold its two-thirds to Fox West Coast Theatres. This transaction, plus the one-third interest Grauman had previously sold them in 1929, made Fox West Coast the *first* 100% corporate owner up to that time.

Subsequent federal legislation forced corporate break-ups resulting in name-change restructuring. Fox West Coast Theatres became National General Theatres, a subsidiary of the National General Corporation, which became the corporate owner of the Chinese. In 1973 the National General Corporation sold its assets to independent theatre owner Ted Mann for $67,500,000. Among those assets was the Chinese Theatre, and Mann thereby became its first 100% *individual* owner. After thirteen years of sole ownership, Mann sold his entire chain of 360 theatres, including the Chinese, to Gulf + Western, the parent company of Paramount Pictures, for

When the prestigious Architectural Digest *magazine published a special Academy Awards issue devoted to Hollywood in April 1990, it featured the Chinese Theatre premiere of* A Tree Grows in Brooklyn (1945) *on the cover. The issue became the most sucessful in their publishing history. (Photograph courtesy* Architectural Digest © *Knapp Communications Corporation.)*

$220,000,000 in 1986. Terms of the sale positioned Mann to remain as Chairman and Chief Executive Officer of Mann Theatres. The latest change in ownership to date occurred in 1987 when Gulf + Western sold 50% of the company to Warner Communications, Inc. Later, at the end of 1990, Mann resigned as chairman and chief executive officer of the Mann Theatre Corporation.

At the 21st annual Academy Awards Presentation, held at the Academy Award Theatre in Hollywood on March 24, 1949, Sid Grauman was presented with one of the highest honors that the film industry can confer: a Special Oscar statuette, for being a "master showman who raised the standard of exhibition of motion pictures." Grauman, who had just turned seventy, quipped, "When I have my thirty-fifth birthday, I'll look back and say, 'They didn't forget me.'" He was later noticed fast asleep in his seat, the Oscar clutched firmly in his hands, the result of having been up late at a Friars Club party the evening before. To this day, Sid Grauman remains the *only* exhibitor ever to have been thus honored by the Academy of Motion Picture Arts and Sciences. (He was also one of its thirty-six founding members in 1927.)

On October 27, 1949, Joseph M. Schenck presided over a testimonial dinner in Sid's honor, sponsored by the Hollywood Chamber of Commerce. According to the Los Angeles *Times*, 375 persons packed the Blossom Room of the Hollywood Roosevelt Hotel across the street from the Chinese Theatre. (Grauman was one of the hotel's four original owners when it opened in 1927.) To introduce Sid Grauman, Schenck proclaimed, "And here is the greatest showman of them all!" Taken within the context of motion pictures, Schenck's remark was not exaggerated. As I.G. Edmonds pointed out in his article "Prince of the Picture Palaces," Sid "...was an exhibitor—a class of showman that people tend to overlook when they think of motion picture genius and contributions to the art of film. But genius this man had in his own special way...."

Less than four months after this tribute, Sid suffered a heart attack and was hospitalized. He seemed to rally, but about two weeks later, another attack occurred, and he died on March 5, 1950, of coronary occlusion. Shortly before his death, Grauman urged theatre operators to return to the showmanship of Hollywood's younger days, saying theatregoers should have a "theatrical dinner, not just popcorn."

Hollywood had long ago agreed that the one man in the film colony without an enemy in the world was Sid Grauman, and hundreds of the community's most famous citizens came to mourn the showman they had affectionately nicknamed "Little Sunshine."

Services were conducted by George Ward, Christian Science reader and a friend of Sid's, at Forest Lawn's Church of the Recessional on March 9. Kenny Baker sang "Shepherd Show Me How To Go" and "The Lord's Prayer." There was not a vacant seat in the church. The services were amplified over a loud speaker system for the hundreds who gathered outside. George Jessel, who knew Grauman for over twenty-five years, delivered the eulogy, which brought many to tears.

Although Grauman had wished that his friends would send money to his favorite charities rather than flowers to his burial, his casket was surrounded by more than sixty floral pieces, including one in the shape of a single heart, made of deep red roses. The name on the card: Norma Talmadge. After the services he was entombed in the Grauman family crypt at Forest Lawn. Both Grauman's Chinese and Egyptian theatres remained dark until 3:30 p.m., opening after the funeral services had concluded.

Grauman's estate was evaluated at $750,000, according to most reports; but incredibly, he left no will. Sid never married and left no close relatives behind. His possessions were sold at public auction.

A few weeks after Grauman died, the California State Assembly passed a resolution on his death, the likes of which had never before (or since) been afforded to any individual in the motion picture exhibition profession. Its final paragraph read:

"...Be it resolved by the Assembly of the State of California that members of the Assembly express extreme regret for the passing of Sid Grauman, one of the truly great showmen of this state."

Los Angeles *Times* columnist Jack Smith probably expressed Grauman's and the Chinese Theatre's legacy best in a 1987 article when he responded to the bleak assertion that Hollywood was dead, and concluded that Hollywood will never die as long as the Chinese Theatre holds fans and tourists spellbound. He wrote:

"The Chinese Theatre probably attracts more visitors than the Washington Monument—and certainly more than the U.S. Supreme Court. It's a testament to the enduring power of our movie stars over our imaginations that this sentimental piece of kitsch is the American mecca....

"I doubt that Hollywood Boulevard will ever die as long as the Chinese Theatre remains as a sanctuary to the memories of the great stars who enlarged and romanticized our lives."

Apart from the tumultuous changes in the film industry over the last six decades, and in spite of all the alterations and adversities of the past, the Chinese Theatre will stand as an historical and indomitable symbol of its—and Hollywood's—glamorous history and promising future.

May 1927: The four original April 15, 1927 imprinted squares belonging to Sid Grauman (left), Norma Talmadge, Douglas Fairbanks, and Mary Pickford are visible along the Hollywood Boulevard curb.

Sid Grauman.   *Norma Talmadge.*   *Douglas Fairbanks.*   *Mary Pickford.*

The Footprint Ceremonies

Lives of great men all remind us
We can make our lives sublime,
And, departing, leave behind us
Footprints on the sands of time.

—Henry Wadsworth Longfellow
From the lyric poem "A Psalm of Life" (1838)

In the late 1970s a tourist from Baden-Baden, Germany, walking along Hollywood Boulevard stopped a stranger and inquired, "Where is the famous footprint theatre? I have come to Los Angeles to see the feet." The stranger was none other than the Chinese Theatre's owner at that time, Ted Mann, who delighted in recounting the incident.

An estimated 2,000,000 tourists a year flock to the theatre from all over the world. They come to see for themselves the celebrated hand and footprints of the stars. (Tourist buses make as many as thirty stops every day.) Los Angeles *Times* columnist Jack Smith likened being asked to leave one's hand and footprints in the wet cement of the theatre's forecourt as "the next best thing to sainthood," and the Mann Theatre Corporation calls the cement artifacts "the world's best known graffiti."

In 1953 Hedda Hopper, a Los Angeles *Times* syndicated columnist, wrote:

"Millions of people have made pilgrimages to Hollywood each year to see their favorite stars at work in a motion picture studio or catch a glimpse of them in a restaurant or night club. Few such dreams are realized....But there is one attraction that all tourists see—the forecourt of the Grauman's Chinese Theatre. New York has its Empire State Building and Paris its Eiffel Tower; but you have to pay to see both....

"There is no admission [charge] to the forecourt at Grauman's where countless millions have wandered about studying the hand and foot prints of famous stars and reading the messages inscribed by the colony's greats. There's never a time from dawn to midnight that a group of visitors can't be found there. It's ironic that in Hollywood where history is written on the wind and where our product deteriorates with time...the cement in Grauman's forecourt is the only lasting memorial to artists who've made Hollywood famous."

The idea of putting the footprints, handprints, and signatures of the stars in cement squares in the forecourt of the Chinese Theatre originated prior to its opening and has proven to be the single most effective, famous, and longest running publicity stunt in the history of the movies. There are many different accounts in print as to how the idea for the custom was born. Published versions of how the idea for the footprints originated include the following:

1) The most widely publicized version states that silent screen star Norma Talmadge accidentally stepped into some wet cement while visiting the construction site of the theatre and that Sid Grauman, witnessing the incident, was inspired with the idea. Variations of this account have Talmadge, Mary Pickford, and Douglas Fairbanks arriving in a car for a visit together, with Pickford inadvertently stepping in the wet cement.

2) Hedda Hopper stated that during the theatre's construction, Sid visited super star Mary Pickford at her studio bungalow on business. There was some wet cement in front of her bungalow, and a passer-by carelessly stepped in it. Seeing this incident, Sid got the idea, summoned Mary, whisked her over to the Chinese site, and had "America's Sweetheart" put her prints in wet cement. Another version of this story has Sid himself stepping into the wet cement outside Pickford's bungalow and telling Mary his idea and that he wanted her to be the first celebrity imprinted.

Zorro, hard at work at the typewriter, with his mistress Mary Pickford (in costume for Dorothy Vernon of Haddon Hall *[1924]) at the Pickford-Fairbanks Studios. She credited the dog with helping her originate the idea of the footprint ceremonies. Charles "Buddy" Rogers, Pickford's third husband, told the authors that Mary and Zorro "were playing in the yard [at Pickfair]. Zorro gets loose—runs across wet cemet. Mary scolds him—then realizes his footprints will be there forever. She called Sid Grauman."*

3) Mary Pickford stated that she had visited the Chinese construction site one afternoon and was returning home to Pickfair where a new cement driveway had just been poured. Her dog Zorro ran across the wet cement, leaving imprints, as Mary was getting out of her car. At first she was upset with the dog's unintentional piece of vandalism, but suddenly an idea clicked, and she called Sid, proposing that she and her husband, the extraordinarily popular silent screen star Douglas Fairbanks, install their prints in the Chinese forecourt and start a tradition. Mary said that she let Sid take credit for the idea since he was the builder of the theatre and a good friend. A similar version of this story has Zorro running through the cement at the theatre's construction site itself.

4) Author Gary Carey offers another Pickford/Fairbanks variation which has Doug and Mary at their Rancho Zorro overseeing improvements they were making on the property. They were building an irrigation dam, and the cement was still wet; they bent down and pressed their hand prints in it and wrote their names. Having recently been to the Chinese site, one of them came up with the idea of stars placing their prints there.

5) Film historian Ronald Haver claims that the chief mason on the project, Jean W. Klossner, performed the centuries-old custom of placing his signature in the form of a hand print in the wet cement. When Sid noticed the imprint, he questioned Klossner about the practice; and from that encounter, with input and advice from Klossner, Sid devised the footprints idea. Another version of this story has Klossner coming up with the idea himself and giving it to Sid.

6) Publicist Arthur S. Wenzel, who worked for Grauman for forty years, wrote to *Variety* in 1975: "...I recall walking with Sid when the Chinese was still incomplete. Sid suddenly slipped off a builder's plank into wet cement. Eyeing his own imprint, he shouted, 'Arthur, I am going to have all the stars recorded here.' That must have been in 1926."

7) Harry Hammond (Ham) Beall, another veteran Grauman publicist, who died in 1952, is "credited with originating" the footprints, according to his obituaries in the Los Angeles *Examiner* and *Variety*. The information as to just *how* he supposedly did this is not supplied. Other obits say only that Hammond "promoted [the] footprinting of famous film stars" at the theatre.

8) Sid's own basic version of the story (told with several variations, as he was a notorious spinner of "tall tales") is that during construction, he accidentally stepped in newly smoothed wet cement. While a worker was bawling him out for ruining the slab, the idea suddenly hit him. He immediately called Douglas Fairbanks, Mary Pickford, and Norma Talmadge at their studios and, in a very agitated state, urged them to come immediately to the Chinese site with no explanation. Thinking he'd gone mad, they all appeared shortly thereafter, at which time Sid told them his idea and persuaded them to make their prints.

Grauman Theatres publicist Harry Hammond Beall.

9) Grauman also said that he was punished as a child for marking some wet cement and that, ever after, he wanted to do it legally.

Of all the versions, Sid's own seems the least credible. Pickford, Fairbanks, and Talmadge, even though close friends and business associates of Sid, had extremely busy and demanding schedules; so it is hard to believe that these three stars could have dropped everything simultaneously on the spur of the moment in the middle of a working day and gone racing over to the theatre's construction site without even knowing why they were headed there. The true and exact story of the origin of the footprint idea may never be known: there are simply too many variations, and the participants in the mystery are now all deceased.

What has been proven, however, is the fact that, for whatever reason, Norma Talmadge, Mary Pickford, Douglas Fairbanks, and Sid Grauman himself were the first celebrities to place their prints at the theatre on April 15, 1927.

A 1927 article entitled "Film Stars Footprinted. Mary Pickford and Others Make Marks for Pavement of a Theatre," datelined Hollywood, April 15, appeared in the New York *Times*. It read:

"The footprints of film stars, done in concrete and signed by the makers, will become flagstones in the forecourt of Sid Grauman's new picture theatre to be opened here in May.

"Mary Pickford, Douglas Fairbanks and Norma and Constance [sic—Constance is mistakenly included in this article] Talmadge stepped today into forms filled with soft concrete to 'make their marks.' Grauman plans to add footprints of others."

In 1953 the brochure "Grauman's Chinese Theatre" stated:

"The story of how the footprint ceremonies came to be a part of the Chinese Theatre goes back to the Spring of 1927 when Sid Grauman took Mary Pickford, Douglas Fairbanks, Sr. and Norma Talmadge to watch the building of the theatre which was to become world-famous.

"As they drove up to the theatre, Miss Talmadge accidentally stepped into the wet cement of the curb as she alighted from the automobile.

"Immediately upon witnessing this, Grauman, a great showman, came up with the idea of also imprinting the hand and footprints of Miss Pickford, Fairbanks and Miss Talmadge.

Filmland's Quaintest Custom—

How it's done is a secret, but it's

1 Famous the world over is the unique way in which stars' footprints and handprints are preserved for posterity by imprinting them in solid cement in the forecourt of Grauman's Chinese Theater on Hollywood Blvd. (above)

2 When new prints are to be made, Cement Sculptor Jean Klosser begins job by taking out original block

3 After the block is all broken up, a hole is cleaned out, prepared for specially treated cement

4 Steel reinforcement (above) is the same used in building bridges. In event collection was ever moved, blocks could be pried up, and steel support would hold them together. To be "hand and footprinted" is a great honor!

5 Treated with Klosser's secret formula, the cement is poured into hole, sets in about 45 minutes

6 Ceremony of "printing" a new star attracts big crowds. Above: The final preparations

The first part of a May 1938 Screen Guide *article entitled "Filmland's Quaintest Custom—Immortalizing Stars in Cement!" illustrates the various steps undertaken by cement artist Jean W. Klossner in order to make each imprinted square.*

October 20, 1936: William Powell (left), Sid Grauman, and Myrna Loy engage in some harmless forecourt frivolity. The two stars hoped these particular shoes would help them "make a bigger 'impression.'"

"Tourists driving up to the theatre today may still see the famous footprints left on the curb by Miss Talmadge...."

In a September 9, 1982, Los Angeles *Times* article entitled "Hollywood Regains Footprints of Stars," Dan Morain writes: "Three cement slabs that had been in front of the Chinese Theatre and bear the faint footprints of Sid Grauman, Mary Pickford and Douglas Fairbanks are back in Hollywood after a twenty-four-year absence." He goes on to describe how the squares had been removed by building contractor J.W. Nicks during the construction of the Walk of Fame on Hollywood Boulevard in the late 1950s. Since no one else wanted them, Nicks held on to them as keepsakes, even taking the squares with him when he moved to Phoenix, Arizona, in 1979.

When Nicks died in 1982, the blocks were purchased by collector Richard Brian, who transported them back to the Hollywood area. The prints are faint—so much so that Brian had to darken them with pencil markings to make them visible—and they were verified as the original blocks by film historian Marc Wanamaker. According to Wanamaker, "They're very crude. It was not the proper kind of cement. They didn't do it right. The cement was already too hard." The three blocks contain signatures and footprints, and Pickford's also contains the date 1927. Wanamaker added, "They are a true part of the history of Hollywood [and]...are not fakes." No photographs of this initial event are known to survive. However, in

Three horses have placed their imprints at the theatre, but a canine has had that distinction only in a fictional film. A scene from Won Ton Ton, the Dog Who Saved Hollywood *(Paramount, 1976). (Photograph © Paramount Pictures.)*

April 1991, Wanamaker discovered a glass negative of the exterior of the theatre taken in May 1927 by an unknown photographer who was standing in the middle of Hollywood Boulevard. The resulting print shows not only the theatre but the four original imprinted squares of Talmadge, Pickford, Fairbanks, and Grauman along the curb.

As for the squares as they exist today in the Forecourt of the Stars, according to film historian Bruce Torrence: "An article and photograph which appeared in the May 1, 1927 Los Angeles *Times* shows Mary Pickford and Douglas Fairbanks placing their hand and footprints in the forecourt of the theatre. The article states that Pickford and Fairbanks were the first to start the now popular tradition. This photograph and others [from Torrence's own collection]...show the block of cement in which Fairbanks made his impressions. The photographs also show part of the smooth, blank cement in which Norma Talmadge subsequently placed her prints." This Pickford/Fairbanks ceremony, held on April 30, was the *second* time they placed their prints, but it was the first footprint ceremony ever actually held in the forecourt. The Pickford/Fairbanks squares are the earliest squares in the forecourt and are still on view to this day.

Scaffolding surrounding the theatre construction site along Hollywood Boulevard is visible in one of the Pickford/Fairbanks photographs. Norma Talmadge, who may indeed have been the first celebrity to place her prints along the curb—cement artist Jean W. Klossner said in 1953, "Norma Talmadge was the first to write her name in my cement"—did not, however, have the first ceremony to take place in the forecourt itself. Nor did her ceremony take place on the occasion of the theatre's opening, although her square contains the date of that event: May 18, 1927. The truth is that Talmadge's square was post-dated and her actual ceremony occurred in the daytime sometime during May prior to the opening. That Talmadge's ceremony was held *after* that of the April 30 Pickford/Fairbanks event is proved by the fact that by the time Talmadge was imprinted photographs show that the scaffolding surrounding the theatre had been removed. Also, the photographers who took pictures of the celebrities arriving at the theatre's opening night premiere of

Stardate 9105.12: "Star Trek's" (1966-1991) Mr. Spock (Leonard Nimoy, left) and Captain Kirk (William Shatner) beam down to the earth's surface from the starship Enterprise *to place their prints at the Chinese Theatre.*

The King of Kings (1927) had their cameras positioned in the forecourt so that many of the guests were shown standing on the Pickford and Talmadge squares. Therefore, Talmadge could not have made her imprints that evening—or even that day—because her prints were dry for the premiere.

The day after the Pickford/Fairbanks ceremony, an article entitled "Stars To Make Stone Record" appeared in the Los Angeles *Examiner* and verified the date of April 30. It read:

"Footprints and handprints of screenland celebrities impressed in squares of the cement paving in the forecourt of Grauman's new Chinese Theatre, Hollywood, a dream of Sid Grauman's ever since the playhouse was first projected, became an actuality yesterday when the first two film notables, Douglas Fairbanks and Mary Pickford, visited the theatre and made their indelible pedal and manual [foot and hand] markings in specially prepared concrete.

"It is Sid Grauman's intention to have not only all of the more important luminaries of the cinema world on record with their footprints, handprints and signatures in the court of his new theatre, but to have world-famous personages, who come to Los Angeles, recorded in concrete in a similar manner...."

The "proper kind of cement" was a special mixture devised by Jean W. Klossner—the formula for which he kept locked in a vault, a jealously guarded secret—and was an essential key to the success and longevity of the footprints. (According to film historian Ronald Haver, Klossner first tried out his special forecourt recipe on his daughter, whose "...footprints were there on the former curb, near the souvenir shop, until...they were supplanted by the Walk of Fame.") Klossner, who was born in France, claimed that the formula had been handed down through the centuries by his ancestors, all masons, who had been in that line of work since the construction of Notre Dame cathedral in Paris. According to Klossner, he spent three days in advance of each ceremony preparing the chemicals that would be incorporated into the final cement mixture to be poured on the crucial day. The final concoction was slow-drying and very malleable, allowing for the registration of fine details, or a quick smoothing over if a mistake was made by the signator, or if any aspect of an imprint seemed unsatisfactory. It also dried into an exceptionally durable final product, which has stood the test of over sixty years of never-ending foot traffic provided by the millions of tourists continually treading on its surface.

July 24, 1942: Henry Fonda (left), Charles Boyer, Rita Hayworth, Sid Grauman (standing), Charles Laughton, and Edward G. Robinson. The stars of Tales of Manhattan (1942) set a forecourt record that stands to this day: Five stars, five individual squares imprinted on the same day. (Fonda had already made his individual square [right]. The other stars would make theirs in this area after posing for this publicity shot.)

Joanne Woodward polishes her Hollywood Walk of Fame star. In 1955 Harry Sugarman, a Hollywood businessman and a member of the city's Chamber of Commerce, was inspired by the Chinese Theatre footprint ceremonies and conceived the idea for the sidewalk that covers thirty-seven blocks of Hollywood Boulevard and Vine Street.

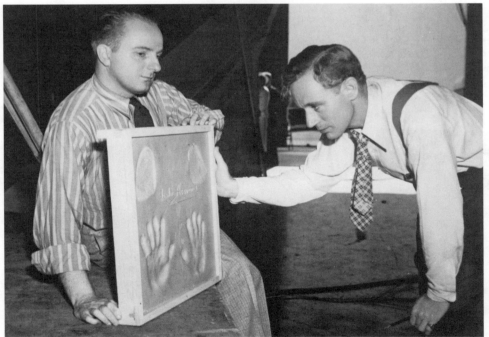

British actor Leslie Howard (right, with unidentified man) examines his imprints and signature which he made for the Rhodes Theatre in Chicago, Illinois, during the production of Stand-In *(1937). The theatre opened that same year and, like the Chinese Theatre, featured concrete imprints of the stars, which were made in Hollywood and shipped back to Chicago.*

As this book was being readied to go to press, Harrison Ford, "Indy" Jones himself, placed his imprints in front of an enthusiastic crowd of fans on June 3, 1992. He wore one blue and one green sneaker to make his impressions. His square is to the east of those belonging to George Lucas and Steven Spielberg and the Star Wars (1977) characters. It was Lucas' casting of Ford as Han Solo in Star Wars that resulted in the actor becoming one of the most successful stars of his generation.

Harrison Ford's square is tinted brown and contains the date ("6.3.92"), his two footprints, two handprints and his signature. That evening he guested on television's "The Tonight Show starring Jay Leno," and Leno joked about the wet cement imprints saying, "We should explain to people this wasn't some 'mob thing' for money you owed." When he asked the actor if he'd been required to take off his shoes, Ford replied, "No, you do it with your shoes on." Leno responded, "So there's no need for a pedicure or anything." Ford placed his prints in connection with the motion picture Patriot Games (Paramount, 1992).

The most recent ceremony in the forecourt occurred on June 15, 1992 when Michael Keaton placed his prints in connection with Batman Returns (Warner Bros., 1992). The picture's world premiere took place at the Chinese Theatre the following evening. The event had been called "the hot ticket of the year," and Los Angeles Times columnist Bill Higgins reported the next morning, "The backdrop included a two-block closure of Hollywood Boulevard; 3,000 star-watching fans— watched by two dozen L.A. police officers and 200 security guards; the Budweiser blimp overhead; plus thirty-three TV film crews and 100 photographers recording the event for history." When the guests were informed that the post-premiere party was to be held at the Warner Burbank lot, one woman commented incredulously, "The premiere's at Grauman's and then you're supposed to drive to...Burbank!?"

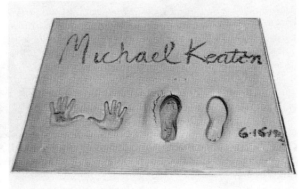

Michael Keaton's square is tinted red and contains the date ("6.15.1992"), his two footprints, two handprints, and his signature. The actor arrived at his ceremony wearing two-tone brown and beige shoes that matched his suit, but he changed into tennis shoes prior to making his imprints. Keaton told the reporters gathered for the event that he had been informed about the ceremony nearly a month before it was to take place, just as he was drifting off to sleep. "I immediately woke up smiling," he confessed, "and I don't think I've stopped since."

October 10, 1939: Mickey Rooney and Judy Garland. She was distressed when the wet cement crept under her false fingernails and hardened. "I thought creeping paralysis had set in," Garland later confessed, "beginning at my fingertips."

Each block is unique in size, shape, and color; no two blocks are the same. When new imprints were to be made, Klossner had the original blank concrete square removed and had the resulting area cleaned out. He then laid down steel reinforcements, the same as those used in building bridges. (This procedure made it possible to pry up and relocate squares, if ever necessary.) The space was then ready for the cement mixture to be poured. Forty-five minutes were required for it to set. At that point, the celebrities were free to make their imprints. The wet cement easily washed off their hands with soap and water, and the ever-present theatre attendants wiped the mixture off their shoes in order to prevent any possible chemical damage.

Making a good impression required skill, and Klossner described the process thusly: "Each finger must be pressed into the cement with the same pressure and then the wrist. The foot must be rolled around so the edges of the shoe make an impression." The concrete surface remained pliable for twenty hours, and Klossner had a reported 150 tools at his disposal to put the final touches on each block. He did nearly all the squares from the beginning through those of Jane Russell and Marilyn Monroe in 1953. Shortly after that occasion, he told host Art Baker in an episode of the television series "You Asked For It" that after twenty-six years on the job and at the age of eighty-two (he was actually only seventy-nine according to his death certificate) he officially retired, adding, "I trained a man to carry on Sid Grauman's wishes."

Klossner's relationship with Grauman was often turbulent. Quite an eccentric character (as was Sid), Klossner often arrived at the printing ceremonies decked out in flowing artist's robes and beret to officially assist the celebrities in the placing of their imprints. He often quarreled with Sid about his fee (in 1938 he reportedly received $100 to $200 per ceremony), haughtily stalking off the job, but eventu-

ally returning when Sid would call in desperation and they would patch up their differences. Grauman tried to replace him more than once but was unsuccessful. Klossner took great satisfaction in the knowledge that the workmanship of the other cement artists did not measure up to his; all non-Klossner squares cracked. He refused many offers to do similar work in front of other buildings.

Klossner died on July 22, 1965. He willed his collection of artifacts relating to the ceremonies (his costume, tools, photographs, and newspaper clippings) to his family; but he took his cement formula with him to the grave. To this day, its exact composition remains a mystery. In 1936 Klossner's daughter Ruth recalled her father placing prints of her bare feet in the sidewalk in front of the entrance to their home shortly after she learned to walk in 1906.

The selection of who is invited to be imprinted in the forecourt has been the decision of the theatre ownership since Sid Grauman's death. (Grauman himself made the decision during his lifetime.) Theatre management claimed it was a secret process, but the honor was usually accompanied by heavy overtones of publicity—often the new honoree had a motion picture to promote that just happened to be playing concurrently at the theatre. Still, many people agree with columnist Sidney Skolsky, who wrote in his December 8, 1961 Hollywood *Citizen-News* column, "I'd say that next to winning an Oscar the greatest tribute that can be shown a movie star is to have the outline of his hand and foot enshrined in concrete at Grauman's Chinese." In recent years, Ted Mann felt that his executives were perhaps overly careful about who was chosen to be honored but reasoned, "We've had offers....The remaining spaces are too important to waste. You need a star who will survive, and how many are there today?" As of this writing, there are still several blank squares waiting to be imprinted.

October 18, 1956: The Los Angeles premiere of Giant.

Mary Pickford, her husband Douglas Fairbanks, and Sid Grauman.

The Stars in the Forecourt

Mary Pickford and Douglas Fairbanks
Ceremony #1: April 30, 1927

The couple were husband and wife at the time of their ceremony. They wed in 1920 and divorced in 1936.

Mary Pickford

Born: Gladys Louise Smith in Toronto, Canada, on April 8, 1892. Died: May 29, 1979.

Mary Pickford, "America's Sweetheart," inspired the following praise from film historian David Shipman: "If popularity were the sole criterion of stardom, then Mary Pickford is without a doubt the greatest star there has ever been." She went on the stage at age five. Touring in stock companies, she developed her talent and finally became a David Belasco actress on Broadway in his 1907 production of *The Warrens of Virginia*. In 1909 she entered the movies at the Biograph Company under the direction of D.W. Griffith. She joined Adolph Zukor's Famous Players Film Company (later Paramount) in 1913, and by 1914 she had become the most popular and highest paid performer in motion pictures.

Possibly the most astute business woman in the history of the movies, Pickford originated the concept that was to become the United Artists Corporation, which was formed in 1919, with Douglas Fairbanks, Charles Chaplin, and D.W. Griffith as her partners.

Famous for her film roles in which she played a little girl with a headful of sausage curls, she also demonstrated versatility by playing a wide range of characters. Pickford thought it best not to age on the screen. She wanted the public to remember her as the embodiment of youthfulness that she had always epitomized.

Her motion picture credits include *The Violin Maker of Cremona* (1909, debut), *Rebecca of Sunnybrook Farm* (1917), *Stella Maris* (1918), *Pollyanna* (1920), *Little Lord Fauntleroy* (1921), *Little Annie Rooney* (1925), *Sparrows* (1926), *My Best Girl* (1927), **Coquette* (1929, talkie debut), and *Secrets* (1933, final film).

In 1976 she received an Honorary Academy Award "in recognition of her unique contributions to the film industry and the development of film as an artistic medium."

*Academy Award winner: Best Actress.

Pickford's square is tinted gray and contains the inscription "Greetings to Sid." Also included are the date ("1927"), her two footprints (made with high heels), two handprints, plus the inscription "Hand and Foot Prints of Mary Pickford [signature]" followed by the drawing of an arrow pointing to her name.

Pickford and Fairbanks posed for photographs during which they practiced making their imprints in a single square which was eventually smoothed over and used by Fairbanks on that day. Pickford placed her prints in a separate block two squares to the left of her husband's. The square dividing them was later occupied with the imprints of Norma Talmadge.

At the time of the ceremony the box-office was a decorative Chinese pagoda in the northeast corner of the forecourt. The squares of Pickford and Fairbanks graced the center of the open area directly in front of the theatre's main entrance doors and were easily viewable from the sidewalk. Today the box-office sits dead center at the forecourt's entrance along Hollywood Boulevard, and the canopy that runs from the box-office to the entrance shades and partially obstructs what was once the choicest area in the forecourt.

Pickford was a friend of the Grauman family, aside

Sid Grauman (left), Mary Pickford, and her husband Douglas Fairbanks.

from being one of Sid's business partners. D.J. Grauman (Sid's father) himself bestowed the nickname "America's Sweetheart" on her in connection with a film which made Mary the most popular woman in the world and saved Zukor's company from bankruptcy. She tells the following story in her memoirs:

"'Pop' [Grauman] put the title 'America's Sweetheart' in electric lights for the first time in 1914, when he was showing my first version of *Tess of the Storm Country* in San Francisco. It was never a pub-

licity 'stunt,' which makes it, to my way of thinking, all the nicer.

"During the war, in 1918, I was marching down Market Street in San Francisco at the head of a Red Cross parade. Hundreds of soldiers and Red Cross workers were marching along together. Flags were flying, bands were blaring, paper coiled through the air; the police were holding back the crowds. Suddenly, through the police lines, I saw a white-haired old gentleman break away from a policeman and, waving frantically, run toward me, shouting, 'Mary, sweetheart!'

"The policeman dashed after him. Certain he was a dangerous crank of some kind, he was raising his club, when I ran up to him and cried, 'Don't, officer, this man is my friend!'

"The truth is I hadn't the slightest idea who the white-haired gentleman was. I had practically to gallop to regain my position at the head of the parade. The old man was now marching along at my side.

" 'How's my boy?' he suddenly asked me. 'Is he all right?'

"'Oh, fine!' I replied without turning my head. I was convinced by then that I had a lunatic on my hands.

"'How is Sid's Million Dollar Theatre in Los Angeles doing?' he asked.

"It was only then that I realized the gentleman at my side must be darling 'Pop' Grauman, whom I had never met—the man who had announced my engagement to the country we both loved and served."

Douglas Fairbanks

Born: Douglas Elton Ulman in Denver, Colorado, on May 23, 1883. Died: December 12, 1939.

By 1900 Douglas Fairbanks was seriously pursuing a career as an actor. He made his Broadway debut in 1902 and by 1913 was an established star with national recognition. An offer from the Triangle-Fine Arts film company of $2,000 per week proved irresistible, and off he went to Hollywood in 1915. He quickly caught on with the movie-going public in a series of jaunty comedies and established an original screen persona: a good-humored, gallant, rugged individual, possessing exuberant optimism, physical agility, moral courage, and a devil-may care attitude. With *The Mark of Zorro* (1920), Fairbanks achieved a major change in image—that of the tanned, mustached, gallant swashbuckler, still basically a comedian, but one who laughed at real danger straight in the face, reducing his adversaries to bumbling fools and performing majestic physical feats while saving the heroine and achieving justice.

His motion picture credits include *The Lamb* (1915, debut), *His Picture in the Papers* (1916), *His Majesty, the American* (1919), *The Three Musketeers* (1921), *Robin Hood* (1922), *The Thief of Bagdad* (1924), *The Black Pirate* (1926), *The Iron Mask* (1929), *Taming of the Shrew* (1929, talkie debut), and *The Private Life of Don Juan* (1934, final film).

Fairbanks was one of the thirty-six founders of the Academy of Motion Picture Arts and Sciences in 1927, as well as its first president (1927-1929). In 1940 that organization voted him a posthumous Special Academy Award "recognizing the unique and

outstanding contribution of Douglas Fairbanks, first President of the Academy, to the international development of the motion picture."

Fairbanks' square is tinted gray and contains the inscription "Good Luck Sid." (The period is Fairbanks'.) Also included are his two footprints, two handprints, and his signature, plus the inscription "Hand and Foot Prints."

Norma Talmadge
Ceremony #2: May 18, 1927

Born: in Jersey City, New Jersey, on May 26, 1897. Died: December 24, 1957.

Although Norma Talmadge once trivialized her talent by stating that her success was built on her ability to provide "sobs and smiles," author Adela Rogers St. Johns wrote in 1926 that she was the movies' "one and only great actress."

She grew up in Brooklyn, New York, the eldest of three sisters. Having done some modeling, she applied for work at the Vitagraph studios in 1910 and was hired. D.W. Griffith took notice of her and gave her a contract with his Triangle-Fine Arts company in 1915. That same year, Talmadge's marriage to Joseph M. Schenck resulted in the crucial turning point of her career. He formed her own production company and assumed the management of her career.

Norma soon hit her stride by establishing as her forte the portrayal of sympathetic women caught up in turbulent romantic and dramatic conflicts. Her films were often set in fabulously sumptuous sur-

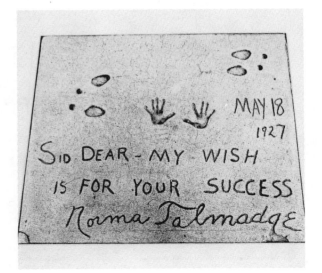

roundings, in which she was gorgeously costumed; thus one critic labeled her "the lady of the great indoors." Talmadge's Brooklyn accent was criticized when she made two talking pictures. She then retired from filmmaking.

Her motion picture credits include *The Household Pest* (1910, debut), *A Tale of Two Cities* (1911), *The Battle Cry of Peace* (1915), *Panthea* (1917), *The Passion Flower* (1921), *Smilin' Through* (1922), *Ashes of Vengeance* (1923), *Secrets* (1924), *New York Nights* (1929, talkie debut), and *DuBarry, Woman of Passion* (1930, final film).

Talmadge's square is tinted gray and contains the inscription "Sid Dear—My Wish Is For Your Success." Also included are the date ("May 18 [sic] 1927"), four of her footprints (made with high heels—Talmadge made two sets of her pair of footprints instead of the customary one set), two handprints, and her signature.

The square is post-dated, as Talmadge actually placed her prints prior to the theatre's May 18 opening festivities.

Joseph M. Schenck, Talmadge's husband, was a long-time friend of Sid Grauman. He knew that Grauman loved to play practical jokes and was a good sport when the tables were turned; so he convinced Sid to rent an apartment in a building Schenck owned. (Sid preferred living in hotels and resided at the Alexandria for years, moving to the Ambassador when it opened its doors in 1921.) Grauman furnished Schenck's apartment at a cost of $27,000 and moved in but didn't care for it. He was an insomniac, and the noise of street traffic disturbed what little rest he got. Grauman loved to gamble. Staying up all night was not a problem for him, as long as he could find a companion. One evening in a poker game, Schenck bet Grauman $18,000. Sid said, "I'll call that with my apartment." Schenck agreed and then proceeded to disclose the winning hand. He sent a moving crew to the apartment early the next morning before Grauman was up and proceeded to move everything out from under Sid as a joke. Grauman never said a word about the incident. He happily returned to his hotel; and Schenck, much to his disappointment, found his joke had fallen flat.

Norma Talmadge and Sid Grauman.

Norma Shearer
Ceremony #3: August 1, 1927

Born: Edith Norma Shearer in Westmount, a suburb of Montreal, Canada, on August 15, 1902. Died: June 12, 1983.

Norma Shearer reigned as a world symbol of chic sophistication, glamor, and feminine elegance throughout the 1930s. Her studio, Metro-Goldwyn-

Sid Grauman and Norma Shearer.

Mayer, billed her as "The First Lady of the Screen."

Still in her teens, Shearer and her sister were taken to New York by their mother in the hope of obtaining stage work. Norma found a job as a pianist in a sheet music store and also did some modeling. Almost ready to give up, she secured a job as a movie extra. Her first sizeable part was in *The Stealers* (1920). Producer Irving G. Thalberg noticed her work and was impressed. When he became production chief for the Louis B. Mayer company in 1923, he quickly signed Norma to a contract and brought her to Hollywood.

Of her initial meeting with the youthful Thalberg, Shearer later said she thought he was an office boy. Mayer, impatient with her lack of experience, insisted she be loaned out to other studios to better learn her craft. Shearer and Thalberg married in 1927, and it was his brilliant handling of her career from that point that elevated her to major stardom.

Her motion picture credits include *The Flapper* (1920, debut), *He Who Gets Slapped* (1924), *The Trial of Mary Dugan* (1929, talkie debut), *Their Own Desire* (1929), **The Divorcée* (1930), *A Free Soul* (1931), *The Barretts of Wimpole Street* (1934), *Romeo and Juliet* (1936), *Marie Antoinette* (1938), and *Her Cardboard Lover* (1942, final film).

*Academy Award nomination: Best Actress.
**Academy Award winner: Best Actress.

Shearer's square is tinted gray and contains the inscription "Good luck always to Sid." Also included are the date ("Aug. 1st 1927"), her two footprints (made with high heels), two handprints, and her signature.

In a letter to the authors, archivist/author Raymond Daum, one of Shearer's most devoted fans, recalls his childhood fascination with motion pictures and the Chinese Theatre:

"...As a nine year old I remember listening to all the movie premieres broadcast from Grauman's Chinese Theatre. For hours I sat by the family's Western Air Patrol radio and listened to the sounds of the excited crowds in front of the theatre, hearing the long black limousines pulling up in a line at the curb to let out the stars so they could be seen as they walked up the long red carpet under the awning to the entrance. It was thrilling to hear the names of the celebrities and the announcer describe the gowns the famous stars were wearing as they emerged from their chauffeur-driven limousines, Packards and Cadillacs. When one of the stars actually spoke into the microphone, I could imagine I was there myself, standing in front of the crowd against the velvet retaining ropes.

"One evening in 1932 I was listening to a premiere at Grauman's, and Norma Shearer spoke directly into the microphone, saying, 'Good evening, everyone!' before the showing of her film *Strange Interlude*. I could no longer bear not being there myself.

"The next day I played hookey from school and determined to go to Grauman's Chinese Theatre. I put on my Union Hardware roller skates and glided all the way from our house near Exposition Park to Hollywood Boulevard, at least eight miles. When I got there, my roller skate wheels were worn down to the nub, but I could still roll around all over the forecourt of the theatre where all the famous stars had made their imprints of hands and feet in wet cement when they became really famous, looking for Norma Shearer's prints with her signature.

"A Grauman's usher dressed in his Chinese costume suddenly appeared and began shouting that I was ruining the footprints of the stars. I didn't think of that in my excitement. I was a big, heavyset kid, but he managed to literally throw me out of the famous forecourt of the Chinese Theatre.

"But I didn't leave. I hung around until he left and went on my private tour of the footprints—this time with my practically wheelless skates flung over my shoulder by the straps.

"After an hour or so I telephoned my mother and told her where I was and that I couldn't skate back home. She said, 'Raymond, my God, what are you doing there?' With no money in my pocket, the nickel for the telephone now spent, she told me to take a taxi and she would be waiting at the door with cab fare money, and she was furious. But I had had a wonderful adventure."

Harold Lloyd
Ceremony #4: November 21, 1927

Born: in Burchard, Nebraska, on April 20, 1893. Died: March 8, 1971.

Charles Chaplin, Buster Keaton, and Harold Lloyd are rightly regarded as the greatest comedians of the silent screen. Lloyd was a Horatio Algeresque "Everyman," personifying aspiring American white-collar youth. Seemingly shy and unassuming, a potential nebbish, he became surprisingly aggressive

Harold Lloyd.

and heroic when danger or injustice loomed and stopped at nothing to right wrongs and save the day.

Lloyd became involved in stock company theatrics as early as 1906. When his family moved to California he found work as an extra with the Edison company in 1912. His earliest documented film appearance is in *Samson* (1914) as an extra. During this period he befriended another extra player named

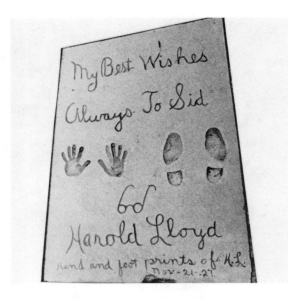

Hal Roach. Roach inherited $3,000 and thereby put Lloyd into his first leading role, "Just Nuts" (1915, short). Pathé offered them a contract; and Lloyd and Roach hit upon the Lonesome Luke character, played by Harold as a sort of variation on Chaplin's tramp.

In 1917 Lloyd conceived his "glasses character," the struggling mild-mannered youth described above. After experimenting with various types of glasses, he finally found the perfect horn-rimmed pair in a small optical shop on Spring Street in Los Angeles for seventy-five cents.

In 1919 Lloyd was badly injured during a still photo session when a supposedly fake bomb prop he was posing with proved to be live and exploded. He lost his right thumb and fore-finger but recovered and amazingly went on to make several "thrill" comedies, in which he found himself in hilarious but physically death-defying situations.

His motion picture credits include "Over the Fence" (1917, short), *Grandma's Boy* (1922), *Safety Last* (1923), *Why Worry?* (1923), *Girl Shy* (1924), *The Freshman* (1925), *The Kid Brother* (1927), *Speedy* (1928), *Welcome Danger* (1929, talkie debut), and *The Sin of Harold Diddlebock* (1947, final film, later re-released as *Mad Wednesday*).

In 1953 he received an Honorary Academy Award as a "Master comedian and good citizen."

Lloyd's square is tinted gray and contains the inscription "My Best Wishes Always To Sid." Also included are the date ("Nov-21-27"), his two foot-prints, two handprints, his signature, the inscription "Hand and foot prints of H.L.," in addition to a drawing of Lloyd's trademark eye glasses.

William S. Hart
Ceremony #5: November 28, 1927

Born: William Surrey Hart in Newburgh, New York, on December 6, 1864. Died: June 23, 1946.

William S. Hart's family moved to the West when he was a small boy. The knowledge he gained of the land, the lifestyle, and culture of the Indians made a strong impression on him that was to influence him the rest of his life.

Hart took a job with the U.S. Post Office, where he remained three years, saving money so that he could launch a career as an actor. He made his stage debut in 1889 and eventually found his way into the movies in 1914, joining Thomas H. Ince's company, which was best known for its Western productions.

Hart strongly disliked the romanticized, artificial, and glamorized depiction of the West usually presented on the screen at that time. He therefore revitalized and changed the course of the entire Western genre by insisting that his films be as authentic as possible in action, characterization, costume, and setting, infusing his pictures with a documentary-like

realism that had scarcely been seen in Western films up to that time.

He retired shortly after his last production, *Tumbleweeds* (1925), but did agree to film an eight-minute sound prologue when the film was re-released in 1939. He lived at the his ranch in Newhall, California, until his death. Fritz, Hart's beloved horse and co-star, is buried there.

William S. Hart (left) and Sid Grauman.

His motion picture credits include "His Hour of Manhood" (1914, short, debut), "The Passing of Two-Gun Hicks" (1914, short), "Cash Parrish's Pal" (1915, short), *Hell's Hinges* (1916), *The Gun Fighter* (1917), *Wolf Lowry* (1917), *The Cold Deck* (1917), *Shark Monroe* (1918), *The Toll Gate* (1920), and *Wild Bill Hickok* (1923).

Hart's square is tinted gray and contains the inscription "To my friend Grauman—lots of luck." Also included are the date ("Nov-28-27"), his two footprints, two handprints, his signature ("Bill Hart"), plus an imprint of Hart's two guns.

Adolph Zukor, who became Hart's employer in 1917 when the actor signed a contract with Paramount, tells the following story in his memoirs:

"One evening I had taken a train in Los Angeles for San Francisco. An hour or so later, in the midst of nowhere, the train struggled to a halt.

"Word flashed from car to car: 'Holdup.'

"We looked out and in the light from the windows could see western badmen up and down the tracks. Passengers began to hide wallets and jewelry in the seats.

"'They're only after the express car,' someone said hopefully.

"'No,' another replied. 'Too many of them just for that.'

"A tall man and a little man, six-shooters drawn, came into the car. The taller wore a slouch hat and a bandanna over the lower part of his face. The shorter had on a huge sombrero and a mask. They headed for me.

"'Hello, Bill,' I said.

"Those steely eyes were too well known to me. In his pictures Hart usually wore a hard-brimmed hat, more like a Canadian Mountie's than a sombrero. He had thought to disguise himself with the old slouch hat.

"'Hello, Sid,' I continued.

"Sid Grauman could have wrapped himself in the Alexandria Hotel's Oriental rug and I would still have known him. Besides, in the event of a practical joke I always looked for Grauman at the bottom of it.

"They announced at once to the other passengers that the holdup was a gag. But even after their departure many didn't believe it. The train crew had been in on the joke, of course, but I have always thought that Grauman and Hart and his cowboys took a long chance. Some passenger with a gun might have opened fire."

Tom Mix and Tony
Ceremony #6: December 12, 1927

Tom Mix

Born: Thomas Edwin Mix, in Mix Run, Pennsylvania, on January 6, 1880. Died: October 12, 1940.

Tom Mix became the greatest Western star of the 1920s by infusing his films with hard-hitting action, humor, and death-defying stunts, which he usually performed himself. While in his teens, Mix lit out for adventure and joined the U.S. military where he became an expert horseman. He later served as a law enforcement officer with the Texas Rangers and as a sheriff in Kansas and Oklahoma.

By 1909 Mix had joined the famed Miller Brothers 101 Ranch, one of the most famous of all the "Wild West" touring shows; but he was discovered by the Selig Polyscope Company of Chicago while working with another show. His early films had an artless, folksy quality and often served primarily as showcases for Mix's spectacular riding stunts, but it was at the Fox Film Corporation that he hit his real stride.

Mix, along with "Tony, the Wonder Horse," became one of the biggest money makers in the industry. In later years, Fox executive Sol M. Wurtzel largely credited the profits from Mix's films for making the construction of both their Western Avenue and Westwood studios possible.

His motion picture credits include *Ranch Life in the Great Southwest* (1909, debut), "Forked Trails" (1915, short), "Six Cylinder Love" (1917, short), *Rough Ri-*

ding Romance (1919), *The Lone Star Ranger* (1923), *The Rainbow Trail* (1925), *The Great K & A Train Robbery* (1926), *Outlaws of Red River* (1927), *Destry Rides Again* (1932, talkie debut), and *The Miracle Rider* (1935, serial, final film).

Tony

Born: 1909. Died: October 12, 1942.

Surely one of the most intelligent horses in history, "Tony, the Wonder Horse" was acquired by Tom Mix for $600 around 1911. A friend of his had originally purchased the horse for less than $20 from a Los Angeles street vendor when Tony was a six-month-old colt. Mix didn't train Tony for film work until 1917, when his first movie horse, Blue, died. Tony made his film debut with Mix in *Cupid's Roundup* (1918). From then until 1932, Tony remained Mix's constant screen co-star and companion.

Only in the most dangerous situations did Mix use a double for Tony. Usually Tony actually did his amazing stunts right along with Mix, such as performing huge leaps from cliff to cliff and plunging down steep ravines. Using his mouth, Tony repeatedly untied ropes binding his master's hands, and he could unhitch his own reins from the post when he had to race off and save the day. Astoundingly, he would even go directly into a burning structure or fiery brush to "save" Mix, if the script called for it.

In 1932 Tony and Mix suffered a very bad fall while filming. The horse was injured, and Mix was knocked unconscious. Tom realized it was time for his aging friend to be retired from filming. Another horse, Tony, Jr. (no relation), was substituted; and the original Tony was sent to live out his retirement at the Mix ranch.

Tony (Tom Mix's horse), Mix, and cement artist Jean W. Klossner.

The Mix/Tony square is tinted gray and contains the inscription "1,000 Good lucks to My Pal and Friend S.G." Also included are the date ("Dec-12-1927"), Mix's two footprints (made with boots), two handprints, and his signature, in addition to a drawing of Mix's trademark ten-gallon hat, Tony's two front hoofprints, and the inscription "Tony's hoof Prints."

The ceremony took place during "Forest Rangers' Night," a special program to which more than 200 rangers, officials, fire wardens, and others interested in forest preservation were invited. It was hoped that the evening would help promote public interest in conservation and fire prevention.

Authors H.M. and F.M. Christeson wrote in *Tony and His Pals:*

"Tom has always given Tony full credit for his share in their success. Where one has gone the other has gone, and when in 1927 Mr. Sid Grauman of Grauman's Chinese Theatre in Hollywood chose to honor Tom Mix, Tony was elected to receive the same distinction...."

Cement artist Jean W. Klossner's family has an account of this ceremony that, although entertaining, may be apocryphal. They claim that Tony was none too cooperative about placing his hoofprints. When the time came for Tony to make his imprints, the horse refused to budge from his trailer, which had been especially backed into the forecourt for the occasion. In desperation, Klossner yanked Tony's tail. Mix was infuriated and slugged Klossner in the jaw. A fight between the two men ensued. When the skirmish was over and cooler heads prevailed, Tom and Tony became a part of the forecourt.

Colleen Moore
Ceremony #7: December 19, 1927

Born: Kathleen Morrison in Port Huron, Michigan, circa August 19, 1900 (sources vary on year). Died: January 25, 1988.

Author F. Scott Fitzgerald wrote, "I was the spark that lit up flaming youth. Colleen Moore was the torch." After Moore snipped off her curly locks and created her famous "Dutch bob," Fitzgerald dubbed the act "the most fateful haircut since Samson's." She raised her skirt hems above the knee, lowered her waistlines down to the hips, and became the archetypal screen flapper.

Completely stage-struck from the age of four, Moore never wanted to be anything else but an actress. In 1916 D.W. Griffith owed Colleen's uncle (managing editor of the Chicago *American*) a favor, as the uncle had helped frustrate attempts to censor his latest release, *Intolerance*. Griffith thought she was just another movie-struck kid but gave her a job with his Triangle-Fine Arts company in Hollywood and a new name.

Moore established a legendary and original screen persona in *Flaming Youth* (1923) and set the mold for a whole school of subsequent screen flappers. As she grew older, Moore discovered that the public wanted her "to go on being the young kid I had been. Now who could do that?" She decided not to try and retired.

Her motion picture credits include *The Bad Boy* (1917, debut), *Dinty* (1920), *The Perfect Flapper* (1924), *So Big* (1924), *Ella Cinders* (1926), *Orchids and Ermine* (1927), *Lilac Time* (1928), *Smiling Irish Eyes* (1929, talkie debut), *The Power and the Glory* (1933), and *The Scarlet Letter* (1934, final film).

Colleen Moore and Sid Grauman.

Moore's square is tinted gray and contains the inscription "May the Chinese Theatre Have Greater Success Every Year Is the Wish of Colleen Moore [signature]." Also included are the date ("Dec. 19th, 1927"), her two footprints (made with high heels), and two handprints.

She tells the following story in her memoirs:

"Determined to have my feet look properly dainty instead of my own size six—now eight—I bought a pair of very tiny shoes with spike heels. Feeling like a Chinese girl with bound feet, I hobbled over to the wet cement and made the prints. When I was in Hollywood recently I went to look at them, and my feet are smaller than my hands!"

Gloria Swanson
Ceremony #8: circa 1927

Born: Gloria May Josephine Swanson in Chicago, Illinois, on May 27, 1899. Died: April 4, 1983.

One of the most important and glamorous actresses of the 1920s, Gloria Swanson was a shy child who surprisingly inquired if she might be photographed when taken on a visit to the Essanay studios in 1914. She soon was a guaranteed stock player. She

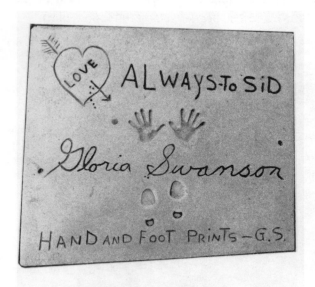

traveled to Hollywood and signed with Mack Sennett's Keystone Film Company in 1916 as a featured comedienne and leading lady.

The turning point in her career came when producer/director Cecil B. DeMille put Swanson under contract at Paramount. Her screen image was transformed into a glamorous, flamboyant, and beautifully

gowned woman of the world. Paramount put her in a series of lavish productions, and Swanson played being "the star" to the hilt. She lived an extravagant life-style and was said to have been the second woman in Hollywood to earn a million dollars and the first to have spent it.

In 1950, after years of relative inactivity in films, Swanson made a stunning impact portraying Norma Desmond, a faded silent screen star, in *Sunset Boulevard. The film provided her with one of the most memorable lines of all time: "I *am* big. It's the *pictures* that got small." Swanson followed a sensible regimen of diet and exercise and was a tireless advocate of healthful living and eating in later years.

Her motion picture credits include "The Fable of Elvira and Farina and the Meal Ticket" (1915, short, debut), "Teddy at the Throttle" (1917, short), *Don't Change Your Husband* (1919), *Male and Female* (1919), *Beyond the Rocks* (1922), *Prodigal Daughters* (1923), *Manhandled* (1924), *Sadie Thompson* (1928), *The Trespasser* (1929, talkie debut), and *Airport 1975* (1974, final film).

*Academy Award nomination: Best Actress.

Swanson's square is tinted gray and contains the inscription "Love Always To Sid." Also included are her two footprints (made with high heels), two handprints, and her signature, the inscription "Hand and Foot Prints—G.S." In addition, the word "Love" is surrounded by the drawing of a heart pierced by an arrow and six drops of blood.

Swanson was a long-time friend of Sid Grauman. One of his famous practical jokes was sending her—deftly made up—to see producer Jesse L. Lasky as an "unknown" hopeful looking for work. Lasky was one of the co-founders of Paramount where Swanson was then under contract. At the time, Gloria was a major star and drew an enormous weekly salary. Grauman hoped Lasky wouldn't recognize her and would try and sign her at $125 per week. Just as Sid had wished, Lasky didn't recognize the real Gloria Swanson under the makeup. However, he declined to hire this "unknown" girl at any price, saying she reminded him too much of somebody already in pictures!

Later, Swanson was away from Hollywood for a period of two years. She made a triumphant return on the occasion of the Los Angeles premiere of *Madame Sans-Gêne* (1925) at Sid's Million Dollar Theatre in downtown Los Angeles. When Gloria and her third husband, the Marquis Henri de la Falaise de la Coudraye, arrived by private train at the Los Angeles depot, they found all Hollywood turned out to welcome them. The crowd cheered; bands played; troops

Gloria Swanson and Sid Grauman. Sunset Boulevard *(1950): When Norma Desmond (Swanson) first encounters Joe Gillis (William Holden), a down-on-his-luck hack writer, she orders him out of her mansion. He replies, "Next time I'll bring my autograph album along, or maybe a hunk of cement and ask for your footprints."*

of policeman were on horseback; Sid's theatre usherettes rode white ponies; flowers were everywhere;
signs and banners contained messages of welcome,
and a ten-foot-wide red carpet had been rolled out.

Later that evening, traffic was jammed in downtown Los Angeles; and people crowded the street for
ten blocks in every direction. They finally made it to
the theatre. Swanson found herself again surrounded
by a cheering throng. Cecil B. DeMille called it a
tribute "that has never been equaled."

On the ride home, Swanson's mother commented,
"Glory, you're so quiet. This should be the happiest
night of your life." Swanson shook her head. "No,
Mother," she said, "it's the saddest. I'm just twenty-
six. Where do I go from here?"

Constance Talmadge
Ceremony #9: circa 1927

*Born: in Brooklyn, New York, on April 19, 1900. Died:
November 23, 1973.*

Composer Irving Berlin labeled Constance Talmadge "a virtuous vamp," and writer Anita Loos
claimed that she was "one of the few genuine *femmes
fatales* I have ever known."

As a child, she was an energetic tomboy with
whom little girls were afraid to play. Following in her
sister Norma's footsteps, Constance began doing
extra work at the Vitagraph studios in 1914. When
Norma moved on to D.W. Griffith's Triangle-Fine
Arts company in 1915, Constance tagged along, too.
She charmed and befriended Griffith, who gave Con-

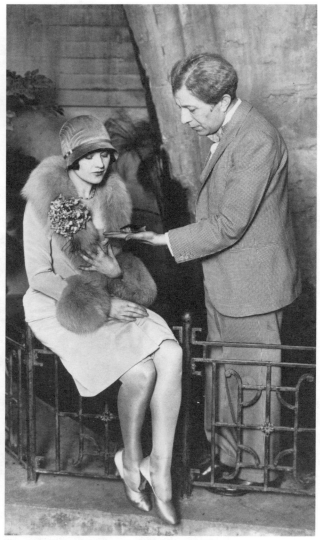

Constance Talmadge and Sid Grauman.

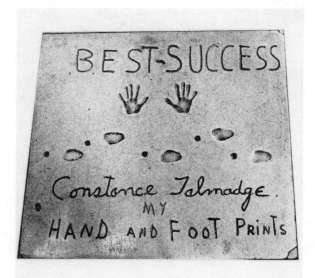

stance her first big break by casting her as The Mountain Girl in his epic *Intolerance* (1916).

Clever, whimsical, and a natural clown, Constance
captivated audiences with a series of sprightly comedies. She claimed that her "shock-proof courage" was
her "main asset," and Griffith once said she had no
knowledge of the word fear. Her style was natural,
light, sophisticated, and hilarious. Talmadge did not
want to make any talking pictures and in 1929 announced, "I'm through with the movies."

Her motion picture credits include "Buddy's First
Call" (1914, short, debut), *A Pair of Silk Stockings*
(1918), *Romance and Arabella* (1919), *Experimental
Marriage* (1919), *Polly of the Follies* (1922), *East Is
West* (1922), *Dulcy* (1923), *The Duchess of Buffalo*

(1926), *Breakfast at Sunrise* (1927), and *Venus* (1929, final film).

Talmadge's square is tinted gray and contains the inscription "Best Success." Also included are five of her footprints (made with high heels—she walked across the cement leaving three imprints of her right foot and two of her left), two handprints, and her signature, plus the inscription "My Hand and Foot Prints."

Charles Chaplin
Ceremony #10: circa January 1928

He placed his prints in connection with the motion picture *The Circus* (United Artists, 1928), in which he starred. He also wrote, produced, and directed the film. His square is no longer in the forecourt (see below).

Born: Charles Spencer Chaplin in London, England, on April 16, 1889. Died: December 25, 1977.

Author George Bernard Shaw called Charlie Chaplin "the one genius created by the cinema." As a child, poverty stricken Charlie began clowning on the streets for money and developed his gifts for performing. At seventeen he joined the Fred Karno theatrical company.

Producer Mack Sennett saw him when the company toured in the United States in 1913 and offered Chaplin a contract with his Keystone Film Company. His first film enjoyed reasonable success, but Sennett was not happy. For Chaplin's second film, "Kid Auto Races at Venice" (1914, short), Sennett instructed him to put on a different sort of comedy make-up. Thus began Chaplin's famous character, "The Little Tramp."

Chaplin learned the mechanics of film making and soon moved on. A 1916 contract with the Mutual Film Corporation promised him full creative control, and he received a $1,000,000 contract with First National Exhibitors Circuit in 1918. In 1919 he co-founded the United Artists Corporation.

As a result of his four marriages, three divorces, a paternity suit in the 1940s (in which he was found innocent), and his alleged "Communist sympathies," Chaplin became a controversial figure. Never having become a citizen, he left the U.S.—with some strong nudging from the State Department—in 1952 vowing never to return.

Twenty years later in 1972 Chaplin found himself back in Hollywood on the occasion when he received an Honorary Academy Award "for the incalculable effect he has had in making motion pictures the art form of this century." In 1975 he was knighted by Queen Elizabeth II.

His motion picture credits as an actor include "Making a Living" (1914, short, debut), and as an actor/director, "The Tramp" (1915, short), *The Gold Rush* (1925), **The Circus* (1928), *City Lights* (1931), *Modern Times* (1936), ***The Great Dictator* (1940, talkie debut), ****Monsieur Verdoux* (1947), *****Limelight* (1952), and *A Countess from Hong Kong* (1967, final film).

In 1929 he received a Special Academy Award "for writing, acting, directing and producing *The Circus*."

   * *Academy Award nominations: Best Actor and Direction.*
  ** *Academy Award nominations: Best Actor and Writing (Original Screenplay).*
 *** *Academy Award nomination: Writing (Original Screenplay).*
**** *Academy Award winner: Music (Original Dramatic Score).*

Chaplin's square is no longer in the forecourt, but one person interviewed by the authors remembers it very clearly. Robert Epstein, son of motion picture publicist Dave Epstein, passed by it often when he was growing up and viewing movies at the Chinese Theatre. He recalls the square was located near those of Mary Pickford, Douglas Fairbanks, and the other silent screen stars who are behind where the present box-office stands.

Epstein says the square contained an inscription to Sid Grauman. Also included were Chaplin's two footprints (the imprints were made with his costume shoes as "The Little Tramp" character and were positioned in his famous duck walk stance), handprints, and his signature, an imprint of "The Little Tramp's" cane (made with same, not drawn in), plus a drawing of the profile of "The Little Tramp's" derby. He does not recall if the square contained the date or any other imprints.

Chaplin was at the height of his fame and popularity when the ceremony took place. Certainly, no one then could have anticipated the intense public hostility that was to develop against him twenty years later. At some point during the Senator Joseph McCarthy-inspired investigations in the early 1950s, the hate campaign directed at Charlie resulted in his square being quietly removed or simply cemented over.

In 1971 film historian Ronald Haver wrote in an article entitled "Out of the Past: Mr. Grauman's Chinese Theatre:" "There is a rumor to the effect that

Charles Chaplin (left) and Sid Grauman signing the contract for the Chinese Theatre's showing of The Circus *(1928). In a 1937 interview, Grauman claimed to have given Chaplin, who had once worked for him on stage in San Francisco, "the letter of introduction that brought him to the screen." Chaplin's square is no longer in the forecourt (see text).*

"The Little Tramp."

in the dead of night, certain footprints have mysteriously disappeared. A spokesman for National General, the present operators of the theatre, denies this, but the footprints of Charles Chaplin, put down in 1928, have quietly vanished and nobody seems to know how."

Fox West Coast Theatres, the owner of the Chinese during the 1950s, insisted that they had no grudge against Charlie; they had just become tired of the nuisance of cleaning up the almost daily vandalism of his square.

Sid Grauman and Chaplin were long-time friends and business partners. Sid once persuaded Charlie to enter a Chaplin impersonation contest—Chaplin won third prize: $1.00. They continually played practical jokes on one another, and Sid often got the best of him. After one episode involving a Grauman "murder victim"—it turned out to be a dummy smeared with catsup—Chaplin commented, "Even if Grauman stood in front of me and said, 'Here I am,' I wouldn't believe a word the so-and-so said!"

However, Chaplin eventually got his revenge. Grauman was very proud of his distinctive haircut and felt it was his signature feature. It certainly attracted a lot of attention. Writer Anita Loos said Grauman "looked like the Mad Hatter, small and wiry with an enormous nose and a halo of fuzzy red hair." A popular joke around town was, "What breed of sheepdog is constantly seen with Joe Schenck?" The answer: "That's no sheepdog; that's Sid Grauman." In a weak moment, Sid agreed to let Charlie cut his hair. Chaplin then proceeded to give Sid the worst haircut he ever had in his life, shearing his famous locks to the skull. Sid didn't speak to him during the months it took his hair to grow out.

Chaplin recalled in his memoirs: "He [Sid Grauman] was an innovator of gimcracks. A fantastic idea of Sid's was to get Hollywood stars to stick their hands and feet in wet cement outside his Chinese Theatre; for some reason they did it. It became an honor almost as important as receiving the Oscar."

Pola Negri
Ceremony #11: April 2, 1928

Born: Barbara Apolonia Chalupec in Janowa, Poland, circa December 31, 1894 (sources vary on year). Died: August 1, 1987.

One of the most tempestuous, outspoken, and flamboyant personalities of the silent screen, Pola Negri was, after Theda Bara, the movies' greatest vamp. She studied at the Imperial Ballet School in St.

Pola Negri.

Petersburg as a girl and made her stage debut as an actress in 1913 and her film debut in 1914.

In 1917 producer/director Max Reinhardt invited her to appear in his stage productions in Germany, and she was soon under contract to the UFA film studios in Berlin. Her acting talents, coupled with her exotic, earthy, and passionate sensuality, made Negri one of Germany's top stars. Soon all the major Hollywood studios were vying to sign her. Paramount won out, bringing Negri to the United States in 1922.

Sadly, Negri found her basic character and screen personality immediately stifled and censored by the newly formed Motion Picture Producers and Distributors of America (commonly referred to as the Hays Office) that had just been set up to control "the moral content" of American films. When the talkies came in, Paramount unceremoniously dropped her in 1928, assuming there was no future for Negri due to her thick accent. She returned to Europe but eventually came back to America and became a U.S. citizen in 1951.

Her motion picture credits include *Niewolnica Zmyslow* (1914, debut, a.k.a. *Love and Passion*), *Carmen* (1918, a.k.a. *Gypsy Blood*), *Madame DuBarry* (1919, a.k.a. *Passion*), *Forbidden Paradise* (1924), *Hotel Imperial* (1927), *Barbed Wire* (1927), *The Secret Hour* (1928), *The Woman He Scorned* (1929, talkie

debit; it is reported Negri was dubbed), *Madame Bovary* (1936), and *The Moon-Spinners* (1964, final film).

Negri's square is tinted gray and contains the inscription "Dear Sid—I love your theatre." (The period is Negri's.) Also included are the date ("April 2th [sic] 1928"), her two footprints (made with high heels), two handprints, and her signature.

The ceremony took place during "Aviators' Night," a special program that was dedicated to Sid Grauman's own aerial squadron, "The Black Falcons." They were Negri's "guard of honor" at the event.

Bebe Daniels
Ceremony #12: May 11, 1929

Born: Phyllis Daniels in Dallas, Texas, on January 14, 1901. Died: March 16, 1971.

Bebe (childhood nickname) Daniels was one of Paramount's most important actresses during the 1920s. She was equally adept at sophisticated comedy, heavy drama, slapstick antics, opulent historical epics, Westerns, modern romances, French boudoir farces, and musicals.

Born to theatrical parents, Bebe's proud father introduced her on stage to an audience when she was a few weeks old. She made her film debut at age nine. A major turning point came when producer/director

Cecil B. DeMille noticed her and put her under contract at Paramount in 1919.

As the talkies loomed, Paramount adopted a policy of shedding their supposedly "over-priced" established silent players while contracting new talent from the Broadway stage. As a result, the studio never even tested Bebe for sound and dropped her in 1928. She quickly signed a new contract with RKO and triumphed in her first picture there, the "all-talking, all-singing, all-dancing" movie version of Ziegfeld's Broadway production *Rio Rita* (1929, talkie debut).

Daniels married actor Ben Lyon in 1930. In 1936 they accepted an offer to appear at the London Palladium. Their act was a hit, and the couple made England their home. During World War II, they became beloved symbols to the English public of Britain's alliance with America.

Her motion picture credits include *The Common Enemy* (1910, debut), *Male and Female* (1919), *The Speed Girl* (1921), *Monsieur Beaucaire* (1924), *Wild, Wild Susan* (1925) *The Campus Flirt* (1926), *A Kiss in*

Bebe Daniels. In their joint memoirs, Daniels' husband Ben Lyon referred to the prints in the forecourt as a "galaxy of 'heels' (the footprints, of course, not the stars)."

a Taxi (1927), *The Maltese Falcon* (1931), *42nd Street* (1933), and *The Lyons in Paris* (1956, final film).

Daniels' square is tinted gray and contains the

inscription "To Sid—Our King of Showmen." Also included are the date ("5-11-29"), her two footprints (made with high heels), two handprints, and her signature.

Marion Davies
Ceremony #13: May 13, 1929

Born: Marion Cecilia Douras in Brooklyn, New York, on January 3, 1897. Died: September 22, 1961.

Although she was a gifted comedienne, today Marion Davies is most widely remembered as the mistress, companion, and confidant of publishing titan William Randolph Hearst.

She began her theatrical career in 1913 in the chorus of a Broadway show, *The Sunshine Girl.* Her extraordinary blonde beauty was immediately noticed, and she swiftly moved from chorine to Ziegfeld show girl. She was spotted on stage by Hearst in 1915, and soon afterwards the relationship began that lasted until his death thirty-five years later. He decided to turn Marion into a movie star and in 1918 formed his own production company, Cosmopolitan Productions, to produce her pictures. Unfortunately, he usually cast her in virginal, demure roles, seldom calling upon Davies' natural comedic talents. In the late 1920s Hearst finally allowed her to prove her

mettle as a comic talent in several films. Despite a stammer, she successfully made the transition from silent films to talkies.

Marion was also famous for her extensive charitable interests, as well as her lavish parties at the fabulous Hearst ranch at San Simeon (known today as the popular Hearst Castle), her Santa Monica beach house, and her bungalow on the Metro-Goldwyn-Mayer lot.

Many people mistakenly assume that the character of the no-talent, unhappy mistress Susan Alexander in Orson Welles' Hearst-inspired film *Citizen Kane* (1941) is an accurate picture of Davies.

Her motion picture credits include *Runaway Romany* (1917, debut), *When Knighthood Was in Flower* (1922), *Little Old New York* (1923), *Janice Meredith* (1924), *The Patsy* (1928), *Show People* (1928), *The Hollywood Review of 1929* (1929, talkie debut), *Not So Dumb* (1930), *Going Hollywood* (1933), and *Ever Since Eve* (1937, final film).

Davies' square is tinted gray and contains the inscription "To Sid Grauman—The Genius Of The Theatre—From Your Pal Marion Davies [signature]." Also included are the date ("May 13th-1929"), her two footprints (made with high heels), and two handprints.

Davies placed her prints at 1:45 in the afternoon during the run of *The Broadway Melody* (1929). Her

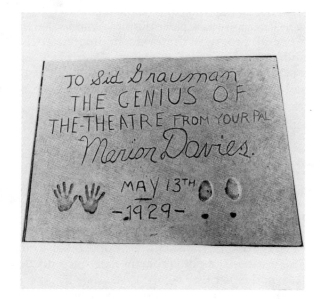

appearance just before the matinee performance caused quite a commotion. Prospective ticket buyers deserted the line at the box-office in order to get a look at her, and those who already had tickets refused to

Marion Davies.

enter the theatre in order to watch the fun in the forecourt. The crowd broke into a cheer at the conclusion of her ceremony.

Janet Gaynor
Ceremony #14: May 29, 1929

Born: Laura Gainor in Philadelphia, Pennsylvania, on October 6, 1906. Died: September 14, 1984.

Janet Gaynor had a pretty, clean-scrubbed look and projected an aura of wholesomeness coupled with a uniquely winning charm. Unsatisfied with jobs as a bookkeeper, office clerk, and usherette, she set her sights on the movies and moved to Los Angeles in 1924. She found extra work at several studios. Her big break came when she was signed by Fox and appeared prominently in *The Johnstown Flood* (1926).

Her roles in **Sunrise* (1927) and ***7th Heaven* (1927) not only turned Gaynor into a major star but along with **Street Angel* (1928) won her the very first Best Actress Oscar ever given by the Academy of Motion Picture Arts and Sciences, presented in 1929.

Fox put her into musicals when the talkies came in. Gaynor sang and danced with refreshing enthusiasm, but she felt she was really at her best in dramas. Her contract was allowed to expire in 1936 when it looked as though her box-office appeal was slipping. Producer David O. Selznick quickly grabbed her for *A Star Is Born* (1937), which became a great personal triumph for Gaynor.

She decided to quit films in 1938 and married Metro-Goldwyn-Mayer studio's distinguished fashion designer Gilbert Adrian in 1939. In later years she primarily occupied herself with painting.

Janet Gaynor.

Her motion picture credits include *Four Devils* (1929, talkie debut), *Sunny Side Up* (1929), *Daddy Long Legs* (1931), *Delicious* (1931), *State Fair* (1933), *Carolina* (1934), *The Farmer Takes a Wife* (1935), *Small Town Girl* (1936), *The Young in Heart* (1938), and *Bernardine* (1957, final film).

In 1978 in conjunction with its fiftieth anniversary celebration the Academy of Motion Picture Arts and Sciences presented Gaynor with a special plaque for her "truly immeasurable contributions to the art of motion pictures and for the pleasure and entertainment her unique artistry has brought to millions of film fans around the globe."

   * *Academy Award nomination: Best Actress.*
  ** *Academy Award winner: Best Actress.*

Gaynor's square is tinted gray and contains the inscription "Continued Success to Sid Grauman— The Master Showman." Also included are the date ("5-29-29"), her two footprints (made with high heels), two handprints, and her signature.

Gaynor's ceremony came just thirteen days after the first Academy Awards presentation, a black-tie dinner which was held across the street from the Chinese Theatre in the Blossom Room of the Hollywood Roosevelt Hotel on May 16.

Joan Crawford
Ceremony #15: September 14, 1929

She placed her prints in connection with the motion picture *Our Modern Maidens* (Metro-Goldwyn-Mayer, 1929).

Born: Lucille Fay LeSueur in San Antonio, Texas, on March 23, 1904. Died: May 10, 1977.

Joan Crawford was one of Hollywood's most durable stars. For nearly half a century she put her indelible stamp on a career full of ups and downs, always managing to triumph and remain at the top.

Working through an impoverished childhood as a laundress, waitress, and shopgirl, Crawford's dream was to be a dancer. She made her first professional appearance as same in a Chicago cafe and eventually appeared on Broadway as a chorus girl. Metro-Goldwyn-Mayer studios executive Harry Rapf saw her, offered her a contract, and brought her to Hollywood in 1925. Her first film job was doubling for Norma Shearer in *Lady of the Night* (1925).

MGM executives feared that "LeSueur" could easily be mispronounced "LeSewer" and briefly called her Joan Arden. A contest was conducted to rename her, and the lucky winner came up with Joan Crawford.

In *The Unknown* (1927) she appeared opposite Lon Chaney, whose dedication to his craft gave her "...the desire to be a real actress." Crawford had great popular success, which continued unbroken into the late 1930s. One of the most iron-willed of all movie stars, she had a tremendous tenacity, grit, and an inner drive that knew no bounds. Labeled "box-office poison" in 1938, she left MGM in 1943, signed with Warner Bros., and made one of film history's most sensational comebacks in **Mildred Pierce* (1945).

Throughout the decades, Crawford continually adapted to the style of the times. She did not want her screen image to be left behind in an ever-changing industry.

Her motion picture credits include *Our Dancing Daughters* (1928), *Untamed* (1929, talkie debut), *Letty Lynton* (1932), *Dancing Lady* (1933) *The Women* (1939), *Susan and God* (1940), *A Woman's Face* (1941), *Possessed* (1947), *Sudden Fear* (1952), and *Trog* (1970, final film).

   * *Academy Award nomination: Best Actress.*
  ** *Academy Award winner: Best Actress.*

Crawford's square is tinted gray and contains the inscription "May This Cement Our Friendship." (The period is Crawford's.) Also included are the date

("9-14-29"), her two footprints (made with high heels), two handprints, and her signature.

Crawford was accompanied by her husband Douglas Fairbanks, Jr. and recalled the following anecdote in her memoirs: "As soon as the picture [*Our Modern Maidens*] was finished, we put our footprints in the courtyard at Grauman's Chinese Theatre and slipped away to New York [to be married]." She was mistaken on two counts. She and Fairbanks had already married in June 1929, and he was not asked to place

his prints alongside hers.

Fairbanks recounts the incident in his memoirs:

"One of the supposed guerdons of film fame was planting one's hands, feet, and signature in wet cement in the forecourt of Grauman's Chinese Theatre in Hollywood. The gimmick had originally been thought up by Sid Grauman himself, but only for Mary [Pickford], Dad, Chaplin, and Barrymore. Later he was pressured by the studios to do the same thing for their Big Names. So when it was MGM's turn to plug its newest star, Joan Crawford, she and I were both sent downtown to a big, searchlight- and police-ridden event in front of the theatre. The report that we both left our marks for posterity was only half true. The film and the star were MGM properties and I was a corporate foreigner from First National. Hence, no provision was made for my recorded hands or feet at all."

Cement artist Jean W. Klossner (kneeling, left), Joan Crawford, and her husband Douglas Fairbanks, Jr.

Ann Harding
Ceremony #16: August 30, 1930

She placed her prints in connection with the motion picture *Holiday* (Pathé, 1930).

Born: Dorothy Walton Gatley in Fort Sam Houston, Texas, circa August 7, 1902 (sources vary on year). Died: September 1, 1981.

Ann Harding's interest in acting was kindled when she got a side job with the Famous Players-Lasky studios as a script reader while working at an insurance company in New York City. She applied as an actress at the Provincetown Players in Greenwich Village and was offered the lead in their upcoming production of a play entitled *Inheritors* in 1921.

Harding acted in various stock companies for two years and made her Broadway debut in 1923 in *Tarnish*. One of Broadway's most important personalities by 1929, she wanted to take a vacation but was deluged with offers from Hollywood. The salaries offered proved irresistible, and she finally signed with Pathé. Her voice recorded with perfect fidelity; so Harding was a natural during the unsure early days of talking pictures. She made her film debut in 1929 and was soon listed among the ten top money-making stars in the early 1930s.

By 1937 Harding had become increasingly dissatisfied with the material she was being offered and

Actor Harry Bannister (left), his wife Ann Harding, and cement artist Jean W. Klossner.

went to England to make films; but more importantly she starred while there in a stage production of George Bernard Shaw's *Candida*. She worked directly with Shaw, who offered aid and counsel at all rehearsals. He declared her the best Candida ever, and Harding personally considered this engagement the greatest professional triumph of her career.

Her motion picture credits include *Paris Bound* (1929, debut), **Holiday* (1930), *The Animal Kingdom* (1932), *When Ladies Meet* (1933), *Peter Ibbetson* (1935), *Enchanted April* (1935), *Eyes in the Night* (1942), *The Magnificent Yankee* (1950), *The Man in the Gray Flannel Suit* (1956), and *Strange Intruder* (1956, final film).

*Academy Award nomination: Best Actress.

Harding's square is tinted gray and contains the inscription "Whatever Success I Have You Make Possible." Also included are the date ("Aug 30, 1930"), her two footprints (made with high heels), two handprints, and her signature.

Cement artist Jean W. Klossner was required to stay after each footprint ceremony to "finish" the squares, a process that took him several hours.

On this occasion, Klossner found himself face-to-face with honoree Harding after she had finished her ceremony and was signing autographs for the enthusiastic crowd. She politely inquired if Klossner would like an autograph. He replied in the affirmative and handed over the only piece of paper he was able to locate on his person—a five-dollar bill. She happily signed it for him.

Although neither of them realized it at the time, Harding started what was to become a tradition for Klossner. Every time he performed a ceremony thereafter, Klossner had the star and/or stars sign a dollar bill. The exceptions were Deanna Durbin, Irene Dunne, and Rex Harrison, who signed two-dollar bills.

Raoul Walsh
Ceremony #17: November 14, 1930

He placed his prints in connection with the motion picture *The Big Trail* (Fox, 1930), which he directed.

Born: Albert Edward Walsh in New York City on March 11, 1887. Died: December 31, 1980.

Raoul Walsh directed over 100 feature films and was regarded as a master craftsman. He made his stage debut in a 1910 production of *The Clansman* in San Antonio, Texas. Later that same year he acquired

work as a cowboy actor at the Pathé studios in New Jersey. By 1912 he had found work as an actor and assistant to director D.W. Griffith at the Biograph company. Griffith cast Walsh as John Wilkes Booth in *The Birth of a Nation* (1915) and also dispatched him to Mexico, where he made his directorial debut (as co-director, with Christy Cabanne) filming both documentary and staged footage of Pancho Villa, resulting in *The Life of General Villa* (1914).

Walsh signed as a director with the Fox Film Corporation in 1915, where he remained steadily, save a few loan-outs, until 1933. It was during the production of *In Old Arizona* (1929, talkie debut) on a desert location that a jackrabbit shattered the window of Walsh's car and blinded him in one eye, resulting in the eye patch that he wore for the rest of his life. Walsh free-lanced through the 1930s until signing a long-term contract with Warner Bros. in 1939.

At Warners he solidified his reputation as a fine director of virile, hard-hitting, tough-minded action and adventure films, starring such legends as James Cagney, Humphrey Bogart, Errol Flynn, and George Raft.

His motion picture credits as a director include *The Thief of Bagdad* (1924), *What Price Glory* (1926), *Klondike Annie* (1936), *The Roaring Twenties* (1939), *They Drive by Night* (1940), *The Strawberry Blonde* (1941), *High Sierra* (1941), *Objective, Burma!* (1945), *White Heat* (1949), and *A Distant Trumpet* (1964, final film).

Walsh's square is tinted gray and contains the date ("Nov. 14-1930"), his two footprints, two handprints, and his signature. Also included is his fist print with the inscription "his Mark."

Robert Parrish was a child actor who later became a film editor, writer, and director. He was fourteen years old when his younger sister, Helen, was cast in a small role in *The Big Trail*, and he was hired as an extra. Parrish later recalled Walsh's Chinese Theatre ceremony in his memoirs:

"...It was the first time that a movie director was invited to sign his name in the cement blocks in the forecourt of the theatre, an honor reserved until then for stars....

"Jack Padjan [an ex-cowboy who 'supplied livestock and wagons to the studios' and had been the head wrangler on *The Big Trail*] brought one of the covered wagons from the picture up to the forecourt of the theatre in the morning. The Fox publicity people spent the day fussing about the wagon....They

Harry E. Jones, president of the Hollywood Chamber of Commerce (left), Dr. John C. Perrish, president of the California Historical Society, Joseph Meller, president of the California Pioneer Association, The Big Trail *(1930) cast members Louise Carver, Tully Marshall, Helen Parrish, Marguerite Churchill, director Raoul Walsh, and Thomas C. Hull, an eighty-seven-year-old pioneer of the original wagon trails.*

also came up with suggestions for something clever for him [Walsh] to write beside his name. This was important....If a star was identified with anything special, he tried to work that in.

"When Walsh arrived, he posed for a photograph in front of Jack Padjan's covered wagon with Emslie Emerson, Louise Carver, Helen Parrish (dressed in her *Big Trail* costume), Marguerite Churchill, and Tully Marshall from the *Big Trail* cast....

"After the photo session, the cement mixer said the block was ready. The publicity man gave Walsh a piece of paper with several suggestions: 'To Sid, On The Big Trail to Happiness,' 'To Sid, The Big Trail

Blazer of Showmanship,' etc. Walsh glanced at the paper, crumpled it up, and put it in his pocket.

"'Where's the wet cement?' he said.

"'Over here, Mr. Walsh....'

"Walsh followed him over to where a movie gossip columnist was waiting with the traditional wooden stick used for signing names in the cement. He signed his name and wrote in the date....Then he put his left fist into the wet cement. Harry Brand, the Fox publicity director said, 'What's that, Raoul?' Walsh looked at him for a moment, then wrote above the imprint of his fist—'his Mark.'"

Cement artist Jean W. Klossner (kneeling, left), Wallace Beery, and Marie Dressler.

Wallace Beery and Marie Dressler Ceremony #18: January 31, 1931

They placed their prints in connection with the motion picture *Min and Bill* (Metro-Goldwyn-Mayer, 1930).

Wallace Beery

Born: in Kansas City, Missouri, on April 1, 1885. Died: April 15, 1949.

Wallace Beery is best remembered for his sound era roles as a tough, rumpled slob who inevitably turns out to be a lovable sort of palooka-rogue with a heart of gold. His brother Noah found work on the Broadway stage and enticed Wallie to try a hand at the theatre, and by 1904 he found himself a chorus boy in New York in *Babes in Toyland*. Later he signed with the Essanay studios to appear in comedy shorts and made his film debut in "His Athletic Wife" (1913, short). In 1914-1915 Beery starred in the successful "Sweedie" comedies, in which he appeared as a female Swedish maid.

He joined the Keystone Film Company in 1916. Leaving the following year, Beery embarked on a series of arch villains, which were to become his specialty. A change of pace as King Richard the Lion-Hearted in Douglas Fairbanks' *Robin Hood* (1922), proved to be his most important role up to that time. He signed with Paramount in 1925.

When the talkies loomed, the studio saw no future for Beery in sound films and let his contract expire in 1929. Metro-Goldwyn-Mayer signed him and put him in *The Big House (1930, talkie debut) as a replacement for an ailing Lon Chaney. Beery and Marie Dressler charmed the world in *Min and Bill* (1930) and *Tugboat Annie* (1933). In later years, MGM teamed Beery with Marjorie Main in an effort to re-kindle the old Beery/Dressler magic.

His motion picture credits include *The Last of the Mohicans* (1920), *Old Ironsides* (1926), **The Champ (1931), *Grand Hotel* (1932), *Dinner at Eight* (1933), *The Bowery* (1933), *Viva Villa!* (1934), *Treasure Island* (1934), *A Date with Judy* (1948), and *Big Jack* (1949, final film).

* *Academy Award nomination: Best Actor.*
** *Academy Award winner: Best Actor.*

Marie Dressler

Born: Leila Marie von Koerber in Cobourg, Canada, on November 9, 1869. Died: July 28, 1934.

Possessed with the radiance of inner beauty, Marie Dressler was one of the most universally beloved of all film stars during her final years. At fourteen she left home and set out for a career on the stage. Dressler made her debut in *Under Two Flags* in Saginaw, Michigan, in 1886; and during the next six years she toured and sang over forty operatic roles. She made a successful Broadway debut in the comic opera *The Robber of the Rhine* in 1892. She made her film debut for producer Mack Sennett's Keystone Film Company in *Tillie's Punctured Romance* (1914), one of the first feature-length comedy films.

In 1919 Dressler became a champion of the Broadway chorus girls in a strike, which led to the official recognition of Actors' Equity as the performers' bargaining agent. As a result of her activism she was blacklisted by theatrical producers and managers, and her career plummeted. A virtual has-been in 1926, Dressler had a chance meeting with director Allan Dwan who hired her for a part in the Fox film *The Joy Girl* (1927).

Once in Hollywood, Marie found a strong ally in the influential writer Frances Marion, who wrote a script especially for Marie, *The Callahans and the Murphys* (1927), and helped Dressler obtain a contract with Metro-Goldwyn-Mayer. Dressler nearly stole *Anna Christie* (1930) from Greta Garbo, who was making her talkie debut; and her greatest triumph came with **Min and Bill* (1930).

Her motion picture credits include "The Scrub Lady" (1917, short), *Bringing Up Father* (1928), *The Patsy* (1928), *The Hollywood Revue of 1929* (1929, talkie

Chinese Theatre usherettes Evelyn Corey and Sue Slamos (not in uniform) watch workmen ready the Beery/Dressler square for relocation (probably in the 1940s). The box-office had been sitting on top of the block for several years.

debut), *Let Us Be Gay* (1930), *Reducing* (1931), **Emma* (1932), *Tugboat Annie* (1933), *Dinner at Eight* (1933), and *Christopher Bean* (1933, final film).

* *Academy Award nomination: Best Actress.*
** *Academy Award winner: Best Actress.*

The Beery/Dressler square is tinted gray and contains the inscription "America's New Sweethearts." Also included are the date ("Jan-31-31"), Beery's two footprints, and his signature ("Wallie Beery"), Dressler's two footprints (made with high heels), and her signature, plus the inscription "'Min and Bill.'" The "s" in "America's" is squeezed in above the "a" and the "New."

Beery's nickname of Wallie has mistakenly been spelled as "Wally" throughout the years. Research has proven that he did indeed spell it, at least some of the time, as it is written in the square.

The Beery/Dressler square is the only one to have been moved to another part of the forecourt in the theatre's sixty-five year history. The cement block had been partially hidden when a new box-office was installed in the mid-1930s. Tourists and visitors complained about the loss of the square; so Fox West Coast Theatres, then owner of the Chinese Theatre, tore the box-office away and moved the slab to its present location (probably in the 1940s). A rededication ceremony took place after the job was completed.

Years before, when Metro-Goldwyn-Mayer's *Hell Divers* (1931) was to run at the Chinese Theatre, Sid Grauman came up with the idea of a traveling ticket office. An MGM star was to go with a wagon to hand out the tickets, assisted by a treasurer to handle the cash receipts.

Certain well-known local sites were to be chosen each day for the convenience of the theatre patrons. If it was inconvenient for the patrons to visit the wagon, they simply had to put in a telephone call; and star, bus, and treasurer would call at their doorstep.

Beery, one of the leads of the picture, was chosen to be the first star to take part in Sid's innovation. Apparently, this idea never came to fruition.

Jackie Cooper
Ceremony #19: December 12, 1931

He placed his prints in connection with the motion picture *The Champ* (Metro-Goldwyn-Mayer, 1931).

Born: John Cooper, Jr. in Los Angeles, California, Circa September 15, 1922 (sources vary on year).

The first major child star to emerge in the movies' early sound era, Jackie Cooper charmed, moved, and amazed audiences with the impressive sensitivity and emotional range of his performances. At age three his grandmother took him to casting offices and got him his first job in a Bobby Clark comedy short. His uncle, director Norman Taurog, shortly thereafter cast him in a few Lloyd Hamilton shorts, which he was directing for the Educational company.

Jackie appeared in fifteen of the "Our Gang" comedies for producer Hal Roach, which led to his being cast in his breakthrough film, *Skippy* (1931). All the major stu-

dios clamored to sign him, and Metro-Goldwyn-Mayer won out. A series of hits followed. Jackie continued successfully into his mid-teens at MGM, but by the late 1930s and into the early 1940s the quality of his films somewhat lessened. In *Glamour Boy* (1941), he parodied himself, playing a former child star making a comeback, though Cooper did not experience a long period off the screen until his three-year stint in the Navy during World War II.

Cooper later forged a successful career in television with two popular series, "The People's Choice" (1955-1958) and "Hennesey" (1959-1962). Thereafter he continued in television as a an actor and director and was in charge of Columbia Pictures Television (1963-1972), while appearing in occasional theatrical films and directing his first in 1972, *Stand Up and Be Counted*.

His motion picture credits as an actor include *Fox Movietone Follies of 1929* (1929, talkie debut), *When a Feller Needs a Friend* (1932), *The Bowery* (1933), *Treasure Island* (1934), *Peck's Bad Boy* (1934), *The Devil Is a Sissy* (1936), *What a Life!* (1939), *Kilroy Was Here* (1947), *Superman* (1978), and *Superman IV: The Quest for Peace* (1987).
*Academy Award nomination: Best Actor.

Jackie's square is tinted gray and contains the inscription "America's Boy." Also included are the date ("Dec-12-31."), his two footprints, two handprints, and his signature, plus the inscription "age 8 Years."

The ceremony took place during the Christmas season, and Jackie was accompanied by a Santa Claus. After Cooper placed his prints, he and Santa hosted over two thousand children who attended a morning screening of *The Champ*.

He wrote in his memoirs:

Jackie Cooper.

"I was, the stories...pointed out, a regular kid. There was nothing sissy or uppity about Jackie Cooper. He was, after all, America's Boy.

"The star treatment was mine.

"I placed my footprints in the forecourt of Grauman's Chinese Theatre.

"I had a fan club....There was a Jackie Cooper newspaper.

"We had someone handling my fan mail. I never saw it and never answered a single letter personally.

"I began to meet other big names, who found it advisable, from a public relations standpoint, to be seen in public with me."

In a telephone conversation with the authors, Cooper recalled that both he and his mother were surprised when Sid Grauman wrote the phrase "America's Boy" in the cement immediately after Cooper made his imprints. Neither of them knew that Grauman was going to make that inscription. Cooper says that not many other squares have a nickname on them like that, and he's right.

He'd forgotten all about the footprints when, years later, he and actor James Garner were filming a television episode of "The Rockford Files" in the 1970s on location in front of the Chinese Theatre. Garner took Cooper to show him where his (Garner's) star was on the Hollywood Boulevard Walk of Fame in front of the theatre. Some of the crew members mentioned that they'd just been in the theatre's forecourt looking at the footprints and saw Cooper's imprints. Cooper and Garner walked over to view the square. "It was quite a thrill," he said, to see his prints after so many years.

Eddie Cantor
Ceremony #20: March 9, 1932

Born: Edward Israel Iskowitz in New York City, on January 31, 1892. Died: October 10, 1964.

One of the truly legendary figures of 20th-century American show business, entertainer Eddie Cantor came to the movies after many years of stardom on the Broadway musical comedy stage. His trademarks were his popping "banjo eyes" and a quick-stepping, hand-clapping, lightning-fast delivery of comedy songs.

Winning first prize in an amateur contest inspired him to make a serious stab at show business, and his first professional job was in the burlesque revue *Indian Maidens* in 1907. Cantor eventually became a star on Broadway. He appeared in Ziegfeld's *Kid*

Boots in 1923 and made his film debut in the successful screen adaptation of the play in 1926.

Whoopee! became another one of his stage hits in 1928, and the 1930 film version led to Cantor's signing a contract with the Samuel Goldwyn company.

His radio program, "The Eddie Cantor Show," made him one of the most popular stars of the medium. As early as 1931 he was credited with inventing and introducing the concept of the live studio audience.

Cantor's final film found him making a cameo appearance as himself during a brief prologue and epilogue in the story of his life, *The Eddie Cantor Story* (1953). He was portrayed by Keefe Brasselle in the film. At the time of his death Cantor was said to have raised more money for charity than any other show business figure in history.

His motion picture credits include *Glorifying the American Girl* (1929, talkie debut), *Palmy Days* (1931), *The Kid from Spain* (1932), *Roman Scandals* (1933), *Kid Millions* (1934), *Strike Me Pink* (1936), *Ali Baba Goes to Town* (1937), *Show Business* (1944), and *If You Knew Susie* (1948).

In 1957 he received an Honorary Academy Award "for distinguished service to the film industry."

Cantor's square is tinted gray and contains the inscription "Here's looking at you Sid." Also included are the date ("3-9-32"), his two footprints, two handprints, and his signature, plus a drawing of his trademark eyes and eyebrows.

In 1922 Sid Grauman saw Cantor in a Ziegfeld show. After the performance they went to supper with a group. Grauman expressed his admiration for Can-

Eddie Cantor (left) and cement artist Jean W. Klossner.

tor and his desire to have him come to Hollywood and star in one of the Grauman prologues at a future date. Cantor replied, "If I ever come to Hollywood and have the chance, it's a deal."

On March 6, 1932 Cantor made good his promise and started a one-week engagement at the Chinese Theatre during the final extended seven days of the Greta Garbo *Mata Hari* (1931) run. He sang, danced, and clowned all through the prologue, opening straight and then making up into his famous blackface character in full view of the audience.

In a letter to the authors, Natalie Cantor Clary, one of Cantor's five daughters, recalled:

"At that time, our family had recently moved here from the East, and we children were great movie buffs. We were enchanted with the glamor of the Chinese Theatre and saw every film that appeared there. Naturally, we were thrilled that my father was shown the respect of the industry by having his prints implanted in the forecourt of the theatre. How wonderful it is to be able to show these prints to our own children and grandchildren today!"

Diana Wynyard
Ceremony #21: January 26, 1933

She placed her prints in connection with the motion picture *Cavalcade* (Fox, 1933).

Born: Dorothy Cox in London, England, on January 16, 1906. Died: May 13, 1964.

Diana Wynyard was a distinguished leading lady of the British theatre who worked much more often on the stage than in films. She studied dramatics at school and made her stage debut in 1925. Joining the Hamilton Dean Repertory Company and then the Liverpool Repertory Company, she once played forty different roles in one year. Her first leading role was in the play *The Devil Passes*, which became a hit. It was transported to Broadway in 1932 with Wynyard in her original role. The play enjoyed a major success in New York; and Metro-Goldwyn-Mayer, impressed with Diana's charm and grace, signed her to a contract and imported her to Hollywood.

Wynyard made her film debut opposite the three Barrymores in *Rasputin and the Empress* (1932). Her most notable Hollywood film came next with *Cavalcade*. The film was the year's biggest grosser at $3,500,000 and won the Best Picture Oscar. Wynyard returned to London and continued her work on the British stage with many more hits and appeared only occasionally in films.

Her motion picture credits include *Reunion in Vienna* (1933), *Where Sinners Meet* (1934), *Let's Try Again* (1934), *On the Night of the Fire* (1939, a.k.a. *The Fugitive*), *Gaslight* (1940, a.k.a. *Angel Street*), *The Prime Minister* (1941), *Kipps* (1941, a.k.a. *The Remarkable Mr. Kipps*), *An Ideal Husband* (1948), *The Feminine Touch* (1956, a.k.a. *The Gentle Touch*), and *Island in the Sun* (1957, final film).
Academy Award nomination: Best Actress.

Wynyard's square is tinted gray and contains the inscription "Happiness always." Also included are the date ("Jan-26-33"), her two footprints (made with high heels), two handprints, and her signature.

Sid Grauman was so delighted with *Cavalcade* that he decided Wynyard should have her prints recorded in the Chinese Theatre forecourt. An audience had gathered for the event; the wet cement was waiting, and Grauman had the cameras all set to take pictures of the historic occasion.

Then he began a lengthy speech, telling the gath-

ering what a wonderful actress the English woman was, so elaborating on her talents that one writer quipped that the likes "...had never been equalled since the days of Mrs. Siddons...." (Sarah Kemble Siddons was a famous English actress in the late eighteenth century.)

Finally, when Sid ran out of superlatives, he turned in exasperation to Wynyard and said, "My dear, I'm sorry, but just what is your name?"

Diana Wynyard.

The Marx Brothers
Ceremony #22: February 17, 1933

They placed their prints in connection with the motion picture *Duck Soup* (Paramount, 1933).

The four Marx Brothers ("Marx" was their true surname) who appeared in film came into the world in New York City as follows: Chico, born Leonard, on March 22, 1887/died: October 11, 1961; Harpo, born Adolph, on November 23, 1888/died: September 28, 1964; Groucho, born Julius Henry, on October 2, 1890/died: August 19, 1977; and Zeppo, born Herbert, on February 25, 1901/died: November 30, 1979.

Zany, irreverent, outrageous, insulting, surreal, and insane—these are just a few of the words that often have been used to describe the comedy of the Marx Brothers. A fifth brother, Gummo (born Milton in 1897) was on stage with their act in early years but left show business before they made films. Their mother, Minna, whose brother became Al Shean of the famed comedy team of Gallagher and Shean, encouraged her sons toward theatrics from boyhood with singing and music lessons.

After years on various vaudeville circuits, they finally made it to Broadway in *I'll Say She Is* in 1924,

in which they scored a hit and became stars. Next on Broadway were *The Cocoanuts* in 1925 and *Animal Crackers* in 1928, both of which ran for two years. Paramount signed them to a contract. They filmed *The Cocoanuts* (1929, debut as a team) by day at the Astoria studios on Long Island, while they performed *Animal Crackers* by night on Broadway.

The Marx Brothers (Harpo [left], Groucho, Zeppo, and Chico) and Sid Grauman. As a joke, the five paraded along Hollywood Boulevard that day dressed in Scottish kilts to protest the new trend in female fashions allowing women to wear slacks!

Duck Soup, their last film for Paramount, was also their last picture with Zeppo, who left the team to become an agent. Irving G. Thalberg at Metro-Goldwyn-Mayer signed the remaining three, and their first two films for the company, *A Night at the Opera* (1935) and *A Day at the Races* (1937), were great successes. Their future pictures were somewhat watered down and not as popular. In 1941 they decided to break up and go their separate professional ways, and filmed together as a team only twice thereafter.

Of all the Marx Brothers, Groucho achieved the greatest success as a solo performer—mainly during his fourteen-year stint, beginning on radio (1947-1958) and then moving into television (1950-1961), with his quiz show "You Bet Your Life." In 1974 Groucho received an Honorary Academy Award "in recognition of his brilliant creativity and for the unequalled achievements of the Marx Brothers in the art of motion picture comedy."

Their motion picture credits include *Animal Crackers* (1930), *Monkey Business* (1931), *Horse Feathers* (1932), *Room Service* (1938), *At the Circus* (1939), *Go*

West (1940), *The Big Store* (1941), *A Night in Casablanca* (1946), and *Love Happy* (1950, final film as a team).

The team's square is tinted gray and contains the inscription "Best Wishes To Sid Grauman From The Marx Bros." Also included are the date ("Feb-17-33"), Groucho's two footprints, two handprints, and two of his signatures (both signatures: "Groucho"); Chico's two footprints, two handprints, and two of his signatures (both signatures: "Chico"); Harpo's two footprints (made with bare feet), two handprints, and two of his signatures (one signature: "Harpo;" the other is a drawing of a harp and the letter "O"); Zeppo's two footprints, two handprints, and two of his signatures (both signatures: "Zeppo").

In his memoirs, writer Arthur Marx had the following to say about his father Groucho and his hand and footprint ceremony:

"There are many things about Hollywood that Father doesn't like, and has tried to avoid...."

"When he first moved to Hollywood, he even balked at putting his footprints alongside those of the other stars in the cement in the forecourt of Grauman's Chinese Theatre.

"'What do I want to do that for?' he'd say, whenever the Paramount Publicity Department brought up the subject. 'What good will it do me?'

"Informed that any publicity was good, Father replied, 'There are an awful lot of actors who have their footprints in there that can't get jobs any more. It's not doing them much good.'

"Under constant pressure, he finally consented, 'But only one foot!' he stipulated. 'If Paramount picks up our option, I'll give you the other foot.'"

Groucho called the Marx Brothers ceremony "a ritual that cemented our foothold in Hollywood...." He went on to recount that when Zeppo left the act, a local newspaper ran a photograph of what had originally been the four Marx Brothers at their Chinese Theatre ceremony, only then it looked as though just Groucho, Harpo, and Chico had placed their prints—Zeppo was gone! Groucho commented, "There was no more conclusive evidence that Zeppo was now a civilian than the neat doctoring job of a Los Angeles tabloid. Zeppo was cut out of one of the pictures of our ritual in concrete at Grauman's and the background was shadowed in. Now we were three."

According to the family of cement artist Jean W. Klossner, Harpo decided it would be amusing to pummel the reporters in attendance with wet cement; and a cement-slinging contest ensued. (The Klossners do not elaborate as to how the reporters reacted to this idea.)

Jean Harlow
Ceremony #23: September 25, 1933

She placed her prints in connection with the motion pictures *Dinner at Eight* and *Bombshell* (both Metro-Goldwyn-Mayer, 1933). Harlow's first square was never placed in the forecourt (see below); one can only assume that it was planned to be located in the same location as her present square, which is #149 on this book's Forecourt of the Stars map.

Born: Harlean Carpenter in Kansas City, Missouri, on March 3, 1911. Died: June 7, 1937.

One of the 1930s' greatest stars, Jean Harlow was revered world-wide as "the platinum blonde bombshell," an image that somewhat obscures her rightful claim to fame as a brilliant and scintillating comic actress.

Her father was a well-to-do dentist, and Harlow received an excellent education at exclusive private institutions. She eloped at sixteen, married a wealthy young socialite, and moved to Beverly Hills. As a rich but bored young wife, she visited the Fox studios with a friend who worked there. On a dare, Harlow found work as an extra at Fox and Paramount, including *Moran of the Marines* (1928), and became a contract player at the Hal Roach Studios. Her marriage soon

ended.

Harlow's major breakthrough came when she was cast in producer/director Howard Hughes' *Hell's Angels* (1930). Hughes signed her to a contact and subsequently loaned her out to appear as a series of sexy floozies. Metro-Goldwyn-Mayer bought her contract from Hughes in 1932 and utilized Harlow's natural ability in comedy. The tragic suicide of her second husband, MGM executive Paul Bern, in 1932, and a short-lived marriage to cinematographer Hal Rosson left emotional scars but never hindered her career.

Everything seemed to be going marvelously for Harlow—critical and commercial success, a promising romance with actor William Powell—when a series of health problems plagued her. She collapsed on the set of her last film, *Saratoga* (1937), and was taken home. Her mother, a Christian Scientist, refused to call a doctor; and when Jean was finally taken to a hospital, it was too late to save her life.

Harlow died of uremic poisoning and cerebral edema nine days later.

Her motion picture credits include "Liberty" (1929, short), *The Saturday Night Kid* (1929, talkie debut), *The Public Enemy* (1931), *Platinum Blonde* (1931), *Red-Headed Woman* (1932), *Red Dust* (1932), *China Seas* (1935), *Wife Vs. Secretary* (1936), *Libeled Lady* (1936), and *Personal Property* (1937).

Harlow's first square contained the inscription "To Sid Grauman—With Sincere Appreciation." Also included were her two footprints (made with high heels), her handprints, and her signature. It is not known whether or not the square contained the date or any other imprints.

Harlow placed her prints in a wet cement slab that had been wheeled on to the actual stage of the theatre—a result of Sid's first attempt to have a footprinting ceremony inside, before a live—and paying—audience. This attempt failed, as the cement dried too quickly. While it was being moved, one half dropped to the floor and smashed into bits in front of the audience.

Harlow was honored with another ceremony at the Chinese Theatre four days later.

Jean Harlow
Ceremony #24: September 29, 1933

Jean Harlow's second square—the first one never made it into the forecourt—is tinted gray and contains the inscription "To Sid—In Sincere Appreciation." Also included are the date ("Sept-29-33"), her two footprints (made with high heels), two handprints, and her signature, plus three black pennies she embedded in the cement for good luck. The pennies have since been pried out.

Harlow agreed to participate in another hand and footprint ceremony so that the new square could replace the block that had been shattered four days earlier when the attempt to hold her ceremony on the stage inside the Chinese Theatre before a ticket-buying audience failed. Unlike the first attempt to record her prints, Harlow's second ceremony took place outside in the forecourt of the theatre before an enthusiastic (and non-paying) crowd.

The family of cement artist Jean W. Klossner has a different account of this ceremony that is entertaining, but apocryphal. According to the Klossner family, Harlow arrived wearing sandals, shoes not appropriate to leave the desired prints. A search was made among the crowd to find her proper shoes. Klossner's

own daughter was present. A Hollywood High School student at the time, she doffed her saddle shoes, and Harlow made her impression in them. However, photographs of Harlow at both her ceremonies clearly show that her prints were made with high heels.

Cement artist Jean W. Klossner (left), Jean Harlow, and Sid Grauman. The ceremony took place on the Chinese Theatre's stage, and Harlow's square broke into pieces as the workers were attempting to move it into the forecourt (see text).

During the time Chevalier was accused of collaboration, considerable pressure was applied in the U.S. in an attempt to force Sid Grauman to remove Chevalier's square from the theatre's forecourt. Grauman completely rebuked any such suggestions and later said, "I refused to move it because I knew the man too well. He couldn't have been guilty, and I knew it."

In the late 1940s Chevalier played a cafe engagement in Hollywood and was delighted when he discovered his imprints were still at the Chinese Theatre.

Jeanette MacDonald

Born: Jeanette Anna MacDonald in Philadelphia, Pennsylvania, circa June 18, 1903 (sources vary on year). Died: January 14, 1965.

Jeanette MacDonald was lovely and vivacious and possessed a glorious soprano voice. Co-star Nelson Eddy called her "the greatest woman movie singer who ever lived." Trained in dramatics, dancing, and singing, Jeanette went to New York City in 1920 and made her Broadway debut in the chorus of *The Demi-Tasse Revue*. She worked her way up to her first important part in *A Fantastic Fricassee* (1922).

Paramount star Richard Dix saw her perform in 1928 and was so impressed that he arranged a screen test for her. Nothing came of the test until a year later when director Ernst Lubitsch saw her footage while searching for the female lead in his next production. He decided at once that she'd be perfect, and Mac-

Sid Grauman (left), Jeanette MacDonald, and cement artist Jean W. Klossner. The ceremony took place on the Chinese Theatre's stage.

lished them as the most popular singing team in film history, and they co-starred together in seven additional films. Her MGM contract ended in 1942; and MacDonald remained active on the concert stage, appearing before sell-out audiences.

Her motion picture credits include *Monte Carlo* (1930), *One Hour with You* (1932), *Love Me Tonight* (1932), *Rose Marie* (1936), *San Francisco* (1936), *Maytime* (1937), *The Firefly* (1937), *Sweethearts* (1938), *Smilin' Through* (1941), and *The Sun Comes Up* (1949, final film).

MacDonald's square is tinted gray and contains the inscription "Continued Success Sid." Also included are the date ("Dec-4-34"), her two footprints (made with high heels), two handprints, and her signature.

The Chevalier/MacDonald ceremony was the last attempt Sid Grauman ever made to have the celebrities record their hand and footprints on wet cement slabs that were wheeled on to the actual stage of the theatre and transferred to the forecourt after they dried. Unlike the first such attempt to record the prints of Jean Harlow, the Chevalier/MacDonald blocks dried properly and were successfully transferred to the theatre's forecourt.

Donald made her film debut opposite Maurice Chevalier in *The Love Parade* (1929). Their pairing resulted in several films that were delightfully sophisticated and subtly risqué.

Jeanette signed with Metro-Goldwyn-Mayer in 1933 and was first teamed opposite baritone Nelson Eddy in *Naughty Marietta* (1935). The picture estab-

Shirley Temple
Ceremony #26: March 14, 1935

She placed her prints in connection with the motion picture *The Little Colonel* (Fox, 1935).

Born: Shirley Jane Temple in Santa Monica, California, on April 23, 1928.

Unquestionably the most popular child star in film history, Shirley Temple was the number one box-office attraction for four consecutive years (1935-1938)—an achievement that no other child performer ever equalled. Millions of moviegoers responded to her sparkling personality, all framed in dimples and curls.

Shirley first appeared in a series of short films featuring moppets entitled "Baby Burlesks" at the Educational company. Her breakthrough came when she was cast to sing the song "Baby Take a Bow" in the Fox production *Stand Up and Cheer* (1934). She stole the picture, and the public clamored to see more of her. Fox quickly put her under contract. The world's adulation dimmed only when Temple approached adolescence.

She signed with Metro-Goldwyn-Mayer, only to be cast in a mediocre programmer, *Kathleen* (1941). In 1943 producer David O. Selznick signed her to a seven-year contract, featured her in *Since You Went Away* and *I'll Be Seeing You* (both 1944), and then loaned her out for the duration of her film career.

Temple married businessman Charles Alden Black in 1950 and announced that she had no further interest in acting in films, although she appeared on television as hostess and sometime performer on two series: "Shirley Temple's Storybook" (1959) and "The Shirley Temple Show" (1960-1961).

In the late 1960s Temple entered politics and was appointed as a special U.S. representative to the United Nations (1969-1970). She was ambassador to Ghana (1974-1976) and served as White House chief of protocol (1976-1977). In 1989 she was made ambassador to Czechoslovakia.

Her motion picture credits include "The Runt Page" (1932, short, debut), *Little Miss Marker* (1934), *The Littlest Rebel* (1935), *Captain January* (1936), *Wee Willie Winkie* (1937), *Heidi* (1937), *Rebecca of Sunnybrook Farm* (1938), *The Little Princess* (1939), *The Bachelor and the Bobby-Soxer* (1947), and *A Kiss for Corliss* (1949).

In 1935 she received a Special Academy Award "in grateful recognition of her outstanding contribution to screen entertainment during the year 1934."

Shirley's square is tinted gray and contains the inscription "Love To You All." Also included are the date ("3-14-35"), her two footprints (made with bare feet), two handprints, and her signature.

Sid Grauman appeared as a guest on a "Lux Radio Theatre" broadcast of *A Star Is Born* in 1937 and had the following recollection about Shirley's ceremony:

"When Shirley came to the theatre to leave her footprints she asked me if I'd mind if she took off her shoes and socks. I told her that we couldn't do that because she'd get her feet all full of concrete. As usual she had an answer ready. 'We can get some warm water and a towel and I'll wash them very carefully.' 'But why,' I asked, 'do you want to make your footprints in bare feet?' 'Mr. Grauman,' she said, 'I just want to be different.' "

Temple recalled in her memoirs:

"For rising movie stars it was noblesse oblige to register hand and footprints in wet cement in the forecourt plaza of Grauman's Chinese....A wall of gaping people pressed in to gawk at my investiture. At this moment of maximum exposure, out fell my first baby tooth, an incisor, right in the middle of my smile. Furtively, I spit it into my hand.

"'Smile for the photographers,' Mother whispered, unaware. With lips pursed, I grinned. The cameras were all on my face.

"[Cement artist] Jean W. Klossner...was beside me in his flowing robe and medieval beret and pointed to a square of glistening wet cement where I should place my foot.

"A-ha, the foot! Get all those cameras and eyes off my face and onto something else.

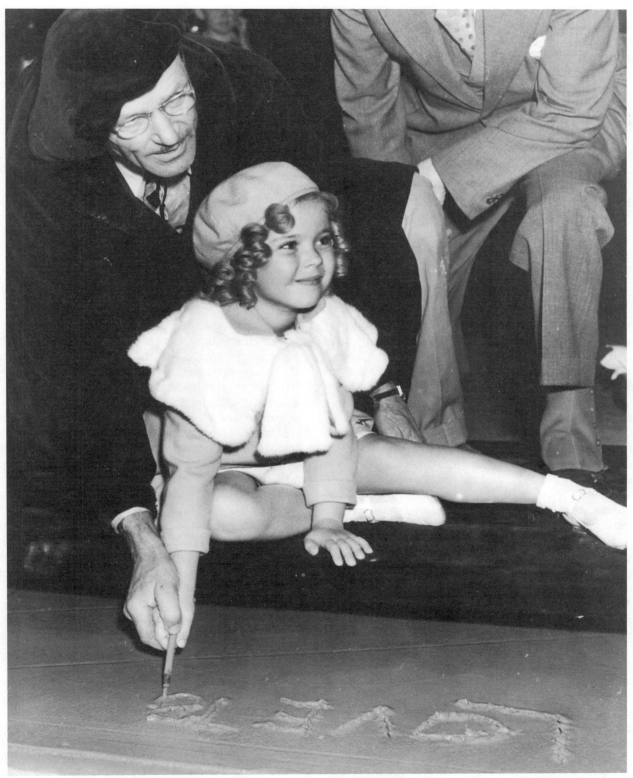

Cement artist Jean W. Klossner and Shirley Temple. Klossner recalled in 1953 that six-year-old Shirley "...was so tiny, I had to help her write her own name."

"'These shoes make my feet too big,' I mumbled behind my palm. 'Can I do it barefoot?'

"Slowly removing one shoe and sock, I wiggled the bare toes to catch camera attention, holding my face pointed down at all times."

From then on Shirley's mother would travel with two or three special spare teeth made just for Shirley by her dentist, tucked away safely in a small box in her pocketbook, along with a can of adhesive powder so that she could glue in a fake tooth in times of emergency. Shirley commented, "So far as the audience could tell, my baby teeth never did fall out. Like me, they were timeless."

Joe E. Brown
Ceremony #27: March 5, 1936

Born: Joseph Evan Brown in Holgate, Ohio, on July 28, 1892. Died: July 6, 1973.

A rubber-faced, sweet-tempered comedian, whose trademark was his wide mouth, Joe E. Brown achieved his greatest film fame playing lovable dolts and outcast underdogs who show surprising energy and resourcefulness when a crisis strikes. At age ten Brown joined the Sells and Downs Circus and became a tumbler and acrobat. By 1906 he was playing in burlesque and vaudeville.

Brown's first legitimate musical comedy lead was on the road in *Listen Lester* in 1919. He made his debut on Broadway in *Jim Jam Jems* in 1920. He entered films in 1928 and played supporting roles in various movies, finally in 1930 landing a starring contract at Warner Bros., where he became one of the most popular comics of the decade.

He spent nearly all of World War II entertaining U.S. troops after the tragic death of his son in a military training accident. After the War, Joe enjoyed the greatest stage success of his career when he appeared in the touring company of the smash hit *Harvey*. He performed in many productions of that play over a fifteen-year period, starting in 1944. Today Brown is best remembered by most for his performance as Osgood Fielding III, the philandering, aging playboy millionaire in *Some Like It Hot* (1959).

His motion picture credits include "Don't Be Jealous" (1928, short, debut), *Hold Everything* (1930), *Local Boy Makes Good* (1931), *The Tenderfoot* (1932), *Elmer, the Great* (1933), *A Midsummer Night's Dream* (1935), *Alibi Ike* (1935), *Earthworm Tractors* (1936), *Show Boat* (1951), and *The Comedy of Terrors* (1963, final film).

Brown's square is tinted gray and contains the inscription "To Sid—With All My Sole." Also included are the date ("3-5-36"), his two footprints, two handprints, and his signature, plus an imprint of his mouth with the inscription "My Mouth Print."

Brown was a long-time friend of Sid Grauman and had worked for Sid and his father, D.J. Grauman, at their Unique Theatre in the early 1900s in San Francisco. He wrote in his memoirs:

"The Unique was an L-shaped theatre (probably that's what made it unique). The early customers sat in the part of the L that faced the stage. The late-comers had to wait in the part of the L that faced a blank wall until they could get seats within sight of the stage. [D.J.] Grauman allowed the show to run its full time if the crowd was only fair. But if his clients came in large numbers, he cut the acts to half or even to a quarter of their length, in order to shorten the show and increase the audience turnover. He couldn't work the hurry-up system if he let the actors go out to eat, so he fed them sandwiches in the wings. Later, taking a lesson from the zoo, he made a special act out of feeding them before the audience. He kept the house happy by his comments on the table manners of the performers.

"He had the right idea about people who played in his theatre, though. He wanted them to come in with the right spirit. He always welcomed everyone and never overlooked the kids. He shook hands with them all."

Cement artist Jean W. Klossner (left), Joe E. Brown, and Sid Grauman.

Al Jolson
Ceremony #28: March 12, 1936

Born: Asa Yoelson in Srednike, Russia, on May 26, 1885. Died: October 23, 1950.

Often called "the greatest entertainer in show business history," Al Jolson had an unparalleled career on stage, screen, radio, and as a recording artist. He was born of Jewish parents who urged him to be a cantor; but he lit out on his own as a boy, joined a circus, and then worked his way into performing in cafes, vaudeville, and burlesque. He appeared with various minstrel troupes and first wore blackface in a minstrel show in 1906.

In 1911 Jolson's performances in the Broadway shows *La Belle Paree* and *Vera Violetta* brought stardom. He made his film debut in 1913 in a scene from one of his Broadway shows. His sound film debut came in the Vitaphone short "Al Jolson in a Plantation Act" (1926), in which he sang "When the Red Red Robin Comes Bob-Bob-Bobbin' Along," "April Showers," and "Rock-a-bye Your Baby with a Dixie Melody."

Jolson's first feature film appearance was in the part-singing/part-talking/mostly silent with music and effects picture *The Jazz Singer* (1927). His line, "Wait a minute, wait a minute, you ain't heard nothing yet!" would become one of the most famous in film history.

Years later, after his stardom had faded, Jolson unexpectedly achieved new-found popularity and a whole new generation of fans as a result of his performing for U.S. troops during World War II. The fresh interest in him brought about the biographical

Unidentified theatre attendant (left), cement artist Jean W. Klossner, Al Jolson, and Sid Grauman. Sid claimed that Al made his first appearance on any stage at Grauman's Unique Theatre in San Francisco.

film *The Jolson Story* (1946) and its sequel, *Jolson Sings Again* (1949, final film). Both pictures were highly successful, and Jolson sang the songs on the soundtrack but was played by Larry Parks on screen.

His motion picture credits include "The Honeymoon Express" (1913, short, debut), *The Singing Fool* (1928), *Mammy* (1930), *Big Boy* (1930), *Hallelujah, I'm a Bum* (1933), *Wonder Bar* (1934), *Go into Your Dance* (1935), *Rose of Washington Square* (1939), *Hollywood Cavalcade* (1939), and *Swanee River* (1939).

Jolson's square is tinted gray and contains the inscription "From Al To Sid." Also included are the date ("3-12-36"), his two footprints, two handprints, and his signature, plus an imprint of Jolson's knees with the inscription "My Knee Prints" and a drawing of two arrows pointing to each of them. Jolson was famous for singing while on bended knee.

Al Jolson and Sid Grauman were friends for many years. In June 1936 Jolson became the vice-president of a mining company (owned jointly by Jolson, Grauman, and several film executives) that dug for minerals in the Black Hills of South Dakota.

In 1949 Grauman was honored with a testimonial dinner, sponsored by the Hollywood Chamber of Commerce, at the Hollywood Roosevelt Hotel across the street from the Chinese theatre. Unable to attend, Jolson made a special recording that was played on that occasion.

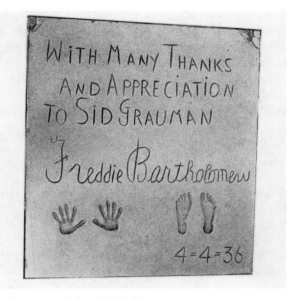

Freddie Bartholomew
Ceremony #29: April 4, 1936

He placed his prints in connection with the motion picture *Little Lord Fauntleroy* (United Artists, 1936).

Born: Frederick Llewellyn in London, England, or Dublin, Ireland (sources vary on location), on March 28, 1924. Died: January 23, 1992.

On screen Freddie Bartholomew was the epitome of the bright and well-mannered British youngster with perfect diction. He was given over to the care of his grandparents at age three, as his parents were hard-pressed financially to care for a third child. His aunt, Myllicent Bartholomew, who also resided with the grandparents, took active charge of Freddie.

As a youngster he was gifted with a natural ability to read and memorize with ease. Soon he was performing at concerts and benefits and even had small parts in a few films. Metro-Goldwyn-Mayer signed him to a contract; and Freddie, accompanied by his aunt, was brought to America by producer David O. Selznick to appear in *David Copperfield* (1935), which brought major stardom.

Between 1936 and 1939 a series of lawsuits began, in which Freddie's family squabbled over the spoils of his income. The litigation and poor professional representation by several agents robbed Freddie not only of his time but of many good roles.

He enlisted in the the U.S. Air Force in late 1942 and, failing to find much film work after his discharge in January 1944, went into theatre and the nightclub circuits as a performer. He also tried television, first

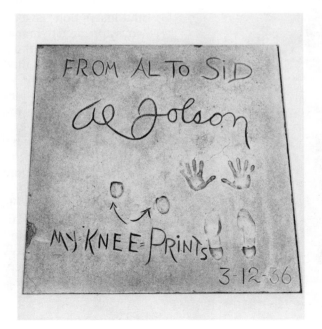

as an afternoon talk-show host and later as a director. He later found great professional success as an advertising executive with Benton & Bowles, one of Madison Avenue's leading agencies.

His motion picture credits include "Toyland" (1930, short, debut), *Anna Karenina* (1935), *Captains Courageous* (1937), *The Devil Is a Sissy* (1936), *Lloyd's of London* (1936), *Kidnapped* (1938), *Lord Jeff* (1938), *Listen, Darling* (1938), *A Yank at Eton* (1942), and *St. Benny the Dip* (1951, final film).

Freddie's square is tinted green and contains the inscription "With Many Thanks and Appreciation to Sid Grauman." Also included are the date ("4=4=36"), his two footprints (made with bare feet), two handprints, and his signature.

Contemporary newspaper accounts which quote his Aunt Myllicent as saying that young Freddie had hoped for the event ever since coming to Hollywood are simply studio publicity hyperbole.

Bartholomew recalled in a telephone conversation with the authors that his tutor had been giving him handwriting lessons earlier in the week prior to the ceremony. He thought that is what accounts for the fact that the four "r's" which appear in his Grauman's signature and inscription have always appeared to him as though they were written by someone other than himself. Apparently he wrote them in that particular way only on the occasion of his ceremony at the Chinese Theatre. "I've never written them that way before or since," he said.

Bartholomew saw his square a number of times over the years and recalled it always seemed to be a forgery done by someone else.

Freddie Bartholomew and cement artist Jean W. Klossner.

Bing Crosby
Ceremony #30: April 8, 1936

Born: Harry Lillis Crosby in Tacoma, Washington, circa May 2, 1904 (sources vary on year). Died: October 14, 1977.

Bing Crosby's fame as a singer propelled him into films. His totally relaxed, casual, and low-key delivery made his performances all seem effortless and easy. The nickname "Bing" came during childhood, as a result of his avid scrutiny of a humor feature entitled the "Bingville Bugle" in the Sunday edition of the Spokane *Spokesman Review*.

His mother hoped he would become a lawyer, but the music profession lured him, and he left college in 1921 to join a band as a drummer. By 1925 he had begun singing and headed for Los Angeles with his partner, Al Rinker, whose sister, singer Mildred Bai-

ley, got them bookings on the Fanchon and Marco vaudeville circuit. They were billed as "Two Boys and a Piano." Paul Whiteman caught their act in 1926. Then the two joined his orchestra with a third partner, Harry Barris, and were thereafter known as "The Rhythm Boys."

Crosby made his film debut in a short subject for Pathé, "Two Plus Fours" (1930), and got his first network radio contract at $600 a week with CBS in 1931. An overnight sensation, Bing's national fame led to a contract with Paramount in 1932, an association that was to last nearly twenty-five years.

In 1940 Bing teamed with Bob Hope and Dorothy Lamour for *Road to Singapore*. Subsequent "Road" pictures led to *Zanzibar* (1941), *Morocco* (1942), *Utopia* (1946), *Rio* (1947), *Bali* (1952), and *Hong Kong* (1962).

Crosby introduced "White Christmas" in *Holiday Inn* (1942). The song won the Academy Award and sold a miraculous 30,000,000 copies—the biggest-selling single record of the century. Throughout his film career, Crosby continued regularly on radio and later, television.

His motion picture credits include *The Big Broadcast* (1932), *We're Not Dressing* (1934), *Waikiki Wedding* (1937), **Going My Way* (1944), *The Bells of St. Mary's* (1945), *Blue Skies* (1946), *Here Comes the Groom* (1951), *The Country Girl* (1954), *High Society* (1956), and *Stagecoach* (1966, final film).

  * *Academy Award nomination: Best Actor.*
  ** *Academy Award winner: Best Actor.*

Bing Crosby (center), in full costume for his role in the motion picture Rhythm on the Range (1936), and cement artist Jean W. Klossner.

Crosby's square is tinted red and contains the inscription "To Sid Grauman from Bing Crosby [signature]." Also included are the date ("4-8-36."), his two footprints (made with boots), two handprints, and his signature, plus a drawing of three bars of music from the song "Where the Blue of the Night Meets the Gold of the Day," with an abbreviated title ("The Blue of The Night") written beneath the bars of music in the cement.

Crosby drew a musical staff with a treble clef, a time signature of three-quarter time (or waltz time), and even included the sign to repeat the chorus ("‖:"). The song is written in the key of G major, and Crosby drew the notes (G, A, B, A, G, and F#) for the lyric that begins the chorus "Where the blue of the night." The notes contain the proper stems with and without flags. Notes G, A, A, and G are eighth notes; and notes B and F# are half notes. (The note-heads of the eighth notes are not filled in as they should be, due to the fact that working in cement is more difficult than one would think!)

The 1931 song had become Crosby's trademark, originating as the theme of his popular radio show, "Fifteen Minutes with Bing Crosby," for Cremo Cigars. The music was composed by Fred E. Ahlert, and the lyric written was by Roy Turk and Bing Crosby.

The song title had been similarly abbreviated in a short subject Crosby made for Mack Sennett in 1933 entitled "Blue of the Night."

Victor McLaglen
Ceremony #31: May 25, 1936

Born: in Tunbridge Wells, England, on December 10, 1886. Died: November 7, 1959.

Victor McLaglen's screen character was usually that of a huge hulk of a man who possessed a sentimental heart underneath a rugged, coarse exterior. In his youth he was a professional boxer. A British producer who saw him fight cast him in his debut film, *The Call of the Road* (1920); and thereafter McLaglen

found himself in demand for film roles. By 1922 he was one of England's most important leading male stars.

In 1924 he was summoned to Hollywood by producer/director J. Stuart Blackton to star in his American debut film, *The Beloved Brute* (1924). After free-lancing at several studios, McLaglen won a contact with First National in 1925. A loan-out to Fox for *What Price Glory* (1926) turned McLaglen into a major star.

As a result of some rather repetitive formula pictures, McLaglen's career was in a slump by 1933. It was revived by two films directed by John Ford: *The Lost Patrol* (1934) and **The Informer* (1935). In the late 1940s Ford again cast him in his classic U.S. Cavalry trilogy: *Fort Apache* (1948), *She Wore a Yellow Ribbon* (1949), and *Rio Grande* (1950).

His motion picture credits include *Beau Geste* (1926), *The Black Watch* (1929, talkie debut), *The Cock-Eyed World* (1929), *Klondike Annie* (1936), *Under Two Flags* (1936), *Wee Willie Winkie* (1937), *Gunga Din* (1939), *The Foxes of Harrow* (1947), **The Quiet Man* (1952), and *Sea Fury* (1958, final film).

　* *Academy Award nomination: Best Supporting Actor.*
　** *Academy Award winner: Best Actor.*

McLaglen's square is tinted gray and contains the inscription "Best Wishes To Sid From Victor Mc.Laglen [signature]." Also included are the date ("5-25-36"), his two footprints, two handprints, and his signature.

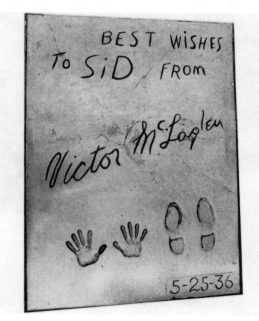

Victor McLaglen (left) and cement artist Jean W. Klossner.

William Powell and Myrna Loy
Ceremony #32: October 20, 1936

They placed their prints in connection with the motion picture *Libeled Lady* (Metro-Goldwyn-Mayer, 1936).

William Powell

Born: William Horatio Powell in Pittsburgh, Pennsylvania, on July 29, 1892. Died: March 5, 1984.

The image of actor William Powell is that of an impeccably groomed, well-dressed, suave, sophisticated, and agreeably cynical epitome of urbanity, with razor-sharp intelligence and wit. His playing in light comedy has a polish that has never been surpassed.

He was bitten by the acting bug after appearing in a high school Christmas play production. Powell studied acting at the American Academy of Dramatic Arts and made his first professional stage appearance in *The Ne'er-Do-Well* in 1912. He made his screen debut in 1922 and won a contact with Paramount in 1925. Powell worked frequently and was usually cast as clever villains, cheats, and roués throughout the 1920s.

After a period with Warner Bros., he signed with Metro-Goldwyn-Mayer in 1934 and was immediately cast opposite Myrna Loy in *Manhattan Melodrama* (1934). They became one of the most popular teams in film history with their next film together, **The Thin Man* (1934). In all, they made six "Thin Man" movies over a period of thirteen years.

Powell was delighted when he was cast in Warner Bros.' **Life with Father* (1947). It was based on one of the longest-running plays in Broadway history, and he had begged MGM to buy the rights to the hit play in 1942 to no avail. In later years he played supporting roles and eventually retired to Palm Springs.

His motion picture credits include *Sherlock Holmes* (1922, debut), *The Last Command* (1928), *Interference* (1929, talkie debut), *The Canary Murder Case* (1929), *One Way Passage* (1932), *The Great Ziegfeld* (1936), **My Man Godfrey* (1936), *Double Wedding* (1937), *How To Marry a Millionaire* (1953), and *Mister Roberts* (1955, final film).

*Academy Award nomination: Best Actor.

Powell's square is tinted gray and contains the inscription "Sid old boy—I am happy to put my foot in it for you." Also included are the date ("10-20-36"), his two footprints, two handprints, and his signature ("Bill Powell").

Powell and Loy were renowned for being "The Perfect Mr. and Mrs. of the Screen." They had appeared together in five films at the time of their ceremony and would later co-star in an additional eight.

When Powell and Loy emerged from their limousine, a roar of laughter was heard from the crowd. Sid Grauman, who had stepped forward to greet them, couldn't figure out what was so funny until he glanced at their feet and cried, "Oh, Bill! Don't do this to me. This is a serious proposition!" Powell recalled his and Loy's ceremony during the filming of *Dancing in the Dark* (1949), part of which was set at the Chinese Theatre:

"We had each put on a pair of those three-foot-long comedy shoes, something like the flippers swimmers wear. Sid went white when he saw them, but hastily pretended he knew it was a gag, and urged us to take them off so we could get on with the ceremony in our real shoes. We played it straight and insisted the flippers were the only shoes we had, and solemnly told him that we'd worn them deliberately so we could

Cement artist Jean W. Klossner (left), Myrna Loy, Sid Grauman, and William Powell.

make a bigger 'impression' than any he had in the forecourt. He began to protest that the slab of wet cement wasn't big enough to hold our imprints, when we finally got our [regular] shoes out of the car to go through with it. But not before we had a considerable discussion during which we kept wriggling our flippers around.

"Since then there have been several funny stunts at the Chinese—John Barrymore allowed his profile to be recorded in the cement, Betty Grable her leg, and Monty Woolley his beard. But I think Myrna and I were the first to gag it up."

Sid Grauman also appeared in *Dancing in the Dark* and on the same occasion as the Powell interview had this to say about the Powell/Loy ceremony and the change in tone brought about by Bill and Myrna:

"It was a solemn, sacred rite until Bill Powell here, gagged it up with Myrna Loy in 1936, by arriving each wearing a pair of Buster Keaton's comedy shoes. I confess I was furious for a minute, at the time, but I turned the tables on Bill by keeping the shoes, for which he had to reimburse Buster."

Myrna Loy

Born: Myrna Williams in Raidersburg, Montana, on August 2, 1905.

For years Hollywood cast Myrna Loy as oriental sirens and half-caste temptresses. She made a successful transition from an exotic to a wholly new persona, the embodiment of "the perfect American wife," in mid-career; and it is in this incarnation she is best remembered, both as a fine dramatic actress and a skilled comedienne.

A visit to Universal studios in 1916 inspired Loy to pursue an acting career. At age twelve, she first appeared in public, dancing at a charity event. Myrna had a job as a dancing teacher during high school and after graduation found work at Grauman's Egyptian Theatre in 1923 as a dancer in the choruses of the prologues. She made her film debut in 1925. An interview at Warner Bros. in 1926 resulted in a five-year contract. Irving G. Thalberg was impressed by her work and signed her at Metro-Goldwyn-Mayer in 1931. Her last oriental role was in *The Mask of Fu Manchu* (1932).

The great turning point in her career came when she was cast opposite William Powell in *The Thin Man* (1934). The film solidly established her new image and made her a genuine star. During World War II, Loy devoted most of her time to work for the American Red Cross and made only one film, *The Thin Man Goes Home* (1945). After the War, she worked for the United Nations and finally returned to the screen in *The Best Years of Our Lives* (1946), in a role that firmly re-established her as a major star.

Her motion picture credits include *Pretty Ladies* (1925, debut), *Noah's Ark* (1928, talkie debut); *The Animal Kingdom* (1932), *Wife Vs. Secretary* (1936), *Too Hot To Handle* (1938), *The Rains Came* (1939), *The Bachelor and the Bobby-Soxer* (1947), *Mr. Blandings Builds His Dream House* (1948), *Midnight Lace* (1960), and *Just Tell Me What You Want* (1980).

In 1988 she was a recipient of the Kennedy Center Honors for lifetime achievement, and in 1991 she received an Honorary Academy Award "in recognition of her extraordinary qualities both on screen and off, with appreciation for a lifetime's worth of indelible performances."

Loy's square is tinted gray and contains the inscription "To Sid—who gave me my first job." Also included are the date ("10-20-36"), her two footprints (made with high heels), two handprints, and her signature.

In 1923 Loy auditioned for Fanchon and Marco, a famous dance team who produced prologues for the nationwide theatre circuits. They hired her for $35 a week, and she soon was engaged to appear at Grauman's Egyptian Theatre. Her first assignment was in the prologue that accompanied Cecil B. DeMille's *The Ten Commandments* (1923).

Loy recalled the following story in her memoirs:

"[Sid] Grauman, the first person really to exhibit movies with style, had created this live prologue concept. His prologues were famous, and he was already something of a Hollywood legend. I didn't know him when I worked there. He was a god; everybody important is a god when you're starting out. You don't know your producer if you're a punk. We were just dancers.

"I saw him in a different light twelve years later, when he asked Bill Powell and me to put our footprints in the forecourt of his Chinese Theatre. Sid was reputedly a great practical joker, so Bill and I decided to have a little fun. We arrived for the ceremony wearing enormous clowns' shoes at least a foot long. Well, I'll never forget Sid Grauman's face. We almost broke his heart. He took that ritual very seriously, and couldn't bear the idea that we were deriding it. We had a terrible time convincing him that it was just a prank. When I finally made my impression in the cement, I wrote: 'To Sid—who gave me my first job,' which somewhat reassured him."

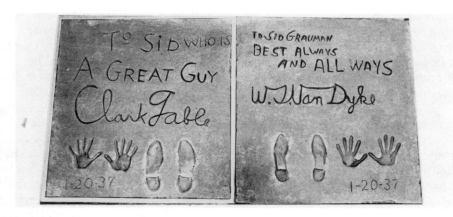

Clark Gable and W.S. Van Dyke II Ceremony #33: January 20, 1937

They placed their prints in connection with the motion picture *Love on the Run* (Metro-Goldwyn-Mayer, 1936); Gable starred, and Van Dyke directed.

Clark Gable

Born: William Clark Gable in Cadiz, Ohio, on February 1, 1901. Died: November 16, 1960.

In 1936 Clark Gable was voted "The King of the Movies" in a public opinion poll. The title sums up Gable's supremacy in Hollywood to perfection. His persona was that of a dashingly handsome, all-American rogue, exceedingly virile and tough, but with a good sense of humor and an underlying heart of gold. His "man's man" image drew male fans to him as well as women admirers, who literally numbered in the millions throughout the globe.

After high school and various non-theatrical jobs, young Gable pursued a stage career. He got into stock companies and eventually went to Hollywood in 1924, finding his first film work as an extra in *Forbidden Paradise* (1924). Getting nowhere in the movies, Gable returned to the stage. Metro-Goldwyn-Mayer finally signed Gable to a contract. He became a star in *A Free Soul* (1931), in which he treated Norma Shearer roughly. Greta Garbo asked for him as her leading man; and soon Gable was in a series of extremely successful films opposite Joan Crawford, Jean Harlow, and Myrna Loy. He reached the zenith of his career in the role of Rhett Butler in *Gone With the Wind* (1939) opposite Vivien Leigh's Scarlett O'Hara.

Gable joined the U.S. Air Force during World War II. He pronounced his comeback film, *Adventure* (1946), "lousy;" and most critics agreed, but he still held on to his huge popularity. After several mediocre films, Gable and MGM parted company before the release of *Mogambo* (1953). The film's success rekindled the studio's interest, and MGM offered him a new contract. Gable, offended by their earlier plans to drop him, would have none of it and went independent.

His motion picture credits include *The Painted Desert* (1931, talkie debut), *Manhattan Melodrama* (1934), **It Happened One Night* (1934), *The Call of the Wild* (1935), *Mutiny on the Bounty* (1935), *Boom Town* (1940), *Honky Tonk* (1941), *Command Decision* (1948), *Teacher's Pet* (1958), and *The Misfits* (1961, final film).

* *Academy Award nomination: Best Actor.*
** *Academy Award winner: Best Actor.*

Clark Gable and cement artist Jean W. Klossner.

Clark Gable (left), W.S. Van Dyke II, Sid Grauman, and cement artist Jean W. Klossner. Gable's distinctive hair style was for his role in the motion picture Parnell *(1937).*

Gable's square is tinted green and contains the inscription "To Sid who is A Great Guy." Also included are the date ("1-20-37"), his two footprints, two handprints, and his signature. There is also a brass border around the square, which was added when the square was rededicated on February 11, 1976.

His appearance drew the largest crowd on record at the ceremonies up to that time.

The 1976 rededication ceremony took place in connection with the motion picture *Gable and Lombard* (1976). The film starred James Brolin and Jill Clayburgh in the title roles and premiered at the Chinese Theatre. The ceremony took place on the morning of that occasion.

Designer Edith Head was on hand and conducted a mini-fashion show of her costumes from the film. (Head designed costumes for both Gable and his wife, actress Carole Lombard, earlier in her career.)

Gable's 1931 yellow Duesenberg was on display in the theatre's forecourt. The car was from the Hollywood Motorama Museum and had been used in the film as well.

W.S. Van Dyke II

Born: Woodbridge Strong Van Dyke II in San Diego, California, on March 21, 1889. Died: February 5, 1943.

W.S. Van Dyke II was one of the most important and successful directors at Metro-Goldwyn-Mayer studios from the late 1920s through the early 1940s. He had a reputation for a skillful, craftsmanlike approach to his work and a talent for bringing in his films ahead of time and under budget. He was called "One-Take Van Dyke," as he felt the first take was almost always the best, and encouraged a quick, improvisational style of playing among his actors.

At age three Van Dyke made his stage debut as Damon's child in *Damon and Pythias*. His first film job was as assistant director to Charles Brabin on *The Raven* (1915). His big break came when he landed a position as one of D.W. Griffith's six assistant directors on *Intolerance* (1916). Van Dyke next found numerous jobs directing features, serials, and shorts. He directed a series of Tim McCoy Westerns at MGM in 1926-1927, and the studio put him under contract.

He was assigned to *Trader Horn* (1931, all-talkie debut), the first American-made, fictional feature sound film to be shot on location in Africa. When MGM decided to follow up the highly successful

Trader Horn with *Tarzan, the Ape Man* (1932), Van Dyke directed and was instrumental in casting swimming champion Johnny Weissmuller in the lead. He directed the sophisticated, urbane detective mystery-comedy *The Thin Man* (1934) in sixteen days and, according to Myrna Loy, was responsible for the casting of herself and William Powell. He also directed the first teaming of Jeanette MacDonald and Nelson Eddy, *Naughty Marietta* (1935).

His motion picture credits as a director include *The Land of Long Shadows* (1917, debut), *Manhattan Melodrama* (1934), *Rose Marie* (1936), *San Francisco* (1936), *After the Thin Man* (1936), *Marie Antoinette* (1938), *Andy Hardy Gets Spring Fever* (1939), *I Love You Again* (1940), *Rage in Heaven* (1941), and *Journey for Margaret* (1942, final film).
Academy Award nomination: Direction.

Van Dyke's square is tinted green and contains the inscription "To Sid Grauman—Best Always and All Ways." Also included are the date ("1-20-37"), his two footprints, two handprints, and his signature ("W.S. Van Dyke").

It appears that Van Dyke was fond of the inscription "Best Always and All Ways." In actor Jean Hersholt's copy of Van Dyke's book *Horning Into Africa* (1931), which deals with his adventures in Africa while shooting *Trader Horn*, the same phrase appears in Van Dyke's handwritten inscription.

Over the years, several Van Dyke films played the Chinese Theatre. MGM's first sound picture (synchronized sound effects and music with fragmentary non-synchronized dialogue) *White Shadows in the South Seas* premiered there on August 3, 1928. The film was a major turning point in Van Dyke's career. He had taken over from director Robert Flaherty and completed the picture, which received rave reviews and was an enormous box-office success.

At the premiere Western star Tim McCoy spoke into the microphone and said the following to the crowd and radio audience:

"I know we're going to see a great picture tonight, for I know the man who made it. He directed most of my best pictures, and I know how he works. Whatever he sets his hand to do has got to be good, or it won't be on film. You don't know who I'm talking about because his name wasn't even mentioned in the papers today. So, I'm going to tell you who he is. His name is W.S. Van Dyke, and you're going to hear a lot about this director from this night on. Mark my word!"

Cement artist Jean W. Klossner (left), Joan Blondell, and her husband Dick Powell.

Dick Powell and Joan Blondell
Ceremony #34: February 10, 1937

The couple were husband and wife at the time of their ceremony. They wed in 1936 and divorced in 1945.

Dick Powell

Born: Richard Ewing Powell in Mountain View, Arkansas, on November 14, 1904. Died: January 2, 1963.

Dick Powell's sprightly, good-natured, brash, and quick-witted characterizations brightened many 1930s musicals. After his graduation from high school, he set out for Louisville, Kentucky, where he obtained professional work as a singer with a dinner orchestra. In 1930 he became the singing emcee at the Stanley Theatre in Pittsburgh. Powell was seen by a Warner Bros. studio talent scout and was soon on his way to Hollywood with a contract.

He made his film debut in 1932. Busby Berkeley directed the musical numbers in Powell's fourth picture, *42nd Street* (1933). It was the first of seven films opposite dancer/actress Ruby Keeler, and it made Powell a star.

Realizing he couldn't be the boy crooner forever, he longed to change his image and by the end of the decade left Warners for Paramount. He was allowed *not* to sing in a few films, but he was still dissatisfied and unfulfilled. He signed with RKO and was cast in

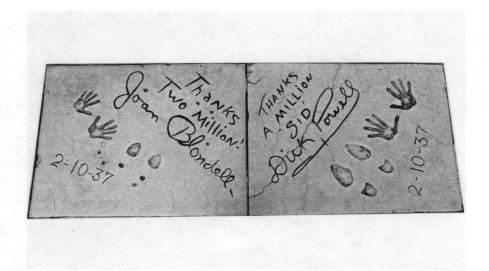

their adaptation of Raymond Chandler's novel *Farewell, My Lovely*, ultimately entitled *Murder, My Sweet* (1945). Powell's performance as the tough detective Philip Marlowe amazed his fans and critics alike and totally changed his image.

In the early 1950s, Powell saw his future in television, not only as an actor, but also as a producer and director. He formed the Four Star Television company with Charles Boyer, Ida Lupino, and David Niven as partners; and it became one of the most important TV companies of the 1950s and 1960s.

His motion picture credits include *Blessed Event* (1932, debut), *Gold Diggers of 1933* (1933), *Footlight Parade* (1933), *Dames* (1934), *Flirtation Walk* (1934), *On the Avenue* (1937), *Johnny O'Clock* (1947), *The Reformer and the Redhead* (1950), *The Bad and the Beautiful* (1952), and *Susan Slept Here* (1954, final film).

Powell's square is tinted gray and contains the inscription "Thanks A Million 'Sid.'" Also included are the date ("2-10-37"), his two footprints, two handprints, and his signature.

Joan Blondell

Born: Rose Joan Blondell in New York City circa August 9, 1906 (sources vary on year). Died: December 25, 1979.

Joan Blondell was one of the best-liked and most affectionately remembered actresses in American films, and her unswerving professionalism inspired enormous respect and admiration from her co-workers for fifty years. She often played tough-talking, brassy, wise-cracking floozies—both cynical and vulnerable—with their heart in the right place. As she herself stated, she was "the happy-go-lucky chorus girl, saucy secretary, flip reporter, dumb-blonde waitress, I'll-stick-by-you broad."

Her parents were vaudevillians, and by age three she had joined their act. In 1929 she appeared on Broadway in a success called *Penny Arcade*, which Warner Bros. acquired and re-titled *Sinner's Holiday* (1930). Warners cast Blondell in the film and gave her a contract. Though the picture was the first Blondell film produced, her second, *The Office Wife* (1930), was released first and became her actual film debut.

She endured an exhausting schedule at Warners, taking whatever was assigned her, and earned the reputation of a "workhorse." Free-lancing by the mid-1940s, Blondell decided her "glamor days" were over and moved into supporting roles. Throughout the 1950s, 1960s, and 1970s, she alternated between stage, film, and television and rarely stopped working. To the end she remained a cheerful, but no-nonsense, hard-working professional.

Her motion picture credits include *The Public Enemy* (1931), *Gold Diggers of 1933* (1933), *Dames* (1934), *Stand-In* (1937), *Cry Havoc* (1943), *A Tree Grows in Brooklyn* (1945), *Nightmare Alley* (1947), **The Blue Veil* (1951), *Desk Set* (1957), and *The Woman Inside* (1981, final film).

* *Academy Award nomination: Best Supporting Actress.*

Blondell's square is tinted gray and contains the inscription "Thanks Two Million!" Also included are the date ("2-10-37"), her two footprints (made with high heels), two handprints, and her signature.

Fredric March
Ceremony #35: April 21, 1937

He placed his prints in connection with the motion picture *A Star Is Born* (United Artists, 1937).

Born: Ernest Frederick McIntyre Bickel in Racine, Wisconsin, on August 31, 1897. Died: April 14, 1975.

Fredric March was one of finest and most distinguished actors in American film and stage history. Early on he was fascinated by finance and economics. He took a job with a bank but was quickly disillusioned in that field and became determined to be an actor, having appeared in several college productions while a student at the University of Wisconsin.

Fredric March.

March made his stage debut in the 1920 Belasco production *Deburau* and was an extra in his first film, *Paying the Piper* (1921). Throughout the 1920s he worked steadily in stock, on and off Broadway. In 1927 he married actress Florence Eldridge, with whom he had a professional co-starring relationship in various plays and motion pictures over the next several decades.

March's entry into sound films occurred as a result of his appearance at the Los Angeles El Capitan Theatre in the touring company of the hit play *The Royal Family* in 1928. He signed a five-year contract with Paramount that same year. March worked steadily in such popular films as **Dr. Jekyll and Mr. Hyde* (1931), *Death Takes a Holiday* (1934), and *A Star Is Born* (1937); but his first love was always the theatre.

In 1938 he returned to Broadway, starting a cycle of alternating between plays and films for the next two decades. In 1956 March enjoyed the greatest theatrical triumph of his career in Eugene O'Neill's *Long Day's Journey into Night*.

His motion picture credits include *The Dummy* (1929, talkie debut), **The Royal Family of Broadway* (1930), *The Barretts of Wimpole Street* (1934), *Anna Karenina* (1935), *Anthony Adverse* (1936), *Nothing Sacred* (1937), *The Buccaneer* (1938), ***The Best Years of Our Lives* (1946), **Death of a Salesman* (1951), and *The Iceman Cometh* (1973, final film).

  **Academy Award nomination: Best Actor.*
  ***Academy Award winner: Best Actor.*

March's square is tinted gray and contains the date ("4-21-37"), his two footprints, two handprints, and his signature.

117

Robson
56: April 22, 1937

...er prints in connection with
...picture *A Star Is Born* (United
...37).

*Born: M... /Jeanette Robison in Melbourne, Australia,
on April 19, 1858. Died: October 20, 1942.*

Distinguished character actress May Robson was affectionately dubbed "the grand old lady of the screen" in the 1930s. She made her theatrical debut in 1883 at the Brooklyn Grand Opera House in *The Hoop of Gold*. In the early 1890s, she formed an alliance with the great Broadway producer Charles Frohman and worked in his productions for twenty-two years. Her first starring role was in 1907 in *The Rejuvenation of Aunt Mary*, which ran for three years. Her association with Frohman ended when he went down with the British liner *Lusitania* in 1915.

From the time of her stage debut until her entry into a full-time film career, Robson never stopped working or missed a theatrical season or performance. Although she dabbled in silent films, Robson didn't really take the movies seriously until the coming of sound, when she made her first talkie, *Mother's Millions* (1931). Published reports regarding her film debut vary. One account has her before Edison's experimental cameras in the 1890s, and another states that she was first filmed for Mutoscopes in 1900. Her first documented film appearance was in *How Molly Malone Made Good* (1915).

Robson played supporting roles in such pictures as *Letty Lynton* and *Red-Headed Woman* (both 1932). The great triumph of her movie career came when she starred as Apple Annie in Frank Capra's **Lady for a Day* (1933).

Her motion picture credits include *The King of Kings* (1927), *Dancing Lady* (1933), *Reckless* (1935), *Anna Karenina* (1935), *Rainbow on the River* (1936), *Wife Vs. Secretary* (1936), *The Adventures of Tom Sawyer* (1938), *Bringing Up Baby* (1938), *Four Daughters* (1938), and *Joan of Paris* (1942, final film).

*Academy Award nomination: Best Actress.

Robson's square is tinted red and contains the inscription "Proud to be Your Friend." Also included are the date ("4-22-37"), her two footprints (made with high heels), two handprints, and her signature.

The only time two performers placed their prints in connection with a picture in which they both appeared, but with the ceremonies on different days, is the instance of Fredric March and May Robson. March placed his the evening *A Star Is Born* premiered at the Chinese Theatre, and Robson placed hers the following evening. A notice announcing the dates of this unusual occurrence appeared in *Daily Variety* on April 20, 1937.

May Robson.

Unidentified theatre attendant (left), Sid Grauman, Tyrone Power, and Loretta Young.

Tyrone Power and Loretta Young Ceremony #37: May 31, 1937

They placed their prints in connection with the motion picture *Cafe Metropole* (20th Century-Fox, 1937).

Tyrone Power

Born: Tyrone Edmund Power III in Cincinnati, Ohio, on May 5, 1914. Died: November 15, 1958.

Tyrone Power's classically handsome looks were both a blessing and a curse. Certainly his face was what initially attracted producers to him and established him with the public, but Power had to fight throughout his career to prove his mettle as an actor.

He was born into a family that boasted a long line of actors dating back to early nineteenth-century Ireland. His father was a prominent Shakespearean actor and matinee idol on the American stage in the early 1900s. Following in his father's footsteps, young Tyrone made his first stage appearance at age seven as a Mexican boy in *La Golondrina*, the annual mission play at San Gabriel, California.

Producer Guthrie McClintic invited Tyrone to join actress Katharine Cornell's prestigious stage company, and in 1935 he appeared in their productions of *Romeo and Juliet* and *Saint Joan*. At this point, Power was tested by 20th Century-Fox and signed a contract. He remained at the studio for the next nineteen years. Power's assured romantic performance in his third Fox film, *Lloyd's of London* (1936), made him an instant star.

In later years, Power longed to go back to the stage, where he found true professional fulfillment. In 1950 he starred in the London production of *Mister Roberts* and in 1953 appeared on Broadway in *John Brown's Body*.

Power was in Spain filming a strenuous dueling scene opposite George Sanders on King Vidor's *Solomon and Sheba* (1959), when he was struck by a heart attack. He was rushed to a Madrid hospital, where he died an hour later. Yul Brynner replaced

Power in the film. The irony of Power's death is that his father had himself been felled by a heart attack while filming *The Miracle Man* (1932). Reportedly, the elder Power died in his son's arms on the set of that production.

His motion picture credits include *Tom Brown of Culver* (1932, debut), *In Old Chicago* (1938), *Alexander's Ragtime Band* (1938), *The Mark of Zorro* (1940), *Blood and Sand* (1941), *Crash Dive* (1943), *The Razor's Edge* (1946), *Nightmare Alley* (1947), *The Eddy Duchin Story* (1956), and *Witness for the Prosecution* (1957, final film).

Power's square is tinted gray and contains the inscription "To Sid—Following in my Fathers [sic]

Loretta Young

Born: Gretchen Michaela Young in Salt Lake City, Utah, circa January 6, 1913 (sources vary on year).

Renowned for her beauty, stunning costumes, immaculate grooming, and yet surprising versatility and poise as an actress, Loretta Young was one of the screen's most popular leading ladies during the 1930s and 1940s. According to Young, she made her film debut in a small part in a picture directed by George Melford and starring Fannie Ward, circa 1917, at the Famous Players-Lasky studios.

Loretta was a schoolgirl when director Mervyn LeRoy telephoned the Young household in the hope of hiring one of her older sisters, Sally Blane, for a role

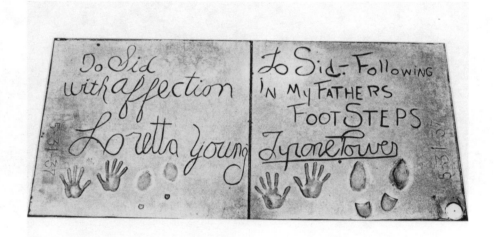

Foot Steps." Also included are the date ("5-31-37"), his two footprints, two handprints, and his signature.

The Power/Young ceremony drew a record crowd, and extra policemen were called upon to hold back the enthusiastic spectators.

Romina Power, Power's eldest child, had the following comments about her father and his ceremony at the Chinese Theatre in a letter to the authors:

"My father died when I was only seven years old. I have lived almost all my life in Europe. As I was growing up, I would occasionally visit the States. Every time I returned to Los Angeles I would visit the Chinese Theatre and measure my hands and feet in his prints to see how much I had grown. By doing this it would make me feel close to him.

"Even now that I am a 'grown-up' I still visit the Chinese Theatre when in town, and I too have followed in my father's footsteps."

in *Naughty but Nice* (1927) at First National. Blane was unavailable; and Loretta, who had answered the phone, got the part. Following a few years at Warner Bros., she was placed under contract to 20th Century Pictures (later 20th Century-Fox) in 1933 and became one of the studio's top stars.

She refused to renew her contract at Fox after starring opposite Don Ameche in *The Story of Alexander Graham Bell* (1939), as she felt that her roles at the studio for the past several years had required her to be beautiful but little else. From then on she free-lanced throughout the major studios.

In later years Young demonstrated her wide range and versatility on television as both a dramatic performer and comedienne in "The Loretta Young Show" (1953-1961), originally entitled "Letter to Loretta." She later appeared in the TV movies "Christmas Eve" (1986) and "Lady in a Corner" (1989).

Her motion picture credits include *Laugh, Clown, Laugh* (1928), *The Squall* (1929, talkie debut), *Zoo in Budapest* (1933), *Ramona* (1936), *Ladies in Love* (1936), *Love Is News* (1937), *Kentucky* (1938), **The Farmer's Daughter* (1947), *Come to the Stable* (1949), and *It Happens Every Thursday* (1953).

   *Academy Award nomination: Best Actress.
   **Academy Award winner: Best Actress.

Young's square is tinted gray and contains the inscription "To Sid—with Affection." Also included are the date ("5-31-37"), her two footprints (made with high heels), two handprints, and her signature.

In a letter to the authors, Young recalled:

"Unfortunately I have no recollection of that particular event outside of the fact I was delighted with the honor of it—then *and* now. Emotionally, that was a very happy period in my life, so I automatically smile when I think of it."

Sonja Henie
Ceremony #38: June 28, 1937

She placed her prints in connection with the motion picture *Thin Ice* (20th Century-Fox, 1937).

Born: in Oslo, Norway, on April 8, 1912. Died: October 12, 1969.

Sonja Henie was one of the greatest figure skaters of all time and the only one who became a major film star. Her films were typically light, sugar-coated ro-

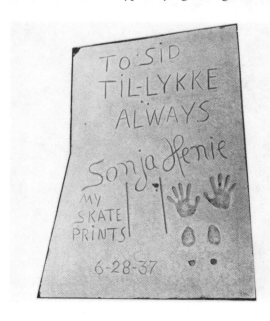

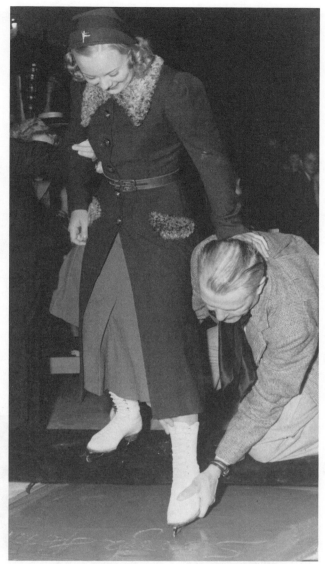

Sonja Henie and cement artist Jean W. Klossner.

mances, and were essentially built around Sonja's spectacular ice-skating production numbers.

Henie received her first pair of skates at age eight as a Christmas present. Her father financed expensive lessons for her in Germany, Austria, Switzerland, and England. She also studied ballet and was inspired at an early age with her original concept of "ballet on ice," which formed the basis for modern figure skating as it is known today.

Henie won the first of *ten* consecutive annual World Championships beginning in 1927 and was the Olympic Gold Medalist in 1928, 1932, and 1936. In between she polished off six Norwegian championships, eight European championships, and gave many command performances for various European royalty and heads of state.

In 1936 Henie turned professional, launched a series of triumphant skating exhibitions in the U.S., and made film her priority career goal. She quickly signed a contract with 20th Century-Fox. Her first Hollywood film, *One in a Million* (1936, talkie debut), was a smash hit, as were most of her subsequent starring vehicles.

When her screen novelty faded, Sonja flung herself into the production of her in-person touring ice-skating spectaculars, entitled "Hollywood Ice Revues."

Her motion picture credits include *Syv Dager for Elisabeth* (1927, debut), *Happy Landing* (1938), *My Lucky Star* (1938), *Second Fiddle* (1939), *Everything Happens at Night* (1939), *Sun Valley Serenade* (1941), *Iceland* (1942), *Wintertime* (1943), *It's a Pleasure!* (1945), and *Hello, London* (1958, final film).

Henie's square is tinted gray and contains the inscription "To Sid—Til Lykke Always." "Til Lykke" is Norwegian for "Good Luck." Also included are the date ("6-28-37"), her two footprints, two handprints, and her signature, plus the imprint of the blades made with a pair of her ice skates with the inscription "My Skate Prints."

The Ritz Brothers
Ceremony #39: September 22, 1937

They placed their prints in connection with the motion picture *Life Begins in College* (20th Century-Fox, 1937).

The Ritz Brothers original surname was "Joachim." They all came into the world in Newark, New Jersey, as follows: Al, born Abraham, on August 28, 1901/died: December 22, 1965; Jimmy, born Samuel, on October 22, 1904/died: November 17, 1985; and Harry, born Heshel, on May 28, 1907/died: March 29, 1986.

Have you ever seen an impression of a man with a double hernia trying to dance an Irish jig? Or of an aging John Barrymore essaying the Charleston while trying to display his profile at all times? Or three grown, hairy men in comedy drag doing an impression of the popular singing trio of the late 1930s and 1940s, the Andrews Sisters? If not, you have never experienced the shtick of the Ritz Brothers. Their burlesques and parodies were among the most outrageous in history. People either loved them or hated them. There simply was no middle ground.

The three tried separate theatrical careers after graduating from high school but were finally brought

The Ritz Brothers (Al [left], Jimmy, and Harry), cement artist Jean W. Klossner, and Sid Grauman.

together as a team in 1925 by a fourth brother, George, who acted as their agent when they made their debut at the College Inn at Coney Island, where they were a hit. They continued in vaudeville and quickly found work at the Fox Folly Theatre in Brooklyn and at the Palace on Broadway in 1929. Showman Earl Carroll spotted them and featured them in several of his annual *Vanities*. They made their film debut in "Hotel Anchovy" (1934, short).

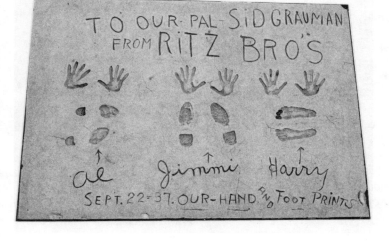

Darryl F. Zanuck signed the Ritz Brothers to a contract at 20th Century-Fox, as the studio was seeking a comedy back-up team for their lavish musicals. Their Fox debut was in *Sing, Baby, Sing* (1936). Subsequent films had them providing comic relief in all-star casts, and then they were featured in their own vehicles. After leaving Fox in 1939, they made several films at Universal. They quit films for good in 1943; and the team returned to the stage, nightclubs, and television, in which media they continued into the 1960s.

Their motion picture credits include *One in a Million* (1937), *On the Avenue* (1937), *You Can't Have Everything* (1937), *The Goldwyn Follies* (1938), *Kentucky Moonshine* (1938), *The Three Musketeers* (1939), *Argentine Nights* (1940), *Behind the Eight Ball* (1942), *Hi Ya, Chum* (1943), and *Never a Dull Moment* (1943, final film as a team).

The team's square is tinted gray and contains the inscription "To Our Pal Sid Grauman From Ritz Bro's." Also included are the date ("Sept. 22-37."), Al's two footprints, two handprints, and his signature ("Al"); Jimmy's two footprints, two handprints, and his signature ("Jimmy"); Harry's two footprints (made with bare feet), two handprints, and his signature ("Harry"); and the inscription "Our Hand and Foot Prints." Each one drew an arrow that points from his name to his footprints.

Unfortunately, Jimmy's signature did not survive as he originally wrote it in the fresh wet cement. The square was tampered with, and by the time it dried

the spelling of his name had been changed to "Jimmi."

The Brothers authored an article entitled "How To Be Different in Hollywood." It was written prior to their ceremony but not published in the Los Angeles *Examiner* until four days after it had taken place. They concluded: "Now comes our real chance to show our originality....What we plan on doing is putting our mugs right down in the goo, and preserving the Ritz pans for posterity."

In the end, the Ritz Brothers didn't go so far as to have their profiles imprinted in the cement. However, they did arrive at the Chinese Theatre wearing raccoon coats and long underwear; and when their ceremony was completed, they passed out wet cement to the crowd for souvenirs.

Eleanor Powell
Ceremony #40: December 23, 1937

She placed her prints in connection with the motion picture *Rosalie* (Metro-Goldwyn-Mayer, 1937).

Born: Eleanor Torrey Powell in Springfield, Massachusetts, on November 21, 1912. Died: February 11, 1982.

In 1929 Eleanor Powell was named "The World's Greatest Feminine Tap Dancer" by the Dance Masters of America. Her mother had enrolled Eleanor in dancing school in the hope that such activity would help her daughter to overcome her shyness. She started with ballet and acrobatic dancing and at thirteen was by chance seen dancing on the beach at Atlantic City by producer Gus Edwards, who immediately offered her a job appearing in his children's reviews.

Powell's ambitions led to Broadway, but she realized she would have to learn to tap to enter that field and invested $35 for ten lessons—the only lessons in tap she was ever to take. Her first major production was in a 1928 revue entitled *The Optimist*. Powell went to Hollywood and made her film debut in *George White's 1935 Scandals* (1935). Metro-Goldwyn-Mayer quickly signed her to a seven-year contract. Her number "Sing before Breakfast" in her first MGM film, *Broadway Melody of 1936* (1935), made her a film star overnight.

In 1943 Powell quietly ended her contract and married actor Glenn Ford. She had her own (non-dancing) television show in Los Angeles entitled "Faith of Our Children," a religious program, in the mid-1950s.

Powell and Ford divorced in 1959. She returned to performing in 1961 at the Sahara in Las Vegas and worked steadily until 1964, when she decided to hang up her dancing shoes forever.

Her motion picture credits include *Born To Dance* (1936), *Broadway Melody of 1938* (1937), *Honolulu* (1939), *Broadway Melody of 1940* (1940), *Lady Be Good* (1941), *Ship Ahoy* (1942), *I Dood It* (1943),

Thousands Cheer (1943), *Sensations of 1945* (1944), and *Duchess of Idaho* (1950, final film).

Powell's square is tinted gray and contains the inscription "To Sid—You're 'Taps' With Me." Also included are the date ("Dec.-23-37"), her two footprints (made with high heels), two handprints, and her signature. In addition, a pair of Powell's heel and toe taps are embedded in the cement.

Don Ameche
Ceremony #41: January 27, 1938

He placed his prints in connection with the motion picture *Happy Landing* (20th Century-Fox, 1938).

Born: Dominic Felix Amici in Kenosha, Wisconsin, circa May 31, 1908 (sources vary on year).

Don Ameche was one of the screen's most popular leading men during the 1930s and 1940s, specializing in smooth romantic leads in light comedies. Ameche appeared in several college theatrical productions and soon was playing in stock companies. His first Broadway role was in *Jerry for Short* in 1929.

He worked in vaudeville with Texas Guinan and in 1931 got a job in radio on the series "The Empire Builders," soon becoming one of the most popular performers on the airwaves. Hollywood took notice, and eventually Ameche was placed under contract to 20th Century-Fox. He made his Fox debut in 1936 and appeared in a string of hits opposite such female stars as Loretta Young, Janet Gaynor, Alice Faye,

Eleanor Powell.

Unidentified theatre attendant (left), Don Ameche, and cement artist Jean W. Klossner.

Sonja Henie, and Betty Grable. *The Story of Alexander Graham Bell* (1939) provided Ameche with his best-remembered role, though his personal favorite is in Ernst Lubitsch's *Heaven Can Wait* (1943).

Ameche's film career declined in the late 1940s; so he relocated in New York and established himself as a major Broadway and television performer. He scored a smash hit on the stage in the musical *Silk Stockings* in 1955. He found himself back in the Hollywood mainstream in the 1980s when he appeared in the hits *Trading Places* (1983) and *Cocoon* (1985).

His motion picture credits include "Beauty at the World's Fair" (1933, short, debut), *Ramona* (1936), *One in a Million* (1936), *In Old Chicago* (1938), *Alexander's Ragtime Band* (1938), *Midnight* (1939), *Hollywood Cavalcade* (1939), *Down Argentine Way* (1940), *Moon over Miami* (1941), and *Oscar* (1991).

*Academy Award winner: Best Supporting Actor.

Ameche's square is tinted gray and contains the inscription "To Sid—Happy Landing." Also included are the date ("Jan-27-38"), his two footprints, two handprints, and his signature.

Fred Astaire (left) and cement artist Jean W. Klossner. It could be said that dancer Fred Astaire and his partner Ginger Rogers, who placed her own imprints in a square beside his the following year on September 5, 1939, have the most famous feet represented in the forecourt.

Fred Astaire
Ceremony #42: February 4, 1938

Born: Frederick Austerlitz in Omaha, Nebraska, on May 10, 1899. Died: June 22, 1987.

Fred Astaire is the most acclaimed dancer in motion picture history. He nearly single-handedly discovered and demonstrated that dance could be effectively and significantly integrated with plot in film. He admitted that his suave, bon-vivant, elegant, devil-may-care image belied his true personality: an absolute perfectionist and relentless taskmaster. He once said, "The only way I know to get a good show is to practice, sweat, rehearse and worry." And he loathed wearing "top hat, white tie, and tails."

Fred and his sister Adele began dancing lessons when they were children and over the years went from vaudeville to stardom in Broadway musicals. Adele married into the British aristocracy and chose to retire; so Fred decided to pursue a film career. RKO put him under contract and cast him opposite the vivacious Ginger Rogers in *Flying Down to Rio* (1933). They were a sensation and quickly became one of the most popular screen duos in the history of film, making a total of ten co-starring vehicles over the years.

Astaire appeared opposite other top-flight dancing partners such as Eleanor Powell and Rita Hayworth in the early 1940s. He announced his retirement in 1946 but was lured back to film when he replaced an injured Gene Kelly in *Easter Parade* (1948). His career took a new turn in the late 1950s when he tired of making musicals and accepted straight acting roles. A modest man, Astaire once said the secret to his success was to "make it look like it's kind of easy."

His motion picture credits include *Dancing Lady* (1933, debut), *Top Hat* (1935), *Swing Time* (1936), *Holiday Inn* (1942), *You Were Never Lovelier* (1942), *The Band Wagon* (1953), *Daddy Long Legs* (1955), *Funny Face* (1957), **The Towering Inferno* (1974), and *Ghost Story* (1981, final film).

In 1950 he received a Special Academy Award "for his unique artistry and his contributions to the technique of musical pictures." In 1978 he was a recipient of the Kennedy Center Honors for lifetime achievement, and in 1981 the American Film Institute presented him with its Life Achievement Award.

*Academy Award nomination: Best Supporting Actor.

Astaire's square is tinted gray and contains the inscription "Thank you Sid." Also included are the date ("Feb-4-38"), his two footprints, two handprints, and his signature.

British actor Michael Crawford appeared in several motion pictures, including *Hello, Dolly!* (1969), and recounted in an April 29, 1990 Los Angeles *Times* article the following incident on the morning of his final Los Angeles performance in the title role of the phenomenally successful stage musical, *The Phantom of the Opera:*

"Grauman's Chinese....The Hollywood premiere for *Hello, Dolly!* was held there. I'd never visited it as a tourist, so early last Christmas morning, I went with...[two] friends to...explore and compare all the footprints.

"I stood in Fred Astaire's and had my picture taken."

Deanna Durbin
Ceremony #43: February 7, 1938

She placed her prints in connection with the motion picture *Mad about Music* (Universal, 1938).

Born: Edna Mae Durbin in Winnipeg, Canada, on December 4, 1921.

In 1936 Universal Pictures was in serious financial trouble, its former glory a fast-fading memory. An unknown girl soprano named Deanna Durbin changed all that. Durbin possessed a superb singing voice, genuine charm as an actress, and exuded irresistible energy, sincerity, and intelligence.

She auditioned at Metro-Goldwyn-Mayer in 1935 for a film that was ultimately never made; but the

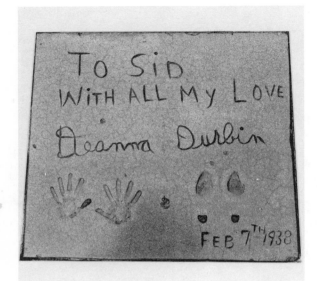

screen the spirit and personification of youth, and as juvenile players setting a high standard of ability and achievement."

Durbin's square is tinted gray and contains the inscription "To Sid—With All My Love." Also included are the date ("Feb 7th 1938"), her two footprints (made with high heels), two handprints, and her signature. A penny was also embedded the cement. It has since been pried out.

Over 2,000 persons were on hand to witness the ceremony. Deanna was accompanied by her father, and Sid Grauman predicted that by age twenty-one she would be the greatest singing star ever seen on the screen.

In a letter to the authors, Deanna Durbin David recalled, "February 7, 1938....it must have been around *Mad about Music* time and I have very few clear memories of these days, when I was making two films a year, two radio shows a week....working on my voice every day....when there was a continuous turmoil!"

She also commented, "I think that your idea of writing about the celebrities who put their foot in it is most amusing....Will you press the first copy [of your book] into the cement of the theatre forecourt?"

studio signed her and put her in a short opposite another newcomer named Judy Garland. Due to an apparent misunderstanding, Deanna was dropped. However, Universal Pictures producer Joe Pasternak and his partner, director Henry Koster, decided she'd be perfect for their upcoming film *Three Smart Girls* (1936). During production, Deanna was signed as a featured performer on radio's "The Eddie Cantor Show," which made her nationally famous. The release of the film turned her into a world sensation.

Her pictures were phenomenally successful, but Deanna herself wasn't happy. She had never wanted to be a movie star and disliked the invasion of her private life. Wanting to retire from the screen before World War II, she was convinced to continue her career throughout the War to boost public morale.

In 1950 Durbin married director Charles Henri David and officially retired. She has refused frequent offers to reactivate her career and shunned publicity and requests for interviews.

Her motion picture credits include "Every Sunday" (1936, short, debut), *One Hundred Men and a Girl* (1937), *That Certain Age* (1938), *First Love* (1939), *It's a Date* (1940), *It Started with Eve* (1941), *Christmas Holiday* (1944), *Can't Help Singing* (1944), *Lady on a Train* (1945), and *For the Love of Mary* (1948).

In 1939 Deanna and Mickey Rooney both received a Special Academy Award "for their significant contribution in bringing to the

Deanna Durbin.

Alice Faye and Tony Martin
Ceremony #44: March 20, 1938

The couple were husband and wife at the time of their ceremony. They wed in 1937 and divorced in 1940. Both placed their prints in connection with the motion picture *Sally, Irene and Mary* (20th Century-Fox, 1938).

Alice Faye

Born: Alice Jeane Leppert in New York City on May 5, 1915.

One of the most popular musical stars of the 1930s and 1940s, Alice Faye possessed a warm, rich contralto voice with which she delivered some of the biggest song hits of her era in a natural and heartfelt style.

Encouraged to take dancing and singing lessons, Faye left school at thirteen, determined to crash show business. After several chorus jobs, her first real breakthrough came when she was hired for the eleventh edition of *George White's Scandals* in 1931. Rudy Vallée was also in the cast and gave Alice a job on his weekly radio program in 1932.

Fox studios signed a deal to film *George White's Scandals* (1934, debut); and, at Vallée's urging, Faye was hired to film just one number. She ended up starring in the film when the star, Lilian Harvey, walked off the picture. Alice was given a contract and by 1938 was among the top ten box-office draws.

Faye married bandleader Phil Harris in 1941. They had two daughters, and Alice's film appearances became less frequent. She introduced "You'll Never Know" in *Hello, Frisco, Hello* (1943). The song became her trademark and won the Academy Award.

Unhappy over how the studio handled her in a straight dramatic role in *Fallen Angel* (1945), Faye quit the movies. She appeared on a popular weekly radio program with Phil Harris starting in 1946 and

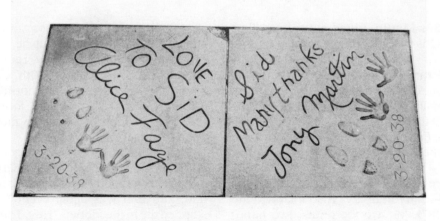

raised her family. Faye starred on stage in the early 1970s in a revival of *Good News* and has made guest appearances on television.

Her motion picture credits include *King of Burlesque* (1936), *On the Avenue* (1937), *Wake Up and Live* (1937), *In Old Chicago* (1938), *Alexander's Ragtime Band* (1938), *Rose of Washington Square* (1939), *Hollywood Cavalcade* (1939), *Lillian Russell* (1940), *State Fair* (1962), and *The Magic of Lassie* (1978).

Faye's square is tinted green and contains the inscription "Love To Sid." Also included are the date ("3-20-38"), her two footprints (made with high heels), two handprints, and her signature.

The Faye/Martin ceremony had originally been scheduled for March 6. It was postponed for two weeks when Faye came down with a brief illness.

Tony Martin

Born: Alvin Morris, Jr., in Oakland, California, on December 25, 1913.

Singer Tony Martin was featured in films from 1936 through the mid-1950s but primarily was involved with recordings, radio, television, and personal appearances in nightclubs and theatres throughout his career. He had been encouraged to sing since childhood and in the early 1930s had jobs playing the saxophone and singing with several dance bands.

He made his film debut in 1935 in an RKO short and had a bit role in *Follow the Fleet* (1936). Cutting himself loose from what he perceived as a dead-end contract with RKO, he landed a job as a featured singer at a posh Hollywood nightclub, the Trocadero, where he was seen by the head of 20th Century-Fox, Darryl F. Zanuck, who signed Martin to a contract. He found immediate popularity in *Poor Little Rich Girl* and *Sing, Baby, Sing* (both 1936). He supplemented further screen success with more club dates and had a regular spot on the George Burns and Gracie Allen radio show in the late 1930s.

Tony Martin (left), his wife Alice Faye, and cement artist Jean W. Klossner.

In the late 1950s Martin drifted away from films and spent most of his time recording and playing club and concert dates.

His motion picture credits include *Banjo on My Knee* (1936), *You Can't Have Everything* (1937), *Ziegfeld Girl* (1941), *The Big Store* (1941), *Till the Clouds Roll By* (1946), *Casbah* (1948), *Two Tickets to Broadway* (1951), *Easy To Love* (1953), *Hit the Deck* (1955), and *Let's Be Happy* (1957).

Martin's square is tinted green and contains the inscription "Sid—Many thanks." Also included are the date ("3-20-38"), his two footprints, two handprints, and his signature.

The Chinese Theatre played a part in an incident that occurred at the time of Martin's big break in motion pictures. He had been cast opposite Shirley Temple and Alice Faye in *Poor Little Rich Girl*. Mack Gordon and Harry Revel had written an original song entitled "When I'm with You" for his character to sing. Martin thought the song was terrific and assumed he'd introduce it, but he was mistaken. Another singer had already recorded it for the soundtrack. The studio—20th Century-Fox—had liked this singer's voice, but not his appearance; so Martin, now cast in the role, found himself in the unhappy position of having to mouth the words to another singer's voice.

He recalled the following story in his memoirs:

"Then came the premiere, at Grauman's Chinese Theatre. Everybody was there. It was a major Fox film, and that was a big event back then. People stopped me in the lobby—'Hey, Tony, you were great, what a voice, great set of pipes'—all that....Everybody was rushing up to me, shaking my hand, saying nice things. I was in—but I felt ashamed because I knew that wasn't my voice they were praising. And, later, the reviews came out and they compared me to Gable and Crosby and said I had a big future as a movie singer. That made me feel even worse."

Edgar Bergen and Charlie McCarthy
Ceremony #45: July 20, 1938

They placed their prints in connection with the motion picture *Letter of Introduction* (Universal, 1938).

Edgar Bergen

Born: Edgar John Berggren on February 16, 1903, in Chicago, Illinois. Died: September 30, 1978.

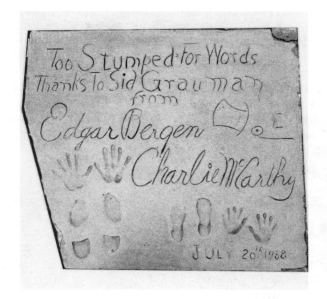

The most famous ventriloquist in history, Edgar Bergen enjoyed a career that spanned more than fifty years. Aside from his ability to create hilarious comic repartee, Bergen's success was mainly attributable to his creation of the top-hatted, monocled dummy, Charlie McCarthy.

By age eleven Bergen discovered he had a gift for mimicry and throwing his voice, and by the end of his high school days he already had created the dummy that became Charlie McCarthy. In 1922 he made his professional debut at Chicago's New Mabel Theatre in a combination ventriloquism and magic act. He finally branched out and played the Chautauqua and Lyceum vaudeville circuits, early on discarding the "magic" part of his act at the urging of management.

After making a hit at the Chez Paree in Chicago, he went to Hollywood and scored a huge success at the Casanova Club.

Bergen and Charlie began appearing in Vitaphone short subjects in 1930 and made about a dozen of them through 1937. Bergen set his sights on radio and was finally given a spot on Rudy Vallée's show in December 1936. By May 1937 Bergen had his own show (entitled "The Chase and Sanborn Hour," a.k.a. "The Edgar Bergen and Charlie McCarthy Show"), which lasted for nineteen years.

In 1938 Bergen and Charlie entered feature films in *The Goldwyn Follies*. That same year Bergen received a Special Academy Award "for his outstanding comedy creation, Charlie McCarthy." Fittingly, the miniature Oscar statuette was made of wood.

Bergen later played straight dramatic roles without Charlie in such films as *I Remember*

Sid Grauman (left), Charlie McCarthy, producer/director John M. Stahl, Edgar Bergen, and cement artist Jean W. Klossner.

Mama (1948) and *Captain China* (1950).

His (and Charlie's) motion picture credits include "The Operation" (1930, short, debut), "The Office Scandal" (1930, short), *You Can't Cheat an Honest Man* (1939), *Charlie McCarthy, Detective* (1939), *Look Who's Laughing* (1941), *Here We Go Again* (1942), *Stage Door Canteen* (1943), *Song of the Open Road* (1944), *Won Ton Ton, the Dog Who Saved Hollywood* (1976), and *The Muppet Movie* (1979, final film).

Charlie McCarthy

The wise-cracking dummy Charlie McCarthy was a sort of alter-ego to ventriloquist Edgar Bergen—Charlie argued with and insulted Edgar and made preposterous, witty, smart-alecky, and deflating remarks to just about everybody. Bergen often seemed astounded that words would come out of Charlie's mouth that could never come out of his own.

Charlie came into being when Bergen was a sophomore at Chicago's Lake View High School. One

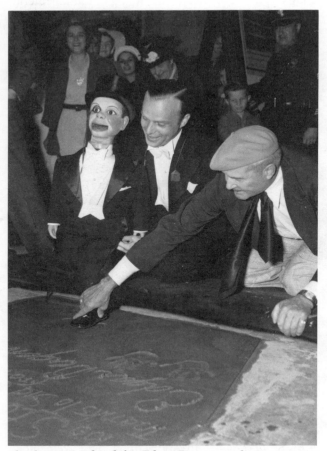

Charlie McCarthy (left), Edgar Bergen, and cement artist Jean W. Klossner.

day in school, Edgar sketched the face of an Irish newsboy who sold papers in the neighborhood and took the drawing to wood-carver Theodore Mack. Bergen showed him the sketch and described the character of the impudent newsboy to Mack, who produced Charlie carved in pine for $35.

Earlier, Bergen had invested 25 cents for a booklet entitled *Herrmann's Wizards' Manual*, with which he taught himself ventriloquism and some magic tricks; so Charlie had a voice from his inception.

Many considered Charlie a real person in his own right; he even received an honorary degree from Northwestern University in 1937, as "Master of Innuendo and the Snappy Comeback." Bergen created additional dummies: Mortimer Snerd in 1939 and Effie Klinker in 1944, but Charlie always remained his star companion. Edgar once asked Charlie, "What would you be without me?," and Charlie replied, "Speechless."

The Bergen/McCarthy square is tinted gray and contains the inscription "Too Stumped For Words—Thanks To Sid Grauman from Edgar Bergen [signature]—Charlie McCarthy [name]." Also included are the date ("July 20th 1938"), Bergen's two footprints, and his two handprints, Charlie's two footprints, and his two handprints, plus a caricature drawing of Charlie in his trademark top hat and right-eye monocle.

In her memoirs, Bergen's daughter actress Candice Bergen had the following to say about the hand and footprint ceremony in which her father and Charlie McCarthy participated:

"In 1938, newsreels and front pages featured Edgar Bergen and Charlie McCarthy—or sometimes simply Charlie, neglecting to mention the man standing conscientiously, inconspicuously behind the dummy.

"At Grauman's Chinese Theatre…, newsreels showed Edgar and Charlie, traditional in their white tie and tails, recording their hand-and-footprints in the famous star-stamped court. Charlie's tiny feet firmly embedded, attendants detach his hands, holding the little extremities high for the cameras as Edgar looks on, somewhat distraught. 'Hey, Charlie! Over here!' yells a photographer and a publicity man lunges to stick his hand through the dummy's backflap to turn him. 'My God, is *nothing* sacred?' Charlie snaps sharply, the man jumps back and Bergen moves in, silent and steely, gently picks up his partner and obediently obliges the press, turning Charlie left and right, the two of them responding as one. 'Hey, Charlie!' 'Over here!' Edgar, Charlie—it's all the same."

The Dionne Quintuplets and Jean Hersholt
Ceremony #46: October 11, 1938

Hersholt placed his prints, and the footprints of the Dionne Quintuplets, in connection with the motion picture *Five of a Kind* (20th Century-Fox, 1938). Their square is no longer in the forecourt (see below). It was located in what are now #138 and #139 on this book's Forecourt of the Stars map. Today the large space is occupied by the two squares of Dorothy Lamour and Bob Hope.

The Dionne Quintuplets

The Dionne Quintuplets were born in Corbeil, Canada, on May 28, 1934. Their official names were Marie Edwilda Yvonne, Marie Lilianne Annette, Marie Emilda Cécile, Marie Jeanne Emilie (died: August 6, 1954), and Reine Alma Marie (died: February 23, 1970); but the world knew them simply as Yvonne, Annette, Cécile, Emilie, and Marie.

When the Quints were born the odds against having such a multiple birth were estimated at over 57,000,000 to one. World fascination with the them was intense, and they instantly became internationally famous phenomena.

Within three days of their birth, their father signed a contract to exhibit them at the Chicago World's Fair/Century of Progress Exposition. Public reaction was so strong that the Canadian government totally wrested control of them from their parents. A government "board of guardians" was appointed and took complete charge over their upbringing, housing (in a private nursery compound), medical needs, education, and financial affairs.

The Quints were turned into a multi-million dollar marketing enterprise, collecting substantial licensing fees as a result of the board's agreement. Included were contracts for Quint photographs, commercial product endorsements, and motion picture appearances. Millions came to stare at them in their compound through a tightly woven wire mesh screen that worked like a one-way piece of glass.

The Quints' doctor, Allan Roy Dafoe, had the last word of approval regarding all contracts, to ensure that no agreement entered into would be unsafe or detrimental to their health.

In 1935 the board signed a contract with 20th Century-Fox for the Quints to appear in movies. Will Rogers was slated to appear opposite them in their feature film debut, *The Country Doctor* (1936); but

when he was killed in a plane crash, he was replaced by Jean Hersholt, who appeared with the Quints in that film as well as their subsequent pictures.

The Quints never left Canada for filming. All footage of them was taken in their nursery compound and limited to thirty minutes of filming time per day.

Their board of guardians served without pay, but a business manager was hired to handle their financial affairs. Their father finally hired a lawyer and won a lawsuit in 1942 giving him control of all monies in the Quints' bank account and all properties and assets held in their names.

They never had been allowed to develop a sense of individual identity and as they grew up had tremendous difficulties adjusting to life in the real world.

Emilie was epileptic and was at a convent in the process of becoming a nun when she died as a result of suffocation by her bed pillows during a severe seizure. Annette, Cécile, and Marie eventually married and had families, while Yvonne remained single and became a nurse.

Their motion picture credits include "The Dionne Quintuplets" (1934, documentary short), "The Quintuplets' Second Christmas" (1935, documentary short), *Reunion* (1936), and *Five of a Kind* (1938, final film).

The Dionne Quintuplets.

Jean Hersholt

Born: in Copenhagen, Denmark, on July 12, 1886. Died: June 2, 1956.

Jean Hersholt was one of the best-loved character actors on the screen. Today his name is most widely recognized as a result of the Jean Hersholt Humanitarian Award, established in his memory by the Academy of Motion Picture Arts and Sciences, and given periodically "to an individual in the motion picture industry whose humanitarian efforts have brought credit to the industry."

Hersholt made stage appearances in his youth, touring in repertory companies. He first appeared on film in the short Danish comedy *On Valpy Hill* (1905, debut). He secured passage to America in 1914 to direct and act in a Danish stage production at the San Francisco Panama-Pacific International Exposition of 1915. He next journeyed to Los Angeles and made his American film debut in "Never Again" (1915, short). His best remembered silent role is that of the villain in *Greed* (1924).

Despite his Danish accent, Hersholt made a successful transition to talkies and appeared mainly in Metro-Goldwyn-Mayer films until he switched over to Fox and was cast as Dr. Allan Roy Dafoe in the films featuring the Dionne Quintuplets. That role resulted in an image change and led to his appearances in the "Dr. Christian" film series. There-

Jean Hersholt.

after, Hersholt was mostly cast in kindly doctor and warm-hearted, grandfatherly parts. Hersholt turned the Dr. Christian character into a radio show and played it on the air for seventeen years (1937-1953).

His motion picture credits include *The Four Horsemen of the Apocalypse* (1921), *Tess of the Storm Country* (1922), *Don Q, Son of Zorro* (1925), *The Student Prince in Old Heidelberg* (1927), *The Climax* (1930, all-talkie debut), *Grand Hotel* (1932), *The Country Doctor* (1936), *Heidi* (1937), *Meet Dr. Christian* (1939), and *Run for Cover* (1955, final film).

He received three Special Academy Awards: in 1940, as president (1938-1956) of the Motion Picture Relief Fund, "acknowledging the outstanding services to the industry during the past year of the Motion Picture Relief Fund and its progressive leadership;" in 1949, "in rec-

The Dionne/Hersholt square is no longer in the forecourt (see text).

Jean Hersholt makes shoe imprints for the Quints.

ognition of his service to the Academy during four terms as president [1945-1949];" and in 1950, "for distinguished service to the motion picture industry."

The Dionne/Hersholt square contained the inscription "Quintuplets' Footprints Placed By Jean Hersholt [signature]." Also included were the date ("Oct 11 1938"), each of the Quints' footprints, their names ("Yvonne," "Annette," "Cecile," "Emilie," and "Marie"), Hersholt's two handprints, and his two footprints, plus an imprint of one of Hersholt's trademark pipes.

Since the Quints never left Canada during their film career, Hersholt made imprints for each little girl using the shoes that they wore in *Five of a Kind*, which

had been shipped to Hollywood especially for the occasion.

The Quints' personal physician since their birth, Dr. Allan Roy Dafoe, sent a telegram in appreciation of the honor done his famous charges.

The square was not made by cement artist Jean W. Klossner. The ceremony took place during one of Klossner's and Sid Grauman's disagreements, and Grauman hired another man to prepare the cement. The square started to deteriorate badly in a matter of weeks and eventually had to be removed.

Hersholt was honored with another ceremony at the Chinese Theatre, when in 1949 he again recorded his hand and footprints.

Mickey Rooney.

Mickey Rooney
Ceremony #47: October 18, 1938

He placed his prints in connection with the motion picture *Stablemates* (Metro-Goldwyn-Mayer, 1938). Rooney's first square is no longer in the forecourt (see below). It was located where #104 is today on this book's Forecourt of the Stars map. Today the spot is occupied by Rooney's second square.

Born: Joe Yule, Jr., in Brooklyn, New York, on September 23, 1920.

Brash, plucky, and exceedingly energetic, actor Mickey Rooney became the ultimate symbol of the idealized American teenager in the late 1930s and early 1940s. His parents were vaudevillians, and Rooney was one year old when he made his stage debut as the "New Year" baby at New York's Palace Theatre wearing a silk hat and a piece of ribbon.

He got his first big film break in 1927 when he landed the lead in the "Mickey McGuire" series of shorts, based on the famous comic strip character by Fontaine Fox. He signed with Metro-Goldwyn-Mayer in 1934 and appeared as a supporting player in several films. The studio's popular "Andy Hardy" series and a string of exuberant musicals opposite Judy Garland made Rooney a major star.

After serving in the Army during World War II, Rooney returned to Hollywood but encountered a different public. His Andy Hardy character was out of step with the times, and he was too old for that kind of role. He free-lanced in films during the 1950s and 1960s, performed in nightclubs, and entered the television medium, in which he gave several compelling dramatic performances.

In 1979 he scored a smash hit on Broadway in *Sugar Babies*, a burlesque revue co-starring actress/dancer Ann Miller, and toured with the show for a decade.

His motion picture credits include "Not To Be Trusted" (1926, short, debut), *Emma* (1932, feature talkie debut), *A Midsummer Night's Dream* (1935), *Boys Town* (1938), **Babes in Arms* (1939), **The Human Comedy* (1943), *National Velvet* (1944), ***The Bold and the Brave* (1956), ***The Black Stallion* (1979), and *Erik the Viking* (1989).

In 1939 Mickey and Deanna Durbin both received a Special Academy Award "for their significant contribution in bringing to the screen the spirit and personification of youth, and as juvenile players setting a high standard of ability and achievement." In 1983 he received an Honorary Academy Award "in recognition of his 60 years of versatility in a variety of memorable film performances."

  * *Academy Award nomination: Best Actor.*
  ** *Academy Award nomination: Best Supporting Actor.*

Mickey's original square contained the inscription "To Sid—Without You, I Wouldn't Be Here." Also included were the date ("Oct. 18, 38"), his two footprints, two handprints, and his signature, plus the inscription of the initial "M."

On the occasion of his first hand and footprint ceremony in 1938, he said, "I've dreamed of this since I was a baby."

Like the Dionne/Hersholt square made a week before his own, Rooney's deteriorated and eventually crumbled into bits, although forty-eight years went by before it was removed.

Mann Theatres officials explained the situation to Rooney, who graciously obliged with another hand and footprint ceremony in 1986.

This Rooney square is no longer in the forecourt (see text).

Nelson Eddy
Ceremony #48: December 28, 1938

He placed his prints in connection with the motion picture *Sweethearts* (Metro-Goldwyn-Mayer, 1938).

Born: in Providence, Rhode Island, on June 29, 1901. Died: March 6, 1967.

Partnering with Jeanette MacDonald, Nelson Eddy was the baritone half of the most popular singing team in film history. His voice thrilled millions; and, for a time, he was the highest paid singer in the world.

In 1922 Eddy made his stage debut in the musical play *The Marriage Tax*. He signed with the Philadelphia Civic Opera company in 1924 and in 1928 began singing solo concerts throughout the United States. He gave an impromptu concert in Los Angeles as a substitute for an ailing Lotte Lehmann in 1933. As a result, Eddy was soon screen tested by several studios, and signed with Metro-Goldwyn-Mayer.

Though *Dancing Lady* (1933) was the first Eddy film produced, his second, *Broadway to Hollywood* (1933) was released first and became his actual debut. MGM let him languish for two years, putting him only in small parts. Discouraged and wanting out of his contract, Eddy was finally given the role that was to turn his career around—the lead opposite Jeanette MacDonald in *Naughty Marietta* (1935). They went on to make seven more extraordinarily popular musical films together.

Nelson Eddy.

Eddy retired from films in 1947 but continued doing concerts until 1952 when he decided to switch to the nightclub circuit. He remained active in the recording industry and branched out into television, as well.

His motion picture credits include *Rose Marie* (1936), *Maytime* (1937), *Rosalie* (1937), *The Girl of the Golden West* (1938), *Balalaika* (1939), *Bitter Sweet* (1940), *The Chocolate Soldier* (1941), *Phantom of the Opera* (1943), *Make Mine Music* (1946, voice only), and *Northwest Outpost* (1947, final film).

Eddy's square is tinted gray and contains the inscription "To Sid Grauman—with every good wish." Also included are the date ("Dec 28 '38"), his two footprints, two handprints, and his signature.

Eddy delighted onlookers by entering into the spirit of the event and helping to mix the cement.

Ginger Rogers
Ceremony #49: September 5, 1939

Born: Virginia Katherine McMath in Independence, Missouri, on July 16, 1911.

On the screen Ginger Rogers typified the image of the hard-working, good-humored, attractive, but tough-minded and honest American girl. Her mother Lela groomed her daughter for a later show business career by giving her singing and dancing lessons, allowing Ginger to embark on a stage career at fourteen after she won a Charleston contest. Her big break came when she was cast in the 1929 Broadway show *Top Speed* and scored a big hit.

In 1929-1930 she appeared in a few short films and made her feature film debut in *Young Man of Man-*

Ginger Rogers.

Judy Garland
Ceremony #50: October 10, 1939

She placed her prints in connection with the motion picture *Babes in Arms* (Metro-Goldwyn-Mayer, 1939).

Born: Frances Ethel Gumm in Grand Rapids, Minnesota, on June 10, 1922. Died: June 22, 1969.

Judy Garland has been called "the greatest entertainer of the 20th century." Her rich singing voice throbbed with passion and sensitivity, and she was also a fine actress and skilled dancer.

She was the youngest of three sisters. Their vaudevillian parents managed a movie theatre, and tiny Frances made her stage debut at age 2-1/2 when she scrambled on to the stage and began to sing "Jingle Bells," the only song she knew. The three girls became an act in vaudeville as "The Gumm Sisters." They joined the Meglin Kiddies troupe and made their film debut in "The Meglin Kiddie Revue" (1929, short). After the sister act was misspelled on a marquee as "The Glum Sisters," headliner George Jessel suggested the name "Garland." Frances herself chose the name "Judy," as she thought it sounded "peppy" and liked the Hoagy Carmichael song of the same name.

Her big turning point came in 1935 when Judy, now a solo act, was signed by Metro-Goldwyn-Mayer. She was cast as Dorothy in *The Wizard of Oz* (1939) and in 1940 received a Special Academy Award "for her outstanding performance as a screen juvenile during the past year." She also appeared in

hattan (1930). Ginger signed with RKO in 1933, and it was her fortuitous casting opposite Fred Astaire in *Flying Down to Rio* (1933) that catapulted the duo into one of the most popular teams in the history of film. The next six years were highlighted by their sublime dancing partnership in a series of eight more RKO musicals.

Always alternating her appearances with Astaire between non-musical comedies and dramatic films, Ginger made a courageous move and broke off their partnership in 1939. Going it alone, she became RKO's most valuable female star and proved her dramatic ability in such films as *The Primrose Path* and *Kitty Foyle (both 1940).

Her film career continued throughout the 1950s and into the 1960s and was augmented by stage and television work. In 1965 she enjoyed a Broadway triumph when she took over the smash hit *Hello, Dolly!* from actress Carol Channing. She starred in that show for eighteen months and toured with it for a year.

Her motion picture credits include *Top Hat* (1935), *Swing Time* (1936), *Stage Door* (1937), *Vivacious Lady* (1938), *Bachelor Mother* (1939), *Tom, Dick, and Harry* (1941), *The Major and the Minor* (1942), *The Barkleys of Broadway* (1949), *Dreamboat* (1952), and *Harlow* (1965).

**Academy Award winner: Best Actress.*

Rogers' square is tinted gray and contains the inscription "To Sid Grauman." Also included are the date ("9-5-39"), her two footprints (made with high heels), two handprints, and her signature.

Mickey Rooney (left), Judy Garland, and her mother Ethel Gumm.

a string of exuberant musicals opposite Mickey Rooney.

During the mid to late 1940s Garland was beset with deeply rooted emotional problems, and the studio dropped her from its payroll in 1950. She next put together a personal appearance act, scoring a triumph at the London Palladium in 1951, and later at the Palace Theatre in New York.

Judy made a spectacular film comeback in *A Star Is Born* (1954). She appeared on the concert stage, television (including "The Judy Garland Show" [1963-1964]), in nightclubs, and made recordings. Her 1961 concert at New York City's Carnegie Hall has been called "the greatest evening in show business history."

Her motion picture credits include *Broadway Melody of 1938* (1937), *Strike Up the Band* (1940), *For Me and My Gal* (1942), *Girl Crazy* (1943), *Meet Me in St. Louis* (1944), *The Clock* (1945), *The Harvey Girls* (1946), *Easter Parade* (1948), **Judgment at Nuremberg* (1961), and *I Could Go On Singing* (1963, final film).

* *Academy Award nomination: Best Actress.*
** *Academy Award nomination: Best Supporting Actress.*

Judy's square is tinted gray and contains the inscription "For Mr. Grauman—All Happiness." Also included are the date ("10-10-39"), her two footprints (made with high heels), two handprints, and her signature.

Garland was assisted at her ceremony by co-star Mickey Rooney. She was wearing her first formal evening gown and later joked that Rooney made a less-than-dignified entrance with her when he whispered in her ear, "Walk around the cement, Jootes, not through it!" ("Jootes" was Mickey's pet name for "Judy.") Garland recalled in 1943:

"What promised to be the most exciting night of my life turned out to be the most embarrassing. It was the premiere of *Babes in Arms*, and the night I placed my hand and foot prints in the forecourt of the Chinese Theatre. I wanted to look more glamorous than ever before. Now I must confess I had the habit of biting my fingernails. I was just sick that I couldn't have long, glittering fingertips. But the manicurist fixed that. She gave me false nails. After I placed my hands in the cement we went inside to see the picture. Suddenly I thought creeping paralysis had set in, beginning at my fingertips. I was in a cold sweat before we left the theatre—then I realized some of the cement had crept under my nails and hardened. The next day I had to have my 'glamour' chipped off."

Garland's mother also attended the event and straightened out a letter in her daughter's signature after the ceremony.

The Chinese Theatre also had an indirect influence on Garland's best-known film, *The Wizard of Oz.* Harold Arlen and E.Y. (Yip) Harburg were the composer and lyricist. Arlen recalled, "We had finished most of the songs, or all of the songs, but the one for Judy in Kansas. And I knew what I wanted, but when it doesn't come it becomes one of those things that bugs you, and most of us don't like to be bugged."

He and his wife Anya decided to go see a movie at the Chinese Theatre. She drove, as Arlen wasn't feeling too well and was nervous about his unsuccessful attempt to come up with the tune he was seeking. "Time was getting short; I was getting anxious," Arlen continued.

As they came to Schwab's drugstore on Sunset Boulevard, Arlen was struck with a "broad, long-lined, melody" and had his wife pull the car over to the side of the road and stop. He took out a little piece of manuscript and jotted down what the world came to know as "Over the Rainbow." "It was as if the Lord said, 'Well, here it is, now stop worrying about it!'" Arlen declared. The song became Garland's trademark and won the Academy Award.

Jane Withers
Ceremony #51: November 6, 1939

Born: in Atlanta, Georgia, on April 12, 1926.

One of the most popular child stars of the 1930s, Jane Withers was the absolute antithesis of that paragon of beauty and perfection, Shirley Temple. The decision to feature Withers opposite Temple in *Bright Eyes* (1934) catapulted young Jane to stardom as "the meanie everyone loves."

Toddler Jane proved a natural performer and at age three made her debut on Atlanta radio. By 1932 she was famous throughout the city for her skits, songs, and impersonations and was alternately nicknamed "Atlanta's Sweetheart" and "Dixie's Dainty Dew-

drop." Her mother took her to Hollywood, and Jane landed a small part at the Fox Film Corporation (later 20th Century-Fox) in *Handle with Care* (1932, debut). The turning point in Withers' career came when she was cast as Shirley's nemesis in *Bright Eyes*.

She made the transition through "the awkward age" and teen years more successfully than most child stars. Withers retired from a full-time screen career in 1947, making only occasional appearances in subsequent feature films. A stand-out was her role as a blowsy, scatterbrained Texas millionairess in *Giant* (1956).

In the 1960s and 1970s Jane became familiar to a whole new generation when she appeared as Josephine, the Plumber, in Comet Cleanser television commercials.

Her motion picture credits include *Ginger* (1935), *The Farmer Takes a Wife* (1935), *Paddy O'Day* (1935), *Little Miss Nobody* (1936), *The Holy Terror* (1937), *Always in Trouble* (1938), *A Very Young Lady* (1941), *Small Town Deb* (1941), *Danger Street* (1947), and *Captain Newman, M.D.* (1963).

Jane's square is tinted gray and contains the inscription "Mr. Grauman—A Hello to You from Jane Withers [signature]." Also included are the date ("11-6-39"), her two footprints, and two handprints, the drawing of a female stick figure that is meant to be Withers with the inscription "me," plus what appears to be two coin imprints. If coins were originally embedded in the cement, they have since been pried out.

In a telephone conversation with the authors, Withers remembered Sid Grauman as a "kind,

thoughtful, and generous man" who "holds a special place in my heart." She explained that Grauman took her under his wing in the early 1930s when she was still an aspiring child performer who had yet to make a film. Even then, Jane was an avid movie fan and autograph hound.

According to Withers, Sid always saved a prominent spot for her on the sidelines of premiere nights at his theatres so that she could have easy access to the stars whom she approached with her autograph book. On these occasions, Grauman made a special point of singling out the eager child to prominent film people as a talented little girl who should have a bright future in films.

In 1935 Jane's first starring film, *Ginger*, premiered at the Chinese Theatre. It was Sid Grauman who personally escorted her and her mother to their reserved seats. He took the opportunity to remind Jane, "You see, I always told you that you'd become a star—and here we are!"

Evidence of his faith in Jane was also visible outside the theatre. Often a banner spanning the width of Hollywood Boulevard was hung to advertise a premiere and/or a picture currently playing at the theatre. On this occasion a banner

reading "YOU'LL LOVE GINGER" was strung across the street; and when Jane and her mother first saw it, they were so thrilled they both cried. As if that weren't enough, a large illuminated sign in the lot on the east side of the building facing Hollywood Boulevard was also used for advertising the current attraction; and during this engagement it read: "JANE WITHERS AS GINGER—HOLLYWOOD'S NEWEST STAR."

Jane Withers.

Linda Darnell.

Linda Darnell
Ceremony #52: March 18, 1940

She placed her prints in connection with the motion picture *Star Dust* (20th Century-Fox, 1940).

Born: Monette Eloyse Darnell in Dallas, Texas, on October 16, 1923. Died: April 10, 1965.

Linda Darnell was a natural beauty who became a very popular leading lady of the screen during the 1940s. She started in roles that cast her as dewy-eyed, virginal heroines and later played lusty, voluptuous temptresses.

In 1938 her ambitious mother learned of a 20th Century-Fox talent scout in Dallas and secured an interview. As a result, her daughter was invited to Hollywood to make a screen test. Viewing her footage, the studio executives decided she wasn't ready for a film career and sent her back to Texas. They called her back for another test in less than a year. This time she was impressive, and Fox signed her to a contract. She made her film debut in *Hotel for Women* (1939) and was so well received by the public

that Fox chief Darryl F. Zanuck yanked her out of a small role in *Drums Along the Mohawk* (1939) and cast her opposite the studio's biggest male star, Tyrone Power, in *Day-Time Wife* (1939).

Fox started casting Darnell in alluring roles in the mid-1940s. She replaced Peggy Cummins as the lead in *Forever Amber* (1947), a vastly ambitious and expensive project that had disappointing results. Her career started to slip after *A Letter to Three Wives* (1949). Fox dropped her in 1952, and she freelanced in films during the rest of the 1950s and 1960s and also tried stage plays and the nightclub circuit.

Her motion picture credits include *Brigham Young—Frontiersman* (1940), *The Mark of Zorro* (1940), *Blood and Sand* (1941), *Summer Storm* (1944), *Hangover Square* (1945), *Anna and the King of Siam* (1946), *Centennial Summer* (1946), *My Darling Clementine* (1946), *Unfaithfully Yours* (1948), and *Black Spurs* (1965, final film).

Darnell's square is tinted green and contains the inscription "To Mr. Sid Grauman—the best always." (The period is Darnell's.) Also included are the date ("March 18. 1940"), her two footprints (made with high heels), two handprints, and her signature.

Star Dust was partly based on Linda's own early experiences in Hollywood. In the film she plays Carolyn Sayres, a young girl who is discovered by a roving Hollywood talent scout. However, Carolyn is rejected because she is too young. Eventually, she does get her big chance and, as a star, places her imprints at the Chinese Theatre.

Rosa Grauman and George Raft Ceremony #53: March 25, 1940

Rosa Grauman

Born: Rosa Goldsmith in Cincinnati, Ohio, circa 1853 (sources vary on year). Died: June 13, 1936.

Sid Grauman said in 1949, "We were great pals, my mother and I. Greater, I suppose, because I never married, and because we had only each other for a good many years."

His parents, Rosa and David J. Grauman, had a total of six children. A kindly, unassuming woman,

Rosa Grauman.

Rosa always shared in her famous son's success. The two became inseparable after the death of her husband in April 1921, and she occupied a suite adjacent to Sid's own at the Ambassador Hotel.

Rosa was involved with many charities and was beloved throughout the film community. She bequeathed her entire estate, valued at more than $200,000, to "my beloved and only son Sidney," then the sole survivor of her six offspring. Sid continued living in the Ambassador Hotel apartments they had both occupied and kept all of Rosa's clothing and mementos.

Rosa Grauman's square is tinted red and contains the inscription "In Eternal Memory of My Dear Mother Rosa Grauman." Also included are the date ("Mar 25-40") and the signature of Sid Grauman.

Rosa was a talented musician and composer and gave many piano recitals during her lifetime, including one broadcast over KFWB radio in Los Angeles in June 1933, when she played her own composition, "Valse Brilliante." Her violin accompaniment that

Sid Grauman (left) and George Raft.

evening was supplied by George Stoll, who was then the conductor of the orchestra at the Chinese Theatre.

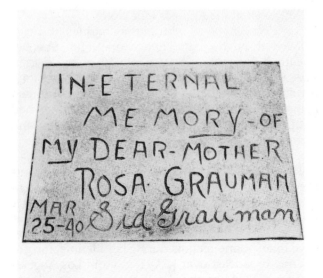

On another occasion several years prior to her radio concert, Sid brought Rosa to the Chinese Theatre and assisted her into the orchestra pit, from which she performed works by Bach, Chopin, and many other composers. He sat in an orchestra seat delightedly listening to his mother's performance.

In honor of Rosa and of Mother's Day, Sid Grauman invited the mothers of several leading film stars in Hollywood to the Chinese Theatre in 1934. He arranged special ceremonies in the forecourt and inside on the stage of the theatre during the run of *The House of Rothschild* (1934) in celebration of the day. More than twenty mothers of screen celebrities accepted his invitation to the festivities.

Once asked why he chose to honor his mother with her own square in the Chinese Theatre forecourt, Sid replied, "Why not? She was a star to me."

The block continues to be an enigma to many of the tourists who visit the theatre. When writer/director Robert Parrish went back for a look at the forecourt during the time he was working on his memoirs,

Rosa Grauman's square stood out among the others; and Parrish commented:

"It's the only block with no handprints, footprints, hoofprints, or snappy greetings, so it's more like a tombstone. When you step from Groucho's slab onto Rosa Grauman's, you suddenly get the feeling that you are in a cemetery and that all the famous movie stars are buried there in a common grave with Rosa Grauman...."

George Raft

Born: George Ranft on September 27, 1895, in New York City. Died: November 24, 1980.

George Raft achieved Hollywood fame in the early 1930s in a series of tough-guy, gangster type roles in films with shady underworld settings. In his teen years, Raft went through a variety of jobs, eventually becoming a "taxi dancer" in some of New York's less respectable "dives" at eighteen. He developed his

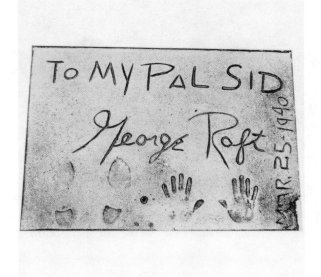

dancing talents and became a prominent ballroom dancer, landing featured spots at many posh nightclubs and touring Europe's better nighteries, as well.

He accepted an offer from a former employer, Texas Guinan, to go to Hollywood for a role in her film, *Queen of the Night Clubs* (1929, debut). His important breakthrough came with *Scarface* (1932), in which his role as a gangster's coin-flipping henchman made him a star and established an indelible image that was to stay with him for life.

In the 1950s Raft made fewer film appearances and was hired as an official greeter for the Flamingo Hotel in Las Vegas. The Nevada Tax Commission

was upset by his connections with gangland figures Owney Madden, Lucky Luciano, and Ben "Bugsy" Siegel. Raft reasoned that he also knew a great many sports figures, saying, "That didn't make me a famous athlete, did it?" In 1966 he shifted to the Colony Club in London but was denied a re-entry visa by the British government, reportedly as a result of his alleged mob connections. The government chose to disregard the fact that Raft had been a close personal friend of the young Prince of Wales (later King Edward VIII) in earlier years.

His motion picture credits include *Night after Night* (1932), *The Bowery* (1933), *Bolero* (1934), *Spawn of the North* (1938), *Each Dawn I Die* (1939), *The House across the Bay* (1940), *They Drive by Night* (1940), *Some Like It Hot* (1959), *Ocean's Eleven* (1960), and *Sextette* (1979, final film).

Raft's square is tinted red and contains the inscription "To My Pal Sid." Also included are the date ("Mar. 25-1940"), his two footprints, two handprints, and his signature. A coin was also embedded in the cement. It has since been pried out.

Raft portrayed a gangster in the motion picture *Scarface*, in which he flipped various coins throughout the film.

John Barrymore
Ceremony #54: September 5, 1940

He placed his prints in connection with the motion picture *The Great Profile* (20th Century-Fox, 1940).

Born: John Sidney Blyth in Philadelphia, Pennsylvania, on February 15, 1882. Died: May 29, 1942.

John Barrymore, "The Great Profile," was one of the consummate actors of the 20th century, as well as one of its most tragic figures. Traumatized by the early death of his father as a result of alcoholism and mental illness, John Barrymore started drinking in his teens and, despite several serious attempts at sobriety, never completely stopped.

He was born into the distinguished Drew/Barrymore theatrical family. Initially he didn't really want to become an actor and pursued a career as an illustrator and cartoonist until 1903, when he was finally enticed to make his stage debut. He achieved a major success in his 1909 Broadway debut, *The Fortune Hunter*. He made his first film in 1914 and in the late teens alternated between the movies and various Broadway triumphs. His compelling perfor-

Sid Grauman pushes John Barrymore's face into the cement. The actor commented, "I feel like the face on the barroom floor."

mance in the film *Dr. Jekyll and Mr. Hyde* (1920) made Barrymore a major movie star.

After his Broadway appearances in the early 1920s as Richard III and Hamlet (the latter a landmark interpretation), he soon embarked wholeheartedly on a film career. He maintained a position as one of the most important stars, first at Warner Bros., and then with United Artists.

Barrymore's health began to fail during the early 1930s. He experienced memory loss, and it began to affect him professionally; thereafter he often had to depend on cue cards to remember his lines. Sadly, some roles near the end of his career found Barrymore parodying himself as a broken-down, once-great but now inebriated ham actor.

His motion picture credits include *An American Citizen* (1914, debut), *Don Juan* (1926), *General Crack* (1929, talkie debut), *Grand Hotel* (1932), *A Bill of Divorcement* (1932), *Dinner at Eight* (1933), *Counsellor at Law* (1933), *Romeo and Juliet* (1936), *Midnight* (1939), and *Playmates* (1941, final film).

Barrymore's square is tinted gray and contains the inscription "To Sid—A Great Show Man." Also included are the date ("Sept-5-40"), his two footprints, two handprints, and his signature, the inscription "My Hand And Foot Print—J.B.," plus the imprint of Barrymore's left profile with the inscription "My Profile—J.B."

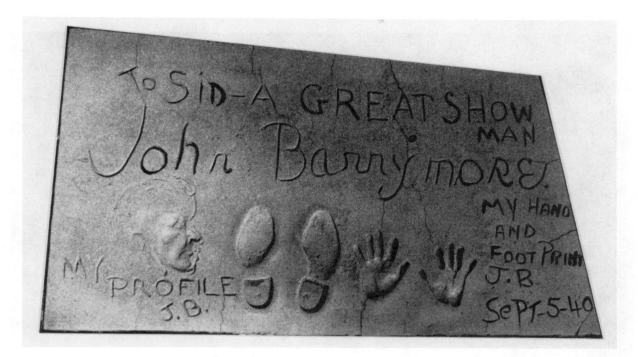

Barrymore misspelled his name in his first attempt at writing his signature ("Jon Barrymore"). The cement had to be smoothed over, and he got it right on the second try.

Sid Grauman told news reporters before the ceremony that photographs would be taken of Barrymore merely placing his cheek next to the cement and added that the actual profile was to be made later from a plaster cast.

A cloth was spread over the wet concrete to protect Barrymore's attire, and he went ahead with the publicity stunt but imprinted his actual profile, without any cast. (Accounts of Grauman's taking it upon himself to sneak up and push Barrymore's face into the cement without forewarning him are questionable.)

Barrymore was none too happy. His muffled obscenities while he was deep in the goo could not be recounted in print by the attending news media. A photograph from one of the local Los Angeles papers covering the event shows a disgruntled Barrymore digging wet cement out of his left ear with his index finger.

Sid drew a few hair strands in the damp concrete while actress Mary Beth Hughes helped clean Barrymore's face with a towel supplied by a theatre attendant. When his limousine drove away, poor John Barrymore was still dabbing his cemented left eye with his handkerchief.

Jack Benny
Ceremony #55: January 13, 1941

He placed his prints in connection with the motion picture *Love Thy Neighbor* (Paramount, 1940).

Born: Benjamin Kubelsky in Chicago, Illinois, on February 14, 1894. Died: December 26, 1974.

Jack Benny was one of the most beloved and talented figures in the history of American comedy. He created a unique and unforgettable comic persona based on stinginess, vanity about his age (an eternal thirty-nine), self-deprecation, and his supposed inability to play the violin.

At age six Benny started violin lessons and initially aimed toward a career as a musician. He started in vaudeville, playing straight, and eventually discovered that he got better audience response by being funny rather than by serious fiddling. Soon his violin became a famous prop for use in his comic monologues.

Benny continued in vaudeville and in Broadway shows throughout the 1920s and made his film debut in the Vitaphone short "Bright Moments" (1928). He made several films for Metro-Goldwyn-Mayer and one for Columbia. With no further film offers forthcoming, Benny set his sights on radio and made his

Writers Hilliard Marx (Jack Benny's brother-in law [standing, left]), Bill Morrow, Sid Grauman, and Jack Benny.

debut on Ed Sullivan's show in 1932. Within a few weeks, he had his own show and became one of the most innovative and definitive masters of the medium, on which he performed continually for over twenty-five years. He alternated between radio and movies (several for Paramount) during the 1930s and 1940s.

In 1950 he invaded television and launched "The Jack Benny Show," which aired through 1965.

His motion picture credits include *The Hollywood Revue of 1929* (1929), *The Big Broadcast of 1937* (1936), *Artists and Models* (1937), *Man about Town* (1939), *Buck Benny Rides Again* (1940), *Charley's Aunt* (1941), *To Be Or Not To Be* (1942), *George Washington Slept Here* (1942), *The Horn Blows at Midnight* (1945), and *A Guide for the Married Man* (1967, final film).

Benny's square is tinted gray and contains the inscription "My [Heart] Belongs To Mary But My Feet Belong To Grauman." Also included are the date ("Jan-13-41"), his two footprints, and his signature.

The "Heart" in the inscription is a drawing of a heart, not the written word; and "Mary" is Benny's wife, actress Mary Livingstone.

The comedian delighted the fans who turned out for the event by pitching in and helping to mix his own cement. He was accompanied on this occasion by writers Hilliard Marx and William Morrow, both of whom started writing for Benny's radio show in 1938.

Livingstone and Marx, who was also Benny's brother-in-law and eventual producer of his radio and television programs, shared an anecdote regarding Jack and the Chinese Theatre in their book, *Jack Benny*:

"Once again, Jack went to work at MGM, starring in a film called *Broadway Melody of 1936* [1935]....The movie was given a big, innovative *afternoon* world premiere at Grauman's Chinese Theatre..., complete with red carpet, stars arriving in limousines, and reporters and cameramen immortalizing the opening, as thousands of fans lined the boulevard waiting to see the celebrities.

"Microphones were set up outside the theatre, and Jack played m.c., entertaining the fans. There was an official ceremony, opened by the simulated roar of Leo the Lion [MGM's trademark that preceded the start of all its motion pictures], followed by a musical medley from the film played by a sizable orchestra. Benny then came out and traded quips with Sid Silvers, turning the whole affair into a quasi 'Jell-O Program' [Benny's own radio show sponsor]. Frances

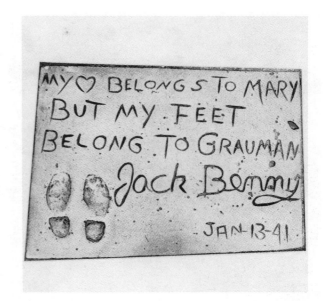

Langford and others from the cast sang. Eleanor Powell did a tap dance. Robert Taylor smiled—and the fans swooned. And Mary Livingstone, there with Jack, read a funny poem like those she had become famous for on radio. Climaxing the festivities, Jack came back on mike personally to thank everyone and to announce Jell-O's six delicious flavors as: 'Strawberry, raspberry, cherry, Metro, Goldwyn, and Mayer.'"

Carmen Miranda
Ceremony #56: March 24, 1941

She placed her prints in connection with the motion picture *That Night in Rio* (20th Century-Fox, 1941).

Born: Maria do Carmo Miranda da Cunha, in the town of Marco de Canavezes, near Lisbon, Portugal, on February 9, 1909. Died: August 5, 1955.

Billed as the "Brazilian Bombshell," Carmen Miranda enlivened movie screens during the 1940s with her singing and dancing in several 20th Century-Fox Technicolor musicals. Her head-to-toe costuming was colorfully flamboyant and consisted of vivid, exaggerated Brazilian native dress, turban headdresses overflowing with fruit and flowers, and three-inch platform shoes.

Her family moved to Rio de Janeiro, Brazil, where, during the 1930s, Miranda became a top star. She made five films, over 300 records, and several triumphant personal appearance tours throughout South America. Broadway impresario Lee Shubert saw her

Theatre attendant James Wong (left), Dr. Mancel Casado, the Brazilian Consul at Los Angeles, and Carmen Miranda.

perform in Brazil and negotiated a three-year contract with her. She arrived in New York in 1939 and made her Broadway debut in Shubert's musical, *Streets of Paris*. The explosiveness of her performance stopped the show and made Carmen an overnight star in America.

Hollywood beckoned, and she signed a long-term contract with 20th Century-Fox, making her American movie debut in *Down Argentine Way* (1940). Other hits included *The Gang's All Here* (1943), in which Carmen's appearance in an outlandish Busby Berkeley production number entitled "The Lady in the Tutti-Frutti Hat" permanently established her as one of the unique popular culture icons of the century.

By the late 1940s her vogue in films had somewhat faded, and she eventually returned to nightclubs with great success in New York, Las Vegas, and even the London Palladium.

Her motion picture credits include *A Voz Do Carnaval* (1933, debut), *Week-End in Havana* (1941), *Springtime in the Rockies* (1942), *Greenwich Village* (1944), *Something for the Boys* (1944), *Doll Face* (1946), *Copacabana* (1947), *A Date with Judy* (1948), *Nancy Goes to Rio* (1950), and *Scared Stiff* (1953, final film).

Miranda's square is tinted gray and contains the inscription "To Sid—Viva! In The South American Way." "Viva!" is Spanish for "Live Life!" Also included are the date ("March 24 1941"), her two footprints (made with her trademark "wedgie" shoes that gave her small frame added height, instead of the customary high heels), two handprints, and her signature.

Over the years Miranda's square has deteriorated, and only her left footprint survives. The area that contained her right footprint has been patched for preservation purposes.

Miranda made a one-week personal appearance engagement at the Chinese Theatre the month following her hand and footprint ceremony during the run of the film *Topper Returns* (1941). Her stage-show played to capacity audiences. Critic Dorothy Manners wrote in the Los Angeles *Examiner* on April 24, 1941:

"Senorita Carmen Miranda has taken over Grauman's Chinese in what is termed a 'personal

appearance' this week, but where Carmen is concerned that is the height of understatement. It's more to the point that Carmen has blown in with the proportions of a personal blitzkrieg and taken over the house lock, stock and barrel.

"Miranda is a personal bombshell that rocked yesterday's audience right out into the aisles. For fifteen minutes this South American honey goes to town singing her numbers as only she can and wearing those fruit-and-flower-packed turbans that would look like truck gardens [farms for the growing of vegetables for the market] on anyone else....

"The lady chants, she swings her South American hips, she makes little animal faces, and 'gives' with a delivery that should do more toward cementing relations between Uncle Sam and South America than anything else."

Barbara Stanwyck and Robert Taylor Ceremony #57: June 11, 1941

The couple were husband and wife at the time of their ceremony. They wed in 1939 and divorced in 1951.

Barbara Stanwyck

Born: Ruby Stevens in Brooklyn, New York, on July 16, 1907. Died: January 20, 1990.

Barbara Stanwyck was a consummate professional, adored by her co-workers both in front of and behind the cameras. Frank Capra and Cecil B. DeMille called her their favorite actress; and Capra wrote, "In a Hollywood popularity contest, she would win first prize hands down."

Orphaned by age four, Stanwyck spent much of her childhood in a series of foster homes and seemed a rootless, lonely outsider. The movie palaces became her escape from a harsh world. She got several jobs as a chorus dancer beginning in 1922 and worked her way up to leads in two Broadway hits, *The Noose* (1926) and *Burlesque* (1927).

Stanwyck arrived in Hollywood in 1929 and shortly thereafter signed two non-exclusive contracts—one at Columbia and one at Warner Bros. Later she signed another non-exclusive deal with RKO. She free-lanced at virtually all the other major studios and chose never to be under long-term exclusive contract to any of them during her career so that she could call the shots.

Stanwyck became a major star after appearing in several films for Frank Capra during the early 1930s.

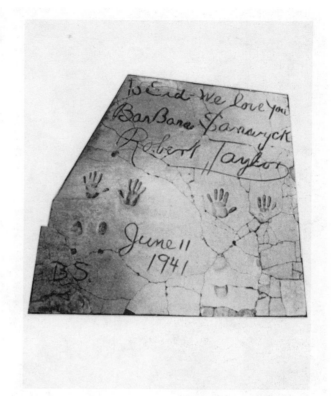

In the 1940s she demonstrated her remarkable versatility by playing such roles as the cold-blooded, calculating temptress of murderous bent in *Double Indemnity* (1944).

The 1950s and early 1960s found her in generally lesser films. Stanwyck appeared on television in such successes as "The Big Valley" (1965-1969) series and the mini-series "The Thorn Birds" (1983).

Her motion picture credits include *Broadway Nights* (1927, debut), *The Locked Door* (1929, talkie debut), *The Miracle Woman* (1931), *Stella Dallas* (1937), *The Lady Eve* (1941), *Meet John Doe* (1941), *Ball of Fire* (1941), *Sorry, Wrong Number* (1948), *Titanic* (1953), and *The Night Walker* (1964, final film).

In 1982 she received an Honorary Academy Award "for superlative creativity and unique contribution to the art of screen acting." In 1987 the American Film Institute presented her with its Life Achievement Award.

Academy Award nomination: Best Actress.

Robert Taylor

Born: Spangler Arlington Brugh in Filley, Nebraska, on August 5, 1911. Died: June 8, 1969.

One of the most devastatingly handsome of all Hollywood actors, Robert Taylor fought a "pretty

Barbara Stanwyck, her husband Robert Taylor, unidentified man (behind Taylor), Sid Grauman, and theatre attendant James Wong.

boy" image in his early career and when he finally landed more masculine and "tough guy" roles proved himself a very good actor indeed.

Attending Pomona College in California, he became involved in student dramatics and appeared in several plays. In 1932 he was seen in one of them by a Metro-Goldwyn-Mayer talent scout who offered Taylor a deal, but Taylor opted to complete school and finally signed with the studio in 1934. He made his film debut that same year and achieved stardom in *Magnificent Obsession* (1935).

MGM quickly put Taylor into a succession of major parts opposite their most important leading ladies, including Joan Crawford, Greta Garbo, Jean Harlow, and Myrna Loy. With *A Yank at Oxford* (1938), Taylor achieved his long-sought image change to more assertively masculine roles and thereafter showed versatility as soldiers, detectives, cowboys, and even gangsters. Taylor served in the U.S.

Navy during World War II as a flying instructor and returned to Hollywood to star in *Undercurrent* (1946).

The 1950s saw him emerge as a symbol of heroic virtue in such period spectacles as *Quo Vadis* (1951) and *Ivanhoe* (1952). He settled his contract with MGM in 1958, leaving with an option to do two more films for the company. He made both and with the last, *Cattle King* (1963), ended a twenty-nine year association with the studio.

His motion picture credits include *Handy Andy* (1934, debut), *Broadway Melody of 1936* (1935), *Camille* (1936), *Three Comrades* (1938), *Waterloo Bridge* (1940), *Johnny Eager* (1942), *Bataan* (1943), *Above and Beyond* (1953), *Miracle of the White Stallions* (1963), and *The Day the Hot Line Got Hot* (1969, final film).

The Stanwyck/Taylor square is tinted gray and contains the inscription "To Sid—We love You."

Also included are the date ("June 11 1941"), Stanwyck's two footprints (made with high heels), two handprints, and her signature, the inscription of her initials "B.S.," Taylor's two footprints, two handprints, and his signature.

Stanwyck's last name is written so that it appears to read "Sanwyck." For years, observers have assumed that she forgot to include the "t." Other Stanwyck signatures from that time period show she was fond of incorporating the "S" and the "t." On close examination of the square, one discovers that the "t" is included and is crossed through the "S."

The square has deteriorated badly over the years. Mann Theatres invited Stanwyck to participate in another ceremony in the mid-1980s, the plan being to remove the Stanwyck/Taylor block and replace it with a new one with her imprints. Stanwyck did not take the theatre up on its offer, possibly realizing that to have done so would have meant the exclusion of Robert Taylor from the forecourt.

Rudy Vallée
Ceremony #58: July 21, 1941

Born: Hubert Prior Vallée in Island Pond, Vermont, on July 28, 1901. Died: July 3, 1986.

Rudy Vallée was the first popular singer to take America by storm, captivate countless thousands of fans, and evoke teenaged girls to scream and swoon. By 1921 he was proficient enough on the saxophone to play professionally. Vallée studied at the University of Maine in 1921-1922 and then went to Yale from 1922 to 1924. He took time off from school to go to London to play at the Savoy Hotel and was an immediate hit. He returned to Yale to complete his education but thereafter headed straight back to show business, having formed his own band—first called "The Yale Collegians" but soon after changed to "The Connecticut Yankees."

Sid Grauman (left) and Rudy Vallée.

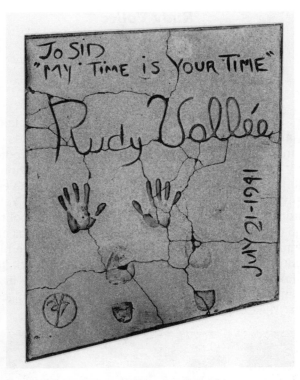

He quickly secured a job at the posh Heigh-Ho Club in New York, from which he made his first broadcast over American radio in February 1928. Vallée and his band were an immediate nation-wide hit, and his show evolved into radio's first major network variety hour.

Hollywood beckoned, and he made his film debut in *The Vagabond Lover* (1929). In 1942 his film portrayal of a prissy, eccentric millionaire in Preston Sturges' screwball comedy, *The Palm Beach Story*, delighted critics and moviegoers alike. In 1961 Vallée scored a triumphant stage hit on Broadway in *How To Succeed in Business without Really Trying*, which ran for three years and was filmed with Vallée in 1967.

His motion picture credits include *Glorifying the American Girl* (1929), *George White's Scandals* (1934), *Gold Diggers in Paris* (1938), *It's in the Bag* (1945), *The Bachelor and the Bobby-Soxer* (1947), *I Remember Mama* (1948), *Unfaithfully Yours* (1948), *Mother Is a Freshman* (1949), *Gentlemen Marry Brunettes* (1955), and *Won Ton Ton, the Dog Who Saved Hollywood* (1976, final film).

Vallée's square is tinted gray and contains the inscription "To Sid—'My Time Is Your Time.'" Also included are the date ("July 21-1941"), his two footprints, two handprints, and his signature, plus a

drawing of a circle; inside is the letter "Y," with the number "2" on the left of the "Y" and the number "7" on the right. This drawing relates to the fact that Vallée was graduated from Yale University and was a member of the Class of 1927.

The inscription is the title of the 1929 song that had become Vallée's trademark and was also the theme of his popular radio show, "The Fleischmann Hour," for Fleischmann's Yeast.

In a letter to the authors, Vallée recalled that his Chinese Theatre ceremony was arranged by Harry Brand, head of the 20th Century-Fox publicity department, and that Harry's wife, Sybil, "really liked [me] and was always trying to find me a wife!" (Vallée married four times.)

Cecil B. DeMille
Ceremony #59: August 7, 1941

He placed his prints in connection with the motion picture *Reap the Wild Wind* (Paramount, 1942), which he produced and directed.

Born: Cecil Blount deMille on August 12, 1881, in Ashfield, Massachusetts. Died: January 21, 1959.

Cecil B. DeMille was one of the most famous producer/directors in film history. His name on the marquee was often a greater draw than those of his stars. He made his debut on the New York stage as an actor in 1900 and toured with many stock companies for several years. DeMille developed a strong interest in motion pictures and in 1913, with Jesse L. Lasky and Samuel Goldwyn, formed the Jesse L. Lasky Feature Play Company (which later evolved into Paramount). DeMille's title was Director-General; and their first production, *The Squaw Man* (1914, directorial debut), became the first feature-length film to be produced in Hollywood.

His first true "epic" was *Joan the Woman* (1916), which depicted the life, trial, and execution of Joan of Arc. From 1919 to 1921 DeMille made a series of high-society, fairly risqué comedy-dramas starring Gloria Swanson. He followed these with his first massive Biblical epic, *The Ten Commandments* (1923).

DeMille left Paramount to form his own company in 1924. The highlight of these years was his production of *The King of Kings* (1927), which opened the Chinese Theatre. He returned to Paramount as an independent producer/director in 1932, where he was to remain for the rest of his career.

Actress/columnist Hedda Hopper (left), Sid Grauman, Cecil B. DeMille, making his imprints for the Chinese Theatre, and actress Martha O'Driscoll on the set of Reap the Wild Wind *(1942). DeMille was unable to take a break during the film's shooting schedule to go to the theatre for the ceremony; so the cement was brought to him instead.*

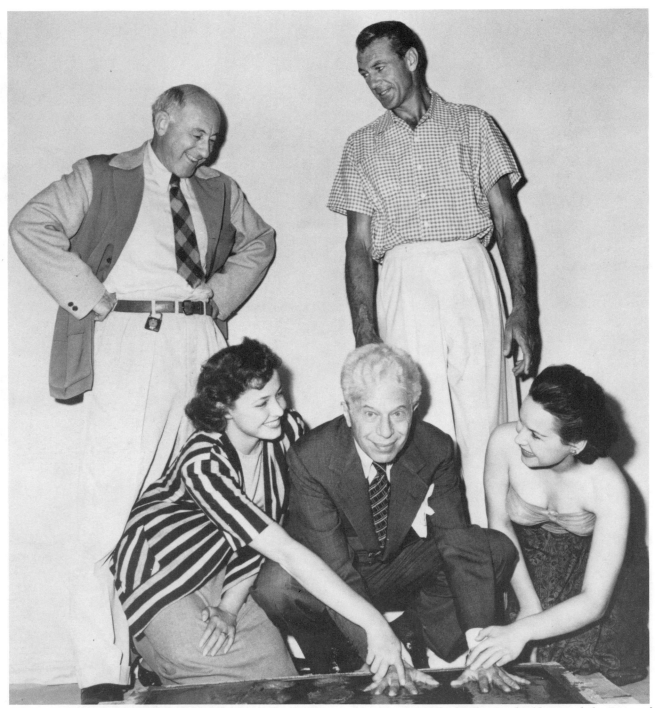

Sid Grauman records his prints for Cecil B. DeMille (left) on the Paramount studio lot during the filming of The Story of Dr. Wassell *(1944). With them are cast members Laraine Day (left), Gary Cooper, and Carol Thurston.*

His motion picture credits as a producer/director include *The Cheat* (1915), *The Little American* (1917), *Male and Female* (1919), *Dynamite* (1929, talkie debut), *The Sign of the Cross* (1932), *Cleopatra* (1934), *Union Pacific* (1939), *Samson and Delilah* (1949), **The Greatest Show on Earth* (1952), and ***The Ten Commandments* (1956, final film).

In 1950 the Academy of Motion Picture Arts and Sciences called him a "distinguished motion picture pioneer" and voted him a Special Academy Award "for 37 years of brilliant showmanship." He also received their Irving G. Thalberg Memorial Award in 1953.

> * *Academy Award nomination: Direction; Academy Award winner: Best Picture.*
> ** *Academy Award nomination: Best Picture.*

DeMille's square is tinted gray and contains the inscription "Greetings to Sid from Cecil B. deMille [signature]." Also included are the date ("Aug-7-1941"), his two footprints (made with boots), two handprints, plus the inscription "Hand and Boot Prints." There is also a brass border around the square, which was added when the square was rededicated on May 24, 1977.

DeMille signed his last name "deMille." The family name was originally spelled with a small "d." DeMille capitalized it for professional purposes but in correspondence and for personal use signed with a small "d."

In 1936 DeMille began a nine-year run as the host of the popular radio program, "Lux Radio Theatre." He had the following to say about the Chinese Theatre during a commercial break on the broadcast of *A Star Is Born* in 1937:

"It was most appropriate that our play [*A Star Is Born*] should end with a scene at Grauman's Chinese Theatre. It was there that the most thrilling premieres in Hollywood history have been held...."

Four years after the "Lux" broadcast, DeMille was asked to place his prints in the Chinese Theatre forecourt. The ceremony took place during a very hectic time period, as he was then shooting his lavish production *Reap the Wild Wind*. It was also held five days prior to his sixtieth birthday. He recounted the following in his memoirs:

"I also achieved a symbol of Hollywood immortality in an unusual way on that birthday: I was too busy on the set [of *Reap the Wild Wind*] to go up to Hollywood Boulevard, so Sid Grauman brought a block of wet cement to the studio to receive the prints of my hands and feet, which tourists will inspect in the forecourt of the Chinese Theatre for generations

to come, and ask each other, 'Cecil B. deMille? Who was he?'"

DeMille was assisted at his ceremony by the film's players Paulette Goddard, Ray Milland, Hedda Hopper, and Martha O'Driscoll. The square was lowered into the theatre's forecourt on DeMille's birthday.

In 1943 DeMille turned the tables on Grauman when he invited him to help dedicate the new DeMille bungalow on the Paramount studio lot. Sid was to come to the studio and record his own footprints, handprints, and a short message in his handwriting, in a slab of cement which was to be displayed on a table in DeMille's office.

All the celebrities who had left their prints in the

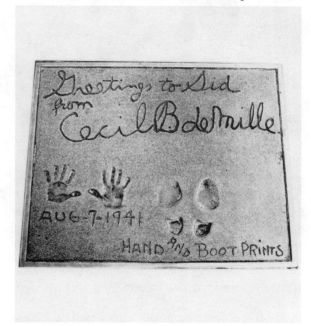

forecourt of the Chinese Theatre were to receive engraved invitations to the event, which was to be held in DeMille's new office building.

Photographs of the event show that it was done either on DeMille's *The Story of Dr. Wassell* (1944) set and/or the still photography gallery. DeMille himself helped Sid place his prints, assisted by three of the film's players, Gary Cooper, Laraine Day, and Carol Thurston. DeMille kidded the on-lookers that gathered by saying, "I'm going to get even with Grauman," as Sid stepped into the wet cement and sank down several inches.

Sid responded, "My, this stuff is sure gooey," but was obviously delighted with the proceedings..

The Grauman square contained the inscription "To Cecil B. DeMille—The World's Greatest Showman." Also included were the date ("Oct 4th 1943"),

Fay Holden (left), Los Angeles Mayor Fletcher Bowron, Judy Garland, Mickey Rooney, Lewis Stone, Ann Rutherford, and Sara Haden. The Judge James K. Hardy family plaque, for reasons unknown, is no longer in the forecourt.

Sid's two footprints, two handprints, and his signature.

When the ceremony was completed, Grauman stepped out of the moist concrete, saying, "What a mess. And to think I can't get another ration coupon [this was during World War II when rationing was rampant] for a pair of shoes."

The 1977 rededication ceremony for DeMille's square took place in connection with a special benefit screening of the motion picture *The King of Kings* (1927) and was part of Mann Theatres' year-long fiftieth anniversary celebration of the Chinese Theatre. The film had opened the Chinese Theatre on May 18, 1927.

Katherine DeMille represented her late father and hosted a reception for the surviving cast and crew members from the production.

Stars of over fifty DeMille films were invited to honor the late producer/director at the rededication of his square.

The Judge James K. Hardy Family Ceremony #60: August 15, 1941

The Hardy family—the fictitious characters of the popular "Andy Hardy" series of films—was honored with a north wall plaque, on the northeast side pillar directly beside the theatre entrance, in connection with the eleventh motion picture of the series, *Life Begins for Andy Hardy* (Metro-Goldwyn-Mayer, 1941). The plaque, for reasons unknown, is no longer in the forecourt.

The "Andy Hardy" Series (Metro-Goldwyn-Mayer, 1937-1958)

In 1937 Metro-Goldwyn-Mayer studios produced *A Family Affair*, a low-budget film based on characters created for a 1928 play entitled *Skidding*, by Aurania Rouverol, that had enjoyed a modest success on

Love Finds Andy Hardy. *Released by Metro-Goldwyn-Mayer (1938).*

Broadway. Produced by Lucien Hubbard and Samuel Marx, directed by George B. Seitz, and written by Kay Van Riper, *A Family Affair* centered around a typical American family, the Hardys, in the small, mythical mid-western town of Carvel, Idaho, population 25,000. The film starred Lionel Barrymore as Judge Hardy and Spring Byington as his wife, Mrs. Emily Hardy—also known as Mother Hardy or Ma Hardy. Their two children who lived at home were played by Mickey Rooney as their son Andrew—better known as Andy—and Cecilia Parker as their daughter Marian. Sara Haden was cast as the family's spinster,

Aunt Milly. Other players included Julie Haydon as another daughter, Joan, Allen Vincent as Joan's husband, and Margaret Marquis as Polly Benedict, a former neighbor of the Hardys whose family has just returned to Carvel.

Some of the cast members had previously appeared in MGM's production of Eugene O'Neill's play *Ah, Wilderness!* in 1935, and the studio hoped to achieve a similar success with this new production. Charming and unpretentious, *A Family Affair* was a surprising hit with audiences everywhere, and MGM received requests from its exhibitors for more films like it. The sets were kept standing, and a sequel was soon in the works. In all, sixteen films dealing with the adventures of the Hardys were made over a twenty-one year period. Mickey Rooney was the only performer to appear in all of them. Inexpensively budgeted, the modest films returned a profit of three or four times their cost and were beloved by the American public.

They also were a good testing ground for up-and-coming female talent under contract to MGM. Players such as Judy Garland, Kathryn Grayson, Donna Reed, Lana Turner, and Esther Williams became major stars after capturing audience interest with their appearances in the Hardy films. The series was the most profitable (considering the low production cost) in Hollywood for many years.

The second Hardy film was *You're Only Young Once* (1937). Producer Lucien Hubbard had left the studio; and J.J. Cohn was assigned as executive producer on the series, which continued without an on-screen producer credit. His associate was writer Carey Wilson. The film contained the cast members that were to become famous in their Hardy family roles. As Judge Hardy, Lewis Stone replaced Lionel Barrymore, who was in England filming *A Yank at Oxford* (1938). Fay Holden took over for Spring Byington as Mrs. Hardy. Ann Rutherford replaced Margaret Marquis as Andy's girlfriend Polly. Mickey Rooney, Cecilia Parker, and Sara Haden reprised their roles. The characters of Joan and Bill were eliminated. The film repeated the success of the first.

Louis B. Mayer, MGM's Vice-President in Charge of Production (1924-1951), was particularly proud of the series and took a great personal interest in it. Years later, Ann Rutherford commented, "There was a certain wholesome quality about the 'Hardys,' and it came across to audiences."

In 1943 Metro-Goldwyn-Mayer received a Special Academy Award "for its achievement in representing the American way of life in the production of the 'Andy Hardy' series of films."

The last of the sixteen pictures, *Andy Hardy Comes Home* (1958), was made after twelve years of dormancy. The film finds Andy married and the father of two youngsters. The picture, an attempt to turn Andy into a young Judge Hardy, did not do well, although it contained several charming scenes from previous Hardy films. Today, the fourth title of the series, *Love Finds Andy Hardy* (1938), in which Judy Garland joined the cast as semi-regular Betsy Booth, is the best remembered of the Hardy pictures.

The Hardy family north wall plaque contained the inscription:

I, Mayor Fletcher Bowron, on behalf
of the citizens of this community,
do hereby proclaim the family of
Judge James K. Hardy, the first
family of Hollywood.

Signed this 15th day
of August 1941

[signatures:]		Fletcher Bowron
Lewis Stone	Mickey Rooney	
Fay Holden	Sara Haden	
Judy Garland	Ann Rutherford	

Los Angeles Mayor Fletcher Bowron presided over the ceremony. The cast members were also given honorary scrolls with wording similar to that of the plaque to commemorate the occasion. Each scroll was signed by the mayor; and, attached in the lower left corner, was the seal of the City of Los Angeles, from which hung a green, yellow, and red striped ribbon.

Rooney, Garland, and Rutherford fittingly arrived for the ceremony in Andy's jalopy. Also present to watch the festivities were various Los Angeles residents actually named Hardy. They sat in bleacher seats specially placed in the forecourt for the occasion. Photos of the event show the irrepressible Rooney happily shaking hands and hugging his Los Angeles "relatives."

In a telephone conversation with the authors, Ann Rutherford recalled that she and the other Hardy family members honored that evening "virtually considered it [the plaque] an Academy Award." She added that "there was little time to savor the event," due to long hours and a six-days-a-week working schedule common at that time. She also remembered that when the cast members arrived for the event the plaque was hidden from view by a small red curtain. Mickey Rooney performed the unveiling honors.

Lou Costello (left), Sid Grauman, and Bud Abbott.

Bud Abbott and Lou Costello Ceremony #61: December 8, 1941

They placed their prints in connection with the motion picture *Rio Rita* (Metro-Goldwyn-Mayer, 1942).

Bud Abbott and Lou Costello both hailed from New Jersey: Abbott, born William Abbott in Asbury Park on October 2, 1895/died: April 24, 1974; Costello, born Louis Francis Cristillo in Paterson on March 6, 1906/died: March 3, 1959.

By 1940 the film careers of Hollywood's three major comedy teams—Laurel and Hardy, the Marx Brothers, and the Ritz Brothers—seemed to be in simultaneous decline. The stage was set for a new pair of comics to take the nation by storm, and Abbott and Costello did just that. Their "Who's on First?" comedy routine is probably the best-known in the world, thanks to the duo's rapid delivery of its classic repartee.

Abbott was the fast-talking con-artist—the lean and snide straight man; and Costello was the roly-poly, bumbling, put-upon stooge who inevitably took the fall in the midst of lightning-fast verbal sparring. Initially they pursued various careers individually, and each found himself working in burlesque by 1930. One night the two were working on the same bill in Brooklyn. Costello's partner didn't show up for the performance; so he and Abbott went on together. They continued working as a team in burlesque for the next seven years with limited success and shifted to radio when New York City Mayor Fiorello LaGuardia closed down the "burlie" houses in 1937.

They achieved national popularity on Kate Smith's radio show in 1938 and were a hit in the Broadway revue *Streets of Paris* in 1939. Hollywood discovered them; and they were quickly signed by Universal, making their film debut in *One Night in the Tropics* (1940). The public was enthusiastic; and their next picture, *Buck Privates* (1941), a modest programmer

that was shot in twenty days, grossed several million dollars.

They sailed through the War years on top, but after 1945 their popularity began to slip. Many criticized them for using the same basic stale burlesque routines and not changing or adapting to the times. But when Universal decided to resurrect their horror film monsters (Frankenstein, Dracula, the Wolf Man, the Invisible Man, and the Mummy) and star Abbott and Costello in a series of films opposite them, the team surged to the top once again.

Their motion picture credits include *In the Navy* (1941), *Hold That Ghost* (1941), *Pardon My Sarong* (1942), *It Ain't Hay* (1943), *Lost in a Harem* (1944), *Bud Abbott and Lou Costello in Hollywood* (1945), *Abbott and Costello Meet Frankenstein* (1948), *Africa Screams* (1949), *Abbott and Costello in the Foreign Legion* (1950), and *Dance with Me Henry* (1956, final film as a team).

The team's square is tinted gray and contains the inscription "To Our Pal Sid." Also included are the month and day ("Dec. 8"), and the year ("1941"), which is written twice, Abbott's two footprints, two handprints, and his signature, plus his inscription "Hi Ya Neighbor," in addition to Costello's two footprints, two handprints, and his signature, plus his inscription "'I'm A Bad Boy.'"

The inscriptions are phrases closely associated with the two. Bud had a life-long problem remembering names. He avoided countless awkward situations by simply greeting everyone and anyone with "Hi ya, neighbor."

As a boy in the fifth grade, Lou was reprimanded by one of his teachers for some infringement of the rules and, as a punishment, was made to write "I am a bad boy" 150 times. He also had to say it aloud after completing each sentence. Costello never forgot the incident and incorporated the phrase "I'm a ba-a-a-d boy" into the team's performances in radio, film, nightclubs, and television.

On December 7, 1941, the day prior to the Abbott and Costello ceremony at the Chinese Theatre, Japanese carrier planes attacked the U.S. naval base at Pearl Harbor, Hawaii. On the date of their ceremony, the U.S. declared war on Japan and entered the second World War.

Comedian Jack Oakie was with Sid Grauman at the theatre that day and said to him, "Hey, Sid, aren't you glad you didn't name it Grauman's Japanese?"

Paddy Costello Humphreys, Lou's eldest daughter, shared her memories of her father on the day he and Bud placed their prints at the theatre in a letter to the authors:

"I must have asked him something like, 'Why are you so happy?' It's interesting what we choose to remember when we're young, but he looked at me with this unbelievable gleam in his eye and said, 'Today I did something really important, Paddy. I placed my hand and footprints in cement at Grauman's Chinese Theatre. What an honor that is.' All I remember thinking, as any child might, was how neat that daddy actually got to write his name in cement!'"

Edward Arnold
Ceremony #62: January 6, 1942

Born: Guenther Edward Schneider in New York City, on February 18, 1890. Died: April 26, 1956.

One of Hollywood's most accomplished and distinguished character actors, Edward Arnold spent nearly his entire life acting but did not achieve great fame until he was into his forties.

At twelve he developed an interest in acting and made a highly successful first appearance as Lorenzo in an amateur production of *The Merchant of Venice*. He immediately decided on an acting career and turned professional at fifteen, finding work with the Ben Greet Shakespearean Players and touring the U.S. for many months in 1906. Soon after, Arnold got work with Maxine Elliott's company and next spent three seasons as a juvenile in Ethel Barrymore's productions.

In 1915 a former associate invited him to join the Essanay company in Chicago. Arnold accepted, and his first documented film role was in "The White Alley" (1916, short). He returned to the stage in 1920 and for the next twelve years appeared in several Broadway shows (including *Easy Come, Easy Go* [1925] and *The Jazz Singer* [1927]), vaudeville, and finally the prestigious Theatre Guild for three seasons.

He finally returned to films in 1932 in *Okay America* (talkie debut) and remained in the movies for the rest of his life. He also worked heavily in radio and later in television.

His motion picture credits include *Diamond Jim* (1935), *Sutter's Gold* (1936), *Come and Get It!* (1936), *You Can't Take It with You* (1938), *Mr. Smith Goes to Washington* (1939), *Johnny Eager* (1942), *Eyes in the Night* (1942), *Mrs. Parkington* (1944), *Command Decision* (1948), and *Miami Exposé* (1956, final film).

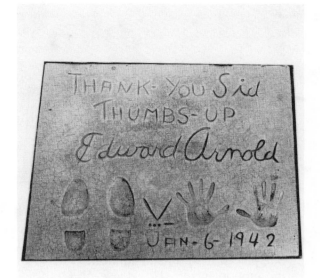

Arnold's square is tinted gray and contains the inscription "Thank You Sid—Thumbs Up." Also included are the date ("Jan-6-1942"), his two footprints, two handprints, and his signature, plus a drawing of the letter "V" on top of three dots and a dash, which is the Morse code for "V."

At that time Arnold was very active working in Hollywood on behalf of World War II-related efforts; and the "V" in his square stood for "V for Victory," a popular phrase during that time.

Edward Arnold.

Joan Fontaine
Ceremony #63: May 26, 1942

She placed her prints in connection with the motion picture *This above All* (20th Century-Fox, 1942).

Born: Joan de Beauvoir de Havilland in Tokyo, Japan, on October 22, 1917.

Joan Fontaine first achieved fame as shy, self-effacing, withdrawn, and sympathetic heroines and found later distinction playing worldly-wise, sophisticated, coolly authoritative women. Both Fontaine and her sister, Olivia de Havilland, pursued acting careers; and Joan made her first professional appearance in 1935 in the play *Kind Lady* in Los Angeles. Jesse L. Lasky noticed her and signed her to a long-term film contract, which he quickly sold to RKO.

Fontaine spent the next three years playing small parts in a few important pictures and leads in programmers. Discouraged and about to quit acting, Fontaine attended a dinner party in 1939 and found herself seated next to producer David O. Selznick, who immediately thought that she would be perfect for the lead in his upcoming production *Rebecca* (1940) and offered her a test for the role. She won the part. The film was a smash hit and made Fontaine a major star.

She parted company with Selznick in 1946 and free-lanced throughout the rest of her movie career. Fontaine punctuated her film appearances with stage work, beginning very successfully on Broadway in *Tea and Sympathy*, when she replaced Deborah Kerr in 1954. She has also made occasional television appearances and in the late 1980s hosted her own cable television celebrity talk show.

Her motion picture credits include *No More Ladies* (1935, debut), *A Damsel in Distress* (1937), **Suspicion* (1941), *The Constant Nymph* (1943), *Jane Eyre*

(1944), *The Affairs of Susan* (1945), *Letter from an Unknown Woman* (1948), *The Emperor Waltz* (1948), *Tender Is the Night* (1962), and *The Devil's Own* (1966).

   *Academy Award nomination: Best Actress.
   **Academy Award winner: Best Actress.

Fontaine's square is tinted gray and contains the inscription "To Sid Grauman—with good wishes and thanks," (the comma is Fontaine's), and the date ("May 26-42"). Also included are her two footprints (made with high heels), two handprints, and her signature.

Joan Fontaine and Sid Grauman.

Red Skelton and Junior
Ceremony #64: June 18, 1942

Skelton placed his prints, and the footprint of the radio character Junior, in connection with the motion picture *Ship Ahoy* (Metro-Goldwyn-Mayer, 1942), in which Skelton starred.

Red Skelton

Born: born Richard Bernard Skelton in Vincennes, Indiana, on July 18, 1913.

One of America's most beloved comedians, Red Skelton has always insisted on being called simply "a clown." First and foremost, Skelton is a brilliant and inspired pantomimist. But he also created characters on the radio, such as Clem Kadiddlehopper, Willie Lump-Lump, Junior, and Bolivar Shagnasty, with the use of only his voice, scoring a nationwide hit while remaining invisible to his audience.

Skelton left home at age ten to join a traveling medicine show. At seventeen he lied about his age in order to become a comedian in burlesque. Between 1935 and 1937 Skelton found considerable success

as a vaudeville comic and made his radio debut in 1937. His film debut, *Having Wonderful Time* (1938), was received tepidly; so he returned to stage and radio appearances until Mickey Rooney, impressed by Skelton, recommended that Metro-Goldwyn-Mayer chief Louis B. Mayer take a serious look at the comedian. A long-term contract with MGM resulted;

and *Whistling in the Dark* (1941), his fourth MGM film, made Red a major star.

"The Red Skelton Show" premiered on radio in 1941 and was a huge hit while Skelton continued very successfully in films throughout the 1940s. In 1951 Skelton began his weekly television show, which was extremely popular and ran for twenty years. In later years, Skelton has also achieved considerable prominence as a painter (most of his images are of clowns). He also writes children's books, designs coloring books, and composes music.

His motion picture credits include *Lady Be Good* (1941), *Whistling in Dixie* (1942), *Du Barry Was a Lady* (1943), *I Dood It* (1943), *Merton of the Movies* (1947), *A Southern Yankee* (1948), *Watch the Birdie* (1950), *Three Little Words* (1951), *The Clown* (1953), and *Those Magnificent Men in Their Flying Machines* (1965).

Junior

Junior, "the mean widdle kid," is one of the many memorable characters created by comedian Red Skelton, who is a skilled child impersonator. The many routines he developed in the 1920s and 1930s in which he acted the role of a little boy eventually culminated in the creation of Junior, a character he enacted on the stage before making him nationally famous on his radio broadcasts. As writer Arthur Frank Wertheim noted, "Skelton's enormous talent for pantomime was obviously lost on radio. Still, he was an exceptional voice imitator who made the character *sound* funny."

Audiences delighted in Junior's antics. The little boy was continually getting himself into some sort of mischief and being rude to his elders.

Junior was finally made visual for the first time to the mass audience in the film *The Fuller Brush Man* (1948). Skelton starred as the title character, and Junior was played by nine-year-old Jimmy Hunt. Starting in 1951, Skelton himself played Junior on his long-running television show and solved the visual problem of playing a little boy by appearing in giant-sized short pants.

The Skelton/Junior square is tinted gray and contains the inscription "Thanks Sid—'We Dood It.'" Also included are the date ("June 18th 42"), Skelton's two footprints, two handprints, and his signature.

On the day the square was made, Skelton recorded imprints honoring Junior. Included were his name ("Jr."), the date ("6-18-42"), Junior's right footprint,

Sid Grauman (left), Red Skelton placing Junior's ill-fated shoe print in the wet cement, and Skelton's wife Edna.

plus the drawing of an arrow pointing from Junior's name and date to the imprint of his right footprint.

The phrase "We dood it" was a variation of Junior's catch-phrase "I dood it," which he said on radio whenever he perpetrated some mischievous act. "The Red Skelton Show" was one of the most popular radio programs of its time, and Skelton's character of Junior was well-known to his listeners. The phrase "I dood it" had become part of the national slang. During World War II, American planes under the command of General James H. Doolittle raided Tokyo and other Japanese cities on April 18, 1942, two months prior to the Skelton/Junior ceremony; newspaper headlines across the nation read: "Doolittle Dood It!"

Unfortunately, Junior's imprints did not survive from the fresh wet cement through the drying process and into the hard block now on view in the forecourt.

Over the years there have been several incidents of squares having been tampered with, none more evident than in this instance.

On the day of his ceremony Skelton clowned for the crowd and helped to mix his own cement. He joked, "That's Hollywood for you. One day you're putting your footprints in it. The next day you're mixing it."

When the ceremony was finished, Skelton turned to his wife Edna and exclaimed, "We dood it!" Sid Grauman walked the couple to their car; and as Red was getting into the vehicle he said to Sid, "You know, there was one thing [that] happened we didn't count on. Just as I finished putting my footprints in the forecourt, Charlie Chaplin's got up and walked out!"

Sid Grauman (left), Red Skelton, and unidentified man.

Mrs. Miniver. *Released by Metro-Goldwyn-Mayer (1942).*

Mrs. Miniver and Greer Garson Ceremony #65: July 23, 1942

Garson placed her prints in connection with the motion picture *Mrs. Miniver* (Metro-Goldwyn-Mayer, 1942). The film's fictional heroine, Kay Miniver, received an honorary plaque and time capsule.

Mrs. Miniver (Metro-Goldwyn-Mayer, 1942)

Based on the 1940 best-selling novel by Jan Struther, *Mrs. Miniver* was one of the most popular and influential films of the early 1940s in that it played a significant role in swaying the sympathy of the American public toward the plight of the British people undergoing the terrors of the "blitz" as perpetrated by the Nazi air force during World War II.

Although the film is about war, it is not a story of soldiers in battle but rather a story of how the war impacts the daily lives of one family, centering on Kay Miniver (depicted by Greer Garson in a Best Actress Oscar-winning performance), a middle-class English woman who shows her true gallantry and courageousness while facing the horrors of warfare on the home front with her husband, played by Walter Pidgeon.

President Franklin D. Roosevelt had the film run in his private screening room before its premiere and was so impressed that he asked for the quickest possible release and urged that everyone see it. The picture premiered at New York City's Radio City Music Hall on June 4, 1942. Directed by William Wyler, it was seen by an unprecedented 1,500,000 people during its ten-week run there.

Critic Bosley Crowther wrote in the New York *Times*: "Certainly it is the finest film yet made about the present war, and a most exalting tribute to the British, who have taken it gallantly."

Mrs. Miniver won the Best Picture Oscar in 1943, plus four additional Academy Awards for Best Supporting Actress; Direction; Writing (Screenplay); and Cinematography (Black-and-White). It received six additional Oscar nominations.

In 1950 MGM produced a sequel, *The Miniver Story*.

In addition to the Mrs. Miniver time capsule housed underneath the square of Greer Garson, the character of Mrs. Miniver was honored with an east wall plaque indicating the position of the time cap-

sule. The plaque (with the initial "M" at the top for "Miniver") contains the inscription:

> Dedicated To The Truly Great
> Heroines Of This War...The
> Millions Of Mrs. Minivers In
> Every Democratic Nation...
> The Mothers, The Wives And
> The Sweethearts Of The Men
> Fighting For Freedom, Liberty
> And Justice, Not Alone For One
> People, But For All.

* * * *

Below the tablet with the signature of Greer Garson a print of the motion picture, "Mrs. Miniver," a copy of the manuscript and of the book have been placed so that future generations may have a pictorial record of the fighting spirit of the people on the home front in 1942

Sailors Dan Gleason of Tacoma, Washington, William Cobb of Houston, Texas, and Greer Garson with the Mrs. Miniver wall plaque.

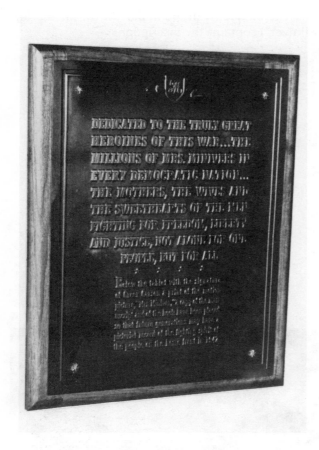

Greer Garson

Born: in County Down, in northern Ireland, on September 29, 1908.

When two of Metro-Goldwyn-Mayer's high-caliber actresses, Greta Garbo and Norma Shearer, retired in 1941 and 1942, respectively, a red-haired, green-eyed beauty named Greer Garson stepped in to fill the void and star in some of the studio's most prestigious films.

She made her London stage debut in 1934 and attracted widespread favorable notice in the play *Golden Arrow* (1935). MGM's chief Louis B. Mayer saw her in a performance of *Old Music* in 1938 and was so convinced he'd found an important new star that he immediately offered her a contract. Garson accepted and went to Hollywood, only to return to England when MGM shot her debut film, **Goodbye, Mr. Chips* (1939), in its London studios. Its success made Garson a major film star.

Back in Hollywood, she was soon cast as Elizabeth Bennet in *Pride and Prejudice* (1940). It was followed by **Blossoms in the Dust* (1941), the first of her eight films opposite actor Walter Pidgeon. They teamed together in ***Mrs. Miniver* (1942), which provided Garson with her best remembered role.

After the War, her popularity slipped a bit, and she made several mediocre films geared toward changing her image. Her MGM contract ended in 1954, and she next appeared in some television dramas and replaced Rosalind Russell on Broadway in *Auntie Mame* in 1958. Garson continued with occasional stage and television work into the 1970s.

Her motion picture credits include *Random Harvest* (1942), **Madame Curie* (1943), **Mrs. Parkington* (1944), **The Valley of Decision* (1945), *That Forsyte Woman* (1949), *The Law and the Lady* (1951), *Julius Caesar* (1953), *Strange Lady in Town* (1955), **Sunrise at Campobello* (1960), and *The Happiest Millionaire* (1967).

*Academy Award nomination: Best Actress.
**Academy Award winner: Best Actress.

Garson's square covers the Mrs. Miniver time capsule. It is tinted gray and contains Garson's inscription "To You Sid." Also included are the date ("July 23-1942"), her two footprints (made with high heels), two handprints, and her signature, plus the inscription "To Greer from Sid Grauman [signature]."

Today the "man" portion of Grauman's signature is covered by the foot of a poster display case. There is also a rectangle imprinted in the upper center of the square indicating the position of the time capsule beneath.

Greer Garson and Sid Grauman fill the Mrs. Miniver time capsule.

Henry Fonda, Rita Hayworth, Charles Laughton, Edward G. Robinson, and Charles Boyer
Ceremony #66: July 24, 1942

They placed their prints in connection with the motion picture *Tales of Manhattan* (20th Century-Fox, 1942).

Henry Fonda

Born: Henry Jaynes Fonda in Grand Island, Nebraska, on May 16, 1905. Died: August 12, 1982.

Henry Fonda personified the quintessential American Everyman, or at least the "Everyman" that most people wished existed—the uncommon common man with innate qualities of integrity, honesty, and basic human decency. He never considered acting until 1925 when Mrs. Dorothy Brando (mother of a then one-year-old Marlon) persuaded young Fonda to appear in a play at the Omaha Community Playhouse. In 1926 he scored a local hit in *Merton of the Movies*.

After eight years of varying success in several stock companies, Fonda finally got a big break on Broadway in *New Faces of 1934*, the first in the popular

revue series. He signed a film contract with producer Walter Wanger and made his film debut in *The Farmer Takes a Wife* (1935), reprising the role he originated on Broadway, and became an overnight movie star. In 1940 he was a memorable Tom Joad in **The Grapes of Wrath*.

Increasingly dissatisfied with most of the films he was handed, Fonda left Hollywood in 1947 to return to his first love, the theatre, and scored the biggest theatrical triumph of his career on Broadway in *Mister Roberts*, which ran for three years. He followed it with more stage roles and returned to Hollywood to make the film version of *Mister Roberts* in 1955.

For the rest of his life, Fonda continued working in film and theatre. His last stage triumph came in 1974 when he created the role of Clarence Darrow in the one-man play of the same name on Broadway.

His motion picture credits include *The Trail of the Lonesome Pine* (1936), *Jezebel* (1938), *Young Mr. Lincoln* (1939), *Drums Along the Mohawk* (1939), *The Lady Eve* (1941), *My Darling Clementine* (1946), *War and Peace* (1956), ****12 Angry Men* (1957, Fonda also produced), *Yours, Mine, and Ours* (1968), and ***On Golden Pond* (1981, final film).

In 1978 the American Film Institute presented him with its Life Achievement Award. In 1979 he was a recipient of the Kennedy Center Honors for lifetime achievement, and in 1981 he received an Honorary Academy Award "as a consummate actor, in recognition of his brilliant accomplishments and enduring contribution to the art of motion pictures."

 * *Academy Award nomination: Best Actor.*
 ** *Academy Award winner: Best Actor.*
 *** *Academy Award nomination: Best Picture.*

Fonda's square is tinted green and contains the inscription "To Sid—A Great Guy." Also included are the date ("July-24-42"), his two footprints, two handprints, and his signature.

Fonda, Rita Hayworth, Charles Laughton, Edward G. Robinson, and Charles Boyer were five of the most popular actors of their time. The stars of *Tales of Manhattan* (1942) set a forecourt record that stands to this day: Five stars, five individual squares imprinted on the same day.

Publicity for the picture boasted "the largest assembly of stars in Hollywood." Other prominent players in the film included Ginger Rogers, Paul Robeson, Ethel Waters, and Eddie "Rochester" Anderson. *Tales of Manhattan* had its world premiere at the Chinese Theatre on August 5. All proceeds from the premiere were donated to World War II charities.

Rita Hayworth

Born: Marguerita Carmen Cansino in New York City on October 17, 1918. Died: May 14, 1987.

Rita Hayworth, Hollywood's "Love Goddess," was the number-one female sex symbol of the 1940s. Her mother, showgirl Volga Haworth, came from a long line of English actors; and her father, Eduardo Cansino, was descended from an Andalusian dancing master and was a vaudeville headliner and head of "The Dancing Cansinos." Young Marguerita was taught to dance as soon as she could walk and eventually became her father's partner on stage.

She was noticed by Fox film executive Winfield Sheehan in 1935. He signed her to a contract, and she appeared in several films as Rita Cansino. In 1937 Columbia Pictures hired her, dubbed her Rita Hayworth, and had her undergo electrolysis treatments to broaden her forehead and accentuate her widow's peak. She also changed the natural brunette coloring of her hair to red.

Rita leaped to stardom as the temptress Doña Sol on a loan-out to 20th Century-Fox in the Technicolor *Blood and Sand* (1941). Columbia's chief, Harry Cohn, quickly realized Hayworth was his studio's greatest asset. She partnered in two films with Fred Astaire, who later said, "Rita danced with trained perfection and individuality." *Gilda* (1946) was the apex of Hayworth's career. In it she played one of the most memorably erotic *femmes fatales* of all time. Her legendary and steamy "Put the Blame on Mame" number still mesmerizes audiences to this day.

Hayworth's popularity began to slip in the early 1950s. But when she co-starred with Frank Sinatra in Columbia's *Pal Joey* (1957), Sinatra said, "Who else but Rita should get top billing? After all, in my mind, she always was and always will be Columbia Pictures!"

Her motion picture credits include "La Fiesta" (1926, short, debut), *...Only Angels Have Wings* (1939), *The Strawberry Blonde* (1941), *You'll Never Get Rich* (1941), *You Were Never Lovelier* (1942), *Cover Girl* (1944), *The Lady from Shanghai* (1948), *The Loves of Carmen* (1948), *Separate Tables* (1958), and *The Wrath of God* (1972, final film).

Hayworth's square is tinted green and contains the inscription "To Sid Grauman—Thank's [sic]." Also included are the date ("7-24-42"), her two footprints (made with high heels), two handprints, and her signature.

The year "42" in Hayworth's date has virtually disappeared as a result of wear and tear over the years.

Hayworth married five times. At the end of 1948 she became romantically involved with the man who would become her third husband, Prince Aly Khan. His father was the spiritual leader of fifteen million Asian and African Ismaili Muslims, and Aly was his heir. She had recently divorced Orson Welles and became the target of harsh criticism because the prince was a married man. Their romance and eventual marriage on the French Riviera the following May created world-wide controversy.

During this period Sid Grauman was asked to remove Rita's square from the Chinese Theatre forecourt. He refused.

Two years later the Khans separated. Hayworth, who had been away from Hollywood for three years, returned to the U.S. and resumed her film career at Columbia, starring in *Affair in Trinidad* (1952) and *Miss Sadie Thompson* (1953). The Khans divorced in 1953. Hayworth later commented on her unsuccessful marriages, saying of her husbands, "They fell in love with Gilda—and woke up with me."

Charles Boyer (left), Sid Grauman, Charles Laughton, Henry Fonda, Edward G. Robinson, and Rita Hayworth.

Sid Grauman (kneeling, left), Charles Boyer, Rita Hayworth, and Edward G. Robinson.

Sid Grauman (left), Charles Laughton, Edward G. Robinson, unidentified man, Charles Boyer, and cement artist Jean W. Klossner (kneeling).

Henry Fonda.

Sid Grauman and Charles Boyer.

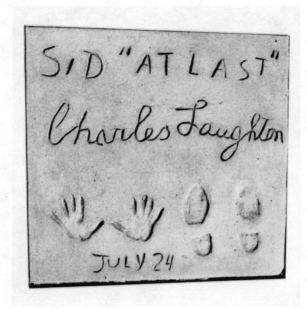

Charles Laughton

Born: in Scarborough, England, on July 1, 1899. Died: December 15, 1962.

Despite a physical appearance that would seem to have limited his box-office potential, Charles Laughton became a film star and one of the century's greatest actors. His heart was set on a theatre career from a very early age. In 1925 he appeared in amateur theatricals and gained admittance for study at the Royal Academy of Dramatic Arts.

In 1929 Laughton married actress Elsa Lanchester, with whom he had a professional co-starring relationship in various plays and films over the next several decades. His first personal smash was in the play *On the Spot* in 1930. *Payment Deferred*, a 1931 hit, was so successful that it went to Broadway and led to a contract with Paramount.

After appearing in *The Devil and the Deep, Payment Deferred*, and *The Sign of the Cross* (all 1932), Laughton returned to England to make the film that made him a major star, **The Private Life of Henry VIII* (1933). He then acted at London's Old Vic during the 1933-1934 season, returning to Hollywood to make a series of enormous film successes, including *Ruggles of Red Gap* (1935).

During the 1940s Laughton began to give readings from great literary works. His *Don Juan in Hell* and *John Brown's Body* met with astounding success in the 1950s, when he performed them extensively. In 1955

he stepped behind the camera and directed *The Night of the Hunter.*

His motion picture credits include "Bluebottles" (1928, short, debut), *Wolves* (1930, talkie debut), *The Barretts of Wimpole Street* (1934), *Les Miserables* (1935), **Mutiny on the Bounty* (1935), *The Hunchback of Notre Dame* (1939), *The Canterville Ghost* (1944), *Young Bess* (1953), *Hobson's Choice* (1954), **Witness for the Prosecution* (1957), and *Advise and Consent* (1962, final film).

　Academy Award nomination: Best Actor.
　**Academy Award winner: Best Actor.*

Laughton's square is tinted green and contains the inscription "Sid—'At Last.'" Also included are the date ("July 24"), his two footprints, two handprints, and his signature.

Edward G. Robinson

Born: Emanuel Goldenberg in Bucharest, Romania, on December 12, 1893. Died: January 26, 1973.

"Short, swarthy, and stocky," was Edward G. Robinson's own description of himself. However, his talents and authoritative presence made him one of the most successful leading actors in film history. Off-screen, he was a passionate art enthusiast and amassed what was considered the finest collection of Impressionist and Post-Impressionist art owned by a private individual.

In 1911 Robinson enrolled in the American Academy of Dramatic Arts and in 1913 made his professional debut with a stock company in Binghamton, New York, in a play entitled *Paid in Full*. From then through the 1920s he worked his way up in the

theatre. He brilliantly played a gangster role modeled on Al Capone on Broadway in *The Racket* (1927).

Robinson made his first film in 1923, but it was the role of the gangster Rico in *Little Caesar* (1931) that made him a major movie star. He transcended typecasting in such memorable films as *The Whole Town's Talking* (1935) and *Double Indemnity* (1944).

In the late 1940s a brush with the House Un-American Activities Committee almost ruined Robinson's career. Even though he was ultimately exonerated of any sympathy for or membership in the Communist party, Robinson found himself being offered mainly undistinguished films during the 1950s until producer/director Cecil B. DeMille cast him in his remake of *The Ten Commandments* (1956). He also worked in television and on stage, scoring a Broadway triumph in *Middle of the Night* (1956).

His motion picture credits include *The Bright Shawl* (1923, debut), *The Hole in the Wall* (1929, talkie debut), *Five Star Final* (1931), *Blackmail* (1939), *Dr. Ehrlich's Magic Bullet* (1940), *The Sea Wolf* (1941), *The Woman in the Window* (1944), *Our Vines Have Tender Grapes* (1945), *Key Largo* (1948), and *Soylent Green* (1973, final film).

In 1973 he was posthumously given an Honorary Academy Award as a man "who achieved greatness as a player, a patron of the arts and a dedicated citizen...in sum, a Renaissance man. From his friends in the industry he loves."

Robinson's square is tinted green and contains the inscription "To Sid—The Prince of Hollywood." Also included are the date ("7-24-42"), his two footprints, two handprints, and his signature.

Charles Boyer

Born: in Figeac, France, circa August 28, 1897 (sources vary on year). Died: August 26, 1978.

Possessed of exotic good looks, deeply probing dark eyes, and a sensuously rich, French-accented speaking voice, Charles Boyer became identified with the screen image of "The Great Lover." After his graduation from the Sorbonne with a degree in philosophy, Boyer enrolled in the Conservatoire National d'Art Dramatique. During the 1920s he worked his way up through several plays in France and was established as a leading matinee idol by the end of the decade.

Boyer had little interest in a film career; but when he made his first sound film, *La Barcarolle d'Amour* (1929), his mesmerizing voice made him a sensation in the new talkie medium. His first Hollywood so-

journ (1929-1932) met with little success, as his command of English was still limited. Returning to France, he studied English seriously and when asked back to Hollywood to film *Caravan* (1934) became a major star in American films. He did *not*, however, utter "Comm wiz me to zee Casbah" to Hedy Lamarr in *Algiers* (1938). That line was invented by a nightclub impersonator.

During World War II Boyer was heavily involved with activities on behalf of the French government and the Free French, becoming one of their chief representatives in the U.S. and giving generously of both his time and his money. By the 1950s Boyer was

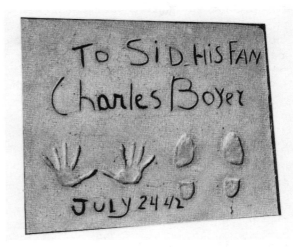

realistically reconciled to the necessity of moving into more character-type roles and away from romantic leads, and began refusing parts he thought too young for him.

His motion picture credits include *L'Homme du Large* (1920, debut), *Mayerling* (1936), *The Garden of Allah* (1936), *Conquest* (1937), *Love Affair* (1939), *All This, and Heaven Too* (1940), *Back Street* (1941), *Gaslight* (1944), *Fanny* (1961), and *A Matter of Time* (1976, final film).

In 1943 he received a Special Academy Award "for his progressive cultural achievement in establishing the French Research Foundation [a library] in Los Angeles as a source of reference for the Hollywood motion picture industry [regarding motion picture production pertaining to France]."

*Academy Award nomination: Best Actor.

Boyer's square is tinted green and contains the inscription "To Sid—His Fan." Also included are the date ("July 24 42"), his two footprints, two handprints, and his signature.

Bob Hope and Dorothy Lamour
Ceremony #67: February 5, 1943

They placed their prints in connection with the motion picture *They Got Me Covered* (RKO, 1943).

Bob Hope

Born: Leslie Townes Hope in Eltham, England, on May 29, 1903.

Comedian Bob Hope has combined careers in film, radio, and television. He has been called the "quintessential American comic" and during the past thirty years has graduated to the status of cultural icon.

Hope entered vaudeville in 1922 and finally scored a major career breakthrough in the Broadway hit *Roberta* in 1933. Between 1932 and 1937 he was on radio several times and made his film debut in a short for Educational, "Going Spanish" (1934). His feature film debut came in Paramount's *The Big Broadcast of 1938* (1938), in which he sang "Thanks for the Memory." The song became Hope's trademark and won the Academy Award.

His own show on radio for Pepsodent on NBC began in 1938. By 1943 his show had the highest rating in the nation, and Hope was famous as one of the quickest ad-libbers in the medium. He became a major film star with *The Cat and the Canary* (1939), and his series of "Road" pictures (beginning with *Road to Singapore* in 1940) with Bing Crosby and Dorothy Lamour catapulted him into one of the biggest box-office draws of the decade.

Hope's characteristic screen persona was a smart-alecky know-it-all who fired off high-speed wisecracks and instantly became a coward when faced with adversity.

In March 1941 Hope made his first broadcast from a U.S. military base and thus began his legendary and ceaseless performances for the armed forces. Hope's film career declined in the late 1950s and 1960s, but his perennial television specials have remained as popular as ever.

His motion picture credits include *The Ghost Breakers* (1940), *My Favorite Blonde* (1942), *The Princess and the Pirate* (1944), *Monsieur Beaucaire* (1946), *The Paleface* (1948), *Sorrowful Jones* (1949), *Fancy Pants* (1950), *The Seven Little Foys* (1955), *That Certain Feeling* (1956), and *Spies Like Us* (1985).

Over the years, Hope has been closely associated with the Academy of Motion Picture Arts and Sciences. He has appeared on twenty-seven annual

Dorothy Lamour, Bob Hope and cement artist Jean W. Klossner. Hope told the authors, "...from the way Lamour is holding me, it looks like I'm drunk!"

Academy Awards shows; and the organization has presented him with two Special Academy Awards, followed by two Honorary Academy Awards: in 1941, "in recognition of his unselfish services to the motion picture industry;" in 1945, "for his many services to the Academy, a Life Membership in the Academy of Motion Picture Arts and Sciences;" in 1953, "for his contribution to the laughter of the world, his service to the motion picture industry, and his devotion to the American premise;" in 1966, "for unique and distinguished service to our industry and

the Academy." He also received the Jean Hersholt Humanitarian Award from the Academy in 1960.

In 1985 he was a recipient of the Kennedy Center Honors for lifetime achievement.

Hope's square is tinted green and contains the inscription "To Sid—Honest <u>Me</u>?" Also included are the date ("2-5-43"), his two footprints, two handprints, and his signature, plus an imprint of the bottom of Hope's nose with the inscription "My Nose" and the drawing of an arrow pointing to the imprint.

Hope was the master of ceremonies at the 18th annual Academy Awards Presentation held at the Chinese Theatre on March 7, 1946 and made reference to his imprint ceremony in his opening monologue, saying, "I don't mind them having my nose print but they had a lot of nerve putting it between Lassie's paw and where Trigger sat down!" (It was a good joke, but Lassie is not represented in the forecourt, and Trigger still had more than three years to wait before his ceremony.)

Dorothy Lamour

Born: Mary Leta Dorothy Slaton in New Orleans, Louisiana, on December 10, 1914.

Exuding tremendous likability and sincerity in her performances, Dorothy Lamour made the sarong her world-famous trademark, becoming Hollywood's number one make-believe South Seas heroine during the 1930s and 1940s.

Aiming for a singing career since childhood, she went to Chicago after winning the title of Miss New Orleans in 1931. At that city's Morrison Hotel, she landed her first professional singing job and then went to New York where she quickly won a contract with NBC radio. When her show was moved by the network to Los Angeles she went with it. There she was spotted by a Paramount talent scout, and the studio signed her to a long-term contract.

The pictures *The Jungle Princess* (1936) and *The Hurricane* (1937) quickly established Lamour's image and made her an important star. The first "Road" picture came with *Road to Singapore* (1940); and Lamour, Bob Hope, and Bing Crosby followed it with six more in the popular series. The studio generally featured Lamour as a singer in comic films when she wasn't playing her romantic sarong-clad characters, and her roles in straight dramas were infrequent.

She left Paramount in 1947 but continued to film on a free-lance basis into the 1950s and 1960s. Beginning in 1967 Lamour enjoyed a huge success touring in a fourteen-month run of the musical play *Hello, Dolly!*. One of her colorful sarongs now resides in the permanent collection of the Smithsonian Institution in Washington, D.C.

Her motion picture credits include "The Stars Can't Be Wrong" (1936, short, debut), *Swing High, Swing Low* (1937), *Her Jungle Love* (1938), *Johnny Apollo* (1940), *Aloma of the South Seas* (1941), *The Fleet's In* (1942), *Masquerade in Mexico* (1945), *The Greatest Show on Earth* (1952), *Donovan's Reef* (1963), and *Creepshow 2* (1987).

Lamour's square is tinted green and contains the inscription "To Sid—Happy Days!" Also included are the date ("2-5-43"), her two footprints (made with high heels), two handprints, and her signature.

Betty Grable
Ceremony #68: February 15, 1943

She placed her prints in connection with the motion picture *Coney Island* (20th Century-Fox, 1943).

Born: Elizabeth Ruth Grable in St. Louis, Missouri, on December 18, 1916. Died: July 2, 1973.

Betty Grable was perceived as the epitome of the all-American golden girl. Throughout the 1940s Grable was a film favorite of audiences the world over, as well as the number one pin-up girl of American servicemen during World War II. Regarding her famous legs, she quipped, "Everyone has to have a gimmick, and I've been standing on mine for years."

Her mother groomed her for performing nearly from the cradle. Betty made her film debut in 1930 and, over the next decade, appeared in various films and was signed—and then summarily dropped—by several studios. She decided to try Broadway and scored a smash hit in the musical *Du Barry Was a Lady* in 1939. Betty soon thereafter signed a contract with 20th Century-Fox, which rushed her into *Down Argentine Way* (1940) to replace an ailing Alice Faye. The film made her a major musical comedy star.

Grable's pictures were often backstage musicals giving her ample opportunity to sing and dance, and were lavishly mounted in Technicolor, with a plot that revolved around a love triangle. Her popularity began to slip after 1951 when blonde newcomer Marilyn Monroe started to supplant her on the Fox lot.

Sergeant B. L. Duckett (left), Betty Grable, Gunner's Mate third class J. O. Buchanan, and Sergeant Albert Woas.

In the late 1950s Grable performed a nightclub act at Hollywood's Moulin Rouge and at Manhattan's Latin Quarter. On stage she opened the Las Vegas production of *Hello, Dolly!* in 1965, toured it for sixteen months, and finally took it to Broadway in 1967.

Her motion picture credits include *Let's Go Places* (1930, debut), *The Gay Divorcee* (1934), *Moon over Miami* (1941), *Springtime in the Rockies* (1942), *Pin Up Girl* (1944), *The Dolly Sisters* (1945), *Mother Wore Tights* (1947), *When My Baby Smiles at Me* (1948), *How To Marry a Millionaire* (1953), and *How To Be Very, Very Popular* (1955, final film).

Grable's square is tinted gray and contains the inscription "Thanks Sid." Also included are the date ("2-15-43"), her two handprints, her signature, an imprint of her right leg and the inscription "My leg" with a drawing of an arrow pointing to same, plus the initials "USA," "USN," and "USMC." The initials stand for United States Army, United States Navy, and United States Marine Corps.

At the time of her ceremony, Betty was the top box-office star in the world. She was flattered and said of her servicemen fans, "A lot of these kids don't have any women in their lives to fight for—I guess what you would call us girls is kind of their inspiration."

The day of her ceremony found Betty assisted by Marine Sergeant B.L. Duckett (USMC—recently returned from duty in the South Seas), Naval Gunner's Mate third class J.O. Buchanan (USN—he fought throughout the Pacific on the cruiser *Vincennes*), and Army Sergeant Albert Woas (USA—formerly of Hollywood). They had volunteered their services as a "thank you" for Grable's many personal appearances at various military establishments throughout the U.S. during World War II.

Newspaper accounts reported that it took an hour and a half to get Grable's leg imprint and that she wasn't wearing stockings. The initial plan was for Buchanan to grasp Grable around the shoulders, Duckett to hold her gently at the waist, and Woas to clasp her at the hips. Sounds easy, doesn't it? It wasn't.

The problem was that the skirt Betty wore on the occasion kept hiking up alarmingly. (Her mother had suggested her daughter wear a bathing suit; but Grable opted for a dress, saying it was more modest.) The servicemen were forced to try again. They regrouped, but Grable's skirt continued to prove a problem, and the proceedings stopped once again.

Trying new leverage, the service men lifted Grable into the air and almost dropped her! Betty let out a scream as her three assistants caught her in time and gently placed her anatomy into the concrete. She exclaimed, "Ooooh, it's cold!" and was a good sport while she waited for the concrete to set up.

At one point, someone's hand slipped, and Grable plopped into the cement. Cement artist Jean W. Klossner told her he could repair the damage done to the square with his trowel but wasn't able to do anything about her dress.

Each serviceman wrote the initials of his branch of the service in the square. When they finished, Betty shook hands with her helpers and hurried home to see if she could remove the wet cement from her skirt before it set. As she departed, Gunner's Mate Buchanan said, "I think that girl was a little nervous. She didn't seem exactly comfortable. I did my best to put her at her ease."

Grable left her ceremony the same way she had arrived—in a taxi driven by her fiancé, bandleader Harry James.

Unidentified workmen (left and right) hold a tray of cement as actresses Jeanne Crain (left) and Jo-Carrol Dennison help Monty Woolley imprint his beard. In 1953 cement artist Jean W. Klossner referred to this imprint as his "greatest masterpiece."

Monty Woolley
Ceremony #69: May 28, 1943

Born: Edgar Montillion Woolley in New York City on August 17, 1888. Died: May 6, 1963.

Monty Woolley sported an impeccably maintained Van Dyke beard with a flaring moustache. He became world renowned for creating shrewd, irascible, curmudgeonly, but highly literate characters and was affectionately dubbed "The Beard."

Woolley's father was wealthy and owned the Bristol Hotel in Manhattan and the fabled Grand Union Hotel in Saratoga Springs, New York. Both establishments were frequented by virtually every theatrical and social celebrity of the era. In 1907 Woolley entered Yale University and became involved with the Yale Dramatic Society. After post-graduate work at Harvard, he returned to Yale as an English professor and an assistant professor of drama.

He directed the hit Cole Porter shows *Fifty Million Frenchmen* (1929) and *Jubilee* (1935) and made his Broadway debut as an actor in Rodgers and Hart's *On Your Toes* (1936). He made his first film in 1937, *Live, Love and Learn*, which was followed by a string of supporting roles in films through 1939. That same year he starred on Broadway as the brilliant, diabolical, arrogant, waspish, but somehow lovable Sheridan Whiteside in *The Man Who Came to Dinner*. The part made Woolley and his beard a national institution, and he repeated the role in the 1941 Warner Bros. film version.

After his last movie, *Kismet* (1955), he retired to his home in Saratoga Springs.

His motion picture credits include *Nothing Sacred* (1937), *Three Comrades* (1938), *The Girl of the Golden West* (1938), *Midnight* (1939), **The Pied Piper* (1942), *Holy Matrimony* (1943), **Since You Went Away* (1944), *Night and Day* (1946), *The Bishop's Wife* (1947), and *As Young As You Feel* (1951).

   * *Academy Award nomination: Best Supporting Actor.*
   ** *Academy Award nomination: Best Actor.*

Woolley's square is tinted gray and contains the inscription "To Sid—Wish You Were Here." Also included are the date ("5-28-43"), his two handprints, and his signature, plus an imprint of Woolley's beard with the inscription "My Beard."

20th Century-Fox starlets Jeanne Crain and Jo-Carroll Dennison, in addition to studio makeup man Roland Ray, were on hand to assist "The Beard."

Instead of the wet cement square residing in its usual place on the forecourt floor, it was contained in a special wooden frame which four workmen were to raise up to Woolley so that he could make his imprints while standing.

A barber chair was brought in for the occasion. Woolley sat while the women combed and waxed his beard prior to its being plunged into the cement. He was worried. Earlier, cement artist Jean W. Klossner had told Woolley that the cement formula contained a small amount of mild acid that enabled Klossner to control the speed of the setting.

Unhappy at the prospect of losing and/or damaging his famed whiskers, Woolley turned in the chair and threateningly muttered to Jeanne Crain in a low voice, "If one hair of this beard gets stuck to the cement, so help me, I'll strangle you!"

The big moment arrived, and Woolley leaned over and plunked his chin into the cement while Crain and Dennison held him down. "Hurry!" he cried. "I feel it hardening on me!"

"The Beard" resurfaced, and the imprint showed that only the end of his whiskers had landed in the wet cement. Makeup man Ray stepped forward and oiled Woolley's whiskers with a rose scent via an atomizer, rubbing it in well so that the beard wouldn't stick to the concrete. Woolley tried again, and this time all went well.

Eager to get the ceremony over with, Woolley was displeased when a newsreel photographer said he needed a shot of him picking the wet cement from his beard.

That was fine with Woolley, until the photographer told him the shade of the wet concrete matched that of his whiskers and wouldn't be visible on black-and-white film. Woolley groaned.

Once again the makeup department came to the rescue. Ray dabbed dark brown grease paint on Woolley's beard to look like wet cement does in the movies.

"How much more of this agony?" Woolley asked.

"Only about fifteen minutes," a press agent reassured him.

"The Beard" glowered.

For the benefit of the news media, Woolley was redunked in the cement five more times. Each time the makeup man washed and reoiled his whiskers.

Finally Woolley grabbed his cane and muttered that the ceremony was the crowning indignity of a life crowded with indignities and headed off for a vacation in New York.

Gary Cooper
Ceremony #70: August 13, 1943

He placed his prints in connection with the motion picture *For Whom the Bell Tolls* (Paramount, 1943).

Born: Frank James Cooper in Helena, Montana, on May 7, 1901. Died: May 13, 1961.

Gary Cooper possibly more than any other film actor embodied the image of the ideal American— honest, courageous, and determined. He played all his parts with an uncanny sense of understatement and subtlety.

After attending college at Wesleyan in Montana and Grinnell in Iowa, he went to Hollywood, where he hoped to obtain work as a cartoonist, having displayed impressive talent in that field for many years. Failing in that ambition, he drifted into extra work in Western films. During 1925 and 1926, he appeared in possibly as many as fifty films as an extra or bit player. The first Cooper film appearance that can be documented was in *The Thundering Herd* (1925).

Cooper's first big break came when he was cast in a small but pivotal role in *The Winning of Barbara Worth* (1926). The public took instant notice of the handsome, lanky cowboy; and by 1928 he was a full-fledged star. His voice was first heard on screen in the final sequences of the part-talkie *The Shopworn Angel* (1928), which was followed by the successful all-talkie *The Virginian* (1929).

Cooper scored brilliantly as a symbol of the honest, decent common man who cannot be corrupted in Frank Capra's *Mr. Deeds Goes to Town* (1936). His career continued to flourish in such films as *Meet John Doe*, **Sergeant York* (both 1941), *The Pride of the Yankees* (1942), and **High Noon* (1952).

His motion picture credits include *Wings* (1927), *Morocco* (1930), *A Farewell to Arms* (1932), *The Lives of a Bengal Lancer* (1935), *Beau Geste* (1939) , *Ball of Fire* (1941), *For Whom the Bell Tolls* (1943), *Saratoga Trunk* (1945), *Friendly Persuasion* (1956), and *The Naked Edge* (1961, final film).

In 1961 he received an Honorary Academy Award "for his many memorable screen performances and the international recognition he, as an individual, has gained for the motion picture industry."

*Academy Award nomination: Best Actor.
**Academy Award winner: Best Actor.

Cooper's square is tinted green and contains the inscription "Sid, I got here at last." Also included are the date ("8-14 [sic] -43"), his two footprints, two handprints, and his signature.

Cooper actually placed his prints on Friday, August 13. Being superstitious, he wrote the date of the following day in the cement instead of the date of the actual ceremony.

Gary Cooper.

Private Joe Brain and Esther Williams.

Esther Williams and Private Joe Brain Ceremony #71: August 1, 1944

They placed their prints in connection with the motion picture *A Guy Named Joe* (Metro-Goldwyn-Mayer, 1943), in which Williams had a featured role.

Esther Williams

Born: Esther Jane Williams in Inglewood, California, circa August 8, 1921 (sources vary on year).

Beautiful Esther Williams, "Hollywood's Mermaid," dazzled audiences of the 1940s and 1950s in her spectacular Metro-Goldwyn-Mayer Technicolor water ballet extravaganzas. She learned to swim as she learned to walk. At fifteen, when Los Angeles Athletic Club coaches saw her in action, they said she could become a champion swimmer in four years. Esther proceeded to do so in two years.

Williams was slated to represent the U.S. in the 1940 Helsinki Olympics, but the onset of World War II caused the cancellation of that event. She turned professional and starred with swimmer/actor Johnny Weissmuller in Billy Rose's Aquacade at the San Francisco World's Fair/Golden Gate International Exposition in 1940. Approached by MGM to appear

Williams not only was the commentator for the newly formed synchronized swimming event during the summer Olympics but was also credited with its invention, as it had been inspired by the water ballets in her pictures (and the Aquacade). She said, "It was a wonderful feeling to sit there...and realize my movies had created a sport."

Her motion picture credits include *Andy Hardy's Double Life* (1943, debut), *Thrill of a Romance* (1945), *Easy To Wed* (1946), *Fiesta* (1947), *Take Me Out to the Ball Game* (1949), *Neptune's Daughter* (1949), *Dangerous When Wet* (1953), *Easy To Love* (1953), *Jupiter's Darling* (1955), and *The Magic Fountain* (1961, a.k.a. *La Fuente Magica*).

Private Joe Brain

Selected to assist Esther Williams with her ceremony, World War II paratrooper Joe Brain was a "typical serviceman" who declared, "Jumping out of a plane in a war zone wasn't half as exciting as doing the footprints!"

The Williams/Brain square is tinted green and contains the inscription "Thanks To Sid—in Honor of G.I. Joe." Also included are the date ("8-1-44"),

in films, she cited her lack of dramatic training and resisted their interest for nearly two years before finally signing a contract in October 1941. *Bathing Beauty* (1944) made Esther a major star.

In 1952 Williams portrayed another famous swimmer/actress, Annette Kellermann, in *Million Dollar Mermaid*; and the role became her favorite. Esther's lavish MGM musical days ended in 1955. In 1984

Williams' two footprints (made with high heels), two handprints, and her signature, Brain's two handprints, and his rank and signature ("PVC [sic] Joe Brain").

Brain also drew a caret (signifying an insert) beside his name in the direction of the "G.I. Joe" in Williams' inscription so that it would be evident he was to represent an average "G.I. Joe."

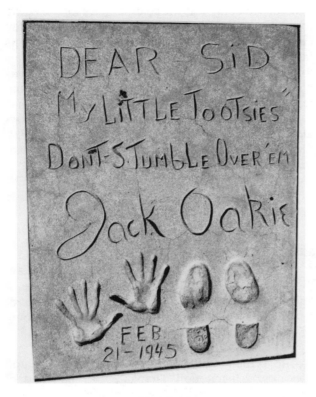

Jack Oakie
Ceremony #72: February 21, 1945

Born: Lewis Delaney Offield in Sedalia, Missouri, on November 12, 1903. Died: January 23, 1978.

During a career that spanned nearly four decades, Jack Oakie delighted moviegoers with his brashly comic portrayals, his trademark "triple take," and his ability to steal scenes from some of Hollywood's greatest stars.

After graduation from high school Oakie obtained a clerk job at a Wall Street brokerage firm, where he apparently spent more time clowning around than attending to business. When his employer staged an amateur show to benefit a charitable group, Oakie performed and proved himself to be a natural comic. He decided to go into show business.

His first professional job came as a hoofer in the Broadway production *Little Nellie Kelly* in 1922. Vaudeville jobs and spots in such New York shows as *Artists and Models* in 1923 and *Innocent Eyes* in 1924 followed. He reportedly appeared in a few films produced in New York during the 1920s, but his participation in these cannot be documented. He headed for California in 1927, where he made his Hollywood film debut in *Finders Keepers* (1928). By 1929 he was under contract to Paramount.

One of his best remembered roles came in Charlie Chaplin's *The Great Dictator* (1940). Oakie also had a popular radio show, "Jack Oakie's College" (1936-1938), and in later years branched out into television appearances.

His motion picture credits include *The Dummy* (1929, talkie debut), *Million Dollar Legs* (1932), *College Rhythm* (1934), *The Call of the Wild* (1935), *The Affairs of Annabel* (1938), *Tin Pan Alley* (1940), *Hello, Frisco, Hello* (1943), *When My Baby Smiles at Me* (1948), *The Rat Race* (1960), and *Lover Come Back* (1961, final film).

*Academy Award nomination: Best Supporting Actor.

Oakie's square is tinted green and contains the inscription "Dear Sid—'My Little Tootsies'—Don't Stumble Over 'em." Also included are the date ("Feb 21-1945"), his two footprints, two handprints, and his signature.

Oakie was a long-time friend of Sid Grauman's and said, "My friendship with Sid Grauman was warm and richly rewarding, but being with Sid was always a risky and unsettling experience. Late one afternoon during World War II, however, the rewards were well worth the gamble."

Oakie had driven out to his ranch in Northridge in the San Fernando Valley after a heavy day's shooting schedule—he was filming *That's the Spirit* (1945)—to do some much-needed work on his property.

Jack was busily working in his orchard, watering his newly planted orange trees, when his housekeeper informed him he was wanted on the telephone. Thinking it was the studio and not feeling up to any nighttime retakes, Oakie told her, "Tell the studio you can't find me."

"It's not the studio," the housekeeper replied. "The man said to tell you to hurry because the cement is getting hard!"

Reluctantly, Oakie went up to the house to answer the phone and find out just what the message meant. The man on the other end of the telephone was Sid Grauman.

Earlier Sid had promised to put Jack's imprints in the Chinese Theatre forecourt. Knowing Sid's well-deserved reputation for practical jokes, Oakie didn't believe him and refused to drive all the way back to Hollywood simply to give Sid a laugh. Jack recalled in his memoirs:

"'Oakie, it's not a joke!' Sid insisted over the phone. 'I'm serious! You've got to come in! And Jack, please hurry. The cement man has the mixture all ready to go and it's getting too dry to pour.'

"'No, Sid.' (I still didn't believe him.) 'I'm watering some baby orange trees and plan to stay out here at the ranch tonight.'

"'All right! I'll tell you what we'll do,' he said in his deep, soft, most gentle con man's voice. 'We'll make your cement green so that people will always know that you have a green thumb and love trees.'

"It was awfully hard to say no to Sid even though I was sure I was the foil in another of his practical jokes. So I took a chance and drove into Hollywood. When I got to the theatre, I could hardly believe it! Sid was truly preparing to put my hand prints and foot prints into a block in the walk of his Chinese Theatre! There was a goodly crowd roped off in the forecourt,

and the cement man was waiting for me, wetting down the green colored mortar that was already poured and smoothed in the block that was to be mine.

"'You see, folks!' Sid shouted to the crowd. 'I told you he'd be here!' He grabbed my arm and led me right down to the edge of that fast-drying cement that every motion picture actor hoped he could step into somewhere down the line in his career. I kneeled down reverently and was handed a special pencillike all-metal pointer.

"I wrote, 'Dear Sid—"My Little Tootsies!"—Don't Stumble Over 'em.'"

Sid Grauman (left) and Jack Oakie.

Jimmy Durante
Ceremony #73: October 31, 1945

Born: Born James Francis Durante on February 10, 1893, in New York City. Died: January 29, 1980.

Nicknamed "Schnozzola" early in his career, Jimmy Durante possessed not only a giant-sized nose, but also a talent and a kind heart to match. He paced the stage frenetically and slapped his sides in mock exasperation. His raspy voice joyously slaughtered the English language as he uttered lines that became national catchphrases, such as "Ev'rybuddy wants ta get into da act," "I got a million of 'em," and his touching and ubiquitous sign-off, "Goodnight, Mrs. Calabash, wherever you are."

Durante fell in love with music at age twelve and displayed great aptitude for playing the piano. Soon he was performing in saloons for clubs and benefits and became known as "Ragtime Jimmy." By the 1920s he had formed a band and invaded the Manhattan nightclub scene, ultimately founding his own establishment, the Club Durant. He played in vaudeville at the Palace Theatre and appeared in Ziegfeld's Broadway hit, *Show Girl*, in 1929.

He made his film debut in Paramount's *Roadhouse Nights* (1930), filmed at their Astoria, New York, studios and finally went to Hollywood when he signed a long-term contract with Metro-Goldwyn-Mayer. By 1935 Durante was back in New York to appear in Billy Rose's spectacular production of the Rodgers and Hart musical, *Jumbo*, at the enormous Hippodrome Theatre.

His career sagged somewhat in the late 1930s and 1940s; but thanks to the television medium, Durante was "re-discovered" by a whole new generation of fans in the 1950s.

His motion picture credits include *The Passionate Plumber* (1932), *Hollywood Party* (1934), *Little Miss Broadway* (1938), *Two Girls and a Sailor* (1944), *Music for Millions* (1944), *It Happened in Brooklyn* (1947), *The Great Rupert* (1950), *Billy Rose's Jumbo* (1962), *It's a Mad, Mad, Mad, Mad World* (1963), and *Those Daring Young Men in Their Jaunty Jalopies* (1969, final film, voice only).

Durante's square is tinted gray and contains the inscription "Sid—Dis is My Schnozzle—Wish I had A Million of em." Also included are the date ("Oct-31-45"), his left handprint, and his signature, plus an imprint of Durante's right profile. Both "z"s in "schnozzle" are written backwards.

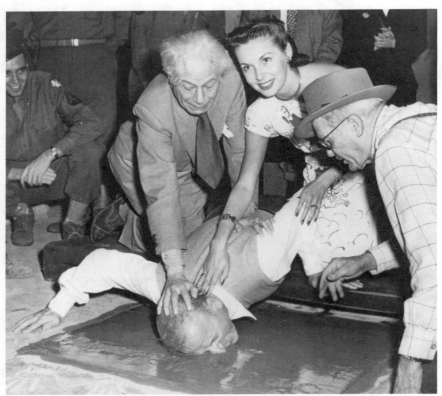

Sid Grauman (left), actress Joan Thorsen, cement artist Jean W. Klossner, and Jimmy Durante (with face in cement). Grauman said of Jimmy, "He hasn't got a heart of gold—he's got two."

Sid Grauman and Gene Tierney.

Sid Grauman and Gene Tierney Ceremony #74: January 24, 1946

Tierney placed her prints in connection with the motion picture *Leave Her to Heaven* (20th Century-Fox, 1945).

Sid Grauman

Grauman's square is tinted gray and contains the inscription "I Am Grateful To All Who Have Made These Hand And Foot Prints Possible." Also included are the date ("Jan. 24th 1946"), his two footprints, two handprints, and his signature, plus a drawing of Grauman's lips.

Just for fun, Sid appeared in a handful of films in which he played himself, including *Hollywood* (1923, debut), *Mad about Music* (1938, talkie debut), *Star Dust* (1940), and *Dancing in the Dark* (1949, final film). During the filming of *Star Dust* it was planned that he would place his prints, along with a drawn outline of his famous wavy hair, in the theatre fore-court in a scene with Linda Darnell at the film's conclusion. The block was to remain in the theatre's forecourt, but the on-screen event never materialized.

Bayard H. Brattstrom came to southern California from Chicago in 1942 when a teenager and lived on El Cerrito Avenue, just a few blocks west of the Chinese Theatre; he is presently a professor of zoology at California State University, Fullerton, and

recalled Sid Grauman and his behavior at the foot-print ceremonies in a letter to the authors:

"It was exciting for me to stand around the inner courtyard watching the workers fix up the area. Sid Grauman, who always had a smile or friendly pat on the back for me and a few other regulars, ran about making sure everything was going well. Sid was very quiet, even shy. Almost nobody knew who he was as he skittered about guests, workmen, and arriving star-watchers. He wanted everything to go right and the *star* to have the main lights. He also wanted his little moment in the photo, so would pop into one or two shots, get thanked, and then back off, often standing back in the courtyard with the few of us who knew how to get into the courtyard the side-way—or did Sid just allow us?"

Over the years, Grauman told several versions of how the idea for the footprints originated. The following dialogue exchange took place when Sid was interviewed during a commercial break on a "Lux Radio Theatre" broadcast of *A Star Is Born* in 1937 by the program's host, producer/director Cecil B. DeMille:

DeMille: "Sid, how did you happen to get that idea of the hand and footprints?"

Grauman: "The answer is 'pure accident.' I walked right in it. While we were building the theatre I accidentally happened to step in some concrete—and there it was. So I went to Mary Pickford. Immediately Mary put her foot into it."

DeMille: "And thereby became the first to sign your concrete autograph album."

Grauman: "Yes—along with Norma Talmadge and Douglas Fairbanks."

In 1949 Sid was interviewed by writer David Ragan for an article entitled "Sid's Sidewalk" that appeared in the Indianapolis *Star* magazine, one of the newspapers in the town of his birth. When asked about the footprints, Grauman said:

"I can't take much credit for that idea. We were just laying the concrete between the theatre and the sidewalk when all that wet cement set the wheels in my head to turning. I ran to the phone, called my friends, Doug Fairbanks, Mary Pickford, and Norma Talmadge, and asked them to hurry on down. Didn't give them any explanation. When they got there they thought I was crazy, but they were game. They were the first."

Sid recalled the following story during the filming of *Dancing in the Dark*, part of which was set at the Chinese Theatre and in which he made a brief appearance as himself:

"Shortly after my Chinese Theatre was completed in 1927, I arrived to supervise [the] final details. I was walking across the forecourt when someone began cursing and yelling unprintable names. I stopped and turned, [and] found the irate workman was addressing me. He didn't know who I was and cared less, but he definitely meant me.

"It seemed the pavement wasn't quite dry, my footprints were visible from the curb to the entrance, and he proceeded to harangue me to this effect: 'Look, you so-and-so, I was all finished, and now I'll have to work hours smoothing this out.' I looked again at the damage I'd done, and that's when the idea hit me.

"Disregarding the curses, I made another set of footprints running back to my car, got into it, broke a few speed laws driving out to the old United Artists studio where I rushed in and breathlessly told Doug

Fairbanks not to ask questions, but to come with me at once. He thought I'd gone crazy, but humored me when I asked where Mary was.

"We picked Mary Pickford up in her dressing room, then stopped by Norma Talmadge's apartment and forced her to come along, and then drove back to the theatre full blast, because I didn't know how fast cement took to dry.

"Those first footprints of Mary and Doug and Norma were imprinted in the curbstone, but the cement was nearly dry, and they were too faint, though they can still be seen there. So a few months later, I had the first formal imprint ceremony, with Mary and Doug and Norma occupying the square in the center close to the theatre entrance....

"So, having to pay for a re-paving job back in 1927 proved an inexpensive prelude to a million dollars worth of world-wide publicity for my theatre and for Hollywood stars."

Grauman died on March 5, 1950. The following day, Sid's obituary in the Los Angeles *Examiner* ended with:

"And anyone around Hollywood who wants to ring a few sentimental changes on that poem phrase, 'footprints on the sands of time,' can argue that no man left them so literally.

"The forecourt of Grauman's Chinese is dotted with them—records of the film greats in enduring concrete.

"They're not Sid's exactly, but nobody is going to forget they were his idea."

Gene Tierney

Born: Gene Eliza Tierney in Brooklyn, New York, on November 20, 1920. Died: November 6, 1991.

Beautiful Gene Tierney, a New York debutante turned actress, possessed chiseled features, high cheek bones, and feline green eyes. She made an impressive success in the hit play *The Male Animal* in 1940 and was highly praised by the critics. Soon after, she was under contract to 20th Century-Fox, where she became one of the studio's most popular stars. In her first film, *The Return of Frank James* (1940), Tierney was rather unsure and stiff in a relatively uninteresting role. She quickly improved her technique and finally hit her stride in Ernst Lubitsch's *Heaven Can Wait* (1943), which was followed by her best remembered role, *Laura* (1944).

Tierney continued filming until 1955; but while her career flourished, her private live was plagued by difficulties—her divorce from fashion designer Oleg Cassini; her parents' disapproval of her career and a bitter financial battle with her father, who mishandled her income; the birth of a retarded daughter due to Tierney's contracting German measles early in pregnancy; and her own mental illness. Tierney committed—and recommitted—herself to mental institutions over a period of several years, and her eventual recovery was a painful process. Finally emerging largely cured, in 1960 she married a Texas oil man,

and took up residence in Houston.

Her motion picture credits include *Tobacco Road* (1941), *The Shanghai Gesture* (1941), *A Bell for Adano* (1945), **Leave Her to Heaven* (1945), *Dragonwyck* (1946), *The Razor's Edge* (1946), *The Ghost and Mrs. Muir* (1947), *On the Riviera* (1951), *The Left Hand of God* (1955), and *The Pleasure Seekers* (1965, final film).

*Academy Award nomination: Best Actress.

Tierney's square is tinted green and contains the inscription "To Sid—Sincere Thanks." Also included are the date ("Jan-24-46"), her two footprints (made with high heels), two handprints, and her signature.

Sid Grauman (left), Irene Dunne, and Rex Harrison.

Irene Dunne and Rex Harrison
Ceremony #75: July 8, 1946

They placed their prints in connection with the motion picture *Anna and the King of Siam* (20th Century-Fox, 1946).

Irene Dunne

Born: Irene Marie Dunn in Louisville, Kentucky, circa December 20, 1898 (sources vary on year). Died: September 4, 1990.

Irene Dunne was a versatile actress who excelled equally in straight dramas, musicals, screwball comedies, and melodramatic tear-jerkers. Her mother decided that young Irene had a singing voice worth training formally. After several years of study, Irene was awarded a diploma from the Chicago Musical College in 1919, and in 1920 she auditioned in New York City for the Metropolitan Opera. This attempt failed; and realizing she didn't have the equipment for grand opera, Irene decided that light opera and

musical comedy would be the proper alternative route. She made a successful stage debut in the Chicago touring company of the musical *Irene* and first played on Broadway in *The Clinging Vine* (1922).

Her big break came when Florenz Ziegfeld cast her in the Chicago road company production of *Show Boat* in 1929. Dunne scored a triumph, which led to a movie contract with RKO. Her second film, **Cimarron* (1931), made her a star; and roles in *Back Street* (1932) and *Magnificent Obsession* (1935) were other tremendous successes in her early screen career. She was finally allowed to display her singing talents on film in *Sweet Adeline* (1934), *Roberta* (1935), and *Show Boat* (1936).

The madcap comedy **Theodora Goes Wild* (1936) was a major career turnabout for Dunne, who thereafter was considered one of the most expert of romantic comediennes. In the 1940s Dunne continued as a major star and retired from filmmaking in 1952.

Her motion picture credits include *Leathernecking* (1930, debut), **The Awful Truth* (1937), **Love Affair*

(1939), *My Favorite Wife* (1940), *Penny Serenade* (1941), *A Guy Named Joe* (1943), *The White Cliffs of Dover* (1944), *Life with Father* (1947), **I Remember Mama* (1948), and *It Grows on Trees* (1952, final film).

In 1985 she was a recipient of the Kennedy Center Honors for lifetime achievement.

*Academy Award nomination: Best Actress.

Dunne's square is tinted green and contains the inscription "To Sid—My Best Always." Also included are the date ("July 8th-1946"), her two footprints (made with high heels), two handprints, and her signature.

In a letter to the authors, Dunne recalled her ceremony by saying, "It was at a time when I was wearing especially high heels. The prints look like they belong to a dwarf!"

Rex Harrison

Born: Reginald Carey Harrison in Huyton, England, on March 5, 1908. Died: June 2, 1990.

Rex Harrison epitomized the elegant, articulate, and witty Englishman. He could be arrogant, egotistical, and waspish but also charming, ingratiating, and devilishly romantic.

At sixteen he was accepted into the Liverpool Repertory Theatre Company. Harrison established himself in London and made his West End debut in *Getting George Married* (1930). He also made his film debut that same year. The New York theatre-going public took favorable notice of him when he appeared in *Sweet Aloes* in 1936; and soon after, British pro-

ducer Alexander Korda offered Harrison a film contract. At that point he began a life-long career pattern of constantly alternating between film and live theatre. So strong was his desire to remain in London that he turned down an offer from Metro-Goldwyn-Mayer of a seven-year contract in 1938. Harrison finally accepted the inevitability of his going to Hollywood and signed a seven-year contract with 20th Century-Fox in 1945.

In 1956 Harrison starred as Professor Henry Higgins in the smash hit Lerner and Loewe musical, *My Fair Lady*, which he played on Broadway for almost two years and then another year in London. He recreated his role in the film version of ***My Fair Lady* (1964), which repeated the success of the play. Working steadily, Harrison continued in many more films and stage roles, also adding television projects to his sphere of performing. He was knighted by Queen Elizabeth II in 1989.

His motion picture credits include *The Great Game* (1930, debut), *Blithe Spirit* (1945), *The Ghost and Mrs. Muir* (1947), *Unfaithfully Yours* (1948), *The Four Poster* (1952), *The Reluctant Debutante* (1958), **Cleopatra* (1963), *The Agony and the Ecstasy* (1965), *Doctor Dolittle* (1967), and *A Time To Die* (1983, final film).

*Academy Award nomination: Best Actor.
**Academy Award winner: Best Actor.

Harrison's square is tinted green and contains the inscription "To Sid Grauman—Sincere Thanks." Also included are the date ("July 8-1946"), his two footprints, two handprints, and his signature.

Margaret O'Brien
Ceremony #76: August 15, 1946

Born: Angela Maxine O'Brien in Los Angeles, California, circa January 15, 1937 (sources vary on year).

Little Margaret O'Brien was a gifted dramatic actress and became the most popular child star of the 1940s. For three generations before her, O'Brien's ancestors had been stage and circus performers. At age three the child expressed a serious desire to pursue acting and posed for magazine covers for photographer Paul Hesse.

Her film debut came with a one-minute shot in Metro-Goldwyn-Mayer's *Babes on Broadway* (1941). Producer Dore Schary, after much deliberation, finally cast her in *Journey for Margaret* (1942), as a neurotic little girl, orphaned during the London blitz. Overnight O'Brien was heralded as a "sensation" and a "child marvel," and MGM signed her to a long-term contract. Angela Maxine also took the name of the film's heroine.

O'Brien remained a major star throughout the 1940s. Her best remembered film is Vincente Minnelli's *Meet Me in St. Louis* (1944). Additional movie successes include *The Canterville Ghost* (1944), *Our Vines Have Tender Grapes* (1945), and *Little Women* (1949), in which she played her favorite role, Beth March.

Although Margaret's popularity faded as she entered her teens, she continued working in films sporadically and did a large amount of stage and television work throughout the 1950s. She continues to take occasional acting assignments.

Her motion picture credits include *Madame Curie* (1943), *Jane Eyre* (1944), *Lost Angel* (1944), *Bad Bascomb* (1946), *The Unfinished Dance* (1947), *Big City* (1948), *The Secret Garden* (1949), *Glory* (1956), *Heller in Pink Tights* (1960), and *Annabelle Lee* (1972).

In 1945, she was presented with a Special Academy Award "for [being the] outstanding child actress of 1944."

Margaret's square is tinted green and contains the inscription "Love To Mr. Grauman From Margaret O'Brien [signature]." Also included are the date ("Aug. 15-1946"), her two footprints (made with bare feet), two handprints, and her signature.

Margaret was accompanied by her mother on the occasion of her ceremony. She tells the following story in her 1947 memoirs (written at age ten):

"Mr. Grauman let me pick out where I would like to sign....I thought I could do it with my shoes on but instead I had to go barefooted. [Columnist Louella O.

Unidentified man and Margaret O'Brien.

Parsons reported O'Brien herself wanted to go barefoot because she didn't want to ruin her shoes.] There were lots of people there and I got embarrassed because they were watching and I got cement all over. Then I put my hand prints in the cement and signed my name underneath. Mr. Grauman said that they will stay there for ever and ever and anybody who has his name there can go to the movies free. That's nice. Jimmy Durante had his face in the cement—I wonder if he really had to put it in the wet cement. Then they took some pictures and Mama and I came home."

In a letter to the authors, O'Brien shared some additional thoughts about her ceremony:

"As you know, I was a very little girl at the time (around eight-years-old) so I do not remember every moment of that ceremony....Most of all I had fun putting my bare feet in the wet cement even though my mother wasn't too pleased with having the job of cleaning it off afterwards. I think I appreciate the ceremony more now as years have gone by than I did at the time."

Humphrey Bogart
Ceremony #77: August 21, 1946

He placed his prints in connection with the motion picture *The Big Sleep* (Warner Bros., 1946).

Born: Humphrey DeForest Bogart in New York City, circa December 25, 1899 (sources vary on month, date, and year). Died: January 14, 1957.

Humphrey Bogart's screen image of iron-willed toughness, cynicism, brutal honesty, bluntness, and sometime arrogance was tempered with a brooding inner pain and emotionalism which his characters tried to suppress. His first public exposure came as an infant when his mother, an illustrator, painted his portrait which was used on labels and advertisements by a baby food company.

While Bogart was growing up, his next-door neighbor was theatre producer William A. Brady, whom he approached for a job after serving in the Navy during World War I. Bogart started as an office boy and worked his way up to road company stage manager. In 1920 he made his stage debut in the road company production of *The "Ruined" Lady*. He entered films in 1930 and between then and 1935 shuttled back and forth from Hollywood to Broadway.

Bogart's big breakthrough came when he won the role of gangster Duke Mantee in the Broadway play *The Petrified Forest* in 1935. He was a hit and recreated the role in the 1936 film version, which resulted in a long-term contract with Warner Bros. *High Sierra* (1941) made Bogart a full-fledged star, and *Casablanca* (1942) provided him with his best remembered role.

Bogart fell in love with his *To Have and Have Not* (1944) co-star, Lauren Bacall, who became his wife. They paired in three additional films. A lover of sailing, Bogart named his production company Santana after his yacht.

His motion picture credits include "Broadway's Like That" (1930, short, debut), *Angels with Dirty Faces* (1938), *The Roaring Twenties* (1939), *The Maltese Falcon* (1941), *The Big Sleep* (1946), *The Treasure of the Sierra Madre* (1948), *Key Largo* (1948), **The African Queen* (1951), *The Caine Mutiny* (1954), and *The Harder They Fall* (1956, final film).

*Academy Award nomination: Best Actor.
**Academy Award winner: Best Actor.

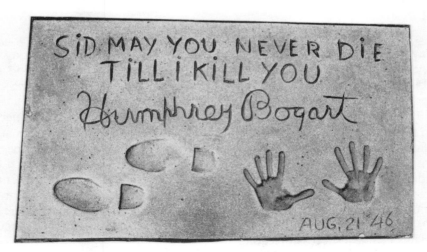

Humphrey Bogart, Sid Grauman (obscured), and actress Lauren Bacall (Mrs. Humphrey Bogart).

Bogart's square is tinted red and contains the inscription "Sid—May You Never Die Till I Kill You." Also included are the date ("Aug. 21 46"), his two footprints, two handprints, and his signature.

The inscription kidded Bogart's tough-guy image as a screen gangster. Earlier in his career he had been known as the screen's "No. 1 Bad Boy." (According to film historian Clifford McCarty, the Warner Bros. publicity department claimed "that a man born on Christmas Day couldn't really be as villainous as he appeared on the screen.") Warner Bros., impressed by the feminine reaction to Bogart's performance in *Dark Victory* (1939), helped him break out of that early stereotype; and he became a successful leading man with considerable romantic appeal.

Bogart, shooting *Dead Reckoning* (1947), worked until the late afternoon on the day of his ceremony. He paused to put on his "lucky" shoes—those he wore in *Casablanca* and *The Big Sleep*—before rushing over to the theatre.

In April 1992 *Casablanca* celebrated its fiftieth anniversary, and the Chinese Theatre was chosen as the Los Angeles site to screen the film. Forty-eight years before, on March 2, 1944, *Casablanca* had won the Best Picture, Direction, and Writing (Screenplay) Oscars at the 16th annual Academy Awards Presentation held at the Chinese Theatre. It was the first time the Oscar ceremony took place there.

Louella O. Parsons
Ceremony #78: September 30, 1946

Born: Louella Oettinger in Freeport, Illinois, on August 6, 1881. Died: December 9, 1972.

"'The first to know' are the most beautiful words in the dictionary to me," wrote gossip columnist Louella Parsons in 1961. Although rival columnist Hedda Hopper, beginning in 1938, gave her a good run for the money, Louella prevailed as the absolute queen of the Hollywood columnists throughout her fifty-one years as a journalist writing on the subject of motion pictures. For several decades she was the most powerful and influential woman in Hollywood.

A budding reporter by sixteen, she was writing social notes for the Dixon (Illinois) *Star*. Louella was a scenario writer for a brief time at the Essanay studios in Chicago around 1912. It was there that she first met and befriended motion picture people and hit on the idea that the public might want to read stories about their daily work and lives. Thus inspired, Louella began writing columns about the film world at the Chicago *Record-Herald* in 1914. Next she tackled New York City and had a job for several years with the *Morning Telegraph*.

Her columns attracted the attention of newspaper tycoon William Randolph Hearst, who gave her a contract to write for his New York *American* in 1922, thereby beginning one of the most remarkable alliances in newspaper history. Parsons remained with the Hearst organization until her retirement in 1965. She always spoke with praise and reverence for "The Chief;" and Hearst said that although Parsons was not his best writer, she was his best reporter.

Hearst established Hollywood as Parsons' home base in 1926, at which point she began to write reportedly the first syndicated movie column to originate from the film capital. During the height of her influence, her column appeared daily in some 1,200 newspapers throughout the globe. Parsons also had her own successful radio show, "Hollywood Hotel," (1934-1938). Health problems forced her to retire in 1965.

She appeared in a handful of films (playing herself), including *Hollywood Hotel* (1938, debut), *Without Reservations* (1946), and *Starlift* (1951, final film).

Parsons' square is tinted green and contains the inscription "To Sid Grauman—That's All Today—See You Tomorrow." Also included are the date ("Sept. 30th-1946"), her two footprints (made with high heels), two handprints, and her signature.

The inscription is the phrase regularly used by Parsons to end her newspaper column, "That's all today. See you tomorrow!" It appeared for the first time on May 8, 1928, and was faithfully used until her last column at the end of 1965. Parsons' final byline appeared on November 30; her assistant of thirty years, Dorothy Manners, took over the column beginning December 1.

Louella was a long-time friend of Sid Grauman, whom she referred to as "Hollywood's own Baron Munchausen." In one of her columns shortly before Sid's death in 1950, Parsons reminisced about his love of practical jokes and shared the following story with her readers:

"There are hundreds of stories about Grauman's jokes, but one that I happen to know very well, since it concerns my husband, Dr. Harry Martin, is the time Sid was supposed to be in New York.

"Faking a long distance call from the East, he asked the doctor to go to his suite in the Los Angeles Ambassador Hotel and get his studs and tuxedo and send them to him in New York. It was during the stock market crash, and Sid lost considerable money and was very depressed.

"Dr. Martin had to go through a lot of red tape to get into the hotel room. When he finally walked in, there was Sid lying apparently dead on the floor—ticker tape all over him and what looked like blood (but was really ketchup) all over his face.

"The bellboy ran screaming from the room, and the manager almost fainted. Finally, the 'dead' man got up, yawned, and greeted everyone!"

Louella was both surprised and touched when Sid asked her to place her imprints in the Chinese Theatre's forecourt, calling it "the highest honor" he ever paid her. Grauman told the crowd of onlookers that had assembled for the occasion: "We are very proud of Miss Parsons in Hollywood. She is the first among many Hollywood columnists."

Sid Grauman and Louella O. Parsons. In 1953 she wrote, "I hope I don't sound boastful when I say that I am the only newspaper reporter to be represented in this galaxy of star celebrities."

Ray Milland
Ceremony #79: April 17, 1947

Born: Reginald Truscott-Jones in Neath, Wales, circa January 3, 1905 (sources vary on year). Died: March 10, 1986.

Ray Milland was considered one of Hollywood's most important and capable leading men, although his rich talent as a dramatic actor was used to complete advantage in only a handful of the more than 100 films he made.

After two years at King's College, University of Wales, Milland left school and joined the elite Household Cavalry of the King's Royal Guards, where he served between 1925 and 1928. He befriended actress Estelle Brody, who suggested he try out for a film part at the Wardour studios in 1929. Milland went to the studio and was cast in a series of small roles in four films.

He was offered a short-term contract by Metro-Goldwyn-Mayer studios and went to Hollywood in 1930. Dissatisfied with the film assignments he was offered, he went back to England, with similarly disappointing results. He went back to Hollywood and back to England and again back to Hollywood for a third and last try in 1933. His being cast in *Bolero* (1934) finally led to a seven-year contract at Paramount.

The Jungle Princess (1936) caused a big jump in his popularity, and *Easy Living* (1937) proved he could deftly handle comedy assignments well. In 1945 Milland reached the pinnacle of his career as the tragic alcoholic in Billy Wilder's **The Lost Weekend*. He continued in films into the 1980s and also performed on stage and in television.

His motion picture credits include *The Flying Scotsman* (1929 debut), *Her Jungle Love* (1938), *Beau Geste* (1939), *The Major and the Minor* (1942), *The Uninvited* (1944), *Kitty* (1946), *The Big Clock* (1948), *Dial M for Murder* (1954), *Love Story* (1970), and *The Sea Serpent* (1985, final film).

*Academy Award winner: Best Actor.

Milland's square is tinted gray and contains the inscription "Thanks Sid For The Honour." Also included are the date ("4-17-46."), his two footprints, two handprints, and his signature.

Ray Milland.

Lauritz Melchior
Ceremony #80: November 17, 1947

He placed his prints in connection with
the motion picture *This Time for Keep*s
(Metro-Goldwyn-Mayer, 1947).

*Born: in Copenhagen, Denmark, on March 20, 1890.
Died: March 18, 1973.*

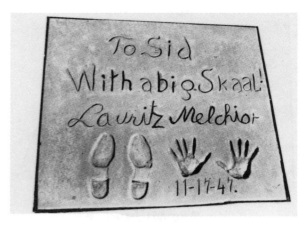

Still considered by many as the greatest helden-
tenor (heroic tenor) in opera history, Lauritz Melchior
sang over 1,000 full-length Wagnerian performances—more than three times the total of any other
singer. He was drawn to a musical career as a boy
and first sang in a church choir. Later Melchior was
admitted to the Danish School of the Royal Opera.

In early adulthood he performed as a baritone until
a colleague convinced him that he was in reality "a
tenor with the lid on." At that, he spent about two
years developing a tenor voice,
studying the rigorous Wagnerian
ritual in Bayreuth and receiving
tutoring directly from Richard
Wagner's widow and son, Cos-
ima and Siegfried.

Melchior's New York debut at
the Metropolitan Opera came in
February 1926, and he remained
there continuously until 1950.
While appearing regularly in
opera, he simultaneously pursued sideline careers in motion
pictures, radio, television, recording, and the concert stage.

Metro-Goldwyn-Mayer pro-
ducer Joe Pasternak heard
Melchior on the radio, thought
he had potential as a film personality, and signed him to a contract with the studio, where
Melchior made his first film,
Thrill of a Romance (1945). He
typically played jovial, robust,
and lovable opera-singing characters in a handful of musical
comedy pictures.

His motion picture credits include *Two Sisters from Boston*
(1946), *Luxury Liner* (1948), and
The Stars Are Singing (1953, final
film).

Melchior's square is tinted
green and contains the inscrip-

tion "To Sid—With a big Skaal!" "Skaal!" is Danish
for "Here's To You!" Also included are the date
("11-17-47."), his two footprints, two handprints, and
his signature.

*Unidentified man (left), Lauritz Melchior, and cement artist Jean W. Klossner.
A 1952 studio biography claimed Melchior's "footprints are the largest to ever
grace Grauman's Chinese Theatre in Hollywood (size 13-½)."*

James Stewart
Ceremony #81: February 13, 1948

He placed his prints in connection with the motion picture *Call Northside 777* (20th Century-Fox, 1948).

Born: James Maitland Stewart in Indiana, Pennsylvania, on May 20, 1908.

As a tall, rather gawky youth, a fresh-faced idealist with a slow, hesitant drawl—sometimes bordering on a stammer—Jimmy Stewart first endeared himself to American audiences in the late 1930s and has enjoyed a career as a great star over the decades. He was graduated from Princeton University in 1932 with a degree in architecture. Classmate Joshua Logan persuaded him to join his University Players at West Falmouth, Massachusetts, and Stewart soon began to take acting seriously. He made his Broadway debut in a small role in *Carrie Nation* (1932), and his first important role came in the play *Yellow Jack* (1934).

Metro-Goldwyn-Mayer signed Stewart to a contract in 1935. Major stardom came with his portrayals in the Frank Capra films *You Can't Take It with You* (1938) and **Mr. Smith Goes to Washington* (1939). Throughout World War II he served with distinction in the U.S. Air Force. On returning from the War, he surprised MGM by rejecting its new contract offer and decided to free-lance. His first post-war film was **It's a Wonderful Life* (1946). "The picture meant more to me than any other," he confessed in 1989.

In 1950 Stewart signed a two-picture contract with Universal, becoming one of the first stars to agree to take a modest up-front salary to be followed by a percentage of the profits. In the late 1940s and 1950s Stewart appeared in four films for Alfred Hitchcock, including *Rear Window* (1954) and *Vertigo* (1958), and in the 1970s starred in two television series, "The Jimmy Stewart Show" (1971-1972) and "Hawkins" (1973-1974).

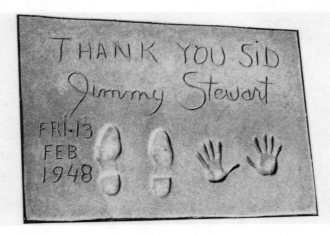

His motion picture credits include "Art Trouble" (1934, short, debut), *Destry Rides Again* (1939), *The Shop around the Corner* (1940), ***The Philadelphia Story* (1940), *Winchester '73* (1950), **Harvey* (1950), *The Greatest Show on Earth* (1952), **Anatomy of a Murder* (1959), *The Man Who Shot Liberty Valance* (1962), and *An American Tail: Fievel Goes West* (1991, voice only).

In 1980 the American Film Institute presented him with its Life Achievement Award, and in 1983 he was a recipient of the Kennedy Center Honors for lifetime achievement. In 1985 he received an Honorary Academy Award "for his fifty years of memorable performances. [And] For his high ideals both on and off the screen. With the respect and affection of his colleagues."

   * Academy Award nomination: Best Actor.
   ** Academy Award winner: Best Actor.

Stewart's square is tinted gray and contains the inscription "Thank You Sid." Also included are the date ("Fri. 13 Feb 1948"), his two footprints, two handprints, and his signature ("Jimmy Stewart").

Unlike his friend, actor Gary Cooper, Stewart was not the least bit hesitant about his ceremony being held on Friday the 13th. Photographs of the event show Stewart holding a black cat—it was on a leash—while posing underneath an opened step-ladder.

In a letter to the authors, Stewart recalled, "I remember that in the footprint ceremony at Grauman's Chinese, I misspelled my first name when I wrote it in the concrete and they had to smooth it over and I tried again."

Archie Henderson, a popcorn salesclerk in the theatre's outdoor snack stand, said in 1985, "People from all over the world come to gawk [at Stewart's footprints]. Only yesterday, a middle-aged woman from London curtsied to them. But that was mild compared to what a lady did a couple of months ago. She was so moved when she saw his handprints that she kept coming back every afternoon with a bucket filled with soap and water. She scrubbed like mad. 'I want Jimmy to always be clean,' she kept explaining."

James Stewart.

Van Johnson (left) and cement artist Jean W. Klossner.

Van Johnson
Ceremony #82: March 25, 1948

He placed his prints in connection with the motion pictures *The Bride Goes Wild* and *State of the Union* (both Metro-Gold-wyn-Mayer, 1948).

Born: Charles Van Johnson in Newport, Rhode Island, on August 25, 1916.

Van Johnson's winning boy-next-door image during the 1940s sent millions of bobby-soxers swooning. He was fascinated with film and theatre from boyhood, and after his education was completed he went to New York City and finally secured a chorus boy job in the revue *New Faces of 1936*. Johnson became one of the "Eight Men of Manhattan," a well-known group which performed in the posh Rainbow Room in Rockefeller Center's RCA building. He had small parts in two Rodgers and Hart Broadway shows, *Too Many Girls* (1939) and *Pal Joey* (1940).

He won a short-term contract with Warner Bros. and went to Hollywood but was dropped after six months. His friend Lucille Ball helped get him a contract with Metro-Goldwyn-Mayer. There he appeared in such films as *Dr. Gillespie's New Assistant* (1942) and *The Human Comedy* (1943) and became a major star in *A Guy Named Joe* (1943). *Two Girls and a Sailor* (1944) paired him with June Allyson. The team became an audience favorite, and they made four more pictures together.

Johnson remained a top star through the 1940s but realized that he could not continue as a juvenile lead forever. The mid-1950s found him free-lancing in

films, and he branched out into television guest spots, stage work, and TV movies. In 1961 he appeared in the London production of *The Music Man* and was seen on Broadway in *La Cage aux Folles* (1985).

His motion picture credits include *Too Many Girls* (1940, debut), *Thirty Seconds over Tokyo* (1944), *Thrill of a Romance* (1945), *Easy To Wed* (1946), *Command Decision* (1948), *Battleground* (1949), *The Caine Mutiny* (1954), *The Last Time I Saw Paris* (1954), *Yours, Mine, and Ours* (1968), and *The Purple Rose of Cairo* (1985).

Johnson's square is tinted green and contains the inscription "God Bless You Sid." Also included are the date ("3-25-48"), his two footprints, two handprints, and his signature.

Johnson recalled his memories of his ceremony at the Chinese Theatre in a letter to the authors:

"I remember a warm sunny day when the MGM people drove me to the fabulous Grauman's Chinese Theatre. Such a crowd of people standing in the courtyard. I thought they [the theatre management] were giving away dishes. The ceremony was a dream come true. As a youngster back in Newport, Rhode Island, I spent all my money on movie magazines and marvelled at the beauty of Mr. Grauman's theatre. And there he was waiting at the curb to open the door—such a kindly man. *Many* years later I stopped by in the pouring rain to see the prints. I stood in them, umbrella in hand. I wonder if they're still there?"

George Jessel
Ceremony #83: March 1, 1949

Born: in New York City on April 3, 1898. Died: May 24, 1981.

An actor, vaudeville and Broadway comedian, producer, director, writer, composer, and song-and-dance man, George Jessel proved himself a multi-talented figure in a show business career that spanned seven decades. Equally famed as a master of ceremonies and after-dinner guest speaker at gala events (including dozens at the White House), Jessel was called the "Toastmaster General of the United States" by five U.S. presidents.

He entered show business at age nine, securing a job at a local movie house as an "intermission singer," accompanying the illustrated song slides flashed on the screen between one-reelers. In 1911 Jessel appeared before cameras at the Edison studios in an early experiment with synchronized sound, and he

major stardom in the Broaday play *The Jazz Singer* (1925).

In 1943 he struck a deal with 20th Century-Fox and became a producer there. Over the next decade he produced more than twenty Fox films, including *The Dolly Sisters* (1945), *Nightmare Alley* (1947), and *When My Baby Smiles at Me* (1948).

His motion picture credits as an actor include *The Other Man's Wife* (1919, first documented film role), *Private Izzy Murphy* (1926), *George Washington Cohen* (1928), *Lucky Boy* (1929, talkie debut), *Happy Days* (1929), *Stage Door Canteen* (1943), *Four Jills in a Jeep* (1944), *Beau James* (1957), *The Phynx* (1970), and *Reds* (1981, final film).

In 1970 he received the Jean Hersholt Humanitarian Award from the Academy of Motion Picture Arts and Sciences.

reportedly appeared in his first released film that same year. Next he got work with Gus Edwards, the famous producer of shows featuring children, and appeared in his lavish vaudeville revues. After that he teamed with Eddie Cantor in an act called "Kid Kabaret." By 1919 he was established as a well-known solo entertainer in vaudeville. He achieved

Jessel's square is tinted green and contains the inscription "Bless You Sid." Also included are the date ("March-1st 49"), his two footprints, two handprints, and his signature ("Georgie Jessel").

Sid Grauman (left), George Jessel, and cement artist Jean W. Klossner. In 1950 Jessel delivered Grauman's eulogy, calling the showman "the soft touch and the soft heart of Hollywood."

Roy Rogers and Trigger
Ceremony #84: April 21, 1949

Roy Rogers

*Born: Leonard Franklin Slye in Cincinnati, Ohio, circa
November 5, 1911 (sources vary on year).*

In 1943 Roy Rogers was dubbed "King of the
Cowboys," a title to which he laid a rightful claim
through another eight years of constant filmmaking
and an additional six years and over 100 episodes of
television's "The Roy Rogers Show" (1951-1957). As
a boy he learned to play the guitar and mandolin. By
1932 he had formed a Western/hillbilly-style singing
duo with a cousin; this evolved into several subsequent groups of various names and sizes over the
next few years until Rogers finally formed the successful "Sons of the Pioneers" with Tim Spencer and
Bob Nolan. By 1935 the group was on the radio and

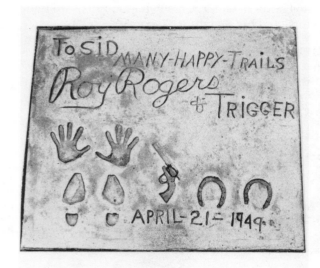

appearing in singing spots in "B" Westerns.

Rogers' big break came in 1937 when Gene Autry,
Republic studio's biggest Western star, left the studio
over a salary dispute. Studio head Herbert J. Yates
signed the newcomer to a contract and cast him in
Under Western Stars (1938), a vehicle originally intended for Autry. When Rogers began getting thousands of fan letters weekly he asked Yates for a raise.
An agreement for a new contract was reached with
Rogers obtaining 100% control and interest in all
outside marketing and product tie-ins involving his
name and image.

He married his frequent co-star, Dale Evans,
"Queen of the West," in 1947. Over the years his

other pursuits have included the annual "Roy Rogers
World's Championship Rodeo," personal appearance tours, his own radio show (1944-1955), recordings, roast beef sandwich shops, and family
restaurants.

His motion picture credits include *The Old Home-
stead* (1935, debut), *Billy the Kid Returns* (1938),
Robin Hood of the Pecos (1941), *King of the Cowboys*
(1943), *Cowboy and the Senorita* (1944, first film with
Dale Evans), *Don't Fence Me In* (1945), *The Golden
Stallion* (1949), *Son of Paleface* (1952), *Alias Jesse
James* (1959), and *Mackintosh and T.J.* (1976).

Trigger

Born: 1932. Died: July 3, 1965.

Trigger, Roy Rogers' golden palomino, appeared
with Rogers in all of his nearly ninety starring film
vehicles (1938-1951), as well as in all 101 episodes
of "The Roy Rogers Show" on television (1951-1957).
Rogers once commented, "I'm the only cowboy in the
business, I think, that started and made all my pictures with one horse." Trigger's trainer, Glenn Randall, said, "He was a very exceptional horse. The title
he had of 'The Smartest Horse in the Movies' absolutely fit. He was almost like a human; you could talk
to him. He could do forty things by word cue." In
addition to his responses to word commands, Trigger
could perform fifty more tricks when given non-verbal
cues.

He was originally owned by the Hudkins Rental
Stable in Hollywood and named Golden Cloud. His
first known screen role was as the steed of Maid
Marian (played by Olivia de Havilland) in *The Adventures of Robin Hood* (1938). Rogers found Trigger
while trying out horses immediately after he signed
his first contract with Republic Pictures. At first the
idea was to rent Trigger, but Rogers decided to purchase the animal and negotiated a sale in the amount
of $2,500. Trigger and Roy first appeared on screen
together in *Under Western Stars* (1938).

Trigger, according to Glenn Randall, had two non-
related understudies: Little Trigger, used for personal
appearances, and Trigger, Jr. Rogers retired Trigger
from performing when the last show in the TV series
was completed in 1957.

When Trigger died the entire Rogers household
was grief-stricken. After much soul-searching, Roy
decided he couldn't bear the idea of burying the horse
and so had him mounted by a taxidermist for placement in the Roy Rogers-Dale Evans Museum in
Victorville, California.

(Left to right) Dale Evans (Mrs. Roy Rogers, kneeling), Pat Brady (standing directly behind her), Trigger (Roy Rogers' horse), Rogers (kneeling), and cement artist Jean W. Klossner (far right).

The Rogers/Trigger square is tinted red and contains the inscription "To Sid—Many Happy Trails." Also included are the date ("April-21-1949"), Rogers' two footprints (made with boots), two handprints, and his signature, plus his gun imprint, Trigger's two front hoofprints, and his name. The signature/name reads "Roy Rogers & Trigger."

The inscription is a reminder that two years later the theme of "The Roy Rogers Show" on television was a song entitled "Happy Trails" (a.k.a. "Happy Trails to You"). It was written by Rogers' wife, Dale Evans.

Rogers' long-time friend and "sidekick" in pictures in the late 1940s and early 1950s and on television, Pat Brady, was present at the ceremony. He congratulated his pal, saying "You've just reached the Hollywood pinnacle. Cowboys aren't usually invited to join the ranks of the all-time movie greats, you know."

Rogers shared his feelings about the event in a letter to the authors:

"It was one of the highlights of my career. I enjoyed meeting Sid Grauman and inspecting all of the other stars' prints represented in the foyer. With my footprints there, I feel honored to be among so many great people, and I feel Trigger feels the same way."

Richard Widmark (left) and Sid Grauman.

Richard Widmark and Charles Nelson Ceremony #85: April 24, 1949

Widmark placed his prints in connection with the motion picture *Down to the Sea in Ships* (20th Century-Fox, 1949). His ceremony also took place on the same day that the theatre held the finals in a talent search contest entitled Talent Quest.

Richard Widmark

Born: in Sunrise, Minnesota, on December 26, 1914.

No one who has seen Richard Widmark's film debut in *Kiss of Death* (1947) can ever forget his performance as the sadistic psychopathic killer—and especially the chilling moment when he sends an old woman in a wheelchair hurtling to her death down a flight of stairs while emitting a blood-curdling, high-pitched laugh. So affecting was this role that Hollywood tried to type Widmark as vicious hoods; but he soon managed to branch out into a wide variety of parts, proving himself a fine and versatile actor.

At Lake Forest College, in Illinois, Widmark was in pre-law studies but was very active in the drama department, appearing in about thirty plays. After graduating in 1936, he stayed on at the college for two years as a drama teacher. In 1938 he went to New York City and quickly found work in radio, working steadily in hundreds of programs over the next decade. In 1943 he made his Broadway debut in the play *Kiss and Tell*. He continued on stage and radio, but his sights were on the screen, and he signed a seven-year contract with 20th Century-Fox in 1947.

Widmark gave many compelling performances in such films as *Panic in the Streets* (1950) and *Pickup on South Street* (1953). He went independent in 1954 and has continued on that basis ever since, filming steadily throughout the 1960s and 1970s. He starred in the television series "Madigan" (1972-1973) and has since appeared in several other TV mini-series and TV movies, including "Cold Sassy Tree" (1989).

His motion picture credits include *Road House* (1948), *No Way Out* (1950), *Don't Bother To Knock* (1952), *Destination Gobi* (1953), *Run for the Sun* (1956), *The Alamo* (1960), *Judgment at Nuremberg* (1961), *The Bedford Incident* (1965), *Murder on the Orient Express* (1974), and *Against All Odds* (1984).

*Academy Award nomination: Best Supporting Actor.

Widmark's square is tinted gray and contains the inscription "To Sid With Sincere Thanks." Also included are the date ("April-24-1949"), his two footprints, two handprints, and his signature.

Charles Nelson

Charles Nelson, a fifteen-year-old baritone from Kansas City, Kansas, was a non-professional who, as the result of winning a talent contest, placed his prints in the Chinese Theatre forecourt.

The contest was entitled Talent Quest, and had been conducted in the hope of finding new discoveries in the field of entertainment. Over 15,000 applicants auditioned and performed in some 600 theatres throughout twenty states. Nine acts were chosen to participate in the week-long national finals held at the Chinese Theatre starting April 14. The contestants vied for prizes totaling $1,850 in cash, merchandise, and a motion picture screen test.

Nelson's square is tinted gray and contains the inscription "Thanks To Sid." Also included are the date ("4-24-49"), his two footprints, two handprints, and his signature, plus the inscription "Talent Quest Winner."

Jeanne Crain
Ceremony #86: October 17, 1949

She placed her prints in connection with the motion picture *Pinky* (20th Century-Fox, 1949).

Born: in Barstow, California, on May 25, 1925.

Jeanne Crain had a wholesome, girl-next-door natural beauty which captivated moviegoers in the 1940s and 1950s. She gave sincere, endearing performances when cast as ingenues and proved herself a capable actress when given serious roles.

Crain was an Inglewood High School student when, on a school tour of RKO studios, Orson Welles spotted her and had her tested for his upcoming *The Magnificent Ambersons* (1942). Welles decided she was too young and inexperienced, but the fact that she was even considered gave Jeanne encouragement, and she decided to pursue an acting career. She won the title of "Miss Long Beach of 1941," was a runner-up in the "Miss America" finals, and was chosen "Camera Girl of 1942."

She was spotted by a 20th Century-Fox talent scout and signed a contract with the studio in 1943. Her winsome, natural qualities were emphasized in her second film, *Home in Indiana* (1944), and she made a hit with the public. *State Fair* (1945) further confirmed her new position as a major personality. In the late 1940s she excelled in more complex and demanding roles such as those in *A Letter to Three Wives* and *Pinky* (both 1949).

In 1945 Jeanne married Paul Brinkman and bore him seven children between 1947 and 1965. By the mid-1950s she was accepting far fewer film roles in order to give more attention to her family.

Her motion picture credits include *The Gang's All Here* (1943, debut), *Winged Victory* (1944), *Leave Her to Heaven* (1945), *Centennial Summer* (1946), *You Were Meant for Me* (1948), *Apartment for Peggy*

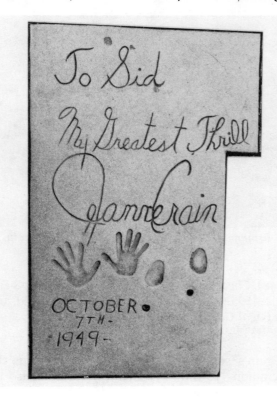

Paul Brinkman, Jr. (left) with his mother Jeanne Crain, Sid Grauman, and cement artist Jean W. Klossner.

(1948), *Cheaper by the Dozen* (1950), *O. Henry's Full House* (1952), *Gentlemen Marry Brunettes* (1955), and *The Night God Screamed* (1975).

    Academy Award nomination: Best Actress.

Crain's square is tinted gray and contains the inscription "To Sid—My Greatest Thrill." Also included are the date ("October-7th- -1949-"), her two footprints (made with high heels), two handprints, and her signature.

Jeanne's very first assignment when she was signed by Fox was to assist Monty Woolley at his Chinese Theatre ceremony in 1943. Six-years later, it was Crain's eldest child, Paul Brinkman, Jr., who played that role in his mother's own hand and footprint ceremony.

Jean Hersholt
Ceremony #87: October 20, 1949

Jean Hersholt's second square—the first one is no longer in the forecourt (see below)—is tinted gray and contains the inscription "'Skaal' to Sid Grauman— My Dear Friend." "Skaal" is Danish for "Here's To You." Also included are the date ("Oct-20-1949"), his two footprints, two handprints, and his signature, plus an imprint of one of Hersholt's trademark pipes.

Hersholt agreed to participate in a second hand and footprint ceremony in order that the new square could replace the deteriorated one from his 1938 ceremony with the Dionne Quintuplets.

Earlier in the year, Hersholt, the eleventh president of the Academy of Motion Picture Arts and Sciences, had presented Sid Grauman with his Special Academy Award at the 21st annual Academy Awards Presentation, held at the Academy Award Theatre in Hollywood on March 24, 1949.

Sid Grauman (left), Jean Hersholt, and cement artist Jean W. Klossner at Hersholt's second Chinese Theatre imprint ceremony (see text).

(*For a description of Hersholt's first ceremony and his biographical write-up, see entry for Ceremony #46: October 11, 1938*).

Anne Baxter and Gregory Peck
Ceremony #88: December 15, 1949

They placed their prints in connection with the motion picture *Yellow Sky* (20th Century-Fox, 1948).

Anne Baxter

*Born: in Michigan City, Indiana, on May 7, 1923.
Died: December 12, 1985.*

Anne Baxter was a gifted actress who, although seldom cast in films worthy of her talent, achieved star status and established a highly respected reputation. At age ten, Anne saw Helen Hayes perform in a play and was immediately inspired to pursue an acting career. Her Broadway debut came at age thirteen in the play *Seen but Not Heard* (1936). She signed a seven-year contract with 20th Century-Fox in 1940, and her first significant role was in *Swamp Water* (1941). Her roles in **The Razor's Edge* (1946) and the title character in *All about Eve* (1950) were the highlights of her years at Fox.

Unhappy over most of her other screen assignments at the studio, Baxter asked to be released from her contract in 1953. She free-lanced and was de-

Gregory Peck (left), Anne Baxter, and Sid Grauman.

lighted to be cast as Nefretiri in the lavish remake of *The Ten Commandments* (1956). In the late 1950s Baxter returned to the stage in several plays and began an intensive career in television that continued steadily for more than twenty years. In 1971 she had a smash Broadway hit when she replaced Lauren Bacall in the musical *Applause*, which was based on the film *All about Eve*—but this time Baxter played the role of Margo Channing instead of Eve Harrington.

In 1983 Baxter took the role of hotel owner Victoria Cabot in producer Aaron Spelling's popular television series "Hotel" (a.k.a. "Arthur Hailey's Hotel") and played it for two years.

Her motion picture credits include *20 Mule Team* (1940, debut), *The Magnificent Ambersons* (1942), *Crash Dive* (1943), *Five Graves to Cairo* (1943), *Guest in the House* (1945), *Smoky* (1946), *You're My Everything* (1949), *Three Violent People* (1957), *Walk on the Wild Side* (1962), and *The Late Liz* (1971, final film).

 * *Academy Award nomination: Best Actress.*
 ** *Academy Award winner: Best Supporting Actress.*

Baxter's square is tinted gray and contains the inscription "Dear Sid—Rain Or Shine I Love You." Also included are the date ("Dec-15th.1949"), her two footprints (made with high heels), two handprints, and her signature, plus the drawings of an umbrella ("Rain"), the sun ("Shine"), and a heart ("Love") beside the inscription.

Baxter's inscription and drawings refer to the fact that it was raining when she and Gregory Peck placed their prints. A tent was erected to protect both the stars and the cement.

Gregory Peck

Born: Eldred Gregory Peck in La Jolla, California, on April 5, 1916.

Throughout his career, Gregory Peck has projected an image of quiet but intense inner strength, moral integrity, righteousness, and compassion, in a notably wide variety of film genres. He became interested in acting while at the University of California at Berkeley and after gradation in 1939 headed for New York City, intent on breaking into stage work. In 1942 he scored an important success on Broadway as the juvenile lead in *The Morning Star.*

After several more plays he went to Hollywood and so impressed motion picture audiences that he soon found himself in the unprecedented position of having signed four contracts (with 20th Century-Fox, RKO, Metro-Goldwyn-Mayer, and David O. Selznick) for a total of sixteen pictures. He was quickly recognized as one of the finest talents and most important male stars to have emerged during the 1940s and was superb in such films as *The Keys of the Kingdom* (1944), *The Yearling* (1946), and *Twelve O'Clock High* (1949).

He stayed at the top throughout the 1950s and 1960s in such hits as *Roman Holiday* (1953) and **To Kill a Mockingbird* (1962), which is widely considered the all-time high point of his career. Since then Peck has continued to appear in films while doing a limited amount of work for television.

His motion picture credits include *Days of Glory* (1944, debut), *Spellbound* (1945), *Duel in the Sun* (1946), *Gentleman's Agreement* (1947), *The Gunfighter* (1950), *The Snows of Kilimanjaro* (1952), *Designing Woman* (1957), *The Big Country* (1958), *The Omen* (1976), and *Other People's Money* (1991).

In 1968 he received the Jean Hersholt Humanitarian Award from the Academy of Motion Picture Arts and Sciences. In 1989 the American Film Institute presented

him with its Life Achievement Award, and in 1991 he was a recipient of the Kennedy Center Honors for Lifetime Achievement.

* *Academy Award nomination: Best Actor.*
** *Academy Award winner: Best Actor.*

Peck's square is tinted gray and contains the inscription "To My Friend Sid—'Mr. Hollywood.'" Also included are the date ("Dec. 15th 1949"), his two footprints, two handprints, and his signature. Three coins were also embedded in the cement. Two have since been pried out, leaving one rather weather-beaten penny.

In a letter to the authors, Peck shared his impressions of the Chinese Theatre as well as his hand and footprint ceremony:

"When the Grauman's Chinese Theatre opened, I was taken as a boy to see the opening film, *The King of Kings* [1927]. The ushers were dressed in Chinese Mandarin garb, the carpets were a foot thick, the air was perfumed with Chinese incense, and along with the movie, a biblical epic, there was a magnificent stage show. Altogether it was a staggering experience for a small-town kid from La Jolla. I have never forgotten it. Compared to that, the footprint ceremony in 1949 was not a great occasion.

"Anne Baxter and I had made a Western, *Yellow Sky*, which was playing at the Chinese. Anne was a wonderful actress. We smiled our way through the history-making event. I couldn't think of anything to write in the cement for ages. Sid Grauman, himself a colorful showman of the old school, suggested that I write, 'To Sid, "Mr. Hollywood,"' or something of the sort. Since the cement was hardening fast, and nothing more brilliant came to mind, that is what I wrote."

Gene Autry and Champion
Ceremony #89: December 23, 1949

Gene Autry

Born: Orvon Gene Autry on a ranch near Tioga, Texas, on September 29, 1907.

Gene Autry was the first singing cowboy to become a major film star. At age twelve he bought his first guitar for eight dollars from a Sears, Roebuck and Co. catalog and began playing and singing, mainly for his own amusement. By 1928 Autry had a job singing on radio station KVOO in Tulsa and became known as "Oklahoma's Yodeling Cowboy."

Autry wanted to be in movies and repeatedly wrote to Nat Levine, president of the Mascot company in Hollywood, asking for a chance in pictures. Levine finally signed him at $100 per week and cast him as a featured singer in a Ken Maynard vehicle, *In Old Santa Fe* (1934, debut). When Maynard left the studio shortly thereafter, Levine put Autry into vehicles previously intended for Maynard, increased their musical content, and built Autry into a star. By that time, Mascot had merged with a few other companies to become Republic Pictures.

Autry's first starring film, *Tumbling Tumbleweeds* (1935), was a huge hit. Over the years, Autry made more than ninety inexpensive "B" Westerns. He also had a popular radio program, "Gene Autry's Melody Ranch" (1940-1956). His recordings sold in the millions, including the Christmas favorite, "Rudolph, the Red-Nosed Reindeer" (1949). In the 1950s he pro-

duced and appeared in ninety-one television episodes of "The Gene Autry Show" (1950-1956).

By 1960 he quit performing altogether to devote his full time to the management of his far-flung corporate and real estate empires, including the ownership of the Los Angeles Angels baseball team (later known as the California Angels). His $54,000,000 Gene Autry Western Heritage Museum opened in Los Angeles in 1988 and documents all aspects of the American West.

His motion picture credits include *The Phantom Empire* (1935, serial), *The Singing Cowboy* (1936), *Git Along Little Dogies* (1937), *Rhythm of the Saddle* (1938), *Blue Montana Skies* (1939), *Shooting High* (1940), **Ridin' on a Rainbow* (1941), *Cowboy Serenade* (1942), *The Last Round-Up* (1947), and *Alias Jesse James* (1959).

> ** Academy Award nomination: Music (Song) ("Be Honest with Me"—music and lyric by Gene Autry and Fred Rose).*

Champion

Champion #1: Born: date unknown. Died: circa 1944.

Billed as "The World's Wonder Horse," Gene Autry's Champion was actually at least three different horses, each of whom also had several stand-ins, understudies, and doubles.

According to Autry, who trained in horsemanship *after* signing for the movies, the original Champion was from Oklahoma; and he purchased the horse at the time he was cast in his first starring film, *Tumbling Tumbleweeds* (1935). Autry used the original Champion continually in his films until World War II interrupted his career. (Between 1942 and 1946, Autry served in the U.S. Air Force.) During the time Autry was overseas, the first Champion died circa 1944.

Autry also explains that the original Champion seen in his films was *not* the same horse used for his personal appearances during that period. That job was filled by Tom Mix's horse, Tony, Jr., a Champion look-alike, who was passed off as the actual Champion for live shows.

After the War, Autry found another horse with similar markings, first called Champion, Jr., and later simply Champion, to appear in Autry's subsequent films. When Autry began his television show in 1950, he retired the second Champion and found a third horse, nicknamed "Little Champ" but officially billed as Champion. This third Champion appeared in both the Autry TV series, as well as a show of his own, "The

Adventures of Champion," (1955-1956), in which Autry did not appear.

The various Champions performed an impressive repertoire of tricks, such as playing dead, outrunning cars and trucks, performing numerous dance steps, and even kneeling "in prayer."

The Autry/Champion square is tinted gray and contains the inscription "To Sid Grauman—A Great Guy And A Great Showman." Also included are the date ("Dec-23 1949"), Autry's two footprints (made with boots), two handprints, and his signature,

Champion's two front hoofprints, and his name ("Champ.").

Autry shared his feelings regarding the inclusion of his and Champion's imprints in the Chinese Theatre forecourt in a letter to the authors:

"I have always been proud to have played a small part in the history of this famous Hollywood landmark. The ceremony was certainly one of the highlights of my career, although I must say that I don't think Champion enjoyed it as much as I did. He was not at all happy about stepping into that wet cement."

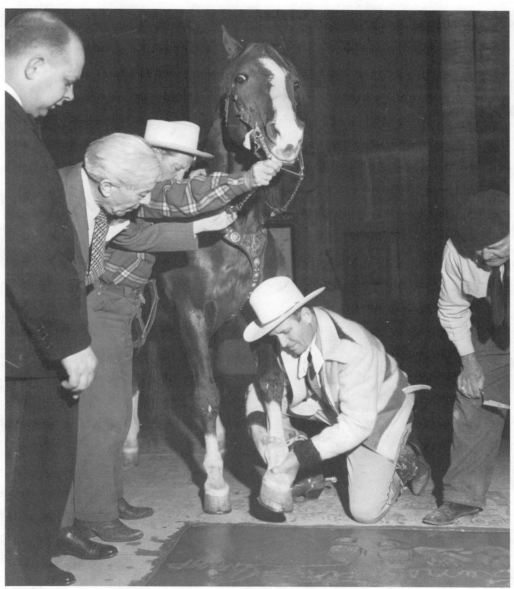

Chinese Theatre manager George Kane (left), Sid Grauman, unidentified man holding Champion (Gene Autry's horse), Autry, and cement artist Jean W. Klossner.

(Kneeling, left) Private Inga Boberg, John Wayne, and Sid Grauman. (Standing, left) Major Gordon West, Lieutenant Colonel C. A. Youngdale, and Colonel J. O. Brauer. Wayne's was the last ceremony at which Sid Grauman officiated. Grauman died March 5, 1950.

John Wayne
Ceremony #90: January 25, 1950

He placed his prints in connection with the motion picture *Sands of Iwo Jima* (Republic, 1949).

Born: Marion Michael Morrison in Winterset, Iowa, on May 26, 1907. Died: June 11, 1979.

A heroic figure, John Wayne created a unique and unforgettable persona as a leather-tough, two-fisted archetypal Westerner. He varied his roles, however, by often playing military men and even occasionally an actual civilian. In 1967 *Time* magazine called him "the greatest moneymaker in film history," his movies having grossed nearly $400,000,000 at that time. (That figure was revised to $700,000,000 in 1979.)

As a boy he had an Airedale dog named Duke, and somehow that name was transferred to Wayne as a permanent nickname. He got his first movie work at Fox studios as a laborer, prop man, and sometime set dresser. Eventually he began doing stunts and bits and was first seen on the screen doubling for Francis X. Bushman, Jr. in *Brown of Harvard* (1926).

Wayne struck up a friendship with director John Ford, who recommended him to Raoul Walsh for the lead in Walsh's upcoming Western epic *The Big Trail*

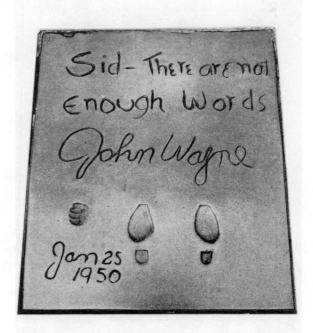

(1930), a breakthrough for Wayne and his first starring role. Wayne spent the next eight years in "B" pictures, primarily at Republic in Westerns, and finally achieved full-fledged stardom in John Ford's *Stagecoach* (1939).

He gained steady momentum during the 1940s, appearing in such popular films as *Fort Apache, Red River* (both 1948), and *She Wore a Yellow Ribbon* (1949). In terms of critical acclaim and stature, the pinnacle of his career came with **True Grit* (1969).

His motion picture credits include *Words and Music* (1929, talkie debut), *The Long Voyage Home* (1940), *Reap the Wild Wind* (1942), *The Spoilers* (1942), **Sands of Iwo Jima* (1949), *The Quiet Man* (1952), *The High and the Mighty* (1954), *The Searchers* (1956), ****The Alamo* (1960, Wayne also produced), and *The Shootist* (1976, final film).
  * *Academy Award nomination: Best Actor.*
  ** *Academy Award winner: Best Actor.*
  *** *Academy Award nomination: Best Picture.*

Wayne's square is tinted gray and contains the inscription "Sid—There are not Enough Words." Also included are the date ("Jan 25 1950"), his two footprints (made with boots), his right fist print, and his signature.

Wayne was assisted by several members of the U.S. Marine Corps, all of whom were stationed at Iwo Jima, the site of a Japanese air base during World War II and an island taken at a great cost by U.S. forces in 1945. The sand used to mix Wayne's cement was literally the "Sands of Iwo Jima" and was shipped from the island to the theatre in two 100-pound sacks for the occasion.

Lana Turner
Ceremony #91: May 24, 1950

Born: Julia Jean Mildred Frances Turner on February 8, 1921, in Wallace, Idaho.

One of the archetypal "movie queens" of the 1940s and 1950s, Lana Turner at once both established and symbolized her own definitive incarnation of glamor. She attended Hollywood High School; and it was at Top's Cafe across the street from the school grounds—not Schwab's drugstore, as legend has it—that Turner was spotted by the owner and editor-in-chief of the *Hollywood Reporter*, Billy Wilkerson. He arranged for her to be represented by Zeppo Marx's agency in 1936, and Turner began her ascent to stardom.

Lana Turner and cement artist Jean W. Klossner. Turner told the authors, "The cement was very wet and cold on my hands."

She was extra in *A Star Is Born* (1937, debut); and her first actual role came that same year with *They Won't Forget*, for Warner Bros., where she was dubbed the "Sweater Girl." At Warners, producer/director Mervyn LeRoy put her under personal contract. When he left Warners for Metro-Goldwyn-Mayer in 1938, Turner went with him.

Melodrama became her forte; and she later gave highly capable and emotional performances in *The Postman Always Rings Twice* (1946), *Green Dolphin Street* (1947), and *The Bad and the Beautiful* (1952). Leaving MGM in 1956, Lana went independent and appeared in the hits *Peyton Place* (1957) and *Imitation of Life* (1959).

In the 1970s Turner had successes touring in several dinner theatre productions, most notably *Forty Carats* (1971). She later made a few guest appear-

ances on the prime-time television soap opera "Falcon Crest" (1982-1983).

Her motion picture credits include *Love Finds Andy Hardy* (1938), *Ziegfeld Girl* (1941), *Honky Tonk* (1941), *Johnny Eager* (1942), *Slightly Dangerous* (1943), *Week-End at the Waldorf* (1945), *The Three Musketeers* (1948), *The Merry Widow* (1952), *Madame X* (1966), and *Bittersweet Love* (1976).
Academy Award nomination: Best Actress.

Turner's square is tinted yellow and contains the date ("5-24-50"), her two footprints (made with high heels), two handprints, and her signature.

Some onlookers who attended the event encouraged Turner to imprint the part of her anatomy that made her Hollywood's "Sweater Girl."

Turner laughed and responded she planned to imprint only her hands and feet and nothing else in order to keep the ceremony "in good taste." She admitted, "I'm so nervous. I've waited a long time for this, you know. I feel like a four-year old."

Her ceremony completed, Lana inquired, "Where are Betty Grable's prints?" and soon left in a mink coat and a black limousine.

A disappointed soldier who had come early in the hope that an imprint of the Turner torso would be enshrined in the forecourt sighed, "Too bad. Oh, well...there's always Jane Russell."

Bette Davis
Ceremony #92: November 6, 1950

She placed her prints in connection with the motion picture *All about Eve* (20th Century-Fox, 1950).

Born: Ruth Elizabeth Davis in Lowell, Massachusetts, on April 5, 1908. Died: October 6, 1989.

Surveying all of cinema history, many consider Bette Davis to be the greatest screen actress of them all. She possessed a striking presence rather than conventional beauty, coupled with flamboyant mannerisms and a distinctive speaking style.

While in high school she decided she wanted to be an actress and enrolled at the John Murray Anderson Dramatic School (1926-1928). She first appeared on Broadway in *Broken Dishes* (1929). At that time she made a screen test for Goldwyn, a failure she described as "ghastly," but soon thereafter signed a short-term contract with Universal studios, making her film debut in *Bad Sister* (1931). Actor George Arliss specifically requested Davis for *The Man Who Played God* (1932) at Warner Bros., and the studio placed her under long-term contract.

She gave an electrifying performance on loan-out to RKO in *Of Human Bondage* (1934), but Warners continued putting her in its routine product, and in 1936 she tried to break her contract. She lost the legal battle; but finally, in 1938, Warners began putting her in only first-rate productions. As a result, Davis became the most acclaimed actress in Hollywood for

Staff Sergeant Jack Spencer (left), Bette Davis, and Technical Sergeant Bert R. Nave. Davis jokingly told the crowd, "It's too bad there's no way to imprint my poached-egg eyes here."

many years and was called "The Fourth Warner Brother."

By the late 1940s Davis' popularity seemed on the wane, and she parted company with Warners in 1949. Her career was quickly and triumphantly revived by the smash hit *All about Eve*, in which she gave what is arguably her best performance. She continued making films and in the 1970s and 1980s appeared in several television movies. Davis called her four-time co-star Claude Rains "the greatest actor I ever worked with."

Her motion picture credits include **Dangerous* (1935), **Jezebel* (1938), *Dark Victory* (1939), *The Letter* (1940), *The Little Foxes* (1941), *Now, Voyager* (1942), *Mr. Skeffington* (1944), *The Star* (1952), *What Ever Happened to Baby Jane?* (1962), and *Wicked Stepmother* (1989, final film).

In 1977 the American Film Institute presented her with its Life Achievement Award, and in 1987 she was a recipient of the Kennedy Center Honors for Lifetime Achievement.

  * *Academy Award nomination: Best Actress.*
  ** *Academy Award winner: Best Actress.*

Davis' square is tinted green and contains the date ("11-6-50"), her two footprints (made with high heels), two handprints, and her signature.

In 1942 Davis helped organize the Hollywood Canteen for World War II servicemen, which was a place in Hollywood for them to be entertained by and socialize with the stars. On the day of her footprint ceremony she was assisted by Canteen Marine Corps veterans Staff Sergeant Jack Spencer and Technical Sergeant Bert R. Nave as a tribute to her work as president of that organization. Davis wrote in 1987, "There are few accomplishments in my life that I am sincerely proud of. The Hollywood Canteen is one of them."

William Lundigan
Ceremony #93: December 29, 1950

Born: in Syracuse, New York, on June 12, 1914. Died: December 20, 1975.

Affable, easy-going, and handsome, William Lundigan typically played all-American "nice-guy" parts, usually in support of a female co-star who was the central focus of the film. As a youngster, Lundigan became fascinated with the broadcasting field. In 1933 he became an announcer at Syracuse radio station WFBL and in two years was the station's production manager.

In 1937 film producer Charles R. Rogers heard him on the air and screen tested him in New York City. Within a month Lundigan was in Hollywood and had won a contract with Universal studios, where he made his screen debut in *Armored Car* (1937).

He primarily appeared in "B" pictures throughout the first eleven years of his film career and became rather discouraged. His big break came when he was cast as the leading man opposite Jeanne Crain in *Pinky* (1949), an important film at 20th Century-Fox, where he was given a contract. He left the studio in 1953.

Sergeant Homer S. Bramble (left), William Lundigan, Sergeant Gladys Bolkow, and cement artist Jean W. Klossner.

He landed the job as host of the prestigious "Climax!" television series (1954-1958) and was spokesman for its sponsor, the Chrysler Corporation. He received more fan mail during this period than he ever had when making films.

His motion picture credits include *Dodge City* (1939), *Santa Fe Trail* (1940), *The Courtship of Andy Hardy* (1942), *Dr. Gillespie's Criminal Case* (1943), *Salute to the Marines* (1943), *What Next, Corporal Hargrove?* (1945), *I'll Get By* (1950), *I'd Climb the Highest Mountain* (1951), *The House on Telegraph Hill* (1951), and *Where Angels Go...Trouble Follows!* (1968, final film).

Lundigan's square is tinted gray and contains the inscription "My Thanks." Also included are the date ("12-29-50"), his two footprints, two handprints, and his signature, plus the imprint of the U.S. Marine Corps symbol. Lundigan served in the Marines during World War II from 1943 to 1945.

The banner portion of the symbol and the motto "SEMPER FIDELIS," which is Latin for "always faithful," are not clearly visible in the imprint in Lundigan's square.

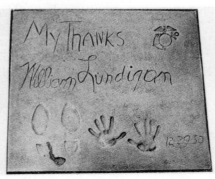

Cary Grant
Ceremony #94: July 16, 1951

He placed his prints in connection with the motion picture *People Will Talk* (20th Century-Fox, 1951).

Born: Archibald Alec Leach in Bristol, England, on January 18, 1904. Died: November 29, 1986.

Cary Grant's ability to delight audiences has proved timeless. At age thirteen he joined the Bob Pender Troupe of traveling acrobats. He became a song-and-dance man and occasional juggler and played music halls in the British provinces and on the Continent.

In 1920 Grant went with the company to New York, where he decided to stay on. He supported himself in small-time vaudeville and at one point was even a stilt-walking ad sign carrier at Coney Island. His first real break came when he landed a good part in the Harbach-Hammerstein Broadway musical *Golden Dawn* (1927). He decided to give Hollywood a try in 1932 and won a contract with Paramount. Appearances opposite Marlene Dietrich in *Blonde Venus* (1932) and Mae West in *She Done Him Wrong* and *I'm No Angel* (both 1933) gave his career a boost, and by the mid-1930s he was well established as a romantic leading man.

The Awful Truth (1937) made Grant a star of the first order; and subsequent pictures such as *Bringing Up Baby* (1938), *His Girl Friday*, and *The Philadelphia Story* (both 1940), established him as the foremost male player of sophisticated and screwball comedy.

In the early 1950s he had a few mediocre vehicles and contemplated retirement. Alfred Hitchcock came to the rescue, however, and gave Grant's career a much-needed rejuvenation with the successful *To Catch a Thief* (1955).

His motion picture credits include *This Is the Night* (1932, debut), *Topper* (1937), *Gunga Din* (1939), *Penny Serenade* (1941), *Arsenic and Old Lace* (1944), *None but the Lonely Heart* (1944), *Notorious* (1946), *North by Northwest* (1959), *Charade* (1963), and *Walk, Don't Run* (1966, final film).

In 1970 he received an Honorary Academy Award "for his unique mastery of the art of screen acting with the respect and affection of his colleagues." In 1981 he was a recipient of the Kennedy Center Honors for Lifetime Achievement.

Academy Award nomination: Best Actor.

Cary Grant.

Grant's square is tinted green and contains the date ("July 16, 1951"), his two footprints, two handprints, and his signature.

Southern California tourist Georgia Douglas just happened to be visiting the Chinese Theatre with her husband on the day of Grant's ceremony and recalled:

"[We] noticed a crowd gathering to await the arrival of a motion picture star who was scheduled to leave an identifying mark in the square of wet cement. In a short time, a big black car drove up and Cary Grant emerged. He was most gracious to the public, shaking hands, joking and standing still while we snapped pictures with our tourist-type cameras. A platform about three inches high had been placed near the wet cement, and he knelt on it, leaned over and left an impression of his hands. An attendant stood by with a basin of water and towel, and after cleaning his hands, he again talked and laughed with the people.

"A short time before this, we had occasion to see another popular star, but his attitude was so cold and unfriendly we never again went to see a movie in which he played an important part.

"Mr. Grant was so congenial and friendly we felt we were lucky to have had the pleasure of watching and talking to him."

Susan Hayward
Ceremony #95: August 10, 1951

She placed her prints in connection with the motion picture *David and Bathsheba* (20th Century-Fox, 1951).

Born: Edythe Marrener on June 30, 1918, in Brooklyn, New York. Died: March 14, 1975.

From the beginning, red-haired actress Susan Hayward was a fighter and a loner who fairly clawed her way to the top. As a child she was raised in poverty and dreamed of becoming a movie star. In 1936 she made her film debut as a fashion model in a Vitaphone short, the title of which is undocumented. After high school she became a professional photographer's model.

In 1937 a picture of Hayward in an edition of *The Saturday Evening Post* caught producer David O. Selznick's eye, and he brought her to Hollywood to test for the role of Scarlett O'Hara in his upcoming production of *Gone With the Wind* (1939). Susan didn't get the part but remained in town. She eventu-

Susan Hayward.

ally signed a contract with Paramount, where she was usually cast in secondary roles.

Hayward left Paramount in 1945 and signed with producer Walter Wanger, who put her career into high gear. The turning point came with *Smash-Up— The Story of a Woman* (1947), which sent her to major stardom. 20th Century-Fox bought her contract from Wanger in 1949 and showcased her in a series of star vehicles over the next few years that put her among the most important of Hollywood actresses.

She reached her career pinnacle as Barbara Graham, who was convicted of murder and died in the California gas chamber, in **I Want to Live!* (1958).

Her motion picture credits include *Beau Geste* (1939), *Adam Had Four Sons* (1941), *Reap the Wild Wind* (1942), *The Hairy Ape* (1944), *Canyon Passage* (1946), **My Foolish Heart* (1949), **With a Song in My Heart* (1952), *Soldier of Fortune* (1955), **I'll Cry Tomorrow* (1955), and *The Revengers* (1972, final film).

*Academy Award nomination: Best Actress.
**Academy Award winner: Best Actress.

Hayward's square is tinted gray and contains the date ("Aug-10-'51"), her two footprints (made with high heels), two handprints, and her signature.

Hayward coated her wet footprints with gold dust to symbolize the queen she played in *David and Bathsheba*—and also to symbolize the profits that Fox hoped to make on this and future Hayward starring vehicles.

Hildegarde Neff and Oskar Werner Ceremony #96: December 13, 1951

Neff placed her prints, and those of Werner's, in connection with the motion picture *Decision before Dawn* (20th Century-Fox, 1951).

Hildegarde Neff

Born: Hildegard Frieda Albertina Knef in Ulm, Germany, on December 28, 1925.

A coolly aloof beauty, Germany's Hildegarde Neff made most of her films in the late 1940s and 1950s. She lived in Berlin during the final years of Hitler's Reich and was an art student with a scholarship to study painting at the UFA film studios art department. She switched from painting to acting in 1944 and made her film debut in *Fahrt ins Glück* (1945, a.k.a. *Journey to Happiness* or *Trip to Fortune*).

After the defeat of Germany Neff built her career, alternating between film and stage appearances. Her first notable success came with *Die Mörder sind unter uns* (1946, a.k.a. *The Murderers Are among Us*). She attained real stardom with *Film ohne Titel* (1947, a.k.a. *Film without a Name*).

In 1948 Neff signed a contract with producer

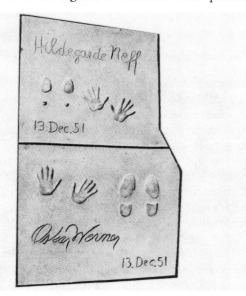

David O. Selznick to appear in American films. Selznick let her sit idle for nearly two years. Frustrated by the inactivity, Neff learned English during the interim and finally obtained a release from her contract. She returned to Germany, and director Anatole Litvak cast her in her first American-produced film,

Hildegarde Neff makes imprints for Oskar Werner using casts of his hands.

Decision before Dawn (1951). It was filmed in Germany and led to a contract for Neff with 20th Century-Fox.

She made a few films for Fox in the early 1950s but again returned to Germany, where she continued in European productions. In 1955 she appeared on Broadway as the star of the Cole Porter musical *Silk Stockings*. In 1984 she returned to Hollywood to guest star in an episode of the "Scarecrow and Mrs. King" television series. She has enjoyed a career as a cabaret chanteuse and an author, reverting professionally to the original spelling of her surname, "Knef." Currently she spells her name "Hildegard Neff."

Her motion picture credits include *Die Sünderin* (1951, a.k.a. *The Sinner*), *Diplomatic Courier* (1952), *The Snows of Kilimanjaro* (1952), *Alraune* (1952), *The Man Between* (1953), *Svengali* (1955), *Die Dreigroschenoper* (1963, a.k.a. *Three Penny Opera*), *The Lost Continent* (1968), *Fedora* (1979), and *L'Avenir d'Emilie* (1984, a.k.a. *Flügel und Fesseln* or *The Future of Emily*).

Neff's square is tinted gray and contains the date ("13-Dec. 51"), her two footprints (made with high heels), two handprints, and her signature.

Oskar Werner

Born: Oskar Josef Bschliessmayer in Vienna, Austria, on November 13, 1922. Died: October 23, 1984.

Although he made only a handful of American films and spent most of his career on the European stage, Oskar Werner made a lasting impression on American audiences with his portrayal in *Ship of Fools* (1965), the first movie he actually made in Hollywood.

At fifteen he got his first part doing a bit in a film as an elevator boy; the title of the film that marked his debut is undocumented. At eighteen he was admitted to the company of Vienna's prestigious Burgtheater and appeared in nearly fifty plays. After Hitler conquered Austria, Werner found himself drafted into the German army in 1941. A pacifist and rabid anti-Nazi, he pretended to be stupid and incompetent and intentionally flunked out of officers' training school within two weeks of enrollment.

After the War, Werner made his first important film appearance in *Der Engel mit der Posaune* (1948, a.k.a. *The Angel with the Trumpet*). Director Anatole Litvak cast Werner in his first American-produced movie, *Decision before Dawn* (1951), which was filmed in Europe. 20th Century-Fox signed Werner to a seven-year contract, and he went to Hollywood for the first time. He languished with no assignments for months, eventually asking to be released from his contract. He returned to Europe, where he launched probably the greatest triumph of his career—his stage production of *Hamlet* (1953). By 1959 he had founded his own

Oskar Werner.

theatrical company, the Theater Ensemble Oskar Werner.

His performance in Francois Truffaut's film *Jules et Jim* (1962, a.k.a. *Jules and Jim*) brought him international praise, and he thereafter made several mainstream movies during the 1960s.

His motion picture credits include *Eroica* (1949), *Das gestohlene Jahr* (1950, a.k.a. *The Stolen Year*), *Der letzte Akt* (1955, a.k.a. *The Last Ten Days*), *Lola Montès* (1955), *Spionage* (1955, a.k.a. *Espionage*), *The Spy Who Came in from the Cold* (1965), *Fahrenheit 451* (1966), *Interlude* (1968), *The Shoes of the Fisherman* (1968), and *Voyage of the Damned* (1976, final film).

Academy Award nomination: Best Actor.

Werner's square is tinted green and contains the date ("13-Dec. 51"), his two footprints, two handprints, and his signature.

Since Werner was in Europe and not able to participate in the ceremony directly, Hildegarde Neff stepped in to do the honors. Casts of Werner's hands and his signature were made in Germany and flown to Hollywood especially for the occasion, along with a pair of his shoes.

Commentators at the time erroneously described the Werner ceremony as the first time a star had been footprinted by proxy, forgetting the Dionne Quintuplets/Jean Hersholt event held thirteen years prior to that of Neff and Werner.

Jane Wyman
Ceremony #97: September 17, 1952

She placed her prints in connection with the motion picture *Just for You* (Paramount, 1952).

Born: Sarah Jane Fulks in St. Joseph, Missouri, circa January 4, 1914 (sources vary on year).

Prior to achieving huge popularity with a whole new generation of fans during the 1980s as the star of the hit television series "Falcon Crest" (1981-1990), Jane Wyman was one of Hollywood's most important stars during the 1940s and 1950s.

Her film debut came as an unbilled chorus girl in *The Kid from Spain* (1932). Next she became a radio singer and toured singing the blues, billed as Jane Durrell. She returned to Hollywood in 1934 and found only a succession of more chorus girl parts.

In 1936 she landed a contract with Warner Bros. and began a long climb through "B" pictures on her way to stardom, creating a stir opposite Olivia de

Havilland in *Princess O'Rourke* (1943). Finally the upper echelons of Hollywood took notice of her, and she was loaned to Paramount for *The Lost Weekend* (1945). Warners realized they had a potential star in its midst. Wyman again triumphed on loan-out to Metro-Goldwyn-Mayer in *The Yearling* (1946), and she reached the pinnacle of her career as the deaf-mute girl in **Johnny Belinda* (1948).

Wyman continued as one of the most popular stars of the 1950s in a wide variety of roles which brought her continued critical praise. On television she hosted and occasionally starred in "Fireside Theatre" (1955-1958). In the 1970s Wyman was generally out of the limelight but was lured back to work with "Falcon Crest."

Her motion picture credits include *Brother Rat* (1938), *Stage Fright* (1950), *The Glass Menagerie* (1950), *Here Comes the Groom* (1951), *The Blue Veil* (1951), *So Big* (1953), *Magnificent Obsession* (1954), *All That Heaven Allows* (1955), *Pollyanna* (1960), and *How To Commit Marriage* (1969.)

* *Academy Award nomination: Best Actress.*
** *Academy Award winner: Best Actress.*

Wyman's square is tinted red and contains the inscription "'Just for You.'" Also included are the date ("9-17-52"), her two footprints (made with high heels), two handprints, and her signature.

A special contest was held at the Chinese Theatre on the evening of Wyman's ceremony. Its winner was to receive a smaller block of cement in its own wooden frame especially inscribed by Wyman. At 7:30 p.m. the holder of the winning ticket was announced. She was Burbank resident Mrs. Lena Evaristo, who was accompanied by her son Larry. After Wyman completed her own ceremony she placed her left footprint in the contest block—it is

tinted green—along with her signature, the date ("9-17 52"), and the inscription "To Lena."

Larry Evaristo, his wife, and son, were vacationing in California at that time and were staying at his parents' home. He recalled the events surrounding the contest in a letter to the authors:

"My wife, Wanda, read in the newspaper that Jane Wyman would be honored with a hand and footprint ceremony at the Chinese Theatre.

"Since Jane Wyman is my favorite actress, my wife teased me and said, 'We'd better go.' My father, Peter, was pessimistic, saying, 'Do you think you're going to get close enough to see her with the crowd that will be there?' We were determined to see her so my wife and I, our son, Michael, and my mother left early that evening for Hollywood.

"As we were looking at all the prints in front of the theatre, we were given tickets for a drawing of an inscribed concrete slab of Jane Wyman's prints.

"Came drawing time, and to our surprise, my mother held the winning ticket! Because of the large crowd, my mother and I were separated from my wife

The contest block.

and son. I didn't want to take the chance of looking for them, as I knew I wouldn't be able to get back into the little circle which included Wyman, Chinese Theatre manager Ralph Hathaway, my mother, and the photographers. In fact, I overheard someone ask, 'Who is that guy with her?,' meaning me. Someone else answered, 'That's her son.' At this point, I thought for sure that I was going to be asked to leave the group, but no one said anything. I was not about to miss this once in a lifetime opportunity to be near my favorite actress. I stood my ground. Not only was I photographed with Jane Wyman, but she leaned on my shoulder for support while she put her footprint in the cement replica. What a moment!

"After the ceremony, we were told to pick up the replica the following day when the cement would be dry.

"When I got up the following morning I had a recurring attack of arthritis in my shoulder and neck and I couldn't turn my head. My wife and mother teased me, 'Ah, Larry, see—you got a stiff neck because Jane Wyman leaned on your shoulder last night at the ceremony.' It was worth it!"

Contest winner Lena Evaristo (left), Jane Wyman, Evaristo's son Larry and the contest block.

Ava Gardner
Ceremony #98: October 21, 1952

She placed her prints in connection with the motion picture *The Snows of Kilimanjaro* (20th Century-Fox, 1952), and in celebration of the twenty-fifth anniversary of the Chinese Theatre.

Born: Ava Lavinnia Gardner in Grabtown, North Carolina, on December 24, 1922. Died: January 25, 1990.

Ava Gardner was considered by many the most beautiful film star of her generation. She was the youngest of six children. During her teens she studied secretarial skills and went to New York City in 1940 in search of a clerical job. Her married sister, Beatrice, was living there; and her husband, Larry Tarr, was a professional photographer who took scores of portraits of Ava. A display of these photos was noticed in a store window by a Metro-Goldwyn-Mayer legal department clerk, and soon thereafter Ava was given a screen test. She signed a contract with the studio in 1941.

Gardner was given extensive coaching in diction (to remove her Southern accent), grooming, and dramatics. Three years of walk-ons and bit parts followed until she was finally given a reasonably noticeable part in *Three Men in White* (1944). Her first major role came in *The Killers* (1946), and *The Hucksters* (1947) brought her major stardom. Soon Ava was Hollywood's number one sex symbol.

Gardner left MGM in 1959 and free-lanced. Her later performances often brought critical acclaim in such films as *On the Beach* (1959) and *The Night of the Iguana* (1964). She lived for a while in Spain and finally took up permanent residence in London, continuing to work whenever she was motivated.

Her motion picture credits include "Fancy Answers" (1941, short, debut), *Pandora and the Flying Dutchman* (1951), *Show Boat* (1951), **Mogambo* (1953), *The Barefoot Contessa* (1954), *Bhowani Junction* (1956), *The Sun Also Rises* (1957), *The Life and Times of Judge Roy Bean* (1972), *Earthquake* (1974), and *Regina* (1987, final film).

*Academy Award nomination: Best Actress.

Chinese Theatre manager Ralph Hathaway (left), Ava Gardner, and cement artist Jean W. Klossner. Gardner reminisced in her memoirs, "My name in a Cole Porter lyric, my footprints in concrete at Grauman's Chinese....As someone who's been there and back, what I'd really like to say about stardom is that it gave me everything I never wanted."

Gardner's square is tinted gray and contains the date ("Oct. 21, 52"), her two footprints (made with high heels), two handprints, and her signature.

Gardner shared her memories of her Chinese Theatre ceremony in a letter to the authors:

"I don't remember much about that day except that I was scared to death, as I always am at any public appearance. I do remember that I wanted to do the footprints barefoot, not because of the film, *The Barefoot Contessa*, but because I always like being barefoot, squelching mud or sand between my toes and as a child I was always barefoot whenever I could be."

Captain Dorothy McDowell (left) and Clifton Webb (kneeling). Others unidentified.

Clifton Webb
Ceremony #99: December 7, 1952

He placed his prints in connection with the motion picture *Stars and Stripes Forever* (20th Century-Fox, 1952).

Born: Webb Parmelee Hollenbeck in Indianapolis, Indiana, circa November 19, 1889 (sources vary on year). Died: October 13, 1966.

Surprisingly, although he enjoyed several decades of fame and success on the stage, Clifton Webb did not became a major film star until the mid-1940s when he was well into middle age. He was on the stage by age seven and at seventeen was singing grand opera. Next he became a highly accomplished dancer and rivaled Vernon Castle during World War I. During the 1920s he became a major star on Broadway. When he had spare time during the 1920s he made a few silent films.

Metro-Goldwyn-Mayer signed him to a contract in 1935 and brought him to Hollywood. However, Webb sat idle for eighteen months. He finally obtained a release from his contract and returned to Broadway, where he appeared in several more hits, the greatest of which was Noel Coward's *Blithe Spirit* (1941). He returned to Hollywood to co-star in **Laura* (1944) for 20th Century-Fox, where he eventually signed a long-term contract. Webb achieved major film stardom in ***Sitting Pretty* (1948) as Mr. Belvedere, the fastidious, decorous, literate bachelor who has to live with a middle-class couple and their children during the post-War housing shortage.

Throughout the 1950s Webb remained an important star, playing Belvedere in two sequels and essaying several other leading roles.

His motion picture credits include *National Red Cross Pageant* (1917, debut), *Polly with a Past* (1920), "The Still Alarm" (1930, short, talkie debut), **The Razor's Edge* (1946), *Cheaper by the Dozen* (1950), *Titanic* (1953), *Mr. Scoutmaster* (1953), *Three Coins in the Fountain* (1954), *The Remarkable Mr. Pennypacker* (1959), and *Satan Never Sleeps* (1962, final film).

> * *Academy Award nomination: Best Supporting Actor.*
> ** *Academy Award nomination: Best Actor.*

Webb's square is tinted red and contains the inscription "Stars and Stripes Forever." Also included are the date ("Dec-7-1952"), his two footprints, two handprints, and his signature.

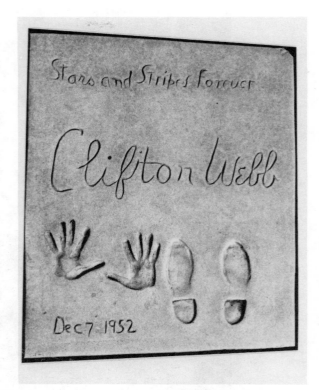

Webb was assisted at his ceremony by several members of the U.S. Marine Corps. The marines were on hand in honor of John Philip Sousa, American bandmaster and composer, who wrote over 100 marches, including "The Stars and Stripes Forever" in 1897. Sousa had learned to play band instruments as an apprentice to the U.S. Marine Band when his father was a member of it and later became the band's leader (1880-1892). Webb portrayed Sousa in the film *Stars and Stripes Forever*.

Olivia de Havilland
Ceremony #100: December 9, 1952

She placed her prints in connection with the motion picture *My Cousin Rachel* (20th Century-Fox, 1952).

Born: Olivia Mary de Havilland in Tokyo, Japan, on July 1, 1916.

Olivia de Havilland was one of Hollywood's most prestigious actresses during the 1940s and 1950s. She became interested in acting during high school in Saratoga, California, and then joined the Saratoga Community Players and was spotted in a local pro-

Olivia de Havilland.

duction of *A Midsummer Night's Dream* in 1934 by an assistant to famed director Max Reinhardt.

De Havilland was signed as the second understudy to Gloria Stuart, the actress playing Hermia, in Reinhardt's production of the play at the Hollywood Bowl that same year. Both Stuart and her first understudy dropped out of the production, and Olivia went on opening night.

She was soon under contract to Warner Bros. and reprised her role in Reinhardt's 1935 film version of the play. Shortly thereafter she was teamed with newcomer Errol Flynn in *Captain Blood* (1935), the first of her eight co-starring films with him. De Havilland wanted more serious roles and got her wish when she was loaned out to Selznick International Pictures for the role of Melanie Hamilton in **Gone With the Wind* (1939).

When her contract with Warners had run its seven-year course, de Havilland wanted to leave the studio but was informed she still owed Warners six months' time for the periods she had been on suspen-

sion. Olivia filed suit against Warners and was off the screen for nearly two years in a lengthy legal battle that culminated in a landmark court ruling in her favor in 1945, known as "The de Havilland Decision." Immediately thereafter, de Havilland proceeded to do the most distinguished work of her career, including ***The Snake Pit* (1948) and ****The Heiress* (1949). She made fewer films in the 1950s after she married *Paris Match* editor Pierre Galante and moved to France in 1955.

Her motion picture credits include *Alibi Ike* (1935, debut), *Anthony Adverse* (1936), *The Adventures of Robin Hood* (1938), *Dodge City* (1939), *The Strawberry Blonde* (1941), ***Hold Back the Dawn* (1941), *In This Our Life* (1942), ****To Each His Own* (1946), *Light in the Piazza* (1962), and *The 5th Musketeer* (1979).

* *Academy Award nomination: Best Supporting Actress.*
** *Academy Award nomination: Best Actress.*
*** *Academy Award winner: Best Actress.*

De Havilland's square is tinted green and contains the date ("Dec-9-1952"), her two footprints (made with high heels), two handprints, and her signature.

In a letter to the authors, de Havilland shared her memories of her ceremony:

"All I recall is that a friend of mine who worked with *Look* magazine at that time, and who later became press representative for Princess Grace [of Monaco], looked out of his office window and, seeing me there across the street, rushed out and invited me to lunch—an invitation which I accepted. His name is Rupert Allan and he was formerly with the State Department."

Adolph Zukor
Ceremony #101: January 5, 1953

He placed his prints in celebration of his fiftieth anniversary in the motion picture industry.

Born: in Riese, Hungary, on January 7, 1873. Died: June 10, 1976.

For many years during the teens and 1920s, pioneer film executive Adolph Zukor was the single most powerful individual in the motion picture industry. He emigrated to the United States in 1888 and by 1903 became fascinated with motion pictures. Zukor invested in penny arcades and by 1905 had advanced to owning some nickelodeons.

By 1910 he had developed a very strong feeling that the public would have an interest in films of greater length than the ubiquitous twelve- to sixteen- minute one-reelers. He felt that distinguished plays, with well-known actors, produced in four-reel or even six-reel lengths, would draw a strong public response. Toward that end, he founded the Famous Players Film Company in 1912, in association with Broadway impresario Daniel Frohman. The company's motto was "Famous Players in Famous Plays," and its policy was to produce only feature-length films.

Zukor's first Famous Players release, the imported *Queen Elizabeth* (1912), starring Sarah Bernhardt, was an enormous success, but by late 1913 Famous Players was in serious trouble. It was Zukor's fortuitous acquisition of Mary Pickford that turned the company around. He had to pawn his wife's jewelry to meet the production budget on Pickford's *Tess of the Storm Country* (1914), but the picture proved to be a smash and saved the studio.

The Paramount Pictures Corporation was formed in 1914 by W.W. Hodkinson to distribute the product of Famous Players and that of the Jesse L. Lasky Feature Play Company, which was founded in 1913. In 1916 Zukor and Lasky acquired fifty per cent of the stock in Paramount, and soon Hodkinson resigned. The two companies then merged to form the Famous Players-Lasky Corporation, with Zukor emerging as president, retaining the Paramount name for distribution purposes.

Zukor remained president until 1935, when the company reorganized as Paramount Pictures, Inc. Barney Balaban became president, and Zukor moved up to the position of chairman of the board.

In 1949 he received a Special Academy Award as "a man who has been called the father of the feature

Singer/actress Rosemary Clooney, who was then Paramount's newest star, Adolph Zukor, and Charles P. Skouras, president of Fox West Coast Theatres.

film in America, for his services to the industry over a period of forty years."

In 1973 Paramount threw an enormous 100th birthday party for Zukor at the Beverly Hilton Hotel.

Zukor's square is tinted gray and contains the inscription "Marking 50 Happy Year's [sic] In Motion Pictures." Also included are the date ("Jany-5th 1953"), his two footprints, two handprints, and his signature.

Zukor insisted on removing his good black shoes and substituted an old pair before he made his footprints. His ceremony at the Chinese Theatre was the first in a series of tributes paid to him during 1953.

Zukor was the man who encouraged Sid Grauman to move to Los Angeles from San Francisco to open movie "palaces" and aided Grauman with financial assistance at that time. He called Sid "the greatest practical joker of them all," and with good reason. H.

Allen Smith recounts the following story about Grauman and Zukor in his book *The Compleat Practical Joker*:

"[Grauman] walked into a meeting of Paramount's board of directors one day wearing overalls and carrying tools. He began tapping with a hammer on a radiator and before long the chairman, Adolph Zukor, was frowning. The tapping grew louder and pretty soon the plumber was whaling away with the hammer, defying Mr. Zukor's orders to leave, even threatening to give Mr. Zukor a couple of clouts on the skull.

"The other directors were about ready to gang [up on] him when he revealed his identity."

Zukor himself recalled in his memoirs, "I don't know how he [Grauman] got the idea of having movie people make footprints in his cement. I wouldn't have dared do it while Sid was alive. He'd have figured out a way to get me stuck in the cement."

Ezio Pinza
Ceremony #102: January 26, 1953

He placed his prints in connection with the motion picture *Tonight We Sing* (20th Century-Fox, 1953).

Born: Fortunato Pinza in Rome, Italy, on May 18, 1892. Died: May 9, 1957.

Ezio Pinza spent most of his career in grand opera, performing on the concert stage, and making recordings. Movies were rather an after-thought for him. His voice was generally classified as a *basso cantante*, although many baritone roles were easily within his range.

Pinza was eighteen when, after failing in his attempts to become a professional cross-country bicycle racer, his father took him to a voice teacher, explaining, "Since all you are good for as an athlete is singing in the shower, you might as well learn to sing right." In 1914 he joined a small opera company near Milan and made his professional debut as a Druid priest in Bellini's *Norma*.

He spent three years at La Scala under the direction of Arturo Toscanini and in 1926 made his first appearance at the Metropolitan Opera house in New York City, scoring an instant success. He remained there for twenty-two triumphant years, playing his last season in 1948. He then signed with Rodgers and Hammerstein to star opposite Mary Martin in their Broadway musical *South Pacific*, which opened in 1949 to ecstatic reviews and became one of the biggest hits in Broadway history.

Chinese Theatre manager Ralph Hathaway (left), Ezio Pinza, and cement artist Jean W. Klossner.

His enormous popular success in the play led to movie offers, which Pinza readily accepted. After his film work, he scored another Broadway hit in the musical *Fanny* (1954).

His motion picture credits include *Carnegie Hall* (1947, debut), *Strictly Dishonorable* (1951), *Mr. Imperium* (1951), and *Tonight We Sing* (1953, final film).

Pinza's square is tinted red and contains the inscription "'Tonight We Sing.'" Also included are the date ("Jan. 26-53"), his two footprints, two handprints, and his signature.

Jimmy Durante assisted Pinza at his ceremony and also placed an imprint of his nose in the Pinza square, not in profile but head-on, executed on the spur of the moment. Durante's nose print did not survive the fresh wet square through the drying process and cannot be seen in the hard block.

Effie O'Connor and Donald O'Connor
Ceremony #103: February 25, 1953

They placed their prints in connection with the motion picture *Call Me Madam* (20th Century-Fox, 1953), in which Donald starred.

Effie O'Connor

Born: Effie Irene Search in Decatur, Illinois, on February 13, 1889. Died: January 11, 1981.

The mother of entertainer Donald O'Connor, Effie O'Connor was a stage actress, circus performer, and vaudevillian. At age five she made her first professional appearance in a stage production of *Uncle Tom's Cabin* at Waycross, Georgia, in 1894. By age thirteen she found herself a "toe and tap dancer" in a carnival tent show and at that young age married John "Chuck" O'Connor, age twenty-five, who was an acrobat with the same outfit. The O'Connors had seven children, only three of whom survived—Jack, Billy, and Donald. They called themselves "The Royal Family of Vaudeville."

Chuck died on stage during the act in 1926 at age forty-seven, and thereafter Effie successfully managed the troupe and continued on the

Chinese Theatre manager Ralph Hathaway (left), cement artist Jean W. Klossner, Effie O'Connor and her son Donald.

boards, dancing and playing the piano. She retired from show business in 1940. The following year Donald signed a contract with Universal Pictures, where he remained for the next fourteen years; so the O'Connor family act disbanded.

Donald O'Connor

Born: Donald David Dixon Ronald O'Connor in Chicago, Illinois, on August 28, 1925.

An exceptionally versatile entertainer, Donald O'Connor was one of the most sprightly, breezy, and cheerful song-and-dance men during Hollywood's "Golden Age" of musicals. He was the seventh child of vaudevillian parents and was introduced into the family act at age one.

In 1938 Donald was spotted by a Paramount talent scout while giving a benefit performance at the Biltmore Hotel in Los Angeles. This led to a contract with Paramount, where his first role was with Bing Crosby in *Sing You Sinners* (1938). Soon after, when O'Connor entered adolescence, Paramount dropped him. He returned to the family act and performed on the road until 1941, when Universal offered him a contract. He became one of the studio's most successful stars. During the World War II years, Donald played in

Universal's teenage "jive" comedy/musicals, often opposite Peggy Ryan.

By 1950 O'Connor's career had slipped a bit, until he starred in *Francis* (1950), opposite the famous "talking" mule. The film was such a hit that O'Connor appeared in five sequels. Universal interspersed O'Connor's parts in the "Francis" films with roles in musicals and comedies, often on loan-out; and during the early 1950s, O'Connor did some of the work

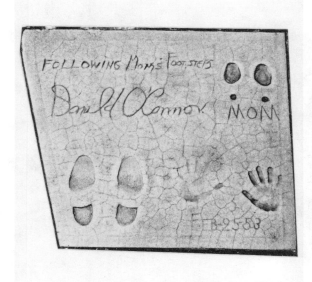

Donald O'Connor and his mother Effie.

for which he is best remembered in such hits as *Singin' in the Rain* (1952) and *There's No Business Like Show Business* (1954). Since the 1950s he has mainly concentrated on live stage and nightclub appearances.

His motion picture credits include *Melody for Two* (1937, debut), *Beau Geste* (1939), *Top Man* (1943), *Something in the Wind* (1947), *Curtain Call at Cactus Creek* (1950), *I Love Melvin* (1953), *Anything Goes* (1956), *The Buster Keaton Story* (1957), *Ragtime* (1981), and *Pandemonium* (1982).

The O'Connor/O'Connor square is tinted yellow and contains the date ("Feb-25-53"), Effie's two footprints, and her signature ("Mom"), Donald's inscription "Following Mom's Footsteps," his two footprints, two handprints, and his signature.

The plans for the ceremony were for Donald only to make his imprints, but when the event took place he insisted that his mother precede him, much to her surprise. When asked how she felt about it, Effie shook her head in wonderment and simply said, "My Donald—he's the best."

In a telephone conversation with the authors, O'Connor recalled that he and his mother had been good friends of Sid Grauman for many years, due to the O'Connor family's career in vaudeville when they worked in many theatres, including the Chinese.

Although Effie never made a movie, it was fitting that she placed her footprints along with those of her son due to her friendship with Grauman, her years in show business as an entertainer, and her membership in the Motion Picture Mothers organization. O'Connor says that, considering his mother's years as a circus performer, both of their careers on stage, and his own work in motion pictures, television, radio and recordings, their square is a complete record of all show business media.

Marilyn Monroe (left) and Jane Russell.

Jane Russell and Marilyn Monroe Ceremony #104: June 26, 1953

They placed their prints in connection with the motion picture *Gentlemen Prefer Blondes* (20th Century-Fox, 1953).

Jane Russell

Born: Ernestine Jane Geraldine Russell in Bemidji, Minnesota, on June 21, 1921.

From the very beginning of her film career in 1941, Jane Russell was hyped and exploited as a sort of aggressive sex symbol with frankly vulgar emphasis directed toward her body in general and her ample bustline in particular. Russell managed to somewhat overcome this one-sided approach to her screen image and often emerged as a warm, likable personality who could handle comic situations with verve and tongue-in-cheek humor.

In 1940 she was discovered by millionaire producer/director Howard Hughes, who signed her to a seven-year contract and cast her in his film about Billy the Kid, *The Outlaw* (debut), in 1940. The film caused a furor due to the photographic emphasis on Jane's upper anatomy and had only a brief run in San Francisco in 1943, another brief and limited release in 1946, and finally a New York opening in 1950. Hughes loaned her out to Paramount to appear opposite Bob Hope in *The Paleface* (1948), in which Jane surprised and delighted critics with her comic skills. *Gentlemen Prefer Blondes*, another loan-out, was her career high point; and she showed an impressive flair for both comedy and musical performance.

In 1955 Hughes renewed her contract, which stipulated that Russell receive $1,000 per week over the next twenty years, with a requirement to appear in five films either under his aegis or on loan-out. She later became a spokesperson for the Playtex company, touting a brassiere in television commercials designed "for us full-figure gals."

Her motion picture credits include *Young Widow* (1946), *His Kind of Woman* (1951), *Macao* (1952), *The French Line* (1954), *Underwater!* (1955), *The Tall Men* (1955), *Gentlemen Marry Brunettes* (1955), *The Revolt of Mamie Stover* (1956), *The Fuzzy Pink Nightgown* (1957), and *Darker Than Amber* (1970).

Russell's square is tinted gray and contains the inscription "Gentlemen Pr," which is the beginning of the title of the film *Gentlemen Prefer Blondes*. The "efer Blondes" is completed in Marilyn Monroe's square. Also included are the date ("6-26-53"), her two footprints (made with high heels), two handprints, and her signature.

Russell recalled the occasion when she and Monroe made their imprints at the Chinese Theatre in her memoirs:

"We were both wearing light, summery dresses and high heels as we posed, arms linked together, for the photographers. We were thrilled beyond words. While I was placing my feet in that square of soggy cement, I thought of all the times when Pat Alexander [a friend of Russell's since their freshman days in high school] and I tried to fit our feet in the footprints of famous actresses and how we figured that they must have worn the tiniest shoes for the occasion. Our feet never fit in. Now my prints were in that cement and I couldn't believe it. I'm sure Marilyn felt the same. Always one for personal comfort, I was wearing my usual big shoes, so no aspiring actress will have any trouble whatsoever getting her feet into my footprints!"

Marilyn Monroe (left) and Jane Russell. Marilyn later confessed that the ceremony made her feel "anything's possible." Mann Theatre Corporation reports that the imprints of Monroe and John Wayne are the most photographed squares in the forecourt.

Marilyn Monroe

Born: Norma Jeane Mortenson in Los Angeles, California, on June 1, 1926. Died: August 5, 1962.

More than any other motion picture personality of earlier generations, Marilyn Monroe seems the most strongly, indelibly, and universally imbedded in the present-day consciousness. Her image appears virtually everywhere, and she remains the most potent symbolic national icon of the phrase "movie star." Film historian Ephraim Katz wrote, "She exuded breathless sensuality that was at once erotic and wholesome, invitingly real and appealingly funny."

Monroe was generally neglected as a child, and her escape from reality became the movies. During World War II Marilyn worked as a paint sprayer in a defense plant and broke into modeling on the side. Howard Hughes saw her photos and was about to make a screen test of her, but 20th Century-Fox beat him to the punch when it signed her to a contract in August 1946. After a year of some extra work and unbilled bits, including *Scudda-Hoo! Scudda-Hay!* (1948), Fox dropped her. Her first really important work came in a supporting role in Metro-Goldwyn-Mayer's *The Asphalt Jungle* (1950).

Fox re-signed her to a seven-year contract in 1951. After she appeared in a succession of supporting parts, they cast her in her first starring role, *Niagara* (1953), which led to the two lavish comedies that firmly established her stardom: *Gentlemen Prefer Blondes* and *How To Marry a Millionaire* (both 1953). She followed them with the smash hit *The Seven Year Itch* (1955).

Marilyn started to reject purely sex-symbol roles and fled to New York City, where she became determined to become a "serious" actress and studied with the Strasbergs at the Actors Studio. Her return to Hollywood in *Bus Stop* (1956) was a critical triumph. By this point Monroe's personal demons had begun to take over her life. By the time she starred in the hit comedy *Some Like It Hot* (1959), she sometimes needed literally dozens of takes to get through a scene. Amazingly, her difficulties are undetectable in the final product.

Director Billy Wilder probably summed up her unique and natural charisma best when he commented, "God gave her everything. The first day a photographer took a picture of her she was a genius."

Her motion picture credits include *Ladies of the Chorus* (1948), *All about Eve* (1950), *Clash by Night* (1952), *Don't Bother To Knock* (1952), *Monkey Business* (1952), *River of No Return* (1954), *There's No Business Like Show Business* (1954), *The Prince and the Showgirl* (1957), *Let's Make Love* (1960), and *The Misfits* (1961, final film).

Monroe's square is tinted yellow—or, in her case, blonde—and contains the inscription "efer Blondes," which is the completion of the title of the film *Gentlemen Prefer Blondes* that was begun in Jane Russell's square. Also included are the date ("6-26-53"), her two footprints (made with high heels), two hand-prints, and her signature.

Monroe embedded a rhinestone in the cement to dot the "i" in "Marilyn." It has since been pried out. In its place is a piece of white frosted glass.

The ceremony drew the largest attendance up to that time. Marilyn told the spectators who gathered, "It [the film] is *Gentlemen Prefer Blondes*, and I am the blonde."

Monroe remembered attending many Saturday matinees at the Chinese Theatre when she was a little girl. Over the years, a quote attributed to Marilyn has surfaced time and time again: "I used to try and fit my hands and feet in the stars' prints. The only ones that fit were Rudolph Valentino's." While it's true that she did visit the theatre, Valentino's prints were not the "ones that fit." He died in 1926, nearly a year prior to the opening of the Chinese Theatre and the origin of the footprint ceremonies.

Marilyn felt that she and Jane Russell should leave imprints other than those of their hands and feet, since the prints were to reflect your public personality:

"I suggested that Jane lean over the wet cement and that I sit down in it and we could leave our prints that way, but my idea was vetoed. After that I suggested that Grauman's use a diamond to dot the 'i' in the 'Marilyn' I scratched in the wet concrete. They finally compromised on dotting it with a rhinestone, but some sightseer chiseled that rhinestone out."

The diamond idea was a reference to her hit song, "Diamonds Are a Girl's Best Friend," from the film.

In a 1960 interview with Georges Belmont, Marilyn was somewhat reflective and recalled being shuttled around from one foster home to another as a child in Los Angeles and Hollywood, including a stay with an English family. She said:

"Through them I learned a lot about the movies. I wasn't even eight. They used to take me to one of the big movie theatres in Hollywood, the Egyptian or Grauman's Chinese. I used to watch the monkeys in the cages outside the Egyptian, all alone, and...I could never get my feet in [the footprints at the Chinese] because my shoes were too big....It's funny to think that *my* footprints are there now, and that other little girls are trying to do the same thing I did."

Her friend, columnist Sidney Skolsky, wrote shortly after her death:

"I read how Marilyn had looked longingly many times at the footprints—especially those of Jean Harlow. She wished and hoped that someday her footprints would be here. I read that she waited two days and two nights for her footprints to dry—and the wooden fence [placed around the wet prints to protect them] taken down. The second night, about two a.m., Marilyn got out of her brass bed, walked from her apartment [near the Chinese Theatre], and, with no one watching her, she stood in her footprints—alone. It was like hearing all the applause in the world."

The Chinese Theatre was remodeled for the engagement of The Robe *(1953). One of the honored guests at the film's premiere was Professor Henri Chrétien, who invented the prototype of the CinemaScope lens in 1927.*

CinemaScope, The Robe (1953), and Jean Simmons
Ceremony #105: September 24, 1953

Simmons placed her prints in connection with the motion picture *The Robe* (20th Century-Fox, 1953). The picture itself and the CinemaScope wide-screen process in which it was shot received an honorary plaque.

CinemaScope

When the influence of television, among various other factors, began having a significantly detrimental effect on movie theatre attendance in the late 1940s and early 1950s, the film industry needed something new, impressive, and dramatic in order to reclaim its dwindling audiences. The idea of a wide-screen process was quickly suggested toward serving that purpose. Cinerama was introduced in 1952; but because it was an expensive and complicated process—three projectors running simultaneously in three separate projection booths, each one with its own projectionist—it was seen only in a few major cities. 3-D also came and went, initially attracting large audiences, but only briefly, as its novelty soon wore thin.

Finally, CinemaScope came to the fore when *The Robe* was given its world premiere at the Roxy Theatre in New York City on September 16, 1953. The camera used a special anamorphic lens while shooting which compressed—or "squeezed"—the image onto standard 35mm film; when projected through another anamorphic lens the image was "unsqueezed" so that

The Robe. *Released by 20th Century-Fox (1953).*

it expanded to fill a screen roughly 2-1/2 times wider than its height.

After some initial refinement, the process achieved better photographic definition and less image distortion. Since 35mm film stock was used, theatre exhibitors had to buy the special anamorphic lenses which were attached to their existing projectors. And they also had to install a new CinemaScope screen as well as stereophonic sound equipment. Theatres which equipped themselves for CinemaScope retained the flexibility of being able to show standard format films when desired. Public response was so favorable that by November 1954 some 9,000 theatres in the U.S. and Canada were able to screen CinemaScope prints; by mid-1955 20,682 theatres throughout the globe had that capability.

The CinemaScope lens, manufactured in the U.S. by Bausch & Lomb, was invented in France by Henri Chrétien in 1927. Great Britain's Rank Organization had an option on the use of the lens, and when it expired 20th Century-Fox picked it up. The Fox organization subsequently licensed it to other studios. By the end of 1953, every major studio with the exception of Paramount, which had its own process called VistaVision, was licensed to use CinemaScope.

CinemaScope was the focus of two Academy Awards in 1954: an Honorary Award, "To 20th Century-Fox Film Corporation in recognition of their imagination, showmanship and foresight in introducing the revolutionary process known as CinemaScope;" and a Scientific or Technical Award (Class I), "To Professor Henri Chrétien and Earl Sponable, Sol Halprin, Lorin Grignon, Herbert Gragg and Carl Faulkner of 20th Century-Fox Studios for creating, developing and engineering the equipment, process and techniques known as CinemaScope."

Other processes and gimmicks came about after the debut of CinemaScope, including Todd-AO, Smell-o-Vision, AromaRama, etc. During the 1960s several spectacular, major budget films, such as *The Sound of Music* (1965), were filmed in 70mm and road-showed in that format in major cities. (Even *Gone With the Wind* [1939] was reformatted in 70mm for rerelease in 1967.) The Panavision process ultimately supplanted CinemaScope.

The Robe
(20th Century-Fox, 1953)

Based on the 1942 best-selling novel by Lloyd C. Douglas, *The Robe* is a fictional story of Marcellus Gallio, a Roman centurion, who wins Christ's robe in a dice game while its owner hangs dying on the cross. Marcellus and Diana, the woman he loves, become Christian converts shortly after the Crucifixion and test their new-found faith when they are condemned to death by the mad emperor, Caligula, at the film's end. The picture was produced by Frank Ross, directed by Henry Koster, and starred Richard Burton, Jean Simmons, Victor Mature, Jay Robinson, and Richard Boone. Philip Dunne wrote the screenplay and Gina Kaus adapted the novel. The musical score was by Alfred Newman.

The film broke box-office records; on its opening day at the Roxy Theatre it grossed an all-time high of approximately $35,000, which was both a premiere day and a one-day record in the twenty-six year history of the Roxy.

Richard Burton recalled that during shooting, "I was told, 'When in doubt, look towards heaven. Be pious.'"

John C. Carlisle wrote in 1981, *The Robe* "...is more important today as the first film in CinemaScope than as a film whose content or directorial style make it memorable."

The Robe received two Oscars in 1954 for Art Direction-Set Decoration (Color) and Costume Design (Color). It was also nominated for Oscars in the following categories: Best Picture, Best Actor, and Best Cinematography (Color).

Jean Simmons

Born: Jean Merilyn Simmons in London, England, on January 31, 1929.

Jean Simmons has long been considered one of the best film actresses in the history of the medium. Delicately beautiful, sensitive, and possessed of a mellifluous speaking voice, she brought rare depth and subtlety to her characterizations. At fourteen she was enrolled at the Aida Foster School of Dancing, was noticed by a film talent scout, and given a small role in *Give Us the Moon* (1944, debut). J. Arthur Rank placed her under contract, and she was soon cast as the young Estella in David Lean's *Great Expectations* (1946). Laurence Olivier was impressed by her performance and cast her as Ophelia in his film of **Hamlet* (1948), which elevated Simmons to stardom. Rank soon sold Simmons' contract to Howard Hughes.

In Hollywood she appeared in generally mediocre films for Hughes' RKO studios. Simmons sued Hughes to get out of her contract and next went to 20th Century-Fox. Free-lancing by the late 1950s, Simmons appeared in such popular films as *The Big Country* (1958), *Spartacus*, and *Elmer Gantry* (both 1960). In the 1970s she toured very successfully in the musical play *A Little Night Music*. Her television appearances include the mini-series "The Thorn Birds" (1983) and the TV movie "Great Expectations" (1989)—not as Estella, of course, but as the eccentric Miss Havisham. Simmons next appeared as Elizabeth Collins Stoddard, matriarch of the Collins family, in the prime-time Gothic soap opera "Dark Shadows" (1991). The role was originally played by Joan Bennett during the run of the popular five-day-a-week daytime series (1966-1971).

Her motion picture credits include *Black Narcissus* (1947), *The Blue Lagoon* (1949), *Angel Face* (1953), *Young Bess* (1953), *The Actress* (1953), *Desiree* (1954), *Footsteps in the Fog* (1955), *Guys and Dolls* (1955), ***The Happy Ending* (1969), and *Going Undercover* (1988).

> * *Academy Award nomination: Best Supporting Actress.*
> ** *Academy Award nomination: Best Actress.*

Simmons' square, which also honors *The Robe* and the CinemaScope process in which the film was shot, is tinted gray and contains Simmons' inscription "In Appreciation." Also included are her two footprints (made with high heels), two handprints, and her signature. The plaque honoring CinemaScope and *The Robe* is in the upper center of the square and contains the inscription:

> In Commemoration Of
> The First CinemaScope
> Picture, "The Robe,"
> Premiered At Grauman's
> Chinese Theatre On
> September 24, 1953.
>
> Goodwin J. Knight [signature]
> Lieutenant Governor
> State Of California

The Chinese Theatre was refurbished for the premiere of *The Robe*. The interior boasted a new CinemaScope screen, seats, draperies, and carpets; the exterior featured a majestic neon sign which swept across the forecourt heralding the CinemaScope process and *The Robe*. It was the first frontal marquee in the history of the theatre. A large illuminated sign, used for advertising the current attraction, stood in the lot on the east side of the building facing Hollywood Boulevard in the 1930s and 1940s. The CinemaScope marquee was mounted

on a lattice-type structure with Chinese ornamentation. The sign was sixty-five feet long and forty feet high, and its bottom was sixteen feet above the forecourt. The theatre had been chosen by 20th Century-Fox as the permanent Southland showcase for Fox's releases. The marquee was ultimately dismantled in 1958.

Jean Simmons.

Danny Thomas
Ceremony #106: January 26, 1954

Born: Muzyad Yakhoob (later changed to Amos Jacobs) in Deerfield, Michigan, on January 6, 1914. Died: February 6, 1991.

Motion pictures were never an integral part of the career of Danny Thomas, who became one of America's most beloved comedians by virtue of his popular television series, "Make Room for Daddy," later called "The Danny Thomas Show," which ran for eleven consecutive seasons (1953-1964).

He quit high school at sixteen, determined to make it in show business. After years of struggling without much success, he was about to give up; but a turning point came in 1940 when he was booked into the 5100 Club in Chicago, where he developed a huge city-wide following. In 1944 a thirty-nine week stint on Fanny Brice's radio show brought him national recognition.

Between 1947 and 1952 Thomas made five Hollywood films while continuing on the night-club circuit and on radio. By that time he was con-vinced that his brightest future lay in the growing television medium. His TV series was one of the most popular programs during its run.

Thomas and Sheldon Leonard formed T & L Productions, which was responsible for such programs as "The Andy Griffith Show" (1960-1968) and "The Dick Van Dyke Show" (1961-1966). Much of his time during the last thirty years of his life was dedicated to his tireless charitable fund-raising efforts in support of the St. Jude Children's Research Hospital of Memphis, Tennessee, which opened in 1962. Thomas was the key figure responsible for the establishment of the facility.

His motion picture credits include *The Unfinished Dance* (1947, debut), *Big City* (1948), *Call Me Mister* (1951), *I'll See You in My Dreams* (1951), *The Jazz Singer* (1952), *Looking for Love* (1964, cameo), and *Don't Worry, We'll Think of a Title* (1966, cameo, final film).

Thomas' square is tinted gray and contains the date ("Jan 26-1954"), his two footprints, two handprints, and his signature, plus the drawing of a Maltese cross.

Pope Pius XII had recently issued a Bulla (an apostolic letter containing an important pronouncement by the Pope) making Thomas, who was a Roman Catholic, a Knight of Malta; therefore, Thomas imprinted the cross. The Knights of Malta is a Catholic charitable organization especially devoted to the care of the sick and the wounded.

Danny Thomas and his wife Rose Marie.

James Mason
Ceremony #107: March 30, 1954

He placed his prints in connection with the motion picture *Prince Valiant* (20th Century-Fox, 1954).

Born: James Neville Mason in Huddersfield, England, on May 15, 1909. Died: July 27, 1984.

James Mason was a superb, authoritative, and intelligent actor. Although he studied architecture at Cambridge University, he decided to try acting when it became evident that very few buildings were being erected during the Depression years of the early 1930s.

After several repertory touring roles, some parts at the Old Vic (1933-1934), and a season (1934-1935) at the Gate Theatre in Dublin, he made his movie debut in 1935 in *The Late Extra*. *The Man in Grey* (1943) made Mason a star and established a persona that was to remain his trademark for several years: that of a ruthless but romantic, sometimes sadistic villain, whose sexuality women nonetheless found irresistible.

Another huge success came with *The Seventh Veil* (1945), which made Mason internationally famous. *Odd Man Out* (1947) brought him his greatest critical acclaim up to that time, and Hollywood became seriously interested in him.

He made his American film debut in *Caught* (1949) and found major critical praise and popularity in Hollywood in such films as *The Desert Fox* (1951), *Julius Caesar* (1953), **A Star Is Born* (1954), and *20,000 Leagues under the Sea* (1954).

From the mid-1950s on, the quality of his films was checkered; but his performances continued to delight audiences.

His motion picture credits include *Fire over England* (1937), *The Wicked Lady* (1945), *Pandora and the Flying Dutchman* (1951), *Five Fingers* (1952), *The Prisoner of Zenda* (1952), *North by Northwest* (1959), *Lolita* (1962), **Georgy Girl* (1966), **The Verdict* (1982), and *The Shooting Party* (1985, final film).

   * *Academy Award nomination: Best Supporting Actor.*
   ** *Academy Award nomination: Best Actor.*

Mason's square is tinted green and contains the inscription "Prince Valiant." Also included are the date ("3-30-54"), his two footprints, two handprints, and his signature.

Mason recalled his ceremony in his memoirs:

"*Prince Valiant* was given a proper Hollywood premiere at Grauman's Chinese Theatre....I had always supposed that it was only the feet of the *enormously* famous that were imprinted on these flag-stones, and now I found that I was to be so immortalized merely because I had top billing on a film....A bit of a let-down I thought—I mean for the public and the Hollywood idolaters—no let-down for me, since I would happily have grabbed any distinction offered to me."

Three of the stars of Prince Valiant *(1954): Janet Leigh, James Mason, and Victor McLaglen.*

Alan Ladd
Ceremony #108: May 12, 1954

Born: Alan Walbridge Ladd in Hot Springs, Arkansas, on September 3, 1913. Died: January 29, 1964.

Alan Ladd projected a tough-guy demeanor that was, as writer Frank Thompson has pointed out, "...precisely appropriate for the dark side of the forties." Ladd enrolled in an actor training program at Universal studios in 1932, remained four months, but was used only in a bit in *Once in a Lifetime* (1932, debut) and then dropped. By 1936 he was working as a grip at Warner Bros. and getting occasional bit parts and extra work.

Ladd had many acting jobs on KFWB radio, on which he was heard by former actress-turned-agent Sue Carol, who summoned him, sight unseen, for an interview because of his impressive voice. As soon as Carol saw him she had a strong hunch he was star material. She signed him in 1939 and spent the next two years persistently pushing Ladd all over Hollywood. They married in 1942.

Ladd's career turning point came that same year as the paid killer in *This Gun for Hire*, the first of four pictures opposite Veronica Lake. Paramount signed him to a long-term contract, and from then on Ladd was a major star and a gold mine for the studio. He spent the rest of his career mainly in rugged action and adventure vehicles but some-

times kidded his own image and still scored big hits in such films as *Lucky Jordan* (1943) and *Duffy's Tavern* (1945).

The critical and popular high point of his career came with George Stevens' classic Western, *Shane* (1953).

His motion picture credits include *The Glass Key* (1942), *China* (1943), *Salty O'Rourke* (1945), *The Blue Dahlia* (1946), *Saigon* (1948), *The Great Gatsby* (1949), *Captain Carey, U.S.A.* (1950), *The Iron Mistress* (1952), *The Proud Rebel* (1958), and *The Carpetbaggers* (1964, final film).

Ladd's square is tinted green and contains the date ("May 12-1954-"), his two footprints, two handprints, and his signature.

On the occasion of his ceremony, Ladd was accompanied by his wife, Sue Carol Ladd, and two of their children, Alana and David.

The caption on the ceremony photo begins: "Alan Ladd, as a boy, was in the forecourt of Grauman's Chinese Theatre for the opening day ceremonies. Alan...looked longingly at the stars, at the footprints and dreamed that some day he might join that great galaxy...."

Alan Ladd. His son, actor/producer David Ladd, told the authors that each of the Ladd family members who had attended the ceremony was allowed to help at the event in some small way.

Edmund Purdom
Ceremony #109: August 30, 1954

He placed his prints in connection with the motion picture *The Egyptian* (20th Century-Fox, 1954). His square is no longer in the forecourt (see below). It was located in what is now #56 on this book's Forecourt of the Stars map. Today the space is occupied by Yul Brynner's square.

Born: Edmund Anthony Cutlar Purdom in Welwyn Garden City, England, circa December 19, 1924 (sources vary on year).

A handsome and intelligent actor, Edmund Purdom enjoyed only a brief career at the top in Hollywood during the mid-1950s. He left college at nineteen and broke into the theatre, joining the Northampton Repertory Company. He was spotted by Laurence Olivier and Vivien Leigh, who gave him a big break by casting him in their 1951 stage productions of *Antony and Cleopatra* and *Caesar and Cleopatra*, in which Purdom appeared in both London and New York.

In 1952 he came to Hollywood and lived in poverty for several months in a tiny garage apartment while he sought film work. After a small part in MGM's *Julius Caesar* (1953), the studio signed him to a contract. The turning point in his career came when he was asked to step in as *The Student Prince* (1954) for Mario Lanza, who was removed from the cast due to his considerable gain in weight. Lanza's singing voice was used on the soundtrack, but Purdom's own good looks and talent were favorably noticed. Soon he replaced another star—this time Marlon Brando—as *The Egyptian* (1954) for Fox.

Edmund Purdom, star of The Egyptian *(1954), which premiered at the Chinese Theatre the following evening, and Eleanor Powell. Someone joked that there was no truth to the rumor that a picture entitled* The Chinese *was going to play down the block at Grauman's Egyptian Theatre!*

After making several more films, Purdom's Hollywood career ended at the close of 1955. The reasons for his demise in Hollywood perhaps can be traced in part to his own personality and conduct. He was widely described as arrogant, egotistical, and outspoken; he alienated the press and received exceptionally unfavorable publicity when he divorced his wife, leaving her with their two little daughters, while he allegedly was having an affair with actress Linda Christian, who was then married to Tyrone Power.

Purdom left Hollywood in 1956. He has continued working in European films and has found roles in both television movies and mini-series, such as "Sophia Loren: Her Own Story" (1980) and "The Winds of War" (1983).

His motion picture credits include *Titanic* (1953, debut), *Athena* (1954), *The Prodigal* (1955), *The King's Thief* (1955), *I cosacchi* (1959, a.k.a. *The Cossacks*), *Moment of Danger* (1960, a.k.a. *Malaga*), *Nefertite, regina del Nilo* (1962, a.k.a. *Queen of the Nile* (1962), *The Yellow Rolls-Royce* (1965), *Witchcraft '70* (1970, a.k.a. *Angeli bianchi...angeli neri*), and *Padroni della città* (1977, a.k.a. *Mister Scarface.*).

Purdom's square contained the inscription "'The Egyptian.'" Also included were the date ("8-30-54"), his two footprints, two handprints, and his signature.

Purdom's ceremony was a part of the Hollywood Chamber of Commerce's first annual Greater Movie Season observance, and a "Footprint Luncheon" was held in the Blossom Room of the Hollywood Roosevelt Hotel on the day he placed his prints. Among the guests of honor were several celebrities who had placed their foot and handprints in the forecourt over the years. Those who attended included Edward Arnold, Bebe Daniels, Jimmy Durante, Jean Hersholt, William Lundigan, Victor McLaglen, Louella O. Parsons, Eleanor Powell, George Raft, the Ritz Brothers, Jean Simmons, Shirley Temple, Danny Thomas, and Clifton Webb. After lunch they toured the Chinese Theatre forecourt.

Later that evening, Purdom's footprint ceremony took place. Almost immediately, controversy ensued over Purdom's inclusion in the forecourt. Hedda Hopper reported in her Los Angeles *Times* column the following day:

"An irate citizen of Hollywood phoned to say she was burned up about Edmund Purdom's getting his footprints into the Grauman's Chinese forecourt. She said, 'I thought this was an honor that had to be earned. When visitors come here they expect to see the footprints and handprints of the stars they have loved over the years—the really great ones who de-

Purdom's square is no longer in the forecourt (see text).

serve it. Haven't we any Americans who have earned the honor?'"

The following year, Purdom told a magazine interviewer that he had not wanted to place his prints in the first place. He refused, only to be coerced by the studio publicity department into changing his mind. Upset by the hostile public outcry brought about by his ceremony, he thought it best not to attend *The Egyptian* premiere the evening after his footprint ceremony. The following day Los Angeles *Examiner* columnist Dorothy Manners reported that Purdom was unable to attend "due to illness."

It's possible that the theatre was pressured into the Purdom ceremony. A Mann Theatres press release regarding the footprints in the late 1970s contained the following bit of information about the Purdom square, although he was not mentioned by name:

"There is an apocryphal story dating from the all-powerful studio days which says a big studio insisted one of their players had to be footprinted. The management [of the theatre] under terrific pressure finally bowed, but after a suitable time lapse the offending prints were quietly removed. So goes the tale."

There is also another possibility as to why his square disappeared without official explanation: an executive in the Fox West Coast Theatre organization decreed that Purdom should be removed on "moral grounds," as he had become romantically involved with Linda Christian, who at the time was married to Tyrone Power. The affair caused a quite considerable scandal.

Sidney Skolsky wrote in his *Citizen-News* column on December 8, 1961, that Purdom:

"...has the hush-hush position of the only star [sic—not true, there were others] to have his footprints removed from the forecourt. After Purdom starred in *The Egyptian*, replacing Marlon Brando, Purdom's footprints were placed with such greats as Bing Crosby, Cary Grant, Lana Turner, Shirley Temple, etc. Then, after Purdom became the industry's bad boy and left town for Europe, the block of stone with his footprints was removed quietly one morning between 2 and 3 a.m. No one missed it until the morning of Natalie Wood's footprint ceremony [December 5, 1961], when I asked, 'What happens to the footprints of a star who is practically run out of town?' and I mentioned Rex Harrison and Edmund Purdom. Harrison's are still there—I guess they've grown accustomed to his feet—but Purdom's have vanished."

Van Heflin.

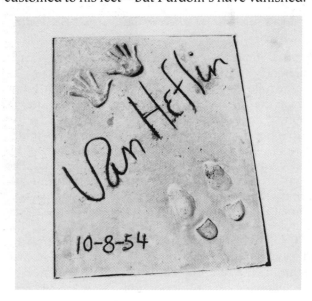

Van Heflin
Ceremony #110: October 8, 1954

He placed his prints in connection with the motion picture *Woman's World* (20th Century-Fox, 1954).

Born: Emmett Evan Heflin, Jr., in Walters, Oklahoma, on December 13, 1910. Died: July 23, 1971.

Van Heflin was rightly considered one of the finest character actors on the American screen. In his boyhood he developed a love of the sea and after high school sailed out of Long Beach, California, and traveled throughout the Pacific. He was living in New York in 1928 and, through a chance meeting with playwright Channing Pollock, made his acting debut in the play *Mr. Moneypenny* (1928), which folded after sixty-one performances.

Heflin went back to the sea for three years but in 1931 became serious about acting and joined the Hedgerow Players in Philadelphia, went to the Yale Drama School, and played a season of stock in Denver. He was spotted by Katharine Hepburn in the Broadway play *End of Summer* (1936), and she suggested Heflin for her film *A Woman Rebels* (1936, debut). In 1939 Heflin's performance opposite Hepburn in the Broadway play *The Philadelphia Story* brought him into star-level prominence.

He signed a long-term contract with Metro-Goldwyn-Mayer in 1941 and scored a sensational success in **Johnny Eager* (1942). He began free-lancing in films in 1950 but found his greatest personal fulfillment and critical acclaim on the stage.

His motion picture credits include *Santa Fe Trail* (1940), *The Feminine Touch* (1941), *Kid Glove Killer* (1942), *Tennessee Johnson* (1943), *The Strange Love of Martha Ivers* (1946), *Green Dolphin Street* (1947), *Madame Bovary* (1949), *Shane* (1953), *Battle Cry* (1955), and *Airport* (1970, final film).

*Academy Award winner: Best Supporting Actor.

Heflin's square is tinted yellow and contains the date ("10-8-54"), his two footprints, two handprints, and his signature.

George Murphy
Ceremony #111: November 8, 1954

Born: George Lloyd Murphy in New Haven, Connecticut, on July 4, 1902. Died: May 3, 1992.

Although George Murphy appeared in dozens of Hollywood films, first as a tap-dancing musical star and later in light romances and dramas, he achieved lasting fame as a result of his public relations efforts on behalf of the film industry and his political activities within the Republican Party, which ultimately resulted in his election as a U.S. Senator from California in 1964.

Murphy attended Yale University but dropped out in his junior year and found work as a runner on Wall Street in New York. He fell in love with dancer Julie Johnson, married her in 1926, and as a result learned to hoof and entered show business as her partner. Murphy went on to appear in several hit Broadway musicals, including *Hold Everything* (1929), *Of Thee I Sing* (1931), and *Roberta* (1933). In Hollywood he was signed by producer Samuel Goldwyn and appeared in *Kid Millions* (1934, debut). Murphy was next awarded a long-term contract with Metro-Goldwyn-Mayer.

By the end of the 1940s, Murphy's involvement with industry and political organizations had overshadowed his career as an actor, and he began to emerge as a sort of unofficial industry-wide spokesperson and ambassador of good will. As a result of all his public relations and political work, Murphy retired from acting in 1952.

His motion picture credits include *Broadway Melody of 1938* (1937), *Little Miss Broadway* (1938),

Broadway Melody of 1940 (1940), *Two Girls on Broadway* (1940), *Little Nellie Kelly* (1940), *Tom, Dick, and Harry* (1941), *For Me and My Gal* (1942), *Bataan* (1942), *Cynthia* (1947), and *Talk about a Stranger* (1952, final film).

In 1951 he received an Honorary Academy Award "for his services in interpreting the film industry to the country at large."

Murphy's square is tinted green and contains the

Theatre chain executive Edwin F. Zabel (left), George Murphy, and General Omar Bradley.

date ("11-8-54"), his two footprints, two handprints, and his signature.

Murphy was assisted at his ceremony by General Omar Bradley, National Chairman of the United Defense Fund. He presented Murphy with a gold medal for the Armed Forces' appreciation of Hollywood entertainers. At that time Murphy was president of the Hollywood Coordinating Committee and had acquired the title "Hollywood's Ambassador of Good Will." Murphy received the medal on behalf of the 2,800 entertainers in the film industry who had given more than 21,000 shows overseas under the Hollywood Coordinating Committee's banner.

Years before, Murphy and his wife were among the crowd that gathered outside the theatre for the premiere of *Hell's Angels* (1930). Murphy recalled in his memoirs:

"All of Hollywood seemed aglow with lights for the occasion, from the Hollywood Hills clear to the Boulevard, and literally hundreds of arc lights swept the sky in a rainbow of colors....It was then I realized the enormous power of the screen and its hold on the imaginations of millions of people all over the world. Many years later, when I became a motion picture industry spokesman, I did all I could to help steer that power toward worthwhile ends. I think that I may have succeeded, at least to a degree. As a matter of fact, I still believe films are the most powerful influence, properly used, in the entire world."

Yul Brynner and Deborah Kerr Ceremony #112: March 22, 1956

They placed their prints in connection with the motion picture *The King and I* (20th Century-Fox, 1956).

Yul Brynner

Born: either Taidje Khan or Youl Bryner in either Vladivostok or Elizabetsk, Russia, or on the Russian island of Sakhalin, on either July 7,11, or 12, in 1915, 1917, or 1920 or...? (sources vary on name, location, date, and year). Died: October 10, 1985.

Yul Brynner's baldness became his trademark; and his handsome Eurasian looks and bold, authoritative, exotic, and sometimes sinister personality made him a unique figure in stage and screen history. He spent his boyhood years in Peking, China. By age thirteen he lived in Paris, France, where he earned his way by singing and playing the balalaika and serving as an acrobat and trapeze artist with a circus. In 1934 he became an apprentice actor with the Pitoeff company in Paris. By 1941 he had arrived in America and made his U.S. stage debut with the Michael Chekhov company in *Twelfth Night*.

A big break came in 1946 when he landed a role opposite Mary Martin in the musical *Lute Song* on Broadway. In 1949 he became a television director and sometime actor at CBS. Brynner co-starred with Gertrude Lawrence in the Rodgers and Hammerstein Broadway musical *The King and I* (1951), one of the century's biggest stage successes. His performance in the film version of **The King and I* (1956) made him one of Hollywood's hottest personalities for the next several years; and other screen hits included *The Ten*

Commandments, Anastasia (both 1956), and *The Magnificent Seven* (1960).

His screen popularity declined during the 1960s and 1970s, but his success on stage in revivals of *The King and I* proved him indestructible. From his opening as the King in 1951, Brynner played the part for

Yul Brynner, in full costume for his role of the King, on the set of The King and I *(1956), makes his imprints for the Chinese Theatre. The reason this event did not take place at the theatre is unknown.*

Deborah Kerr, in full costume for her role of Anna, on the 20th Century-Fox studios lot during production of The King and I *(1956), makes her imprints for the Chinese Theatre. The reason this event did not take place at the theatre is unknown.*

four consecutive years and starred in several long-running revivals throughout the globe until June 30, 1985, at the Broadway Theatre, when he took his last curtain call after 4,625 performances as the monarch.

His motion picture credits include *Port of New York* (1949, debut), *The Brothers Karamazov* (1958), *The Buccaneer* (1958), *The Journey* (1959), *The Sound and the Fury* (1959), *Solomon and Sheba* (1959), *Taras Bulba* (1962), *The Madwoman of Chaillot* (1969), *Westworld* (1973), and *Con la rabbia agli occhi* (1976, a.k.a. *Death Rage*, final film).

Academy Award winner: Best Actor.

Brynner's square is tinted gray and contains the inscription "The King," which is the beginning of the title of the film *The King and I*. The "and I" is com-pleted in Deborah Kerr's square. Also included are his two footprints (made with sandals), two hand-prints, and his signature.

There is a faint imprint of what appears to be a failed first attempt at his signature above the finished version.

The ceremony, for reasons unknown, took place on a 20th Century-Fox sound stage containing one of the interior sets for the production. Brynner's square was then transported outside the stage and placed along side the one readied for his co-star, Deborah Kerr.

The King and I premiered at the Chinese Theatre on June 29, three months after the Brynner/Kerr ceremony.

Deborah Kerr

Born: Deborah Jane Kerr-Trimmer in Helensburgh, Scotland, on September 30, 1921.

In the 1950s Deborah Kerr was the embodiment of the English gentlewoman on the screen—wholesomely sincere, innately genteel, but also highly spirited. She trained as an actress at a drama school in Bristol, England. She got some radio jobs and then began getting walk-ons in plays in London. She was signed by producer Gabriel Pascal and made her film debut in *Major Barbara* (1941). She played three distinct roles in *The Life and Death of Colonel Blimp* (1943), and the film made her a star. Her performance in *Black Narcissus* (1947) brought Hollywood interest, and Metro-Goldwyn-Mayer purchased her contract from Pascal.

Her first American film was *The Hucksters* (1947). Roles in such popular pictures as *King Solomon's Mines* (1950) and *Quo Vadis* (1951) soon followed, but Kerr was generally unhappy with the often insipid parts MGM handed her. She begged to be loaned out to Columbia and cast against type as the adulterous wife in *From Here to Eternity* (1953). The successful film proved Kerr's versatility and broke her image mold forever. Inundated with good offers, she chose to go to Broadway to star in *Tea and Sympathy* (1953), another tremendous hit. Her role as Anna in the screen version of the Rodgers and Hammerstein musical *The King and I* (1956) was a marvelous plum.

In the 1970s she returned to the theatre in such plays as *The Day after the Fair* (1972), *Long Day's Journey into Night* (1977), and *Candida* (1977). She has appeared on television in the mini-series "A Woman of Substance" (1984) and its sequel, "Hold the Dream" (1986).

Her motion picture credits include *Perfect Strangers* (1945, a.k.a. *Vacation from Marriage*), *Edward, My Son* (1949), *Tea and Sympathy* (1956), *Heaven Knows, Mr. Allison* (1957), *An Affair To Remember* (1957), *Separate Tables* (1958), *The Sundowners* (1960), *The Innocents* (1961), *The Night of the Iguana* (1964), and *The Assam Garden* (1985).

Academy Award nomination: Best Actress.

Kerr's square is tinted gray and contains the inscription "And I." (the period is Kerr's), which is the completion of the title of the film *The King and I* that was begun in Yul Brynner's square. Also included are the date ("3-22-56"), her two footprints (made with high heels), two handprints, and her signature.

The ceremony, for reasons unknown, took place on the 20th Century-Fox lot during the production of the film.

Kerr shared her recollections of the event in a letter to the authors:

"If my memory serves me right, my two young daughters, Melanie and Francesca, were with me for the ceremony, and although *I* was thrilled at the honour, THEY were absolutely thrilled at the idea of Mummy plunging her hands into wet cement! They would have loved to have done it, too!"

Elizabeth Taylor, Rock Hudson, and George Stevens
Ceremony #113: September 26, 1956

They placed their prints in connection with the motion picture *Giant* (Warner Bros., 1956); Taylor and Hudson starred, and Stevens produced and directed.

Elizabeth Taylor

Born: Elizabeth Rosemond Taylor in London, England, on February 27, 1932.

Violet-eyed Elizabeth Taylor could be referred to as the last bona fide "movie queen" created by the original Hollywood studio system, which perished during the 1950s, and was one of the few child stars whose adult fame eclipsed that of her youth. She has widely been called "The Most Beautiful Woman in the World," but her beauty was often an obstacle to her being taken seriously as an actress.

Her family relocated to California shortly before the start of World War II in 1939. Elizabeth made her screen debut in a Universal programmer, *There's One Born Every Minute* (1942); but the studio dropped her contract shortly thereafter. She then signed with Metro-Goldwyn-Mayer to do *Lassie Come Home* (1943) and remained with MGM until 1960. An excellent horsewoman, Elizabeth captured the role of the horse-crazy young girl in *National Velvet* (1944) and became a major star.

A *Place in the Sun* (1951) gave Taylor her first taste of acclaim as an adult performer. She received a well-publicized one million-dollar salary for *Cleopatra* (1963), which was the first of ten pictures opposite Richard Burton, who later became her husband. In 1966 Taylor surprised her detractors who thought she was too young and too beautiful to star in **Who's Afraid of Virginia Woolf?* by submerging her famed good looks to play the role of Martha. She appeared on the Broadway stage in *The Little Foxes* (1981) and has devoted much of her time in recent years to raising funds to find a cure for AIDS.

Her motion picture credits include *Father of the Bride* (1950), *Ivanhoe* (1952), *The Last Time I Saw Paris* (1954), **Raintree County* (1957), **Cat on a Hot Tin Roof* (1958), **Suddenly, Last Summer* (1959), ***Butterfield 8* (1960), *The Sandpiper* (1965), *The Taming of the Shrew* (1967), and *Il Giovane Toscanini* (1988, a.k.a. *Young Toscanini*).

* Academy Award nomination: Best Actress.
** Academy Award winner: Best Actress.

Taylor's square is tinted green and contains the inscription and date "Giant-56." Also included are her two footprints (made with high heels), two handprints, and her signature.

George Stevens, Jr., who in 1967 became the founding director of the American Film Institute, shared his memories of the Taylor/Hudson/Stevens ceremony in a letter to the authors:

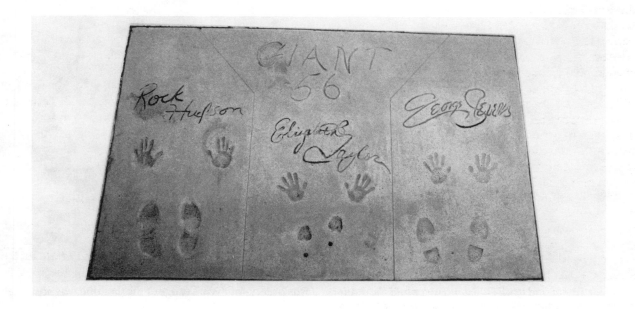

Elizabeth Taylor and Rock Hudson. Taylor told the authors, "I was twenty-four years of age at the time and was absolutely thrilled to be joining such a select group of personalities."

"The only recollection I have is that Elizabeth Taylor who, along with Rock Hudson and my father, was part of the program, arrived, as was her custom, a little bit late and the cement was drying and there was some question as to whether they were going to be able to remove their hands and feet from the rapidly congealing (is that what cement does?) cement."

Rock Hudson

Born: Roy Harold Scherer, Jr., in Winnetka, Illinois, on November 17, 1925. Died: October 2, 1985.

For over a decade Rock Hudson personified the ideal romantic hero of the screen. Although in his early career most critics thought him merely another Hollywood "beefcake" creation of limited ability, Hudson proved himself an actor of skill, charm, and versatility.

He arrived in Los Angeles in 1946 with little acting experience, save appearances in school plays, but was eager to learn, cooperate, and work hard. He had some portrait photos made of himself and sent them all over Hollywood. He received only one response; but it came from agent Henry Willson, who signed him and set the wheels in motion for the start of his career.

In 1949 Hudson was placed under contract to Universal, which gave him solid training and a major publicity build-up as they molded him. *The Lawless Breed* (1953) provided him with his first role of any depth, and he achieved stardom in *Magnificent Obsession* (1954). Producer/director George Stevens cast Hudson in **Giant* (1956), and the film proved a turning point in his career. After several more romantic leads, Hudson starred in the comedy *Pillow Talk* (1959), opposite Doris Day. The picture was an enormous hit, and he and Day co-starred in two additional films.

He starred in the popular television mystery series "McMillan and Wife," (1971-1976), opposite Susan St. James, as a likable San Francisco police commissioner. It ran for an additional season as "McMillan" (1976-1977), without St. James.

His motion picture credits include *Fighter Squadron* (1948, debut), *Taza, Son of Cochise* (1954), *All That Heaven Allows* (1955), *Written on the Wind* (1956), *A Farewell to Arms* (1957), *This Earth Is Mine* (1959), *Lover Come Back* (1961), *Send Me No Flowers* (1964), *Seconds* (1966), and *The Mirror Crack'd* (1980, final film).

*Academy Award nomination: Best Actor.

Hudson's square is tinted green and contains his two footprints, two handprints, and his signature.

At the time of his ceremony, Hudson was married to Phyllis Gates, the former secretary of agent Henry Willson. When *Giant* premiered at the Chinese Theatre on October 18, Phyllis and two of Hudson's friends (actor George Nader and Mark Miller) were finishing work on a home movie detailing the events of Rock's footprint ceremony and *Giant*'s east and west coast premieres in order to surprise Hudson on his birthday a few weeks later.

The movie was entitled "Rock Goes A-Bunting!"— "bunting" being the pet name Hudson and Gates called one another—and opens with Rock placing his prints in the forecourt. Elizabeth Taylor is shown pounding on his shoes to plant them deeper in the wet cement.

Next, the Hudsons are shown attending the New York premiere of *Giant* at the Roxy Theatre. The film finishes with them back at the Chinese for the Los Angeles premiere of *Giant*. Hudson was delighted with the home movie and exclaimed, "This is terrific. How'd you guys do this? I never saw a thing!" He was nearsighted and in true movie star fashion at the time, never wore his glasses in public.

George Stevens

Born: George Cooper Stevens in Oakland, California, on December 18, 1904. Died: March 8, 1975.

Producer/director George Stevens was a meticulous craftsman who always took painstaking care with all aspects of his films. He brought his special touch to dramas, comedies, Westerns, adventures, and even musicals with equal success.

His parents were well-known stage actors on the West Coast, and by age five Stevens was acting. In 1921 he landed a job as a motion picture camera assistant. By 1924 he was a full-fledged cameraman and worked as such for five years, mostly on two-reel comedies, eventually at the Hal Roach studios, where he often filmed Laurel and Hardy. In 1929 Stevens was given a chance to direct some shorts for Roach and next directed a few more at both Universal and RKO.

Stevens' first directorial assignment on a feature film came with *Cohens and Kellys in Trouble* (1933) at Universal. Next came a contract with RKO, where he began with low-budget features in 1934. His career turning point came when Katharine Hepburn asked that he direct *Alice Adams* (1935), his first film of real substance. Subsequent Stevens successes included

Theatre chain executives Edwin F. Zabell (kneeling left) and Frank H. Ricketson, Jr. with George Stevens (both standing); Elizabeth Taylor and Rock Hudson.

Swing Time (1936), considered by many to be the best Fred Astaire/Ginger Rogers film; *Vivacious Lady* (1938), his first as his own producer; and *Woman of the Year* (1942), which began the teaming of Katharine Hepburn and Spencer Tracy.

During World War II Stevens served in the U.S. Army Signal Corps and had responsibility for motion picture coverage of some of the War's most grisly events, including the liberation of the inmates at the Dachau concentration camp.

He returned from the War a profoundly shaken and matured man. Emotionally, he went from a prewar optimism to a postwar disillusionment that pervaded his subsequent films. He never again made a comedy and thereafter concentrated on films with serious dramatic themes. His career reached its apex in the 1950s with ***A Place in the Sun* (1951), **Shane* (1953), ***Giant* (1956), and **The Diary of Anne Frank* (1959).

His motion picture credits as a director include *Kentucky Kernels* (1934), *Annie Oakley* (1935), *A Damsel in Distress* (1937), *Gunga Din* (1939), *Penny Serenade* (1941), *The Talk of the Town* (1942), ***The More the Merrier* (1943), *I Remember Mama* (1948), *The Greatest Story Ever Told* (1965), and *The Only Game in Town* (1970, final film).

In 1954 he received the Irving G. Thalberg Memorial Award from the Academy of Motion Picture Arts and Sciences.

  * *Academy Award nomination: Direction.*
  ** *Academy Award nominations: Direction and Best Picture.*
  *** *Academy Award winner: Direction; Academy Award nomination: Best Picture.*

Stevens' square is tinted green and contains his two footprints, two handprints, and his signature.

Elmer C. Rhoden
Ceremony #114: September 16, 1958

He was honored with a plaque from the Leif Erikson Foundation in connection with the motion picture *Windjammer* (National Theatres, 1958). The film was shot in the Cinemiracle wide-screen process, which was developed by Russell H. McCullough under the direction of Rhoden.

Born: in LeMars, Iowa, on May 15, 1893. Died: July 14, 1981.

Elmer C. Rhoden was the president of National Theatres Corporation during the development of Cinemiracle and the production of *Windjammer* (1958), a semi-documentary adventure/travelogue. Rhoden was largely responsible for the company's decision to invest over $5,000,000 in the purchase and perfection of the wide-screen process.

His first connection with the motion picture business came in 1912 when he got a job with the General Film Company as a shipper.

By 1954 Rhoden had become the vice president of the newly formed California-based National Theatres, created when the parent company, 20th Century-Fox, was ordered to divest itself of all theatre operations. Fox owned more than 500 theatres at that time. By November, Rhoden was elected president of the company.

In 1955 he announced the development of Cinemiracle, touted as "seamless Cinerama" because it largely eliminated the visibility of the joining lines—or "seams"—between the three screen sections, which had been distractingly evident in Cinerama productions. Though the system was a success, *Windjammer* was the one and only feature film ever produced in the wide-

screen Cinemiracle process.

Rhoden retired as National Theatres president in 1958.

Rhoden's square is tinted gray, and its plaque contains the inscription:

[illustration of a ship]

S.S. Christian Radich	Louis de Rochemonts [sic]
Star Of The First	"Windjammer"
Cinemiracle Production	World Premiere
	Chinese Theatre
	April 8, 1958

the first
Special Merit Award
Conferred By The
Leif Erikson Foundation
Upon
Elmer C. Rhoden
Whose Foresight And Leadership Culminated
In The Development Of The Cinemiracle Process Of
Motion Picture Photography And Projection.
September 10, 1958

Dr. Vaino A. Hoover, president of the Leif Erikson Foundation (left), actress Karen von Unge, and Elmer C. Rhoden.

Note that the September 10, 1958 date on the plaque is not the date of the ceremony, which took place September 16.

Louis de Rochement was the producer of *Windjammer*, which chronicled the exploits of a group of eighty-five cadets making their first sea voyage on the Norwegian ship, the *Christian Radich*.

The Leif Erikson Foundation was established in 1956 and incorporated in Los Angeles in 1958 as a cultural and educational foundation dedicated to the public recognition of the pioneering spirit in modern life. The organization gave periodic awards to outstanding institutions or individuals who showed leadership in any field of human endeavor.

Cinemiracle's camera had been unveiled to the press in August 1957, and actual footage was shown the following November. Its "wall-to-wall" projection was first publicly demonstrated on a gigantic new forty by 100-foot curved screen at the Chinese Theatre's world premiere of *Windjammer* on April 8, 1958.

The theatre was refurbished for the occasion. Extensive changes were made in the interior, including a new Cinemiracle screen, seats, and carpets. The exterior CinemaScope marquee extending across the forecourt was removed, and smaller—without CinemaScope—marquees were placed on each side of the theatre. Critic Bob Sabel commented in his April 9, 1958 *Citizen News* column:

"The screen is huge, all right. In fact it sprawls from wall to wall. In this connection, an expensive rehabilitation job has been done on the Chinese. The theatre is now thoroughly modernized and sans much of the Oriental gingerbread which was so astounding in the late Sid Grauman's day."

The Chinese Theatre was again remodeled for the engagement of Windjammer *(1958), and the exterior vertical signs bearing the name "Grauman's" were removed.*

Rosalind Russell
Ceremony #115: February 19, 1959

She placed her prints in connection with the motion picture *Auntie Mame* (Warner Bros., 1958).

Born: in Waterbury, Connecticut, circa June 4, 1907 (sources vary on year). Died: November 28, 1976.

Rosalind Russell's performances fairly crackled with the electricity of her intelligence and wit. At Marymount College she became involved in dramatics and by 1929 had broken into stock company work. In 1930 she first appeared on Broadway, doing sketches and singing in the last *Garrick Gaieties*.

She signed with Metro-Goldwyn-Mayer in 1934 and made her film debut in a small part in *Evelyn Prentice* (1934). The role of the outrageously funny and caustic Sylvia Fowler in *The Women* (1939) made Russell a major star. She gave a breakneck-speed performance in Howard Hawks' *His Girl Friday* (1940) and scored another hit in *My Sister Eileen* (1942).

During the 1940s Russell was often typed as a brainy, highly coiffed, immaculately dressed, ultra-successful career woman; but she also managed to prove her versatility in such serious dramatic films as *Sister Kenny* (1946) and *Mourning Becomes Electra* (1947).

She detected somewhat of a career decline by 1949 and decided to return to the stage, first in a tour of *Bell, Book and Candle* (1951), and next in the Broadway hit, *Wonderful Town* (1953), an adaptation of *My Sister Eileen*. In 1956 she was again on Broadway as *Auntie Mame*. It was the greatest triumph of her career, and the film of *Auntie Mame* was a smash hit as well.

Her motion picture credits include *China Seas* (1935), *The Citadel* (1938), *No Time for Comedy* (1940), *Take a Letter, Darling* (1942), *Flight for Freedom* (1943), *Roughly Speaking* (1945), *The Velvet Touch* (1948), *Picnic* (1955), *Gypsy* (1962), and *Mrs. Pollifax-Spy* (1971, final film).

In 1973 she received the Jean Hersholt Humanitarian Award from the Academy of Motion Picture Arts and Sciences.

Academy Award nomination: Best Actress.

Russell's square is tinted gray and contains the inscription "Auntie Mame was here." Also included are the date ("Feb 19 '59"), her two footprints (made with high heels), two handprints, and her signature.

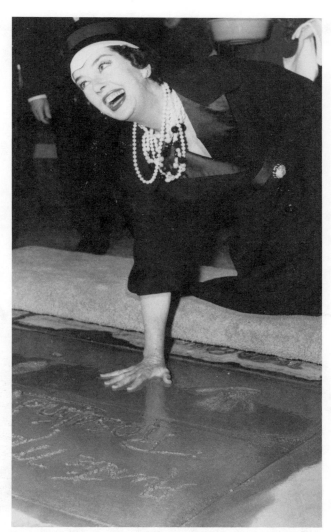

Rosalind Russell. She wrote of the ceremony in her memoirs, simply stating, "It had taken me twenty-five years to get there."

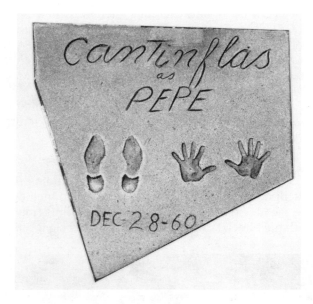

Here's the Point), *Ni sangre ni arena* (1941, a.k.a. *Neither Blood Nor Sand*), *El gendarme desconocido* (1941, a.k.a. *The Undercover Cop*), *Los tres mosqueteros* (1942, a.k.a. *The Three Musketeers*), *Romeo y Julieta* (1943, a.k.a. *Romeo and Juliet*), *El señor fotógrafo* (1953, a.k.a. *Mr. Photographer*), *El extra* (1962, a.k.a. *The Extra*), *Un Quijote sin mancha* (1969, a.k.a. *A Quixote without La Mancha*), and *El barrendero* (1982, a.k.a. *The Streetsweeper*).

Cantinflas' square is tinted gray and contains the inscription "as Pepe." Also included are the date ("Dec 28-60"), his two footprints, two handprints, and his signature.

Cantinflas
Ceremony #116: December 28, 1960

He placed his prints in connection with the motion picture *Pepe* (Columbia, 1960).

Born: Mario Moreno Reyes in Ciudad de los Palacios, Mexico, circa August 12, 1911 (sources vary on year).

Cantinflas, the most famous and popular figure in the history of Spanish-language cinema, introduced his character, the *peladito* (little tramp) over fifty years ago. The character is a symbol of the poorest class of Mexico—the peon, a social underdog, but one of comic buoyancy, optimism, idealism, and a genuine concern for justice and his fellow man.

Cantinflas' parents were poor, and as a boy he often shunned school to sing and dance in the streets for the few *pesos* that might be flung his way. By 1930 he had joined a *carpa* (traveling tent show), and it was there that he learned the essentials of comedy. He graduated to stage appearances in Mexico City's largest theatre and made his film debut in 1936. He was an immediate sensation. By the early 1940s not only Mexico but all of Latin America had succumbed to his talents.

In 1956 he made his first film outside Mexico, Michael Todd's *Around the World in 80 Days*, which was a huge success and made Cantinflas an internationally known celebrity. However, after only one more U.S.-produced film, *Pepe* (1960), he returned to filming exclusively in Mexico.

His motion picture credits include *No te engañes, corazón* (1936, debut), *Ahí está el detalle* (1940, a.k.a.

Cantinflas. He attended the premiere of Pepe *(1960) the night before at the Stanley Warner Beverly Hills Theatre and returned to Mexico City the day after the ceremony.*

Doris Day
Ceremony #117: January 19, 1961

Born: Doris Mary Anne von Kappelhoff on April 3, 1924, in Cincinnati, Ohio.

Actress Doris Day was and is natural, congenial, and ebullient. One fan said, "She looks as if she drinks a pint of liquid sunshine every day." At sixteen she joined Barney Rapp's band in Cincinnati as lead singer; he changed her name to Day when she had a hit with the song "Day after Day." She next had stints with the Bob Crosby and Les Brown bands. During this period, Day first appeared on film in three "Soundies" shorts, including "My Lost Horizon" (1941, debut). After an unsuccessful marriage, Day returned to the Brown band.

In Los Angeles she was down on her luck and ready to return to Cincinnati when she was cast in *Romance on the High Seas* (1948) at Warner Bros. Day was an immediate hit. During her early Hollywood career she usually appeared in sprightly musicals but alternated with occasional dramatic roles, including *Love Me or Leave Me* (1955) and *The Man Who Knew Too Much* (1956). Day sang "Whatever Will Be, Will Be" ("Que Sera, Sera") in the latter, and the song became her trademark.

Day achieved greater popularity than ever before in the comedy *Pillow Talk* (1959), the first of three pictures opposite Rock Hudson. She later starred in the successful television series, "The Doris Day Show" (1968-1973) for five seasons. Since then, Day has been one of the foremost celebrity champions of animal rights, devoting most of her time and energy toward that cause.

Her motion picture credits include *My Dream Is Yours* (1949), *On Moonlight Bay* (1951), *Calamity Jane* (1953), *Teacher's Pet* (1958), *Midnight Lace* (1960), *Lover Come Back* (1961), *The Thrill of It All* (1963), *Send Me No Flowers* (1964), and *With Six You Get Egg Roll* (1968).

Academy Award nomination: Best Actress.

Day's square is tinted gray and contains the date ("Jan 19 1961"), her two footprints (made with high heels), two handprints, and her signature.

George Gibson, who had staged the footprint ceremonies for three decades, said the Day event was "the biggest turnout since Sid Grauman 'accidentally' started this event back in 1927. Clark Gable in 1937 drew the biggest crowd until today, but Doris Day far outstripped that gathering." (Note: Other ceremonies since Gable that have been heavily attended by fans and members of the news media have claimed "record crowds" as well.)

Doris told the excited on-lookers, "I can remember the time I walked around here, admiring other footprints but never dreaming I would be invited to be a part in such a ceremony."

When it was pointed out to Day that her inscribed "Jan" date looked more like "June," she hastily grabbed the trowel, smoothed the cement over, and began again. "I must be correct," she laughed.

Carl H. Anderson, president of the Hollywood Chamber of Commerce (kneeling left), Doris Day, and theatre chain executive Roy Evans. Doris was also given a "Star of Stars" award that day by the Chamber for being "Hollywood's foremost star" based on recent box-office grosses.

Natalie Wood
Ceremony #118: December 5, 1961

She placed her prints in connection with the motion picture *West Side Story* (United Artists, 1961).

Born: Natasha Gurdin in San Francisco, California, on July 20, 1938. Died: November 29, 1981.

Natalie Wood spent thirty-nine of her forty-three years in front of motion picture cameras. She was a successful child actress who easily made the transition to teenage star and next achieved the difficult metamorphosis of becoming a respected adult performer and dramatic actress.

Wood made her film debut in a bit part in *Happy Land* (1943), which was filmed on location near her home. Director Irving Pichel was so impressed that he remembered her two years later and called her to Hollywood for a noticeable role in *Tomorrow Is Forever* (1946). From then on she worked steadily. Her most memorable child part came in *Miracle on 34th Street* (1947), as the little girl who literally becomes acquainted with Santa Claus.

Rebel without a Cause (1955) proved a major turning point and established Wood as a star. **Splendor in the Grass* (1961) won her critical acclaim as a serious adult actress. In the late 1960s she was off the screen for three years but made an impressive return in the smash hit *Bob & Carol & Ted & Alice* (1969).

Her box-office magnetism declined in the 1970s, during which she filmed occasionally and turned to television, where she appeared in TV movies and mini-series, including "Cat on a Hot Tin Roof" (1976) and "From Here to Eternity" (1979).

Her motion picture credits include *The Ghost and Mrs. Muir* (1947), *The Searchers* (1956), *Marjorie Morningstar* (1958), *Gypsy* (1962), ***Love with the Proper Stranger* (1963), *Sex and the Single Girl* (1964), *The Great Race* (1965), *Inside Daisy Clover* (1965), *The Last Married Couple in America* (1980), and *Brainstorm* (1983, final film).

   * *Academy Award nomination: Best Supporting Actress.*
   ** *Academy Award nomination: Best Actress.*

Wood's square is tinted gray and contains the date ("12-5-61"), her two footprints (made with high heels), two handprints, and her signature.

At the ceremony, Wood kneeled to make her footprints, removed her shoes, and pressed each one into the wet concrete. The theatre management felt that by using this method the imprint would be harder and better defined, in addition to the fact that the cement would not become deformed when honorees re-

Natalie Wood.

moved their feet. Wood posed for photographers with her foot daintily poised above her empty shoe, as though she had simply stepped into the cement.

Her friend, columnist Sidney Skolsky, was on hand for the event and was told, "Until a few years ago the cement had to be imported from Europe."

Janet Shulf, a long-time Natalie Wood fan, approached the star after the ceremony. Wood thought she was going to ask for an autograph and was surprised when she inquired, "May I just hug you, Natalie Wood? I've wanted to do it for a long time." Natalie smiled and said, "Sure," and Shulf carried through her request.

Natalie was thrilled to be included in the forecourt and felt being asked validated her success in the industry. She told writer Joe Hyams, "It would be ridiculous to say that now I'm a serious actress with no more personality of my own and I won't give any more autographs and I don't want to be recognized on the street. I'm still me....Finally, I'm beginning to think I've got more going for me than optimism."

Charlton Heston
Ceremony #119: January 18, 1962

He placed his prints in connection with the motion picture *El Cid* (Allied Artists, 1961).

Born: Charlton Carter in Evanston, Illinois, on October 4, 1923.

Charlton Heston achieved his greatest fame in costume dramas produced on an epic scale. At age five he made his first stage appearance as Santa Claus in a school play. He received a scholarship to Northwestern University, where he majored in drama and speech, and also made his film debut there in a 16mm production of *Peer Gynt* (1941).

In 1948 Heston went to New York where he landed a part in Katharine Cornell's production of *Antony and Cleopatra*. He found his first notable success in television's early days by playing leads on "Studio One" and other dramatic programs. His role as Rochester in a TV production of "Jane Eyre" (1948) caught the eye of film producer Hal B. Wallis, who signed him to a personal contract. Heston's first Hollywood film was Paramount's *Dark City* (1950); but it was his second, Cecil B. DeMille's *The Greatest Show on Earth* (1952), that firmly established him as a star. His next blockbuster was DeMille's *The Ten Commandments* (1956), and his career pinnacle came in the title role of *Ben-Hur* (1959).

Heston has always alternated film with stage work as time permits and has successfully appeared in such plays as *A Man for All Seasons* (1965) and *The Crucible* (1972). In 1990 he starred as Long John Silver in the TV movie "Treasure Island."

His motion picture credits include *The President's Lady* (1953), *The Naked Jungle* (1954), *Touch of Evil* (1958), *The Big Country* (1958), *Major Dundee* (1965), *The Agony and the Ecstasy* (1965), *Planet of the Apes* (1968), *Will Penny* (1968), *Earthquake* (1974), and *Almost an Angel* (1990).

In 1978 he received the Jean Hersholt Humanitarian Award from the Academy of Motion Picture Arts and Sciences.

*Academy Award winner: Best Actor.

Heston's square is tinted gray and contains the inscription "Thanks." Also included are the date ("1/18/62"), his two footprints, two handprints, and his signature, in addition to an imprint of a key in the

lower left corner. It is not known if the key was actually embedded in the cement and has since been pried out or if it was supposed to be just an imprint.

When Heston wrote his last name, he left out the "t" and had to squeeze it in above the "s" and the "o." Also, the "s" in "Thanks" is written below the rest of the letters and underneath Heston's left footprint.

In 1983 the Los Angeles *Times* commented on the errors in Heston's square, noting that, as Moses, Heston "had worked with stone tablets in *The Ten Commandments*."

Charlton Heston and his wife Lydia Clarke Heston, who is a professional photographer.

At the ceremony Heston carried and displayed Tizona, the replica of El Cid's fabled sword used in the film.

Comments from the crowd included, "Mr. Heston, will you autograph this before you wash your hands?" One spectator questioned, "Wonder what they're going to do with his shoes? I'd like to have them for souvenir bookends."

Heston's wife, Lydia Clarke Heston, a professional photographer, also attended the event and recorded the ceremony with her own lens. She said, "I am just as excited today as I was when I came here when I was sixteen."

Heston kept a journal for many years, and his entry on the day of his Chinese Theatre ceremony reads:

"I dutifully went through the ancient tribal ritual at Grauman's, putting my foot in wet cement, attended by a full complement of photographers and fans. So now I'm immortalized right on top of Marilyn Monroe and Jane Russell. (How many men can make that statement?)"

In individual letters to the authors, the Hestons shared their memories of the ceremony. Charlton Heston wrote:

"It's one of Hollywood's more endearing rituals. (One of the more enduring ones, too, come to think of it.) As far as I know, it doesn't cause cancer or "do harm to living things," so I guess it's O.K. It certainly was a lot of fun...kind of like playing mud pies. Which among us hasn't longed to step on a slab of freshly laid sidewalk?"

His wife recalled:

"The two photographs you sent of our happy day at the Chinese Theatre brought back nostalgic memories. The whole thing meant a great deal to me because my first memory of Los Angeles had been Ginger Rogers' dancing feet recorded in that historic entryway. I see several items of interest to me personally in the photos. Did we really still wear hats in 1962? I'm wearing a wool suit that Coco Chanel had made for me in Paris—I still have that, and of course it's a museum piece now. I have two Leicas in the picture, always the quietest [still] camera on a movie set. Photographers are seldom photographed, I find, and love having some record of where they were when."

Sophia Loren
Ceremony #120: July 26, 1962

She placed her prints in connection with the motion picture *Boccaccio '70* (Embassy International, 1962).

Born: Sofia Villani Scicolone in Rome, Italy, on September 20, 1934.

Voluptuous Sophia Loren is the most popular star ever produced in the history of Italian cinema. She grew up in poverty in Pozzuoli, an industrial suburb of Naples. After World War II she journeyed to Rome and found her first film work as an extra in 1950 in the American production *Quo Vadis* (1951). (Another screen appearance, *Cuori sul mare* [1950, a.k.a. *Hearts at Sea*], was released first and became her actual debut).

After extra work in many more pictures, Loren was spotted by producer Carlo Ponti, who became her champion, mentor, and in 1957 her husband. It was under the direction of Vittorio De Sica that she achieved real stardom in *L'oro di Napoli* (1954, a.k.a. *The Gold of Naples*).

Ponti negotiated a Hollywood deal with Paramount, where Loren filmed *Desire under the Elms* (1958), her first Hollywood film. The quality of her

Sophia Loren.

Hollywood productions was checkered, but she became an international major star as a result. When she returned to Italy in 1960, she became an even bigger international name than she had been in Hollywood.

The critical highlight of her career came with **La Ciociara (1960, a.k.a. Two Women). Loren continued with enormous success into the 1960s and 1970s, often in films with Marcello Mastroianni. During the 1980s she appeared in the television mini-series, "Sophia Loren: Her Own Story" (1980), in which she starred as herself, and a four-hour remake of "Two Women" (1989).

Her motion picture credits include Boy on a Dolphin (1957), The Pride and the Passion (1957), Houseboat (1958), It Started in Naples (1960), El Cid (1961), Ieri, oggi e domani (1963, a.k.a. Yesterday, Today and Tomorrow), *Matrimonia all'italiana (1964, a.k.a. Marriage, Italian Style), A Countess from Hong Kong (1967), Una giornata speciale (1977, a.k.a. A Special Day), and Sabato, domenica e lunedi (1990, a.k.a. Saturday, Sunday and Monday).

In 1991 she received an Honorary Academy Award as "one of the genuine treasures of world cinema who, in a career rich with memorable performances, has added permanent luster to our art form."

  * Academy Award nomination: Best Actress.
  ** Academy Award winner: Best Actress.

Loren's square is tinted green and contains the inscription "Solo per sempre," which is Italian for "alone forever." Also included are the date ("7 26-62"), her two footprints (made with high heels), two handprints, and her signature.

Loren, accompanied by her husband, flew in from Rome on the morning of July 26 for a one-day stay in Hollywood. The first scheduled stop on her itinerary was at the Chinese Theatre, where she placed her prints.

As she stood in the cement, Loren wiggled her hips back and forth in order to make a deeper impression in the wet concrete.

Newsmen noticed that Loren did not remove her wedding ring from her right hand nor a huge sapphire and diamond ring from her left when she plunged her hands into the cement.

She said her mother told her "to make one fingerprint in the cement for her. She couldn't believe I was going to have my feet and hands in the cement. She asked me if they would be there for eternity and I told her they would."

That evening the Pontis attended a dinner party in her honor at the Beverly Hills Hotel. Loren had not attended the 34th annual Academy Awards Presentation held on April 9, 1962 when she was announced the winner of the Best Actress Oscar for her performance in Two Women. She was the first performer in a foreign-language film to be nominated for an Academy Award.

At the party at the Beverly Hills Hotel following her Chinese Theatre ceremony, Loren finally picked up her officially inscribed prize.

Kirk Douglas
Ceremony #121: November 1, 1962

Born: Issur Danielovitch (later changed to Demsky) in Amsterdam, New York, on December 9, 1916.

Although his performances are usually aggressive and intense, Kirk Douglas tempers his portrayals with a sensitivity and convincingness that makes them movingly believable.

As a boy he grew up in extreme poverty and had many jobs. He saved what money he could and worked his way through four years of college at St. Lawrence University. On a scholarship he spent two years (1939-1941) at the American Academy of Dramatic Arts and made his Broadway debut in Spring Again (1941). On Lauren Bacall's recommendation, producer Hal B. Wallis saw Douglas, signed him to a contract, and cast him in The Strange Love of Martha Ivers (1946, debut) for Warner Bros.

Kirk Douglas gets a lift from Donald O'Connor. Others unidentified.

He played a ruthless boxer in *Champion* (1949), which made him a major star. Suddenly Douglas was Hollywood's newest sensation, and all the major studios were after him. Warner Bros. got him, but only briefly, as in 1952 he became one of the first stars to buck the studio system by forming his own production company, named Bryna, after his mother.

Douglas not only starred in *Spartacus* (1960) but was also the executive producer and helped bring about an end to the Hollywood blacklist by hiring writer Dalton Trumbo for the picture and, more importantly, giving him screen credit.

His motion picture credits include *A Letter to Three Wives* (1949), *Young Man with a Horn* (1950), *Detective Story* (1951), **The Bad and the Beautiful* (1952), *20,000 Leagues under the Sea* (1954), **Lust for Life* (1956), *Gunfight at the O.K. Corral* (1957), *Paths of Glory* (1957), *Lonely Are the Brave* (1962), and *Oscar* (1991).

In 1991 the American Film Institute presented him with its Life Achievement Award.

*Academy Award nomination: Best Actor.

Douglas' square is tinted red and contains the date ("Nov. 1, '62"), his two footprints, two handprints, and his signature.

The ceremony coincided with a "Footprint Reunion" of many of the celebrities who had placed their prints in the forecourt. The event was sponsored by the Hollywood Film Council and the Los Angeles County Board of Supervisors.

Eugene V. Klein, the president of the National General Corp., wrote the following in a letter inviting all the honorees to participate: "We believe this reunion of 'Footprint Alumni' will serve as a reminder to the world of Hollywood's great past, present and future and that it will reaffirm that Hollywood remains the world's film and glamour capital."

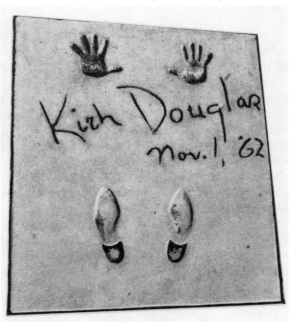

A crowd of over 1,000 fans waited outside in the forecourt and on Hollywood Boulevard for the footprint ceremonies to begin while the celebrities attending the event had cocktails inside on the empty theatre's stage. The participants included Bud Abbott, Gene Autry, Jackie Cooper, Jeanne Crain, George Jessel—he doubled as master of ceremonies—William Lundigan, Jack Oakie, Donald O'Connor, Jane Withers, and Jane Wyman.

After Douglas made his imprints, he turned to comedian/photographer Ken Murray and proceeded to wipe his cement-laden hands on Murray's cheeks, instead of the customary towel. Murray wasn't amused and complained, "This wasn't in the script. I only came to this shindig as a photographer."

He wasn't the only one who was unhappy. Due to the large number of celebrities hovering around Douglas when he made his imprints, many eager spectators who had been waiting for hours to get a glimpse of the event found their views blocked and actually booed.

Paul Newman and Joanne Woodward
Ceremony #122: May 25, 1963

The couple are husband and wife. They wed in 1958.

Paul Newman

Born: Paul Leonard Newman in Cleveland, Ohio, on January 26, 1925.

One of the biggest box-office stars of the 1960s and 1970s, Paul Newman has also proved himself one of the finest actors of his generation. He studied during 1951-1952 at Yale University's School of Drama. He next went to New York City and made his Broadway debut in the hit play *Picnic* (1953). In 1954 he signed a long-term contract with Warner Bros., but his film debut in *The Silver Chalice* (1954) proved embarrassing. He fled back to New York, where he redeemed himself with a compelling performance on stage in *The Desperate Hours* (1955).

Returning to Hollywood, Newman appeared in *Somebody Up There Likes Me* (1956), which made him a star. He had success with *Cat on a Hot Tin Roof* (1958) and then a series of smash hits in his so-called "lucky 'H'" pictures: *The Hustler* (1961), *Hud* (1963), *Harper* (1966), and *Hombre* (1967). He made his directorial debut with ***Rachel, Rachel** (1968, Newman also produced), starring Joanne

Woodward; and they mutually enjoyed one of their greatest critical triumphs.

Newman ended the 1960s opposite Robert Redford in the huge hit *Butch Cassidy and the Sundance Kid* (1969). In 1973 they co-starred again with even greater success in *The Sting*. All the profits from his line of "Newman's Own" salad dressings, spaghetti sauce, natural popcorn, and lemonade are donated to charities and social welfare organizations.

His motion picture credits as an actor include *The Long, Hot Summer* (1958), *The Young Philadelphians* (1959), *Sweet Bird of Youth* (1962), *The Outrage* (1964), *Cool Hand Luke* (1967), *Fort Apache, the Bronx* (1981), **Absence of Malice* (1981), **The Verdict* (1982), ***The Color of Money* (1986), and *Mr. and Mrs. Bridge* (1990).

In 1986 he received an Honorary Academy Award "in recognition of his many and memorable compelling screen performances and for his personal integrity and dedication to his craft."

   * *Academy Award nomination: Best Actor.*
  ** *Academy Award winner: Best Actor.*
*** *Academy Award nomination: Best Picture.*

Joanne Woodward

Born: in Thomasville, Georgia, circa February 27, 1930 (sources vary on year).

A superb and subtle actress, Joanne Woodward inhabits her roles so believably that she has never developed a so-called screen "persona" of her own. She always wanted to be an actress and appeared in several plays in both high school and at Louisiana State University. Next she joined a little theatre

Joanne Woodward and her husband Paul Newman.

group, played summer stock, and went to New York City, where she studied for two years at the Neighborhood Playhouse School of the Theatre. A big break came when she was hired to understudy both lead actresses in the Broadway hit *Picnic* in 1953. During its 477-performance run, Woodward went on fifty times and attracted much favorable attention.

In 1955 20th Century-Fox producer Buddy Adler signed her to a seven-year contract. She was quickly loaned out for three fairly minor films before Fox got around to actually using her in one of its own pictures: **The Three Faces of Eve* (1957). The film was a triumph for Woodward and propelled her to stardom. Woodward was very selective about her scripts and turned down many. She was a serious actress, didn't care about publicity, and would have none of the usual Hollywood hype games.

Over the years Woodward and Paul Newman have co-starred in ten films with varying success. She has also appeared in TV movies, including "Come Back, Little Sheba" (1977) and "See How She Runs" (1978).

Her motion picture credits include *Count Three and Pray* (1955, debut), *The Long, Hot Summer* (1958), *The Stripper* (1963), *A Fine Madness* (1966), *Rachel, Rachel* (1968), *They Might Be Giants* (1971), *The Effect of Gamma Rays on Man-in-the-Moon Marigolds* (1972), *Summer Wishes, Winter Dreams* (1973), *The Drowning Pool* (1975), and *Mr. and Mrs. Bridge* (1990).

> * Academy Award nomination: Best Actress.
> ** Academy Award winner: Best Actress.

The Newman/Woodward square is tinted green and contains the inscription "Thanks!" Also included are the date ("May 25 1963"), Newman's inscription "His," his two footprints (made with bare feet), two handprints, and his signature, in addition to Woodward's inscription "Hers," her two footprints (made with high heels), two handprints, and her signature.

Jack Lemmon and Shirley MacLaine
Ceremony #123: June 29, 1963

They placed their prints in connection with the motion picture *Irma La Douce* (United Artists, 1963).

Jack Lemmon

Born: John Uhler Lemmon III in Boston, Massachusetts, on February 8, 1925.

One of the few stars who has excelled equally in comedy and drama, Jack Lemmon has been delighting and amazing movie audiences for almost forty years. Lemmon epitomized the common man—sort of the nice young accountant living up the street.

He participated in dramatics at Harvard, where he earned both a B.A. and a B.S. in 1947, and then headed straight for New York City. His first job was playing piano in a saloon that showed silent movies. Lemmon soon obtained steady television work and estimated he appeared in over 500 live TV shows during the early 1950s. He made his Broadway debut in a revival of *Room Service* (1953) and was spotted by a talent scout for Columbia, who recommended him to director George Cukor for *It Should Happen to You* (1954, debut). His captivating performance in *Mister Roberts* (1955) sent him on the way to stardom.

His career soared after **Some Like It Hot* (1959); and some of his biggest successes during the 1960s include **The Apartment* (1960), **Days of Wine and Roses* (1962), and *The Odd Couple* (1968). The critical pinnacle of his career came with ***Save the Tiger* (1973).

His triumph on Broadway in the stage play *Tribute* (1978) put Lemmon's career in a whole new phase by thrusting him into a sort of distinguished "elder statesman" class in Hollywood, allowing him to pick

Shirley MacLaine and Jack Lemmon.

and choose among the best roles and finest scripts available for any actor of his age range in the business.

His motion picture credits include *My Sister Eileen* (1955), *Operation Mad Ball* (1957), *Bell, Book and Candle* (1958), *Cowboy* (1958), *The Notorious Landlady* (1962), *The Great Race* (1965), **The China Syndrome* (1979), **Tribute* (1980), **Missing* (1982), and *JFK* (1991).

In 1988 the American Film Institute presented him with its Life Achievement Award.

* Academy Award winner: Best Supporting Actor.
** Academy Award nomination: Best Actor.
*** Academy Award winner: Best Actor.

Lemmon's square is tinted red and contains the inscription "Magic-Time." Also included are the date ("6/29/63"), his two footprints, two handprints, and his signature, plus the imprint of the cork from the bottle of champagne from which Lemmon and Shirley MacLaine drank a celebration toast during their ceremony.

"Magic-Time" is what Lemmon always says just before he goes before the camera to film a scene.

In what he described as a "hasty note [to the authors regarding his ceremony] from backstage in London,"—he was appearing at the Haymarket Theatre in *Veteran's Day* (1989)—Lemmon admitted, "Really have no specific recollections or anecdotes regarding placing [my] prints at Grauman's. ('Nice day, lots of press, and enjoyed it,' etc.) Dull, what?"

Shirley MacLaine

Born: Shirley MacLean Beaty in Richmond, Virginia, on April 24, 1934.

In 1955 Shirley MacLaine burst on the Hollywood scene as a fresh and original new type of movie star. She personified the average and vulnerable young woman, with whom just about every American working woman or housewife could identify.

Trained as a dancer since childhood, MacLaine set her sights on the musical comedy stage and in 1950 began working in a series of chorus jobs, both in New York City and in road companies. She was in the chorus of the Broadway hit *The Pajama Game* (1954) and was understudying star Carol Haney when Haney broke her ankle shortly after the opening night. MacLaine took over for her and was spotted by Hollywood producer Hal B. Wallis. Wallis signed her to a long-term contract, and soon Shirley was before the cameras in Alfred Hitchcock's *The Trouble with Harry* (1955, debut) for Paramount.

After a few more films, she was propelled to major stardom by *Some Came Running* (1958). High points in her career during the 1960s include *The Apartment* (1960) and *Irma La Douce* (1963). During that period MacLaine became a political activist, championing civil rights and other liberal causes. In 1975 she produced and co-directed the feature-length documentary ***The Other Half of the Sky: A China Memoir*. The critical high-point of her career came with her performance in **Terms of Endearment* (1983).

A seeker of self-awareness, MacLaine gave instruction to others in her "Connecting with the Higher Self" seminars in the 1980s.

Her motion picture credits include *Around the World in 80 Days* (1956), *Can-Can* (1960), *Two for the Seesaw* (1962), *Sweet Charity* (1969), *Two Mules for Sister Sara* (1970), *The Turning Point* (1977), *Being There* (1979), *Madame Sousatzka* (1988), *Postcards from the Edge* (1990), and *Waiting for the Light* (1990).

* *Academy Award nomination: Best Actress.*
** *Academy Award winner: Best Actress.*
*** *Academy Award nomination: Documentary (Feature).*

MacLaine's square is tinted red and contains the inscription "MeanTime." Also included are the date ("6/29/63"), her two footprints (made with high heels), two handprints, and her signature.

Mervyn LeRoy
Ceremony #124: October 15, 1963

He was honored with a commemorative plaque in connection with the motion picture *Mary, Mary* (Warner Bros., 1963), which he produced and directed.

Born: in San Francisco, California, on October 15, 1900. Died: September 13, 1987.

During a career that spanned over forty years, Mervyn LeRoy directed and/or produced over seventy feature films; and the record of his work certainly proves him to have been a talent of extraordinary versatility.

He broke into show business in 1914, playing a bit in the play *Barbara Frietchie*. By 1923 LeRoy had found work in the movies, beginning as a wardrobe assistant. Next he got a place in the film developing lab and soon graduated to an assistant cameraman position. He also played bits and had steady work as a gag writer.

At First National Colleen Moore suggested he be given a chance to direct, and his first assignment was *No Place To Go* (1927). He learned his craft, and then the turning point of his career came: *Little Caesar* (1931), the Warner Bros.-First National picture that started the gangster film genre in the talkies and established LeRoy as a major talent.

LeRoy moved from Warner Bros. to Metro-Goldwyn-Mayer in 1938, where he produced some films, including the milestone *The Wizard of Oz* (1939), as well as directing many pictures at that studio. In 1945 he directed and co-produced a short subject, **"The House I Live In," which dealt with racial and ethnic intolerance. LeRoy returned to Warners in 1954,

where he made such pictures as *Mister Roberts* (1955) and *Gypsy* (1962).

His motion picture credits as a director include *Hot Stuff* (1929, talkie debut), *I Am a Fugitive from a Chain Gang* (1932), *Gold Diggers of 1933* (1933), *Anthony Adverse* (1936), *Waterloo Bridge* (1940), *Johnny Eager* (1942), **Random Harvest* (1942), *Thirty Seconds over Tokyo* (1944), *Quo Vadis* (1951), and *Moment to Moment* (1966, final film). In addition he assisted John Wayne in the direction of *The Green Berets* (1968) but was uncredited.

Kitty LeRoy (left), her husband Mervyn, and Natalie Wood.

In 1976 he received the Irving G. Thalberg Memorial Award from the Academy of Motion Picture Arts and Sciences.

    * *Academy Award nomination: Direction.*
    ** *Academy Award winner: Special Award.*

LeRoy's square is tinted gray, and its plaque contains the inscription:

Mervyn LeRoy
***
In Grateful Appreciation For
His Artistic Contributions To
Hollywood And Commemorating
His 75th Motion Picture Production
October 15, 1963

Friends and co-workers who had worked with LeRoy over the years participated in his ceremony, including Nick Adams, Jack Benny, Karl Malden, Lana Turner, James Stewart, and Natalie Wood—the latter two also co-hosted the event.

LeRoy recalled the occasion in a letter to the authors:

"The ceremony took place on my sixty-third birthday and the thought that went through my mind at the time was, 'Gee, Mervyn, aren't you too old to be playing in the mud like this!'"

National General Corp. thoughtfully surprised LeRoy with a birthday cake.

Hayley Mills
Ceremony #125: February 22, 1964

Born: Hayley Catherine Rose Vivian Mills in London, England, on April 18, 1946.

From age thirteen to nineteen, Hayley Mills literally grew up in front of the motion picture camera and charmed millions as one of the most skillful and captivating child stars ever.

The daughter of actor John Mills and writer Mary Hayley Bell, she first appeared before the motion picture cameras when an infant in one of her father's films, *So Well Remembered* (1947, debut). Hayley never particularly considered an acting career seriously, regardless of her heritage. But her acceptance of a major role in *Tiger Bay* (1959) launched one of the most successful childhood careers in film history.

Hayley attracted the attention of Walt Disney, who personally met with her and signed her to a five-year contract. Her first Disney film, *Pollyanna* (1960), brought glowing praise from the critics; and for this portrayal Hayley received an Honorary Academy

The Mills family: Hayley (kneeling, center) with her parents, John and Mary Hayley Bell.

Award for "the most outstanding juvenile performance during 1960." Next came *The Parent Trap* (1961), which was a box-office smash. Several other Disney films followed, and her last for the studio was *That Darn Cat* (1965).

By 1968, however, Hayley found that producers decided she had outgrown her image; and then she had trouble securing adult roles. In 1986 and 1989 she was back at Disney to film two TV movie sequels to the biggest hit of her career: "The Parent Trap II" and "Parent Trap III."

Her motion picture credits include *Whistle Down the Wind* (1961), *In Search of the Castaways* (1962), *Summer Magic* (1963), *The Chalk Garden* (1964), *The Moon-Spinners* (1964), *The Truth about Spring*

(1965), *The Trouble with Angels* (1966), *The Family Way* (1966), *Take a Girl Like You* (1970), and *Appointment with Death* (1988).

Hayley's square is tinted green and contains the inscription "Fab." Also included are the date ("2/22/64"), her two footprints (made with high heels), two handprints, and her signature, plus the inscription "'Dad's Birthday.'" A coin was also embedded in the cement. It has since been pried out.

The inscription "Fab" was an exclamation popular with British teenagers at the time and was an abbreviation of "Fabulous."

In 1959 when she first came to the U.S. after being signed by Disney, the studio sent her to the Chinese

Theatre to pose gazing fondly at the prints of another famous child actress—Shirley Temple.

Hayley was assisted at her ceremony by her parents. She couldn't resist making faces and sticking out her tongue in response to the feeling of the wet cement on her hands. Her reactions were captured by news photographers and appeared in newspapers and magazines throughout the world. She said, "It's so silly, but I always seem to do it at just the wrong moment, and then afterward I regret it bitterly."

When someone told her that she was one of the youngest persons to be so honored, Hayley expressed surprise and pleasure: "Really? Well, it was great fun, and I didn't fall in, thank heavens. Imagine being entombed at Grauman's!"

In her memoirs, Bell recalled her daughter's attitude toward her career in the film industry's capital:

"And truly, Hollywood never did hurt Hayley. She was impervious. Natural and spontaneous, completely unselfconscious, she lived her life as she would have lived it anywhere, and for that reason was loved....The adulation and applause she received never for an instant turned her fair head or gave her a moment of conceit, whether it was placing her hands and feet in the cement next to Shirley Temple's at Grauman's Chinese Theatre, or being met at Tokyo Airport at midnight by three thousand children waving flags with her name on it."

In a letter to the authors, Hayley wrote:

"I am afraid my recollections of that day in 1964 outside the Grauman's Chinese Theatre are rather imperfect but I do remember that everybody laughed a great deal, that the sun shone very brightly, that it was my father's birthday and that there were two good excuses for us to go off and have a celebration."

Dean Martin
Ceremony #126: March 21, 1964

Born: Dino Paul Crocetti in Steubenville, Ohio, on June 17, 1917.

Once the straight-man half of one of the world's most popular comedy teams—the other member of the duo was comedian Jerry Lewis—Dean Martin subsequently became a major star in his own right.

He began singing at a local cafe and within a few years was playing the nightclub circuits. In 1946 he first appeared with Jerry Lewis at a club in Atlantic City. They were both booked there as separate acts; but when each failed to generate much audience enthusiasm, the two started to team, at first on the

spur of the moment, ad-libbing wildly, and running rampant with physical, chaotic, free-for-all comedy in which they created mayhem both on stage and in the audience.

Almost overnight, Martin and Lewis found themselves the hottest comedy team in the business. They were spotted by producer Hal B. Wallis, who signed the duo to a long-term contract; and the two made their film debut in *My Friend Irma* (1949) for Paramount. Martin and Lewis became the most highly paid and successful movie comedy team of the 1950s, making sixteen films together.

After the team split up in 1956, rather acrimoniously, Martin's first solo effort, *Ten Thousand Bedrooms* (1957), was not a success; but he rallied with a smash nightclub engagement in Las Vegas, several hit records, and solid dramatic roles in *The Young*

Dean Martin (kneeling, center) and family. Martin was also presented with citations that day for his efforts to raise funds on behalf of the 1964 United States Olympic team.

Lions, Some Came Running (both 1958), and *Rio Bravo* (1959).

In the 1960s he made several films with Frank Sinatra and his other "Hollywood Rat Pack" cronies and also appeared in four films as detective Matt Helm. In addition, Martin found enormous success with his own television series, a variety program, "The Dean Martin Show" (1965-1974).

His motion picture credits include *At War with the Army* (1951), *Jumping Jacks* (1952), *Artists and Mod-* els (1955), *Bells Are Ringing* (1960), *Sergeants 3* (1962), *Airport* (1970), *Toys in the Attic* (1963), *The Sons of Katie Elder* (1965), *The Silencers* (1966), and *Cannonball Run II* (1984).

Martin's square is tinted gray and contains the inscription "Thanks." Also included are the date ("3-21-64"), his two footprints, two handprints, and his signature.

Peter Sellers
Ceremony #127: June 3, 1964

He placed his prints in connection with the motion picture *A Shot in the Dark* (United Artists, 1964).

Born: Peter Richard Henry Sellers in Southsea, England, on September 8, 1925. Died: July 24, 1980.

Peter Sellers gained international stardom during the 1960s as a comic actor of remarkable versatility and range. He worked as an actor and musician as a boy and during World War II toured as an official entertainer of the troops of the R.A.F., performing mimicry, impersonations, and comedy routines. After the War Sellers became a comedian at the Windmill Theatre in London. He became a nationally known

Peter Sellers and his wife Britt Ekland.

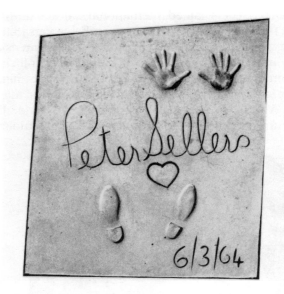

figure on British radio's "The Goon Show," which debuted in 1951.

Sellers began appearing on television while making some short films with his fellow "Goons." *The Ladykillers* (1955) was his first big break in feature films and made him a popular movie personality in England.

In 1959 he produced and starred in the short **"The Running, Jumping and Standing-Still Film," which won four international festival awards. *Lolita* (1962) and *Dr. Strangelove or: How I Learned To Stop Worrying and Love the Bomb* (1964), in which he gave a triple-character performance, made him a well-known figure to American audiences.

However, it was *The Pink Panther* (1964) that gave Sellers the role for which he is best remembered—Inspector Clouseau, the idiotic, bumbling, accident-prone French police detective who fancies himself a brilliant crime solver and great ladies' man, but who more often than not falls flat on his face. Sellers repeated his Clouseau characterization in five follow-up films.

The critical high point of his career came with *Being There* (1979).

His motion picture credits include *Penny Points to Paradise* (1951, debut), *The Mouse That Roared* (1959), *I'm All Right Jack* (1959), *Waltz of the Toreadors* (1962), *The World of Henry Orient* (1964), *The Wrong Box* (1966), *I Love You, Alice B. Toklas!* (1968), *The Party* (1968), *Murder by Death* (1976), and *Trail of the Pink Panther* (1982, final film).

 * *Academy Award nomination: Best Actor.*
 ** *Academy Award nomination: Short Subject (Live Action).*

Sellers' square is tinted green and contains the date ("6/3/64"), his two footprints, two handprints, and his signature, plus the drawing of a heart.

Sellers' wife, actress Britt Ekland, accompanied him at the ceremony and also inscribed her initial "B" in the wet cement after Sellers finished. The "B" did not survive from the fresh wet cement through the drying process and into the hard block now on view in the forecourt.

News media accounts of the ceremony mentioned that Sellers had just recovered from a massive and nearly fatal heart attack that he suffered on April 7 in Hollywood.

Debbie Reynolds
Ceremony #128: January 14, 1965

She placed her prints in connection with the motion picture *The Unsinkable Molly Brown* (Metro-Goldwyn-Mayer, 1964).

Born: Mary Frances Reynolds in El Paso, Texas, on April 1, 1932.

Debbie Reynolds exuded a freshness and bouncy exuberance that made her one of America's most celebrated stars in the 1950s and 1960s. Her staple was performing in light-hearted fare—almost always musicals and comedies.

When Debbie was eight her family relocated to Burbank, California. Reynolds won the title of "Miss Burbank" in 1948; and the resulting attention secured her a contract at Warner Bros., where she made her film debut in a small part in *June Bride* (1948). The

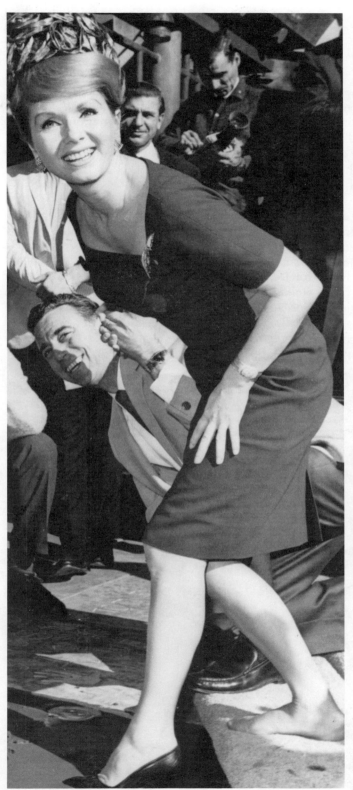

Debbie Reynolds. Assisted by unidentified man.

studio dropped her after eighteen months. Metro-Goldwyn-Mayer quickly snapped her up, and the turning point in her career came with her role in the musical *Singin' in the Rain* (1952), which brought stardom. The critical pinnacle of her career came with the success of **The Unsinkable Molly Brown (1964).*

Her screen popularity began to slide in the late 1960s, and in 1973 Reynolds turned to the stage and scored a smash hit in a revival of *Irene*. Since then she has worked constantly in other shows and toured her nightclub act with great success.

Reynolds devotes a large amount of time to the Thalians, a charitable organization which assists emotionally disturbed children and adults. She has worked with the group since 1955 and currently serves as its chairwoman.

Her motion picture credits include *Two Weeks with Love* (1950), *I Love Melvin* (1953), *Susan Slept Here* (1954), *The Tender Trap* (1955), *Bundle of Joy* (1956), *Tammy and the Bachelor* (1957), *The Rat Race* (1960), *How the West Was Won* (1963), *What's the Matter with Helen?* (1971), and *That's Entertainment!* (1974).

* Academy Award nomination: Best Actress.

Reynolds' square is tinted red and contains the inscription "Many Thanks." Also included are the date ("1/14/65"), her two footprints (made with high heels), two handprints, and her signature.

Reynolds had been an admirer of the footprints in the Chinese Theatre's forecourt while a student at John Burroughs High School in Burbank. Early in her career Debbie attended openings at the theatre—and other famous Hollywood spots—with various up-and-coming actors under the watchful eye of the studio publicity department.

On the day of her ceremony, Reynolds was ill with a twenty-four-hour virus, but that didn't stop the show. She told the crowd that gathered for the event, "I'd have gotten out of a death bed to be here!"

She recalled the time of her footprint ceremony in her memoirs:

"I put my hands and feet in the wet cement outside Grauman's Chinese in Hollywood, and at Cape Canaveral, Florida, Gus Grissom and John Young lifted off to outer space for the third manned space flight ever in a capsule christened 'The Molly Brown.'"

Marcello Mastroianni
Ceremony #129: February 8, 1965

Born: Marcello Vincenzo Domenico Mastroianni in Fontana Liri, Italy, circa September 28, 1924 (sources vary on day and year).

Handsome and virile, but also elegant and re-fined, Marcello Mastroianni has enjoyed a distin-guished career spanning the last four decades and is the most popular and famous actor in the history of the Italian cinema. He has achieved some of his biggest successes in a series of films opposite his friend and colleague Sophia Loren.

In his adolescence Mastroianni began working as an extra in films to help support his family. His first documented film appearance was in *Marionette* (1938). He aspired to become an architect, but during World War II he was sent to a forced-labor camp by the Germans.

After the War Mastroianni found a job as a clerk with the Italian office of the film firm Eagle-Lion, while joining a group of stage players at the University of Rome. In the late 1940s, director Luchino Visconti invited him to join his highly regarded theatrical company, where Mastroianni appeared in several important productions while beginning to branch out into film. A career turning point came with Visconti's *Le notti bianche* (1957, a.k.a. *White Nights*), which made Mastroianni a well-known personality.

His pivotal role in Federico Fellini's *La dolce vita* (1960) made him a major international star. In Fellini's view, Mastroianni is "the actor I prefer above all others;" and the director cast him as his alter-ego in *Otto e mezzo* (1963, a.k.a. *8 1/2*).

His motion picture credits include *Una domenico d'agosto* (1949, a.k.a. *Sunday in August*), *I soliti ignoti* (1958, a.k.a. *The Big Deal on Madonna Street*), *La notte* (1961, a.k.a. *The Night*), **Divorzio all'italiano* (1961, a.k.a. *Divorce—Italian Style*), *Ieri, oggi e domani* (1963, a.k.a. *Yesterday, Today and Tomorrow*), *Matrimonia all'italiana* (1964, a.k.a. *Marriage Italian Style*), **Una giornata speciale* (1977, a.k.a. *A Special Day*), *Ginger e Fred* (1986, a.k.a. *Ginger and Fred*), **Oci ciornie* (1987, a.k.a. *Dark Eyes*), and *Stanno tutti bene* (1991, a.k.a. *Everybody's Fine*).

*Academy Award nomination: Best Actor.

Marcello Mastroianni.

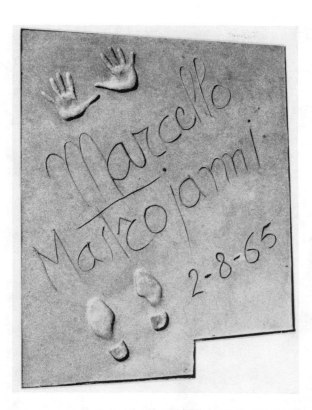

Mastroianni's square is tinted red and contains the date ("2-8-65"), his two footprints, two handprints, and his signature.

After completing his ceremony, Mastroianni spent time shaking hands and signing autographs for the people who turned out for his ceremony, all the while smoking a cigarette.

One woman kissed him on the cheek. Another almost fainted when he smiled at her. One *did* faint when he kissed her—she had also been at the airport the previous day when he flew into Los Angeles, crying, "Marcello, I love you!"

A three-year-old child pushed his own stroller behind the crowd while his mother waited for an autograph. After being jostled around several times, he cried, "Mommy, when can we leave?"

An elderly woman was almost knocked down. A teenager had Mastroianni sign a copy of the book *Goals in Spelling*—she'd been standing in line doing her homework!

Mastroianni attended the 22nd annual Hollywood Foreign Press Association's Golden Globe Awards that same evening at the Ambassador Hotel, where he and Sophia Loren were named the 1964 "World Film Favorites." Mastroianni accepted the awards for both of them.

Frank Sinatra
Ceremony #130: July 20, 1965

He placed his prints in connection with the motion picture *Von Ryan's Express* (20th Century-Fox, 1965).

Born: Francis Albert Sinatra in Hoboken, New Jersey, on December 12, 1915.

He started out as a scrawny-looking, obscure nightclub singer; but Frank Sinatra was quickly transformed into the musical idol of millions of swooning bobby-soxers during the early 1940s, ultimately becoming one of the most important artists in both the recording and motion picture industries.

In high school he started performing as a singer for dances, benefits, and other social functions. Sinatra finally landed a spot on the radio with "Major Bowes' Original Amateur Hour" and as a result toured with Bowes for about three months in 1937. That same year he landed a job as a $15-a-week singer, headwaiter, and emcee at an obscure Jersey roadhouse in Englewood Cliffs called the Rustic Cabin, where he remained for eighteen months. Sinatra was spotted there by bandleader Harry James, who offered him a singing job with his orchestra in 1939. In 1940 Sinatra

Frank Sinatra.

moved on as a singer with the Tommy Dorsey orchestra.

Sinatra's first major motion picture role came in RKO's *Higher and Higher* (1943). He was soon under contract to Metro-Goldwyn-Mayer and enjoyed a huge success in *Anchors Aweigh* (1945), becoming a genuine motion picture star.

After a few unsuccessful films in the late 1940s, some unfavorable publicity, and vocal problems caused by a hemorrhage of blood vessels, Sinatra found his career in a disastrous slump by 1952. But in 1953 he made an impressive return to the film mainstream in **From Here to Eternity*, which established him as a serious dramatic actor. Sinatra's subsequent films included a few vehicles with his so-called "Hollywood Rat Pack" cronies.

He announced retirement in 1971 but returned to performing with his television special "Ol' Blue Eyes Is Back" (1973). Since then Sinatra has continued with hugely successful concert and nightclub appearances throughout the globe.

His motion picture credits include "Major Bowes' Amateur Theatre of the Air" (1935, short, debut), *Ship Ahoy* (1942), *Take Me Out to the Ball Game* (1949), *On the Town* (1949), **The Man with the Golden Arm* (1955), *High Society* (1956), *Pal Joey* (1957), *Ocean's Eleven* (1960), *The Manchurian Candidate* (1962), and *Who Framed Roger Rabbit* (1988, voice only).

In 1971 he received the Jean Hersholt Humanitarian Award from the Academy of Motion Picture Arts and Sciences. In 1983 he was a recipient of the Kennedy Center Honors for Lifetime Achievement.

  * *Academy Award nomination: Best Actor.*
  ** *Academy Award winner: Best Supporting Actor.*

Sinatra's square is tinted green and contains the date ("7-20-65"), his two footprints, two handprints, and his signature. Three coins were also embedded in the cement. They have since been pried out.

A crowd of 3,000 gathered to watch the Sinatra ceremony. Some on-lookers even climbed the trees in the forecourt to get a better view.

The northwest corner of the forecourt, in which Sinatra's prints reside, has been referred to as the Chinese Theatre's "Little Italy," due to the neighboring squares of Sophia Loren, Dean Martin, and Marcello Mastroianni.

Julie Andrews
Ceremony #131: March 26, 1966

She placed her prints in connection with the motion picture *The Sound of Music* (20th Century-Fox, 1965). She was also honored for her work in the motion pictures *Mary Poppins* (Buena Vista, 1964) and *The Americanization of Emily* (Metro-Goldwyn-Mayer, 1964).

Born: Julia Elizabeth Wells in Walton-on-Thames, England, on October 1, 1935.

After having achieved Broadway stardom in the 1950s, Julie Andrews became one of the most popular film stars of the 1960s. When Julie was a child, it was discovered that she had the larynx of an adult and a vocal range of four octaves. Singing lessons ensued; and Andrews made her professional stage debut in 1947, singing an aria in a revue entitled *Starlight Roof*, and promptly stole the show. In 1952 she lent her vocal talents to the motion picture *The Rose of Bagdad* (a.k.a. *The Singing Princess*, debut, voice only), the English-language version of the Italian animated film *La rosa di Bagdad* (1949).

Her first big break came when she was brought to New York City to star on Broadway in *The Boy Friend* (1954). Next Andrews landed the plum role of Eliza Doolittle in *My Fair Lady* (1956), which became one of the greatest hits in the history of musical theatre. She played it two years on Broadway and eighteen months in London. In 1960 she was back on Broadway in *Camelot*.

Though she lost the film version of *My Fair Lady* (1964) to Audrey Hepburn, Andrews triumphed in Walt Disney's **Mary Poppins** that same year, the first time she was actually seen on the motion picture screen. She next played Maria in *The Sound of Music, one of the biggest money makers of all time.

Julie took the plunge into a well-received television series during 1972-1973, "The Julie Andrews Hour." Her later film successes include her roles in *10* (1979) and *Victor/Victoria* (1982).

Her motion picture credits include *Torn Curtain* (1966), *Hawaii* (1966), *Thoroughly Modern*

Julie Andrews, Eugene V. Klein, president of National General Corp. (kneeling), and unidentified man.

Millie (1967), *Star!* (1968), *Darling Lili* (1970), *The Tamarind Seed* (1974), *Little Miss Marker* (1980), *S.O.B.* (1981), *Duet for One* (1986), and *Tchin-Tchin* (1991).

     * *Academy Award nomination: Best Actress.*
   ** *Academy Award winner: Best Actress.*

Andrews' square is tinted red and contains the date ("3:26:66"), her two footprints (made with high heels), two handprints, and her signature.

At her ceremony Andrews stepped into the wet concrete with both feet. Her shoes sank so deeply into the cement that she had to step out of them and remove them by hand. After that, the theatre made it a rule that honorees could imprint only one foot at a time.

In a telephone conversation with the authors, Andrews commented on the extremely high-heeled shoes that were fashionable at the time and gave her so much trouble, saying that it was a great challenge to balance herself in the wet cement. She added she wished she could have worn her costume shoes from *Mary Poppins*—if she'd been able to do so she would not have had any difficulty standing firmly in the mixture. She also said that the shoes "from my *Mary Poppins* era better represented my [public] image at the time."

Andrews also noted that she has a rather large, flamboyant signature and found it extremely difficult to write her name in her usual style in the wet concrete.

Dick Van Dyke
Ceremony #132: June 25, 1966

He placed his prints in connection with the motion picture *Lt. Robin Crusoe, U.S.N.* (Buena Vista, 1966).

Born: in West Plains, Missouri, on December 13, 1925.

Dick Van Dyke achieved stardom as a tall, gangly, rubber-faced, and seemingly rubber-boned, comedian in both television and motion pictures. During his high school years he appeared in school plays and civic theatre productions. After serving in the Air Force during World War II, he put together a comedy team act called "The Merry Mutes." He worked nightclubs until 1953 and eventually become the host of several local television programs in Atlanta, Georgia, and New Orleans, Louisiana.

In 1955 Van Dyke moved to New York City and broke into network television on CBS as emcee of "The Morning Show." In 1958 he left the network to free-lance on TV and appeared on the programs of such personalities as Garry Moore, Phil Silvers, Ed Sullivan, and Andy Williams.

In 1960 Van Dyke scored a big hit on Broadway as the star of *Bye Bye Birdie* and in 1961 finally got

Dick Van Dyke.

the comical, singing and dancing chimney sweep in Walt Disney's *Mary Poppins* (1964).

Since the 1960s Van Dyke has appeared only sporadically in films but has had another successful TV series, "The New Dick Van Dyke Show" (1971-1974), and a not-so-successful one, "The Van Dyke Show" (1988).

His motion picture credits include *What a Way To Go!* (1964), *Divorce American Style* (1967), *Fitzwilly* (1967), *Never a Dull Moment* (1968), *Chitty Chitty Bang Bang* (1968), *Some Kind of a Nut* (1969), *The Comic* (1969), *Cold Turkey* (1971), *The Runner Stumbles* (1979), and *Dick Tracy* (1990).

Van Dyke's square is tinted red and contains the date ("June 25, 1966"), his two footprints, two handprints, and his signature.

Van Dyke was accompanied at his ceremony by his wife Marjorie and their four children. In a letter to the authors, Van Dyke recalled:

"Along with my footprints in the wet cement, my wife added a 1948 penny right next to them, as 1948 was the year that we were married....The next time we went back, the penny was gone. Someone had pried it out of the block!"

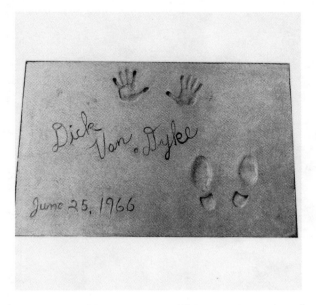

his own weekly TV series, "The Dick Van Dyke Show," which ran until 1966, and was one of the most popular and critically acclaimed series in television history. He made his film debut in *Bye Bye Birdie* (1963); but his best remembered screen role is that of

Steve McQueen. Over McQueen's left shoulder is his wife Neile Adams. Directly behind her is theatre chain executive William F. Hertz.

Steve McQueen
Ceremony #133: March 21, 1967

He placed his prints in connection with the motion picture *The Sand Pebbles* (20th Century-Fox, 1966).

Born: Terrence Stephen McQueen in Beech Grove, Indiana, on March 24, 1930. Died: November 7, 1980.

Steve McQueen created an image of a tough, intense loner who seemed to perform heroic deeds in spite of himself and became one of the biggest stars of his generation. His characters were almost always anti-authoritarian and succeeded in bucking whatever system they were up against.

The rebellious young McQueen got into trouble with the law while in his early teens and was sent to a school for troubled youths at Chino, California, where, said McQueen, "they straightened me out." At seventeen he joined the U.S. Marine Corps for a three-year stint, and in 1950 he landed in New York City.

In 1951 he was struck with the idea of becoming an actor and did his first theatrical work in Sanford Meisner's class at the Neighborhood Playhouse. He was eventually accepted as a student at The Actors Studio. McQueen's first big break came when he replaced Ben Gazzara on Broadway for three months in *A Hatful of Rain* (1956), for which he received rave notices. He made his film debut that same year and became a television star when he landed his own series, "Wanted: Dead or Alive" (1958-1961).

Real Hollywood stardom came with *The Great Escape* (1963). The greatest critical acclaim of his career was for *The Sand Pebbles* (1966), and he reached the apex of his popularity with *Bullitt* (1968).

His motion picture credits include *Somebody Up There Likes Me* (1956, debut), *The Blob* (1958), *The Magnificent Seven* (1960), *Soldier in the Rain* (1963), *Love with the Proper Stranger* (1963), *The Cincinnati Kid* (1965), *The Thomas Crown Affair* (1968), *The Getaway* (1972), *Papillon* (1973), and *The Hunter* (1980, final film).

Academy Award nomination: Best Actor.

McQueen's square is tinted gray and contains the inscription "Thanks!!" Also included are the date ("3/21/67"), his two footprints, two handprints, and his signature.

This is one of only two squares that face south toward Hollywood Boulevard. The other was placed

by actress Ali MacGraw, who was the second of McQueen's three wives.

McQueen was accompanied by his first wife, dancer/actress Neile Adams. A large number of fans were able to attend the event, as it occurred during Easter vacation. Adams, now Neile McQueen Toffel, recalled the event in her memoirs:

"Over 2,000 fans were there and God knows how many photographers. In true Hollywood fashion, we arrived in Steve's burgundy Ferrari as the crowd cheered. Amid the pandemonium we learned that Steve had set an attendance record, equaling that of Marilyn Monroe and Jane Russell."

Although McQueen appreciated the honor, he commented later that "all the hoopla bugged me. I mean, you can't say no to something like this, but the whole scene is like a circus act with you as the performing elephant."

Sidney Poitier
Ceremony #134: June 23, 1967

He placed his prints in connection with the motion picture *In the Heat of the Night* (United Artists, 1967). He was also honored for his work in the motion picture *Lilies of the Field* (United Artists, 1963).

Born: in Miami, Florida, on February 24, 1924.

Sidney Poitier, the first black super-star of the movies, paved the way for the entry of other black actors into the mainstream of film-making.

He was his parents' eighth child and grew up in extreme poverty on the Bahamian Island of Cat, 100 miles from Nassau. He moved to New York City in 1943. Frustrated and depressed by the seemingly inescapable routine of manual labor and menial jobs, Poitier came across an ad in 1945 for the American Negro Theatre and was struck by the idea of becoming an actor. He was eventually accepted by the ANT and appeared in several plays, including a small role in an all-black production of *Lysistrata* (1946) on Broadway.

Poitier says that his first work before a camera was as an extra in *Sepia Cinderella* (1947), although several sources state that he made his film debut in the U.S. Army Signal Corps film "From Whence Cometh Help" (1949, short). His Hollywood debut came at 20th Century-Fox with *No Way Out* (1950), in which he was well received; but subsequent roles were difficult to find.

His compelling part in *Blackboard Jungle* (1955) brought favorable attention, and *The Defiant Ones (1958) made Poitier a genuine star. His greatest career triumph to date came with **Lilies of the Field (1963).

In 1967 he starred simultaneously in three of the biggest hits of the year: *To Sir, with Love, In the Heat of the Night*, and *Guess Who's Coming to Dinner*. Shortly thereafter, Poitier formed his own production company and in the 1970s started a successful additional career as a director.

His motion picture credits as an actor include *Cry, the Beloved Country* (1952), *Something of Value* (1957), *Porgy and Bess* (1959), *A Raisin in the Sun* (1961), *A Patch of Blue* (1965), *The Slender Thread* (1965), *For Love of Ivy* (1968), *They Call Me MISTER Tibbs* (1970), *Uptown Saturday Night* (1974), and *Little Nikita* (1988).

In 1992 the American Film Institute presented him with its Lifetime Achievement Award.

  * *Academy Award nomination: Best Actor.*
  ** *Academy Award winner: Best Actor.*

Poitier's square is tinted green and contains the date ("6/23/67"), his two footprints, two handprints, and his signature. A dime was embedded in the cement. It has since been pried out.

Poitier admitted that the dime he embedded in the square bore no special significance, save it was "the only thing I had in my pocket."

When asked how it felt to be the person chosen to integrate the forecourt, he replied,

"Well, I feel just like the first Negro putting his footprints and handprints in the Grauman's Chinese Theatre thing."

Poitier responded thusly when questioned later about the ceremony:

"I could give you all of the pat answers about what a great day it was in my life. But to be honest, I didn't feel anything special. It was a nice day, my friends Bill Cosby and Ivan Dixon were on hand, and it was nice to see them.

"But one of the things I find most difficult at a time like that ceremony is to see myself as such gestures indicate. They imply 'movie star' and I ain't no movie star, in my own feeling.

"The word 'actor,' when I hear it applied to me, is a foreign term. I'm a creative worker. I happen to enjoy what I do but I work like everybody else does. I go to work, I go home, eat dinner, watch a little television, prepare for the next day's work, and go to bed.

"That's why I was really a little embarrassed by the ceremony."

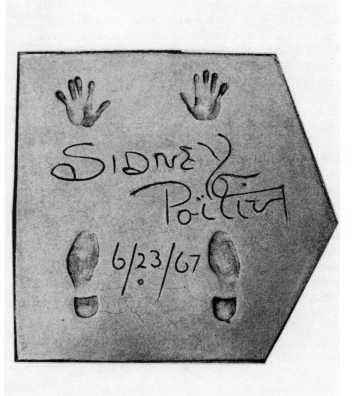

Theatre chain executive William F. Hertz (second from left) and Sidney Poitier (kneeling). Others unidentified.

Anthony Quinn
Ceremony #135: December 21, 1968

He placed his prints in connection with the motion picture *The Shoes of the Fisherman* (Metro-Goldwyn-Mayer, 1968).

Born: Anthony Rudolph Oaxaca Quinn in Chihuahua, Mexico, on April 21, 1915.

Anthony Quinn became a major motion picture star after fifteen years on the screen during which he nearly always played bit and supporting parts, often in "Bs" and programmers. He decided he wanted to become an actor while working as a janitor at an acting school. Mae West gave Quinn his first big break in *Clean Beds*, a play she was producing in Hollywood in 1936.

Though Quinn says his first film job was as an extra in *The Milky Way* (1936), his first recognizable film appearance was in *Parole* (1936). He next conned producer/director Cecil B. DeMille into believing he was a full-blooded Cherokee Indian, thereby landing a small part in *The Plainsman* (1936). Quinn signed a contract with Paramount in 1937 and for years was a highly visible player in their efficiently run "B" unit. He also managed to get himself into a few "A" pictures, such as *Union Pacific* (1939) and *Road to Morocco* (1942).

In 1948 he appeared on stage as Stanley Kowalski in the national touring company of *A Streetcar Named Desire*, garnering rave notices. He returned to Hollywood and found a career turning point in **Viva Zapata!* (1952). His best remembered role came as ***Zorba the Greek* (1964).

Anthony Quinn and three of his children.

In the 1980s Quinn repeated his success as Zorba in a musical stage version of the film, touring the show for over four years in more than 1,200 performances.

His motion picture credits include *Blood and Sand* (1941), *They Died with Their Boots On* (1941), *La Strada* (1954), **Lust for Life* (1956), ***Wild Is the Wind* (1957), *The Guns of Navarone* (1961), *Requiem for a Heavyweight* (1962), *Lawrence of Arabia* (1962), *The Secret of Santa Vittoria* (1969), and *Jungle Fever* (1991).

    * *Academy Award winner: Best Supporting Actor.*
    ** *Academy Award nomination: Best Actor.*

Quinn's square is tinted gray and contains the inscription "Dreams do come true." Also included

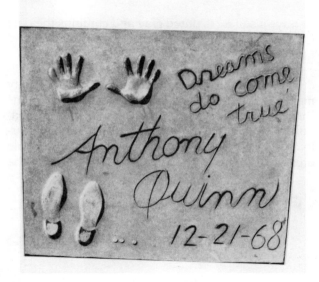

are the date ("12-21-68"), his two footprints, two handprints, and his signature, in addition to three 1968 pennies, which are embedded in the cement.

Quinn was accompanied at the ceremony by his wife Iolanda and three of his children: Francesco, Daniele, and Lorenzo.

When he signed his name Quinn forgot to dot the "i" because he was distracted by his sons. The little boys were to participate in their father's ceremony and could no longer contain their excitement. Each child stood by Quinn on the knee stand provided by the theatre for the ceremonies and placed a penny in the cement.

John Tartaglia, theatre chain maintenance and decorating official, who had been footprinting celebrities since 1954, cautioned Quinn to place just one foot at a time in the cement, citing the Julie Andrews mishap two years before. When Quinn stepped out

of the cement, he confessed, "I've got a hole in my left shoe."

When Quinn first wrote the date he placed the year ahead of the day. This was unacceptable. The cement was trowled over; and Quinn re-wrote the date, inscribing the year after the month and day.

He then washed up and faced the on-lookers who gathered for the event. In the crowd was a Mexican man holding a sign that read "Viva Chihuahua—Viva el gran actor Anthony Quinn." (Spanish for "Long live Chihuahua—Long live the great actor Anthony Quinn.") Chihuahua, Mexico, was the place of Quinn's birth. When he saw the man and his sign, Quinn reached for the chopstick with which he had previously signed his name and the date and kneeled down once again to write the inscription "Dreams do come true."

He told columnist James Bacon that he had once applied for a job as an usher at the theatre, only to be turned down. "The guy who was hiring ushers said I looked too Mexican to work in a Chinese theatre," Quinn said.

Danny Kaye
Ceremony #136: October 19, 1969

He placed his prints in connection with the motion picture *The Madwoman of Chaillot* (Warner Bros.-Seven Arts, 1969).

Born: David Daniel Kominsky (sources vary regarding spelling of last name) in Brooklyn, New York, on January 18, 1913. Died: March 3, 1989.

Danny Kaye's staccato delivery of tongue-twisting, double-talk lyrics, and his rubber-faced and rubber-limbed buffoonery, combined with sharp wit and his heart-felt humanitarianism, made him one of the most beloved figures in American entertainment.

He entered vaudeville in 1933. After playing on the "Borscht Circuit" in the Catskills, Kaye made his Broadway debut in *The Straw Hat Revue* (1939), for which Sylvia Fine composed music and lyrics. They married the following year, and Fine was responsible for most of his subsequent specialty songs.

His first big-time club date was at New York's La Martinique, where he scored a smash and was seen by playwright Moss Hart, who immediately hired him for the Broadway musical *Lady in the Dark* (1941), the show that made Kaye a star. After another huge hit on Broadway in *Let's Face It* (1941), Kaye agreed

Danny Kaye. That day Kaye was also presented with the Hollywood Chamber of Commerce's Humanitarian Award for his efforts on behalf of UNICEF.

to go to Hollywood and signed a contract with Samuel Goldwyn. Kaye was showcased in lavish productions by the producer in such films as *Up in Arms* (1944) and *The Secret Life of Walter Mitty* (1947), usually cast in the role of a milquetoast who miraculously becomes a hero.

In 1948 he scored a triumph at the London Palladium when he performed his act there. He had his own television series, "The Danny Kaye Show"

(1963-1967), and in 1970 had a Broadway hit as Noah in the musical *Two by Two*.

His motion picture credits include "Dime a Dance" (1937, short, debut), *The Kid from Brooklyn* (1946), *On the Riviera* (1951), *Hans Christian Andersen* (1952), *Knock on Wood* (1954), *White Christmas* (1954), *The Court Jester* (1956), *Merry Andrew* (1958), *The Five Pennies* (1959), and "The Pied Piper" (1972, UNICEF short, final film).

In 1955 he received an Honorary Academy Award "for his unique talents, his service to the Academy [of Motion Picture Arts and Sciences], the motion picture industry, and the American people." In 1982 he received that organization's Jean Hersholt Humanitarian Award, and in 1984 he was a recipient of the Kennedy Center Honors for Lifetime Achievement.

Kaye's square is tinted gray and contains the date ("10/18/69"), his two footprints, two handprints, and his signature.

Kaye's ceremony was attended by nearly 500 children in colorful Halloween costumes, along with sixty members of the famed UNICEF (United Nations International Children's Emergency Fund) International Children's Choir. They were sponsored by various southern California chapters of that charitable organization and turned out to honor Kaye for the

many years he labored on behalf of UNICEF. Kaye became associated with UNICEF in 1954 and during the last thirty years of his life spent a vast amount of time touring on its behalf, entertaining throughout the world and raising funds.

Kaye's wife, composer/lyricist Sylvia Fine, in a letter to the authors, shared one of their "favorite family stories" that happened to include his ceremony at the Chinese Theatre:

"In 1943 when Danny had made his first [feature] picture, *Up in Arms*, he went one afternoon to keep an appointment with [producer] David O. Selznick at Selznick International studios. A few hours later he came home obviously in high, good spirits, and bounced into the room where I was having a meeting with our then New York lawyer. He kissed me hello and said, 'You'll never guess what happened.' So I didn't guess. And he said, 'Shirley Temple asked me for my autograph. Can you imagine Shirley Temple asking *me*?' The lawyer looked up at him and said, 'What are you so excited about?' He then added quite seriously, 'What are you going to do when they ask you to put your footsteps in Grauman's Chow Mein?'

"So on the day that you speak of, when Danny put his footprints and handprints into that celebrated sidewalk, he came home and said, 'You'll never guess what.' So I didn't guess. And he said, 'I just put my footprints into Grauman's Chow Mein.'"

Gene Kelly
Ceremony #137: November 24, 1969

He placed his prints in connection with the motion picture *Hello, Dolly!* (20th Century-Fox, 1969), which he directed.

Born: Eugene Curran Kelly in Pittsburgh, Pennsylvania, on August 23, 1912.

Gene Kelly was one of Metro-Goldwyn-Mayer's most accomplished and innovative artists. His mother ran a dancing school, and young Gene began teaching there. The school became very successful and was ultimately named The Gene Kelly Studio of the Dance when he was about twenty-one.

Next Kelly appeared in vaudeville and small-time nightclubs. He got a job as a chorus boy on Broadway in the Cole Porter musical *Leave It to Me* (1938), and his first important break came with a leading part in the play *The Time of Your Life* (1939). But it was his handling of the title role in the Rodgers and Hart musical *Pal Joey* (1940) that made Kelly a star.

Producer David O. Selznick signed him to a film contract in 1941; but since Selznick had no immediate plans for any musicals, he soon sold Kelly's contract to MGM, where he made his film debut in *For Me and My Gal* (1942). He scored a triumph in *On the Town* (1949), a genuine break-through in the musical genre and his first picture as co-director. His greatest career peaks came with *An American in Paris* (1951) and *Singin' in the Rain* (1952), which many regard as the definitive movie musical.

Kelly geared himself more toward non-dancing roles and direction when it became evident that the Hollywood musical was on its way out. He directed the Broadway hit *Flower Drum Song* (1958) and starred in the television series "Going My Way" (1962-1963).

His motion picture credits as a performer include *Cover Girl* (1944), *Anchors Aweigh* (1945), *The Pirate* (1948), *The Three Musketeers* (1948), *Take Me Out to the Ball Game* (1949), *Summer Stock* (1950), *Brigadoon* (1954), *Invitation to the Dance* (1956), *Inherit the Wind* (1960), and *Xanadu.* (1980).

In 1952 he received an Honorary Academy Award "in appreciation of his versatility as an actor, singer, director and dancer, and specifically for his brilliant achievements in the art of choreography on film." In 1982 he was a recipient of the Kennedy Center Honors for Lifetime Achievement, and in 1985 the American Film Institute presented him with its Life Achievement Award.

Academy Award nomination: Best Actor.

The Gene Kelly family: Gene (kneeling, center) with his wife, dancer/choreographer Jeanne Coyne, son Timothy, and daughter Bridget. Unknown theatre attendant at right. Five days prior to the event, Kelly was honored with a U.S. Congressional Record tribute for his "great contribution to American art, culture and entertainment, matched by his record of public service."

Kelly's square is tinted green and contains the date ("11-24-'69"), his two footprints, two handprints, and his signature.

His ceremony had originally been scheduled to take place on November 20 but was changed at his request for reasons unknown.

On the day of the ceremony a band played "Hello, Kelly!," a parody of the famous *Hello, Dolly!* title song. Plans mentioned in a 20th Century-Fox in-house memo dated November 6, 1969, called for Kelly to arrive at the ceremony in a vintage automobile; and, while the band played, the hope was that he might be able to "do a time-step up to the cement block, literally dancing in the concrete if possible."

Francis X. Bushman
Ceremony #138: November 17, 1970

He was posthumously honored with a plaque. It was awarded in connection with the fact that Bushman, his first wife Josephine, and their five children lived in their private residence from 1913 to 1915 on the site where the theatre now stands.

Born: Francis Xavier Bushman in Baltimore, Maryland, on January 10, 1883. Died: August 23, 1966.

The first star to be called "King of the Movies" was not Clark Gable, but rather Francis X. Bushman, whose cinema reign spanned the teens. Between 1914 and 1917 he was the most popular leading man in motion pictures.

By 1903 Bushman was playing small parts in stock companies and supplemented his income by posing for many prominent sculptors. In 1911 he was enticed by the movies and joined the Essanay company in Chicago, where he made his film debut in *His Friend's Wife* (1911). He soon surpassed the popularity of other early male screen idols.

However, when the public discovered that Bushman had been married since 1902, had five children, and divorced his first wife to marry his leading lady, Beverly Bayne, in 1918, his popularity plummeted. By 1920 he was considered all but washed up in the movies. Bushman turned to vaudeville, did some plays, and was off the screen for three years.

In 1923 his luck changed when he was signed to play Messala in the Metro-Goldwyn-Mayer produc-

tion of *Ben-Hur* (1925). The film was a smash hit, and it seemed his career might be revitalized; but, according to Bushman, he was blacklisted because of a

Francis X. Bushman.

"stupid misunderstanding" with Louis B. Mayer and found it nearly impossible to obtain work at any major studio for many years thereafter. He made a comeback on radio, doing thousands of broadcasts over the years.

His motion picture credits include "Out of the Depths" (1912, short), *One Wonderful Night* (1914), *Graustark* (1915), *Romeo and Juliet* (1916), *Red, White and Blue Blood* (1917), *The Lady in Ermine* (1927), *The Call of the Circus* (1930, talkie debut), *Wilson* (1944), *David and Bathsheba* (1951), and *The Ghost in the Invisible Bikini* (1966, final film).

Bushman was honored with a west wall plaque, which contains the inscription:

> To The Memory Of
> Francis X. Bushman
> Noted Motion Picture Star
> Whose Home
> Occupied This Site Prior To
> The Construction Of The
> Grauman's Chinese Theatre

The plaque was presented by the Women's Division of the Hollywood Chamber of Commerce, which had suggested that Bushman and his home site be honored by the Chinese Theatre as early as 1962.

Ali MacGraw
Ceremony #139: December 14, 1972

She placed her prints in connection with the motion picture *The Getaway* (National General, 1972).

Born: Elizabeth Alice MacGraw in Pound Ridge, New York, circa April 1, 1938 (sources vary on year).

In 1969 Ali MacGraw had her first starring film role in *Goodbye, Columbus*, and in the early 1970s she seemed destined to become *the* counter-culture heroine of the decade. But it all came to a grinding halt in 1972, at the height of her "bankability," when she began a five-year hiatus from filming to raise her infant son.

MacGraw worked her way through Wellesley College, with the assistance of scholarships, and was graduated with honors. Soon after, she became an

Ali MacGraw.

assistant editor to the legendary Diana Vreeland at *Harper's Bazaar* magazine and next a photographer's stylist in the fashion industry. When a model didn't appear for a session on one occasion, Ali was pressed into service as a substitute and from then on enjoyed a prestigious career in the modeling field.

She began auditioning for film roles. After her hit in *Goodbye, Columbus*, she starred in one of the most successful movies of all time, **Love Story* (1970). She scored a third consecutive hit in *The Getaway* and then withdrew from availability for future roles.

MacGraw chose to return to the screen in *Convoy* (1978) and in 1983 appeared in the highly praised TV mini-series "The Winds of War." She was also seen on television in the role of Lady Ashley Mitchell in the popular series "Dynasty" in 1985.

Her motion picture credits include *A Lovely Way To Die* (1968, debut), *Players* (1979), and *Just Tell Me What You Want* (1980).

*Academy Award nomination: Best Actress.

MacGraw's square is tinted green and contains the inscription "Peace & Love." Also included are the date ("14 12-72"), her two footprints (made with high heels), two handprints, and her signature. A coin was also embedded in the cement. It has since been pried out.

This is the second of only two squares that face south toward Hollywood Boulevard. The other was placed by actor Steve McQueen, who was the third of MacGraw's three husbands.

A group of protesters paraded outside the theatre during the ceremony. They were upset that MacGraw was being honored by the theatre so early in her career—after all, they contended, *The Getaway* was only her third starring role on the screen. Their placards read "Let us give credit where credit is due—Ali MacGraw, who are you?"

On December 28, just fourteen days after her ceremony, two men in their late twenties were caught trying to cover MacGraw's square by placing wet cement on top of her footprints. No damage was done, as the cement was discovered before it set and was quickly washed off the square. The two men escaped in a taxi.

It was theorized that this act of vandalism was committed for the same reason that the ceremony drew protestors—some people felt that MacGraw was enshrined in the forecourt too early in her career.

Jack Nicholson
Ceremony #140: June 17, 1974

He placed his prints in connection with the motion picture *Chinatown* (Paramount, 1974).

Born: in Neptune, New Jersey, on April 22, 1937.

Jack Nicholson has been one of the most critically acclaimed and highly successful actors at the box-office during the past two decades. His performances are both charismatic and delicately shaded with subtle levels of meaning, and his piercing smile can be alternately genial or menacing. Nicholson is drawn to roles that he can relate to on a personal level, often refusing films that obviously will be commercial blockbusters, in favor of smaller projects that he finds more artistically rewarding.

Jack Nicholson.

After high school graduation he turned down a scholarship to the University of Delaware and opted to set out for Los Angeles in 1954, aiming to write for the movies. Nicholson's first industry job was as an office boy in the Metro-Goldwyn-Mayer animated cartoon department at $30 a week. He joined an acting group called The Players' Ring, studied under Jeff Corey, and found himself involved with the Hollywood-fringe productions of Roger Corman, as a writer, producer, director, and actor. His film debut as an actor was for Corman in *The Cry Baby Killer* (1958).

Nicholson long struggled to break down the seemingly impenetrable walls of the major studios. *Easy Rider* (1969), a low-budget film which shook the industry by becoming one of the year's biggest critical and popular hits, sent Nicholson into the mainstream. He suddenly became one of the most important stars in Hollywood and has since consistently scored in hit after hit, including such personal triumphs as ****One Flew over the Cuckoo's Nest* (1975), **Terms of Endearment* (1983), and ***Prizzi's Honor* (1985).

His additional motion picture credits as an actor include *The Little Shop of Horrors* (1960), ***Five Easy Pieces* (1970), *Carnal Knowledge* (1971), ***The Last Detail* (1973), ***Chinatown* (1974), *The Shining* (1980), *Reds* (1981), ***Ironweed* (1987), *Batman* (1989), and *The Two Jakes* (1990).

    * *Academy Award nomination: Best Supporting Actor.*
    ** *Academy Award winner: Best Supporting Actor.*
    *** *Academy Award nomination: Best Actor.*
    **** *Academy Award winner: Best Actor.*

Nicholson's square is tinted green and contains the date ("June 17, 1974"), his two footprints, two handprints, and his signature.

Mayor Tom Bradley and Ted Mann
Ceremony #141: May 18, 1977

Mayor Tom Bradley

Born: Thomas Bradley in Calvert, Texas, on December 29, 1917.

First elected to the office of Mayor of the city of Los Angeles on May 29, 1973, Tom Bradley became the first black mayor of an American city with a predominately white population. He is currently serving an unprecedented fifth term in that office.

In high school, Bradley was a good student and a Los Angeles all-city football tackle. He obtained an athletic scholarship to UCLA and became a track star there. He quit college in 1940 and joined the Los Angeles Police Department, where he remained for the next twenty-one years.

During the 1950s Bradley began studying law at night and in 1956 obtained his LL.B. degree from Southwestern University. In 1957 he was admitted to the California Bar, and in 1961 he retired from the police department and established a private law practice in Los Angeles. He soon became active in local politics and in 1963 was elected to the Los Angeles City Council, becoming the first black elected to that body.

Although Bradley failed in a mayoral challenge against incumbent Sam Yorty in the election of 1969, he defeated Yorty in the election of 1973. The Bradley administration has seen the emergence of Los Angeles as a city of unparalleled ethnic and cultural diversity, the financial center of the Western U.S., and the "Gateway to the Pacific Rim."

Ted Mann

Born: Theodore Mann in Wishek, North Dakota, on April 15, 1916.

Ted Mann is the former chairman and chief executive officer of the Mann Theatre Corporation, which owned the Chinese Theatre. He became the first and only individual to be the 100% sole owner of the Chinese in 1973, a distinction he retained for thirteen years.

His family relocated to Minneapolis, Minnesota, where as a teenager, Mann spent summers working in theatres. He initially entered the film exhibition field as a young man in 1935 and later acquired two theatres in St. Paul (the Oxford and the Gem), building these into a chain of more than twenty theatres. Mann achieved extraordinary success, ultimately developing his holdings into a theatre circuit that stretched across the upper Middle West to Washington, D.C.

He entered the field of film production in 1967. Mann served as co-producer of *The Illustrated Man* (1969) and executive producer of *Buster and Billie* (1974), *Lifeguard* (1976), and *Brubaker* (1980).

In 1970 Mann sold his Mid-West chain to General Cinema and moved permanently to Los Angeles, where in 1973 he acquired the National General theatre chain of nearly 270 screens as sole owner for $67,500,000. He re-christened the firm the Mann Theatre Corporation and ultimately sold it to Gulf +

TV personality Monty Hall (left), William F. Hertz, by then the director of theatre operations for Mann Theatres, Los Angeles Mayor Tom Bradley, and Ted Mann.

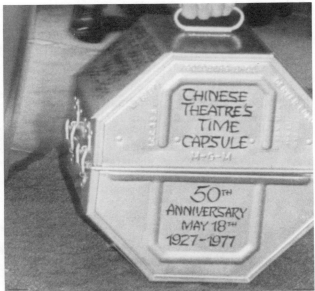

The 50th anniversary time capsule; actually, a motion picture film canister.

Western in 1986. By 1988 the circuit had grown to over 450 screens. Mann launched an eighty-five-screen expansion program for southern and northern California in mid-1990, to eventually give the chain 535 screens at 117 complexes.

Mann settled his five-year contract as Chairman and Chief Executive Officer of the 510-screen Mann Theatres on December 31, 1990, ten months prior to its scheduled expiration in October 1991. The chain is currently the flagship circuit of Cinamerica Theatres, a joint venture of Paramount Communications and Time Warner. His current plans include activities for Ted Mann Productions, headquartered on the Paramount lot in Hollywood in a non-exclusive deal, where he has several projects in active development as of this writing.

The Chinese Theatre's Fiftieth Anniversary Ceremony #142: May 24, 1977

On May 18, 1977, Mayor Tom Bradley and Ted Mann placed their prints in connection with the fiftieth anniversary of the Chinese Theatre's opening with the premiere of Cecil B. DeMille's production of *The King of Kings* (Producers Distributing Corp., 1927). Their square also includes the Chinese Theatre's fiftieth anniversary time capsule, which was placed on May 24, 1977.

The Bradley/Mann/fiftieth anniversary square is tinted red and contains the inscription "All Los Angeles Congratulates Ted Mann [signature] and the Chinese Theatre." Also included are the date ("May 18 1977"), "Tom Bradley [signature]—Mayor," and the inscription "For 50 Great Years." A plaque in the lower left corner of the square indicates the position of the time capsule with the inscription:

> Chinese
> Theatre
> 50th
> Anniversary
> Time
> Capsule

An additional plaque honoring the fiftieth anniversary of the Chinese Theatre—a reproduction of a Los Angeles City resolution—is in the upper right corner and contains the inscription:

> City Of
> Los Angeles
> State Of California
> Resolution
> Wheres [sic],
> Mann Theatres
> Is Observing The
> Fiftieth Anniversary
> Of The Dedication Of
> Hollywood's Chinese Theatre

(The rest of the city resolution follows on the plaque but is not included here.)

The ceremonial program for the day included the burial of a time capsule in the forecourt in the afternoon, the rededication of Cecil B. DeMille's square at 7:30 p.m., and an anniversary screening of *The King of Kings* (1927) at 8:00 p.m.

The capsule was a film canister and contained mementos of the 1927 premiere of *The King of Kings*, a copy of the fiftieth anniversary premiere program, an official City Council resolution signed by the Mayor and the fifteen City Council members

The Los Angeles City resolution plaque.

commemorating the fiftieth anniversary of the theatre, clips from famous Chinese films (i.e., the country of China, not motion pictures that had played at the theatre), plus Chinese artifacts depicting the design and construction of the theatre. It is to be opened in 2027.

Mann was assisted by William F. Hertz, the director of theatre operations for Mann Theatres, who coordinated the Chinese Theatre's participation for the day's programming.

The afternoon festivities began at 12:15 p.m. and included the unveiling of the new Bradley/Mann block. In a brief speech, Mann praised Chinese Theatre founder Sid Grauman for his vision, talent, and foresight and proudly noted, "The Chinese Theatre is still one of the great theatres in the country."

The Consul General of the People's Republic of China coordinated the participation of the Chinese community. Half of the forecourt was reserved to accommodate a demonstration and exhibit of Chinese culture and arts that included entertainment by Chinese dancers.

That evening, the stars and invited dignitaries who attended the premiere were encouraged to dress in 1927 fashions and to arrive at the theatre in vintage pre-1928 automobiles in an effort to recreate the atmosphere of the original gala opening.

A donation $1.50 per person was required. This was the 1927 post-premiere regular ticket price.

Star Wars (1977) characters See-Threepio, Artoo-Detoo, and Lord Darth Vader, and Anthony Daniels Ceremony #143: August 3, 1977

See-Threepio/Anthony Daniels, Artoo-Detoo, and Lord Darth Vader placed their prints (in that order) in connection with the motion picture *Star Wars* (20th Century-Fox, 1977).

Star Wars (20th Century-Fox, 1977)

In early 1977 advance posters for *Star Wars* announced that the picture was "Coming To Your Galaxy This Summer." The film starred Mark Hamill, Harrison Ford, Carrie Fisher, and Alec Guinness; and when it opened on May 25 it quite literally took the world by storm. The picture was brilliantly imaginative; and its events and characters—Luke Skywalker, Han Solo, Princess Leia Organa, Ben (Obi-Wan) Kenobi, arch villain Darth Vader (the Dark Lord of the Sith), Chewbacca the Wookie, and the robots See-Threepio and Artoo-Detoo—almost immediately became a part of our contemporary mythology.

The primary creative force behind the film was its writer and director, George Lucas. He said, "I want to give young people some sort of faraway exotic envi-ronment for their imaginations to run around in." The action was set "A long time ago in a galaxy far, far away...;" and Lucas conceived his story as an expression of his idealized boyhood fantasy life and his love for Flash Gordon and the films, comics, books, and television shows of his youth. From this inspiration he transformed his ideas into a film of amazing technical wizardry, combining breathtaking action in outer space with romantic fantasies of sword and sorcery.

The picture was the most successful up to that time and was followed by two eagerly awaited and equally popular sequels: *The Empire Strikes Back* (1980), which introduced the characters of Yoda and Lando Calrissian, and *Return of the Jedi* (1983), which featured the Ewoks. The three pictures were conceived by Lucas as the middle trilogy of a nine-film adventure saga. The other six films have not yet been realized.

The saga's philosophy, "May the Force be with you," has been translated into many languages throughout the globe; and its successful merchandising campaigns—including toys, video games, and bubble gum—are rivaled only by those of the Walt Disney company.

Pat H. Broeske wrote in 1984, "Credited with revitalizing public appetite for science fiction and fantasy—in print as well as on the screen—the *Star Wars* films belong to a select group of titles distinguished by everlasting youth. Along with *King Kong* (1933), *The Wizard of Oz* (1939), quintessential screen lovers Scarlett O'Hara and Rhett Butler [of *Gone With the Wind* (1939)], and a handful of others, the *Star Wars* films....belong to audiences, especially youthful ones, everywhere."

Star Wars was produced by Gary Kurtz for Lucasfilm Ltd. Productions and won seven Academy Awards: for Art Direction-Set Decoration; Film Editing; Music (Original Score); Sound; Visual Effects; Costume Design; and a Special Achievement Award "for the creation of the alien, creature and robot voices featured...." It received four additional Oscar nominations, including Best Picture.

Anthony Daniels.

Anthony Daniels

Born: in Salisbury, England, on February 21, 1946.

Anthony Daniels is best known to audiences as the lovable android See-Threepio of the *Star Wars* trilogy.

He trained in acting from 1970 to 1973 at the Rose Bruford Drama School. He then won a six-month engagement as a member of the BBC Radio Drama Repertory Company. In 1974 he made his stage debut in *She Stoops To Conquer* at the Palace Theatre, Watford, just outside London. He soon joined the Young Vic Company and appeared in several of their touring stage productions (*Macbeth, Much Ado about Nothing,* and *Rosencrantz and Guildenstern Are Dead*), while dabbling in radio and television on the side.

Daniels strongly felt that he did not want to do *Star Wars* when it was initially offered to him. But upon reading the script he promptly fell in love with the See-Threepio character and quickly changed his mind. Because of the harrowing logistical difficulties involved with working inside the elaborate golden robot costume, Daniels found the making of the picture to be "...agony, intellectually and physically" but was ultimately both amazed and pleased with the final results.

Daniels also provided the voice of See-Threepio for National Public Radio's adaptations of *Star Wars* and *The Empire Strikes Back*. In costume as See-Threepio, Daniels has guest-conducted the London Symphony Orchestra and the Boston Pops. Daniels also provided the voice for one of the characters in the animated motion picture *The Lord of the Rings* (1978), in addition to writing children's stories and plays for the BBC Radio.

The *Star Wars* square is tinted gray and contains the inscription "Star Wars." Also included are the date ("Aug 3-1977"), Artoo-Detoo's three footprints, and his signature ("R2D2"); Lord Darth Vader's two footprints, and his signature ("Darth Vader"); See-

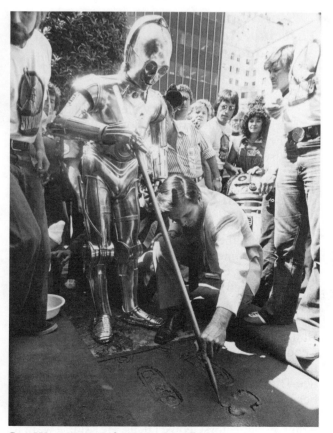

Star Wars *(1977) character See-Threepio.*

Threepio's two footprints, and his signature ("C3PO"); and Daniels' signature.

The ceremony set the theatre's all-time attendance record—a crowd of 8,000 turned up for the event! The occasion was also another "first" for the theatre in that the film officially re-premiered that same day and moved back into the house for a resumed regular run. The picture had originally opened on May 25, 1977, at the Chinese Theatre, the Avco Center Cinema in Westwood, and Plitt's City Center Cinema in Orange.

Just as the eager spectators had hoped, Darth Vader was properly menacing, See-Threepio/Anthony Daniels delivered an enthusiastic thank you speech, and little Artoo-Detoo made his customary whistles, sighs, and beeps, much to the crowd's delight.

David Prowse, assisted by the voice of James Earl Jones, portrayed Lord Darth Vader; and Kenny Baker portrayed Artoo-Detoo in the three films. But of all the performers in the *Star Wars* trilogy, only Anthony Daniels, in costume as See-Threepio, signed his name in the cement during the ceremony in the

Star Wars *(1977) character Artoo-Detoo.*

Chinese Theatre forecourt. Shortly after, Daniels commented, "Compared to the stars that are there, I am a bit embarrassed that I am there at all."

Author Adela Rogers St. Johns wrote about the impact the film had on the youth of the day and a changing Hollywood in 1978:

"I saw *Star Wars* the other day in the company of some of my great-grandchildren who belong to the *post*-post-Hoppy [Western star Hopalong Cassidy] generation and they were vastly taken with the movie and the tall gold humanoid robot, C-3PO, who speaks with a British accent and the little mechanized robot, R2-D2, who bubbles and squeaks....These two new stars were immortalized in cement in front of Grauman's Chinese Theatre not far from the prints of Tom Mix and his horse, Tony. I have to admit that...whether I like it or not, and I don't, the Old West as a frontier is being replaced, in the imagination of the young at any rate, by the new frontier of Space. The glamour of the cowboy now rests with spacemen and robots while the trusty horse is, I suppose, the computer although I'm not too sure how far we should go with this."

Star Wars *(1977) character Lord Darth Vader.*

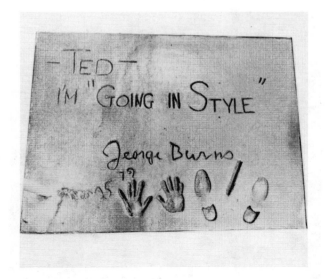

George Burns
Ceremony #144: January 25, 1979

He placed his prints in connection with the motion picture *Going in Style* (Warner Bros., 1979).

Born: Nathan Birnbaum in New York City on January 20, 1896.

After eighty-nine years in show business, George Burns has become not only a living legend but also somewhat of a national treasure, with his ubiquitous cigar, raspy voice, and never-ending repertoire of quips and anecdotes.

At seven Burns organized a group of neighborhood kids to sing together, calling them the "Pee Wee Quartet." At fourteen he adopted his trademark cigar and began stand-up comedy, playing small-time vaudeville circuits, usually with little success.

He was twenty-seven when he met Gracie Allen, a young actress/dancer who had given up show business and was studying to become a stenographer. Burns talked her into returning to vaudeville as a team and married her three years later in 1926. Together they became one of the most successful comedy teams in history, and by the late 1920s they were major stars playing the "big-time" circuits.

Their teaming was a match made in heaven, with Burns the perfect foil for her dizziness and inspired illogical lunacy. They worked together consistently until her retirement in 1958. In 1929 they began filming a series of comedy shorts and in 1930 made their radio debut on the BBC while touring England. After guesting on several top radio shows, they began their own series in 1932, which ran until 1950 when they successfully made the change-over to television with "The George Burns and Gracie Allen Show" (1950-1958).

Gracie's untimely death from a heart attack in 1964 left Burns stunned and deeply depressed. For a while it looked as though he would quietly slip into retirement, but he turned himself around and went back into entertaining full force, as a solo act, with great success.

His motion picture credits include "Lambchops" (1929, short, debut), *The Big Broadcast* (1932), *The Big Broadcast of 1937* (1936), *A Damsel in Distress* (1937), *College Swing* (1938), *Honolulu* (1939, his final film with Gracie), **The Sunshine Boys* (1975),

William F. Hertz, director of theatre operations for Mann Theatres and then the president of the Hollywood Chamber of Commerce (left), George Burns, and actress Dorit Stevens.

Oh, God! (1977), *Just You and Me, Kid* (1979), and *18 Again!* (1988).

In 1988 he was a recipient of the Kennedy Center Honors for Lifetime Achievement.

Academy Award winner: Best Supporting Actor.

Burns' square is tinted red and contains the inscription "Ted—I'm 'Going in Style.'" Also included are the date ("Nov 25 79"), his two footprints, two handprints, and his signature, plus an imprint of Burns' trademark cigar. In order to obtain the best imprint possible, a wooden cigar model was used.

Before Burns arrived for his ceremony, a workman had written the inscription Burns wanted included in the cement "Ted—I'm 'Going in Style.'" When Burns saw it, he joked, "I'm 'going in style,' but not for a hell of a long time."

William F. Hertz, the director of theatre operations for Mann Theatres, who was then also president of the Hollywood Chamber of Commerce, presided over the event. Burns told him, "If you want to live a long time you have to smoke cigars, drink martinis and dance close."

Burns bantered with the on-lookers, saying, "When I first started out, I sang 'The Sidewalks of New York.' [a.k.a. ' East Side, West Side.'] Now here I am seventy-six years later working the sidewalks again."

When someone noted that Burns signed his name in the wet cement with a ballpoint pen, Chinese Theatre manager Elmer Haines explained that the honorees of the past used chopsticks and other instruments to write their signatures and inscriptions, but the imprints were sometimes rough and unsatisfactory; so ballpoint pens were substituted.

John Travolta
Ceremony #145: June 2, 1980

He placed his prints in connection with the motion picture *Urban Cowboy* (Paramount, 1980).

Born: in Englewood, New Jersey, on February 18, 1954.

During the late 1970s and early 1980s, John Travolta was the most exciting and popular film star of his generation. His good looks and the rhythmic way he moved his body were all framed by the personality of someone who seemed street-wise and hip but simultaneously good-hearted, vulnerable, and lovable.

Travolta was drawn to the acting field from childhood of his own volition. He was allowed to drop out of high school at sixteen in order to seriously pursue acting and dancing as a profession. After a string of commercials, small parts on television, and several musicals on stage, his big break came in 1975 when he landed the part of Vinnie Barbarino in the TV series "Welcome Back, Kotter" (1975-1979).

He generated excitement on the motion picture screen in a small role in *Carrie* (1976) and impressed the critics with his acting ability in the TV movie "The Boy in the Plastic Bubble" that same year, but it was *Saturday Night Fever* (1977) that sent his career skyrocketing to astounding heights. He followed *Fever* with *Grease* (1978), the most profitable musical in film history.

However, his next picture, *Moment by Moment* (also 1978), was a flop. His stature was largely recovered with the successful *Urban Cowboy* (1980), but a series of disappointing films put Travolta's career in serious jeopardy. By the mid-1980s his popularity had slipped precipitously. In 1989 he had his first genuine hit in several years with *Look Who's Talking*, a modestly budgeted comedy which became a box-office smash.

His motion picture credits include *The Devil's Rain* (1975, debut), *Blow Out* (1981), *Staying Alive* (1983), *Two of a Kind* (1983), *Perfect* (1985), *The Experts* (1989), *Look Who's Talking Too* (1990), and *Shout* (1991).

Academy Award nomination: Best Actor.

Travolta's square is tinted green and contains the inscription "Ted, It's Great to Be Here, Thanks!" Also

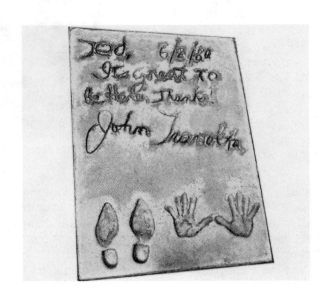

John Travolta and William F. Hertz (kneeling, right), director of theatre operations for Mann Theatres.

included are the date ("6/2/80"), his two footprints (made with boots), two handprints, and his signature.

Travolta arrived for his ceremony at the theatre decked out in new Western attire, including boots, as befitted his film role. He was concerned that his brand-new, expensive boots might be damaged by the wet concrete and had to be reassured that no harm would come to them. When he stepped out of the cement attendants quickly rushed to his aid and cleaned the soggy residue from them.

Travolta was amused when he saw how much larger his size twelve boot prints were than those of his forecourt neighbor John Wayne.

Burt Reynolds
Ceremony #146: September 24, 1981

He placed his prints in connection with the motion picture *Paternity* (Paramount, 1981).

Born: Burton Leon Reynolds, Jr., in Waycross, Georgia, on February 11, 1936.

Only two stars in film history have ever been voted the number one box-office attraction for five consecutive years: Bing Crosby (1944-1948) and Burt Reynolds (1978-1982). His good-ol'-boy macho image is tempered with sensitivity, self-deprecation, and genuine likability.

He intended to be a professional football player, but an auto accident caused an injury that shattered his plans. Reynolds became interested in acting while a student at Palm Beach Junior College. He won a scholarship to the Hyde Park Playhouse in New York and made his New York stage debut in a revival of *Mister Roberts* (1956). Soon after, he signed a long-term television contract with Universal.

Reynolds appeared in several TV series, including "Riverboat" (1959-1960), "Gunsmoke" (1962-1965), "Hawk" (1966), and "Dan August" (1970-1971). He began frequently guesting on several network TV talk shows; and his witty, irreverent personality made him hugely popular with audiences. His spread as the first nude male centerfold in history (in *Cosmopolitan*, April 1972), which Reynolds intended as a humorous put-down of *Playboy* magazine, set the nation on its ear and won him countless new fans.

Burt Reynolds.

Then came the film that proved a major turning point and made him a full-fledged star: *Deliverance* (1972). For the next twelve years it was nearly all uphill for Reynolds as he starred in (and sometimes directed) a series of box-office smash hits.

Reynolds' film career declined somewhat after the early 1980s. He opted to return to TV in the series "B.L. Stryker" in 1989 and since 1990 has appeared in the series "Evening Shade."

His motion picture credits as an actor include *Angel Baby* (1961, debut), *Sam Whiskey* (1969), *The Longest Yard* (1974), *Smokey and the Bandit* (1977), *Semi-Tough* (1977), *Hooper* (1978), *Starting Over* (1979), *The Cannonball Run* (1981), *Sharky's Machine* (1981), and *All Dogs Go to Heaven* (1989, voice only).

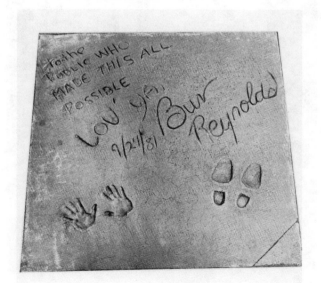

Reynolds' square is tinted gray and contains the inscription "to the Public Who Made This All Possible—Lov' Ya," (the comma is Reynolds') and the date ("9/24/81"). Also included are his two footprints (made with boots), two handprints, and his signature.

Reynolds told the spectators who gathered for his ceremony, "When I came here in 195...[deliberately slurring the exact date], I remember standing in Douglas Fairbanks' prints. And I remember thinking how small they seemed."

Reynolds chose to wear his largest pair of boots when his turn came to be footprinted and joked, "I want people to think *everything* is in proportion."

Rhonda Fleming
Ceremony #147: September 28, 1981

Fleming is married to Ted Mann, who was
the chairman and chief executive officer of
the Mann Theatre Corporation at the time
of her ceremony. The couple wed in 1978.

*Born: Marilyn Cheverton Louis in Los Angeles, Cali-
fornia, circa August 10, 1923 (sources vary on year).*

Famous for her beautiful features, burnished red-
gold hair, and perfect complexion, Rhonda Fleming
photographed ideally in color and appeared in a
string of starring vehicles during the late 1940s and
1950s.

She attended Beverly Hills High School, appeared
in school plays, and started taking singing lessons at
fifteen. After an impressive showing on Jesse Lasky's
"Gateway to Hollywood" radio show, she caught the
eye of agent Henry Willson, who got her a six-week
stint on stage in Ken Murray's *Blackouts.* She made
her film debut in a bit part in *Hello, Frisco, Hello*
(1943).

Producer David O. Selznick signed her to a seven-
year contract and first used her in a small but impres-
sive dramatic part in *Spellbound* (1945), in which
Rhonda proved effective and gained favorable notice.
Selznick often loaned her out to other studios; and
Fleming fought hard for, and won, the much-coveted
lead in Paramount's *A Connecticut Yankee in King
Arthur's Court* (1949), opposite Bing Crosby.

After parting with Selznick, Rhonda signed a contract with Paramount for several films and later free-
lanced. She plunged into stage work during the
1970s. Fleming made her Broadway debut in *The
Women* (1973). In 1976 she starred as Lalume in a
special ten-week engagement of *Kismet* at the Los
Angeles Music Center's Dorothy Chandler Pavilion.
This run led to a highly successful one-woman concert at the Hollywood Bowl.

Her motion picture credits include *The Spiral Stair-
case* (1946), *Adventure Island* (1947), *Out of the Past*
(1947), *The Redhead and the Cowboy* (1951), *Little
Egypt* (1951), *Tennessee's Partner* (1955), *Gunfight at
the O.K. Corral* (1957), *Home before Dark* (1958),
Alias Jesse James (1959), and *The Nude Bomb* (1980).

Fleming's square is tinted green and contains the
inscription "To my Mann, Ted—Love Rhonda Fleming [signature]." Also included are the date ("9-28-
81"), her two footprints (made with high heels), and
her two handprints.

Appropriately, Ted Mann, then the owner of the
Chinese Theatre, assisted his wife in placing her
prints.

Rhonda Fleming.

Ted Mann (left), Sylvester Stallone, and unidentified man.

Sylvester Stallone
Ceremony #148: June 29, 1983

He placed his prints in connection with the motion picture *Staying Alive* (Paramount, 1983), which he directed, co-produced, and co-wrote.

Born: Michael Sylvester Stallone in New York City on July 6, 1946.

Usually projecting an image of Italian-American machismo, Sylvester Stallone became one of the most popular film stars of the 1970s and 1980s, primarily on the basis of two characters he played in film after film: Rocky Balboa, the boxer who raises himself from obscurity to championship status, and John Rambo, the Vietnam veteran whose patriotic zeal leads him on heroic but violent and harrowing missions.

Stallone spent two years in the drama department of the University of Miami studying to become an actor. He moved to New York City in 1969 and found some off-Broadway parts. Stallone landed a good role in *The Lords of Flatbush* (1974), which was well received by the critics but not a commercial success.

Just when he felt himself at a dead end, Stallone was inspired with the idea for the screenplay for *Rocky (1976), which made him a star. He wrote the first draft in long-hand in three days and was determined to play the role himself. At one point, with $106 to his name he turned down a $265,000 offer for the script because the potential producer would not agree to cast him in the picture. Finally, producers Robert Chartoff and Irwin Winkler agreed to pay him $75,000 for the script *and* star him in the film, which won the Best Picture Oscar.

His next two films, *F.I.S.T.* and *Paradise Alley* (both 1978), were not successful; so he returned to his tried-and-true character in *Rocky II* (1979) and *Rocky III* (1982), both of which were hits.

Stallone's first appearance as Rambo was in *First Blood* (1982), in which his new larger-than-life character eclipsed his Rocky persona. He made two more pictures as that character.

His motion picture credits as an actor include *Party at Kitty and Studs* (1970, debut, a.k.a. *Italian Stallion*), *Bananas* (1971), *Capone* (1975), *Cannonball* (1976), *Nighthawks* (1981), *Victory* (1981), *Rhinestone* (1984), *Cobra* (1986), *Over the Top* (1987), and *Oscar* (1991).

> * *Academy Award nominations: Best Actor and Writing (Screenplay Written Directly for the Screen).*

Stallone's square is tinted gray and contains the inscription "To Ted, Keep Punchin', America!" Also included are the date ("6/27/83"), his two footprints, two handprints, and his signature.

Stallone forgot to cross the "t" in his signature, and workers later corrected that omission for him before the cement dried.

The "punchin'" in the inscription is a reference to the popular "Rocky" series of films in which Stallone portrays boxer Rocky Balboa. Three "Rocky" pictures had been made at the time of the ceremony.

Later that evening the world premiere of *Staying Alive* raised money on behalf of the Stallone Fund for Autism Research, in affiliation with the Los Angeles Chapter of the National Society for Autistic Children. Stallone is the father of two sons. His second child, Seth, is autistic.

Dan Rothschild (son of famed Los Angeles photographer Otto Rothschild) worked as a security guard at the time of the ceremony. In a telephone conversation with the authors, he recounted that the cement was too thinly mixed and refused to dry in the usual twenty-four-hour time frame.

Rothschild was hired (complete with guard dogs) to protect the site from any possible tampering during the time it took the square to harden. He worked four fourteen-hour shifts on four consecutive days; and his partner worked four ten-hour shifts, thereby giving the square around-the-clock security for ninety-six hours until it was completely dry.

George Lucas and Steven Spielberg
Ceremony #149: May 16, 1984

They placed their prints in connection with the motion picture *Indiana Jones and the Temple of Doom* (Paramount, 1984). Lucas co-produced and co-wrote, and Spielberg directed.

George Lucas

Born: in Modesto, California, on May 14, 1944.

During the early 1970s George Lucas emerged as one of the most successful producer/directors in the history of film. His forte is fantasy and high-action wizardry resulting in unique and spectacular imagery.

As a youth Lucas spent much of his time souping up old cars and drag racing. His initial ambition was to become a professional race driver, but a nearly fatal auto accident a few days before his high school graduation dissuaded him from that career.

As a social sciences major at Modesto Junior College, he became fascinated with the film medium and began experimenting with a friend's 8mm camera. Cinematographer Haskell Wexler befriended Lucas and advised him to enroll in the USC Cinema School. Lucas directed several student films there including *THX 1138: 4EB* (1967). At this point, producer/director Francis Ford Coppola recognized Lucas' talent and gave him encouragement and support.

In 1969 Coppola persuaded Warner Bros. to sign Lucas to direct a feature-length version of *THX 1138* (1971). To attract major-studio interest, Coppola lent his name as producer to Lucas' next directorial outing, his autobiographical **American Graffiti* (1973). The film was a smash and thrust Lucas to the top of his profession.

In 1975 Lucas founded his Industrial Light & Magic company to deal with the special effects preparation of his next production, **Star Wars (1977), which became the highest grossing film up to that time. After that, Lucas abdicated the director's chair and chose to serve only as producer and/or writer of the productions of his Lucasfilm Ltd., which he founded in 1978.

His motion picture credits as director and/or producer include "Look at Life" (1965, debut, animated short, USC student film), "Filmmaker" (1968, documentary short), *More American Graffiti* (1979), *The Empire Strikes Back* (1980), *Raiders of the Lost Ark* (1981), *Return of the Jedi* (1983), *Howard the Duck*

Steven Spielberg (left) and George Lucas.

(1986), *Labyrinth* (1986), *Willow* (1988), and *Indiana Jones and the Last Crusade* (1989).

In 1992 he received the Irving G. Thalberg Memorial Award from the Academy of Motion Picture Arts and Sciences.

> * *Academy Award nominations: Direction and Writing (Best Story and Screenplay—based on factual material or material not previously published or produced).*
> ** *Academy Award nominations: Direction and Writing (Screenplay Written Directly for the Screen).*

Steven Spielberg

Born: in Cincinnati, Ohio, on December 18, 1947.

Steven Spielberg had by his fortieth birthday directed and/or produced seven of the twenty highest-grossing films of all time. His films combine technical virtuosity and dynamic imagery with a sense of innocence and adventure.

At age twelve he completed his first film, a 3-1/2-minute 8mm opus depicting a stagecoach robbery which he produced for ten dollars. Because of inadequate grades, Spielberg could not get into any of the prestigious University film schools; so instead he enrolled at California State University at Long Beach as an English major.

In the mid-1960s he crashed the gate at Universal studios by simply dressing in a suit, carrying a briefcase, and pretending to work there while he observed professionals on sets for several months. After he produced an impressive 35mm short entitled "Amblin'" in 1968, Universal signed him to a

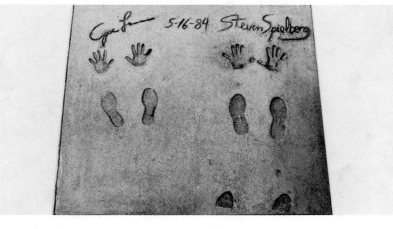

contract as a director the following year. His first professional directorial assignment was the pilot episode of Rod Serling's "Night Gallery" television series in 1969.

After more television assignments, including the TV movie "Duel" (1971), Spielberg directed his first theatrical feature, *The Sugarland Express* (1974). His next was *Jaws* (1975), which sent him to the top of his profession. Other enormously successful films followed, including **Close Encounters of the Third Kind* (1977), **Raiders of the Lost Ark* (1981), and the phenomenally popular ***E.T. The Extra-Terrestrial* (1982).

In 1984 Spielberg founded his Amblin Entertainment company and subsequently served as producer or executive producer of several more hits, and director of ***The Color Purple (1985) and *Indiana Jones and the Last Crusade* (1989).

His motion picture credits as director and/or producer or executive producer include *I Wanna Hold Your Hand* (1978), *1941* (1979), *Poltergeist* (1982), *Gremlins* (1984), *Back to the Future* (1985), *Young Sherlock Holmes* (1985), *An American Tail* (1986), *Empire of the Sun* (1987), *Who Framed Roger Rabbit* (1988), and *Hook* (1991).

In 1987 he received the Irving G. Thalberg Memorial Award from the Academy of Motion Picture Arts and Sciences.

> * *Academy Award nomination: Direction.*
> ** *Academy Award nominations: Direction and Best Picture.*
> *** *Academy Award nomination: Best Picture.*

The Lucas/Spielberg square is tinted red and contains the date ("5-16-84"), Lucas' two footprints (made with tennis shoes), two handprints, and his signature, Spielberg's two footprints (made with tennis shoes), two handprints, and his signature. Partial upper-portion footprints of Spielberg's feet are in the bottom edge of the square.

The Cole Porter song "Anything Goes" from the *Indiana Jones and the Temple of Doom* soundtrack (sung by the film's female star Kate Capshaw and Chinese chorus girls in Chinese) played from loudspeakers into the courtyard. The ceremony was to have started at 10:30 a.m., but Walter Mondale was in Los Angeles campaigning for the Democratic presidential nomination; so there were no available police escorts to accompany Lucas and Spielberg from the Burbank airport, where they landed in a private jet. Consequently, they didn't arrive at the theatre until 11:10.

The film *Indiana Jones and the Temple of Doom* was the first motion picture in history to open at all three Chinese Theatres simultaneously. Ted Mann introduced Lucas and Spielberg to the crowd and joked, "If their picture doesn't gross a lot of money, I'll wind up as a doorman here." (He need not have worried. The film was released on 1,685 screens throughout the country and grossed $42,267,345 in six days, the highest-grossing opening of any movie in history up to that time.)

By the time Lucas and Spielberg were ready to make their prints, the wet cement had started to harden, and a fresh layer had to be applied. They signed their names with ball point pens. When they made their footprints Lucas explained, "We want to be the first people to have tennis shoe prints." Afterwards they both carefully scraped the brand names of the shoes off their imprints.

Neither Lucas nor Spielberg seemed comfortable in front of the news reporters that turned out for the event. Lucas said ruefully, "We had snakes in the last ['Indiana Jones'] picture. We have bugs in this picture. But probably the greatest fear man has is of public speaking, and I think I'm evidence of that."

Spielberg nervously commented, "This is the greatest honor I've ever been exposed to."

Donald Duck and Clarence "Ducky" Nash
Ceremony #150: May 21, 1984

They placed their prints in celebration of the fiftieth anniversary of Donald's creation.

Donald Duck

Born: on June 9, 1934, at the Walt Disney studios, then located on Hyperion Avenue in the Silver Lake district of Los Angeles, California.

In terms of the total number of his screen, television, and comic book appearances, Donald Duck is the most prolific animated character in the history of the Walt Disney studios. His popularity is immense and challenges even that of Mickey Mouse, the "king of the lot."

The irascible, hot-tempered, easily flustered duck has been delighting audiences since 1934 when he made his debut in a supporting role in the cartoon short "The Wise Little Hen." Walt Disney had been toying with the idea of a duck character since about 1932; and in late 1933 when Clarence Nash, who became the voice of Donald, auditioned his many

animal sounds and bird calls for Disney, he let fly with what was initially intentioned to sound like a baby billy goat, whereupon Walt declared, "There's our talking duck!" There was no doubt about the force of Donald's personality, and he was truly an overnight sensation.

Throughout the years several of Donald's cartoon shorts received Academy Award nominations, but only one received the Oscar: "Der Fuehrer's Face" (1942, Short Subjects: Cartoons). He also appeared in a few feature films, most notably *The Three Caballeros* (1945).

In the early 1960s the Disney cartoon shorts were phased out of production, but Donald continued with television appearances and made a few educational shorts. After a long hiatus, he made a comeback in the 1983 short "Mickey's Christmas Carol."

His motion picture credits in cartoon shorts include "Orphans' Benefit" (1934), "The Band Concert" (1935), "Modern Inventions" (1937), "Donald's Nephews" (1938), "Donald's Dilemma" (1947), "Tea for Two Hundred" (1948), "Bee at the Beach" (1950), "Canvasback Duck" (1953), "Donald in Mathmagic Land" (1959), and "The Prince and the Pauper" (1990).

Clarence "Ducky" Nash

Born: in Watonga, Oklahoma, on December 7, 1904.
Died: February 20, 1985.

For fifty years, only one man did the voice of Donald Duck. He was Clarence "Ducky" Nash, who joined the Disney organization in December 1933. Growing up in a rural area, Nash became an expert imitator of all the various types of barnyard animal and bird sounds that continually surrounded him. From age five he felt drawn toward show business, and he hoped his imitations would get him work as an entertainer.

When Nash heard that the Disney company was searching for people with wide-ranging and/or novelty vocal talents for use in recording the sound tracks of its cartoon productions, he decided to audition there. Disney felt that the talking duck character he had in the planning stages and Nash were meant for each other; so Nash signed on and stayed for the rest of his professional life. He became a master at recording the complex and difficult cartoon tracks and over the years essayed several other non-duck voices, but Donald was always his staple.

Nash was seen on the screen in *The Reluctant Dragon* (1941), during which humorist Robert Benchley is given a tour of the Disney studios, and on television in "A Day in the Life of Donald Duck" (1956). The latter begins at the studio as live action and animation blend together during a scene in which Donald screams into his office intercom, "Send my voice in here!" Nash enters only to have Donald confront him regarding his fan mail: "All the letters say the same thing! They can't understand a word you say!"

In addition to providing the on-screen voice of Donald, Nash toured and made hundreds of personal appearances on behalf of the Disney company over the decades with a two-foot Donald replica, often performing at schools, orphanages, and children's hospitals throughout the U.S.

Donald Duck (left), Clarence "Ducky" Nash, unidentified man (partially obscured), and Daisy Duck.

The Donald/Nash square is tinted red and contains the date ("5-21-84"), Donald's two footprints (made with webbed feet), and his signature, in addition to Nash's signature ("C. Ducky Nash").

Nash was delighted when he heard earlier in the year that "Donald will be putting his feet in wet cement someplace." Donald's long-time girlfriend, Daisy Duck, was on hand for the footprint ceremony, which was only one of many celebrations during the year-long birthday festivities for Donald Duck's fiftieth anniversary.

That same year the world's best known fowl was saluted at the 56th annual Academy Awards Presentation, the Indianapolis 500 Parade, and the Kentucky Derby. He also received a star on the Hollywood Walk of Fame. Los Angeles Mayor Tom Bradley issued a proclamation commemorating Donald's first screen appearance fifty years before, and June 9 was officially declared "Donald Duck Day" in Los Angeles. His career was the subject of an hour-long CBS television special, a four-week retrospective of his work in New York City, as well as an exhibition of Donald Duck animation art.

The Disney company was pleased. Disney executive Jack Lindquist, said, "Donald is a character very much into one-upmanship, so we wanted him to have one-up on Mickey Mouse, whose fiftieth birthday [in 1978] was a national event."

Clint Eastwood
Ceremony #151: August 21, 1984

He placed his prints in connection with the motion picture *Tightrope* (Warner Bros., 1984). He starred and was co-producer.

Born: Clinton Eastwood, Jr., in San Francisco, California, on May 31, 1930.

Clint Eastwood is the only star in history to have appeared on the list of top-ten box-office draws nineteen consecutive times (1968-1986). His screen image is that of a lanky, laconic, cool, tight-lipped hero, facing seemingly unconquerable odds in his quest for justice. He has also directed several of his starring films.

After high school graduation and a stint in the Army, he decided to try acting, having met several

Clint Eastwood. Unidentified man to his right. Eastwood's ceremony attire included a jacket that advertised his company, Malpaso Productions, on the front left side.

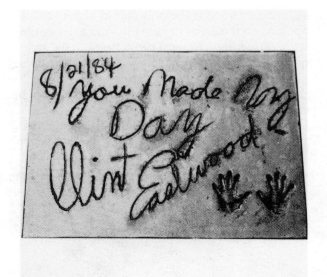

actors while in the service. An Army buddy who was working at Universal got Eastwood a screen test there, which resulted in a standard contract for him in 1955. He got his big break as one of the co-stars of the TV series "Rawhide" (1959-1966), which made him a nationally known personality.

Eastwood decided to go to Italy while on hiatus from "Rawhide" to film Westerns for director Sergio Leone, thinking it was a good way to see Europe and have his expenses paid. A trilogy of low-budget so-called "spaghetti westerns" became world-wide smash hits; and Eastwood's portrayal of the steely, cigar-chomping mercenary gunfighter, the "Man with No Name," made him an international sensation.

In 1971 he made his directorial debut and starred in *Play Misty for Me*. *Dirty Harry* (1972) introduced the public to Eastwood's characterization of the tough, unorthodox, compulsive cop, which he has reprised in four highly successful sequels.

His best known ventures outside Hollywood have been in the picturesque city of Carmel along the California coast where he served a term as Mayor (1986-1988) and where he owns a successful restaurant—the Hog's Breath Inn.

His motion picture credits as an actor and/or actor/director include *Revenge of the Creature* (1955, debut), *Per un pugno di dollari* (1964, a.k.a. *A Fistful of Dollars*), *Il buono, il brutto, il cattivo* (1966, a.k.a. *The Good, the Bad, and the Ugly*), *Two Mules for Sister Sara* (1970), *High Plains Drifter* (1973), *Magnum Force* (1973), *Every Which Way but Loose* (1978), *Escape from Alcatraz* (1979), *Bronco Billy* (1980), and *The Rookie* (1990).

Eastwood's square is tinted green and contains the inscription "You Made My Day." Also included are the date ("8/21/84"), his two handprints, and his signature.

The inscription is a variation on the famous line of dialogue from the motion picture *Sudden Impact* (1983), the fourth film of the popular "Dirty Harry" series. Eastwood portrays Harry Callahan, a streetwise San Francisco homicide detective, and confronts a would-be robber in The Acorn coffee shop with a loaded gun—a .44 Magnum—and the words, "Go ahead, make my day." The line is also reprised at the end of the film when Harry chases a villain down in an amusement park.

Over 3,000 fans and members of the news media witnessed the event, the largest turnout in many years. Eastwood chatted with various persons in the crowd and graciously signed autographs.

Mickey Rooney
Ceremony #152: February 18, 1986

Mickey Rooney's second square—the first one is no longer in the forecourt (see below)—is tinted gray and contains the inscription "To Sid & Ted—Without you Both I wouldn't be here." Also included are two dates ("Oct. 18-38" and "Feb 18-86"), his two footprints (made with bare feet), two handprints, and his signature.

Rooney agreed to participate in a second hand and footprint ceremony in order that the new square could replace the deteriorated one from his 1938 ceremony. Shortly before the date of the new ceremony, Mann

Unidentified man (left) steadies Mickey Rooney at Rooney's second Chinese Theatre imprint ceremony (see text). Those two events plus the honorary plaque awarded to the "Andy Hardy" series (in which Mickey starred) and its cast members in 1941, make three-time honoree Rooney the most honored individual at the theatre.

Theatres removed the old square and readied the area so that Mickey would still occupy the same site in the forecourt.

In a telephone conversation with the authors, Rooney shared some comments about Hollywood and the Chinese Theatre: "Back in the days when Gable, Harlow, Garland, Barrymore, etc., were represented at the theatre, that meant something; and it was fitting that these great Hollywood stars were honored."

Over the years, Rooney has been outspoken about what he feels is the loss of Hollywood's glamour and the great days of the studio system. He commented at a surprise 1984 luncheon in his honor at the Vine Street Brown Derby restaurant, "I love this town. It's more than a sign on a hill."

(*For a description of Rooney's first ceremony and his biographical write-up, see entry for Ceremony #47: October 18, 1938*).

Eddie Murphy (kneeling, center), unidentified man, and William F. Hertz, by then the director of marketing and public relations for Mann Theatres (kneeling, right).

Eddie Murphy and Hollywood's 100th Anniversary Ceremony #153: May 14, 1987

Murphy placed his prints in connection with the motion picture *Beverly Hills Cop II* (Paramount, 1987). He starred and co-wrote the story. His ceremony also took place on the same day that the Chinese Theatre celebrated the 100th anniversary of Hollywood. The city received an honorary plaque.

Eddie Murphy

Born: in Brooklyn, New York, on April 3, 1961.

Since 1982 comic actor Eddie Murphy has been among the most popular stars in the film medium. In 1988 his films were reported to have grossed in excess of one billion dollars, a first for a black performer. His image is that of a street-smart, lighting-quick fellow with razor-sharp wit and intelligence.

As a little boy he began doing imitations of cartoon characters such as Bugs Bunny and Tom and Jerry. His first step toward professionalism came when he hosted a talent show in 1976 at the Roosevelt Youth Center.

After appearing in many small nightclubs, Murphy got his first real break when he was signed as a player on the 1980-1981 television season of "NBC's Saturday Night Live," where he remained for four years and became a national sensation. Audiences loved his irreverent take-offs on such personalities as Bill Cosby, Muhammad Ali, and Stevie Wonder. Murphy also created such memorable characters as a grumpy Gumby, a grown-up version of the "Little Rascal" Buckwheat, and Little Richard Simmons (a send-up of television exercise enthusiast Richard Simmons and the 1950s rock 'n' roll star Little Richard).

Murphy's first film, *48 Hrs.* (1982), was a smash hit, as was his second, *Trading Places* (1983). Murphy

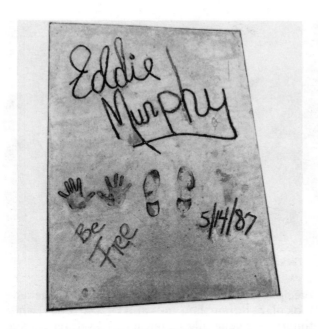

then signed a deal with Paramount studios, which guaranteed him a multi-million-dollar salary per film and financial backing for the newly established Eddie Murphy Productions.

His motion picture credits include *Best Defense* (1984), *Beverly Hills Cop* (1984), *The Golden Child* (1986), *Beverly Hills Cop II* (1987), *Eddie Murphy Raw* (1987), *Coming to America* (1988), *Harlem Nights* (1989), and *Another 48 Hrs.* (1990).

Murphy's square is tinted gray and contains the inscription "Be Free." Also included are the date ("5/14/87"), his two footprints, two handprints, and his signature.

It was estimated that 5,000 people attended the event.

Hollywood, California

A stranger in this funny town
Will think he's had a dream.
Until he looks around to find
Things are not what they seem.
—Anonymous
From the poem "The Town of Make-believe"

Of all the major studios that were located in the section of Los Angeles known as Hollywood, today only Paramount remains; but Hollywood is still synonymous the world over with the American motion picture industry, along with the excitement, luxury, glamour, and celebrity which are immediately associated with the movies. Its population currently numbers 140,000, and its borders contain 1,700 acres

consisting approximately of the area bounded by Franklin Avenue on the north, Western Avenue on the east, Melrose Avenue on the south, and La Brea Avenue on the west.

Hollywood and the film business have been portrayed in countless motion pictures, most notably *A Star Is Born*, which was filmed twice (1937 and 1954) with the movie industry as its theme, and was based in part on an earlier film, *What Price Hollywood?* (1932). Other well known Hollywood-themed pictures include *Merton of the Movies* (1922), *Show People* (1928), *Movie Crazy* (1932), *Once in a Lifetime* (1932), *Bombshell* (1933), *Hollywood Hotel* (1938), *Hollywood Cavalcade* (1939), *Sunset Boulevard* (1950), *Singin' in the Rain* (1952), *The Bad and the Beautiful* (1952), and *The Day of the Locust* (1975).

As an oft-repeated saying goes, Hollywood is not a place; it's a state of mind. In the sense that Hollywood stands as a symbol of the entire history of the film industry, along with all that implies, this statement is a true one, especially in that the Hollywood which survives has sadly faded from its glory days of the 1920s, 1930s, and 1940s, when it was a beautiful, up-scale, thriving, fashionable area. But even now, many of Hollywood's original landmarks survive intact; and various civic and preservationist groups continue to strive to revitalize and restore it.

In 1886 when Harvey H. Wilcox, who had come from Kansas to Los Angeles in 1883, purchased 120 acres of land at $150 per acre in what is now the core of central Hollywood, the area was a tranquil pastoral region, dotted with farms, bean fields, and orange,

avocado, and lemon groves. Wilcox quickly subdivided his parcel and offered lots for sale. His wife, Daeida, remembered the name of an acquaintance's home back East, Hollywood, and suggested the name to her husband for the new area. The name Holly-

The Hollywoodland sign shortly after its construction in 1923. Today the landmark simply reads "Hollywood."

wood first appeared officially when Wilcox filed a claim for subdivision purposes with the Los Angeles county recorder on February 1, 1887.

Hollywood grew slowly but steadily and got its first post office in 1897. Although filming had taken place in the southern California area as early as 1907, the Nestor Film Corporation was the first to film in what is actually the Hollywood area in 1911. Carl Laemmle's Universal company was next on the scene in 1912. The first feature-length film to be produced in Hollywood was *The Squaw Man* (1914), a Jesse L. Lasky Feature Play Company production, directed by Cecil B. DeMille and Oscar Apfel, which began production on December 29, 1913.

Throughout the teens filming in Hollywood increased rapidly and soon became the principal business activity in the area. Motion picture production established itself as one of the nation's major industries. By 1920 the population of Hollywood had grown to 36,000. In 1925 Douglas Fairbanks called the town "The Holy City of the Movies." By 1930 the population had swelled to over 150,000.

Writer Richard Alleman has commented:

"As Hollywood made the transition from village to metropolis, a great boulevard kept pace with the new city's growth and came to be the center of its wealth, power, and glory. Edged with movie palaces, stately hotels, glamorous restaurants and apartment buildings, Hollywood Boulevard was, in its heyday, one of the most dazzling thoroughfares in the country."

Downtown Hollywood continued to hold its own until the old studio system began to collapse in the early 1950s, surrendering to the encroachment of television, independent production, a tendency to make more films on location, and other factors. The

precipitous decline of the Hollywood area in general took place during the 1960s and 1970s. Today, while things look generally better, much work remains to be done.

Several historical sites and landmarks remain in Hollywood, and looking down on them is perhaps the most famous icon of them all—the Hollywood sign, which was most recently restored in 1978 and presides over the community in its fifty-foot-high/270-foot-wide glory.

Hollywood's 100th anniversary square is tinted gray, and its plaque contains the inscription:

> In Commemoration
> The 100th Anniversary of Hollywood

Paramount	Mann
75th	Chinese
Anniversary [logo]	Theatre
A	60th Anniversary
Gulf + Western ™	
Company	
Frank Mancuso	Ted Mann
[signature]	[signature]

> May 14, 1987

In 1928 Sid Grauman wrote an article in which he discussed the growth of the Hollywood community and its famous theatres. The showman said in part:

"...My attention was directed to Hollywood in the first place as an unexploited field for the showman....It has...the supreme advantage of being the world's film center, despite many attempts to shear it of this glory by other ambitious communities and cities...."

"Star Trek's" Twenty-fifth Anniversary (1966-1991); and its creator Gene Roddenberry, and featured players William Shatner, Leonard Nimoy, DeForest Kelley, James Doohan, Walter Koenig, Nichelle Nichols, and George Takei Ceremony #154: December 5, 1991

The players placed their prints in connection with the motion picture *Star Trek VI: The Undiscovered Country* (Paramount, 1991). Nimoy was also the executive producer and co-wrote the story. "Star Trek" and its creator received an honorary plaque on the television series' twenty-fifth anniversary.

"Star Trek"

—Created by Gene Roddenberry—
(Paramount)

Space, the final frontier. These are the voyages of the starship Enterprise. *Its five-year mission: to explore strange new worlds, to seek out new life and new civilizations; to boldly go where no man has gone before.*

—*Captain James T. Kirk*

These words, followed by the image of the U.S.S. *Enterprise* speeding through the galaxy, accompanied by Alexander Courage's now classic theme music, were heard at the beginning of each of the seventy-nine one-hour television episodes of "Star Trek," a weekly series which aired on the NBC network from September 8, 1966 through September 2, 1969. Set in the 23rd century, the adult science fiction program received mediocre ratings. When the network decided to cancel the show after two seasons, its loyal supporters banded together and wrote over one million letters that kept "Trek" on the air for just one more year.

The enormous popularity of "Star Trek" began when its reruns were syndicated shortly after its initial run. Like its Vulcan greeting, "Live long and prosper," "Trek" went on to become the most successful "failure" in the history of television. It attracted millions of fans who became known as "Trekkies" or "Trekkers," as they now prefer to be called. Gene Roddenberry, creator of the series and executive producer, called them "incredible people," adding, "They are people who believe in humanity, and who believe we *are* going to make it!"

By "Star Trek's" twenty-fifth anniversary, Roddenberry found himself the creator of an international cult phenomenon. His vision of a brighter future had spawned six multimillion dollar feature films, an animated TV series (1973-1975), novels, comic books, records, videotapes, audiotapes, fan publications, a theme-park attraction, conventions, a reported half billion to one billion dollars in merchandising sales, and television's "Star Trek: The Next Generation," the highest-rated weekly syndicated series in America, which premiered in 1987 with a new cast, new characters, and a new, more luxurious *Enterprise*, now on a "continuing mission...where no one has gone before."

Roddenberry was born Eugene Wesley Roddenberry in El Paso, Texas, on August 19, 1921. His interest in science fiction began as a boy with *Astounding Stories* magazine. He served as a B-17 pilot in World War II and began writing for flight magazines while working as a commercial pilot for Pan American World Airways (1945-1949). Roddenberry wrote poetry for several publications and became a Los Angeles Police Department sergeant (1949-1953). He sold his first teleplay in 1951. By the mid-1950s, he was writing for such TV shows as "Dragnet" and "Have Gun Will Travel."

In 1963 Roddenberry created and produced his first television series, "The Lieutenant" (1963-1964), for Metro-Goldwyn-Mayer. He had conceived "Star Trek" in 1960 as a sort of "'Wagon Train' to the stars," alluding to the hit TV series (1957-1965). Desilu finally expressed interest in "Star Trek" in 1964, and Roddenberry had to make two pilot episodes ("The Cage" and "Where No Man Has Gone Before") be-

Gene Roddenberry.

fore NBC committed to air it. Jeffrey Hunter was initially cast as Captain Christopher Pike, Commander of the U.S.S. *Enterprise*; but the role was rewritten, renamed, and recast with William Shatner as Captain Kirk, who Roddenberry said he modeled after his vision of a top pilot. A few days before "Trek" went on the air, Roddenberry said that many people "seem to equate science fiction with the monster-who-gobbled-up-Tokyo sort of trash" and wished he could make the series create an entirely different public perception of the genre.

The combined talents of "Star Trek's" cast members, directors, writers, guest stars, technicians, and the wizardry of three leading special effects companies gave its audience a look at such wonders as alien planet surfaces, cities on the edge of forever, troublesome balls of fluff called tribbles, hortas who tunnel their way through solid rock, the races of Vulcans, Klingons, and Romulans, phasers, stardates, and the

ability to transport a being from a spacecraft to a planet surface in an instant. "Star Trek" showed worlds more tolerant, ecologically sensitive, and largely free of racial prejudice. Shatner commented in 1989, "'Star Trek' was more than just a unique TV show; it was about dreams and ideals. People saw 'Star Trek' and they wanted to believe that that future was possible."

Paramount acquired "Star Trek" when it purchased Desilu in 1967. Roddenberry, who produced *Star Trek - The Motion Picture* in 1979 and was the executive consultant on the next four sequels, admitted in 1987 that:

"I don't make 'Star Trek' to please the fans. I make it to please me. And if I'm fortunate that the audience likes it too, they're welcome to come along....It provides a sense of the challenge of tomorrow, a sense that we're able to grow, we're becoming something. 'Star Trek' is a story, I guess, of becoming."

In 1974 an eleven-foot scale model of the U.S.S. *Enterprise* was presented by Paramount to the Smithsonian Institution's National Air and Space Museum in Washington, D.C., which celebrates the history of man's quest in airborne travel from the Wright brothers at Kitty Hawk to the *Apollo* astronauts on the face of the moon. The *Enterprise* is hung from the ceiling beside Charles Lindbergh's *The Spirit of St. Louis*, in which Lindy made the first solo, nonstop transatlantic flight from New York to Paris in 1927. Two years later the National Aeronautics and Space Administration (NASA) named its first space shuttle the *Enterprise* after the most famous craft in science fiction history.

In 1969 Roddenberry married actress Majel Barrett, who had played chief nurse Christine Chapel on the original "Trek" series. He was about to retire in 1986 when Paramount convinced him to be the executive producer of "Star Trek: The Next Generation." Roddenberry would later liken both shows to his family, calling the "Star Trek" series his "original children" and "The Next Generation" series his "children by a second marriage." He died on October 24, 1991, two days after screening *Star Trek VI: The Undiscovered Country*. The picture was released the following December 6 and bore the simple dedication: "For Gene Roddenberry."

Leonard Nimoy, "Star Trek's" Mr. Spock, said in 1991, "The series has undeniably had a very profound effect on audiences everywhere. I mean, does anybody still talk this way about 'Gilligan's Island' [1964-1967]?"

William Shatner

Born: in Montreal, Canada, on March 22, 1931.

William Shatner has become so thoroughly identified with his "Star Trek" (1966-1969) role as Captain James T. Kirk, the dashing, ambitious Commander of the U.S.S. *Enterprise* and its 430-member crew, that it surprises people to realize he made scores of television appearances on other shows both prior to and after the "Star Trek" years.

He decided on an acting career at age eight and began his professional life as a child performing on the Canadian Broadcasting Company. As a young man he joined the Canadian Repertory Company and made his stage debut in 1952. He next joined the Stratford Shakespeare Festival in Ontario (1954-1956), where he appeared in several of the Bard's plays. He also acted in films for the National Film Board of Canada. He made his U.S. film debut in *The Brothers Karamazov* (1958).

Shatner appeared on television in such programs as "Alfred Hitchcock Presents" and "The Twilight Zone" and on the Broadway stage in *The World of Suzie Wong* (1958) and *A Shot in the Dark* (1961). He starred in the short-lived TV series "For the People" (1965). The following year the "Star Trek" series came along. After "Trek" he had two additional starring TV stints in "The Barbary Coast" (1975-1976) and "T.J. Hooker" (1982-1985).

He has directed several TV shows and the film *Star Trek V: The Final Frontier* (1989). He also co-wrote the story.

His motion picture credits as an actor include *The Explosive Generation* (1961), *Judgment at Nuremberg* (1961), *The Intruder* (1962), *The Outrage* (1964), *Big Bad Mama* (1974), *The Devil's Rain* (1975), *Kingdom of the Spiders* (1977), *Visiting Hours* (1982), *Airplane II: The Sequel* (1982), and all six *Star Trek* movies.

Leonard Nimoy

Born: in Boston, Massachusetts, on March 26, 1931.

Of all the principal "Star Trek" (1966-1969) characters, Leonard Nimoy's Mr. Spock, the non-emotional, ultra-rational, half-human/half-alien First Officer and Chief Science Officer aboard the U.S.S. *Enterprise*, is undoubtedly the most visually original and compelling, with his large pointed ears, cropped hair style, and upswept eyebrows. When Spock was first seen by one network executive, he was taken aback and told producer Gene Roddenberry, "Get rid of the guy with the funny ears." Roddenberry re-

fused; and soon after, the immensely positive audience response to Nimoy as Spock proved his instincts correct. Mr. Spock quickly became a world-famous cult hero.

Nimoy began acting as a child and first appeared on stage in 1939 at the Elizabeth Peabody Playhouse in Boston. At eighteen he moved to California and studied at the renowned Pasadena Playhouse. He then slowly built his career and appeared in numerous stage plays, films, and television shows, including "Dragnet" and "The Man from U.N.C.L.E." After nearly two decades in the business, however, his first steady acting job came with "Star Trek." Suddenly the heretofore little known Nimoy was a star.

After the "Star Trek" series was cancelled, Nimoy next starred in the hit series "Mission: Impossible" (1969-1971). He has also directed several TV shows and motion pictures, including *Star Trek III: The Search for Spock* (1984) and *Star Trek IV: The Voyage Home* (1986). He also co-wrote the story for the latter. In 1991 Nimoy appeared as Spock in "Unification," the two-part 100th episode of "Star Trek: The Next Generation."

His motion picture credits as an actor include *Queen for a Day* (1951, debut), *Kid Monk Baroni* (1952), *Them!* (1954), *The Brain Eaters* (1958), *Seven Days in May* (1964), *Deathwatch* (1966), *Seconds* (1966), *Catlow* (1971), *Invasion of the Body Snatchers* (1978), and all six *Star Trek* movies.

DeForest Kelley

Born: in Atlanta, Georgia, on January 20, 1920.

DeForest Kelley created the "Star Trek" (1966-1969) role of Dr. Leonard "Bones" McCoy, Senior Ship's Surgeon and Head of the Life Science Department on board the U.S.S. *Enterprise*—an outspoken, somewhat cynical and eccentric, but ultimately likable character, who is at heart a true Southern gentleman. In his pre- "Star Trek" days Kelley usually specialized in sinister villains in film, television, and stage productions.

Kelley fell in love with southern California when he came to Long Beach to visit an uncle after graduating from high school. He decided to stay and become an actor, doing theatre work at the Long Beach Theatre Group. During World War II, the U.S. Army loaned him to the Navy for a training film, *Time To Kill*. In 1946, shortly after his military discharge, Kelley signed a contract with Paramount. He stayed two-and-a-half years and later appeared in many major films at other studios. In television he found

"Star Trek" (1966-1991): The crew members of the U.S.S. Enterprise *pose on the starship's bridge. (Front left) DeForest Kelley, William Shatner, and Leonard Nimoy. (Back, left) James Doohan, Walter Koenig, Majel Barrett, Nichelle Nichols, and George Takei. (Photograph © Paramount Pictures.)*

himself in steady demand for such popular shows as "Bonanza," "Gunsmoke," "Rawhide," and "Playhouse 90."

At the inception of his "Star Trek" role, Kelley's image as a screen heavy came to an abrupt halt as he established a new persona that was to make him world famous as a figure of heroic proportions.

In 1987 he appeared in "Encounter at Farpoint," the initial episode of "Star Trek: The Next Generation," as a 137-year-old Dr. McCoy.

His motion picture credits include *Fear in the Night* (1947, feature film debut), *Variety Girl* (1947), *Gunfight at the O.K. Corral* (1957), *Raintree County* (1957), *The Law and Jake Wade* (1958), *Warlock* (1959), *Where Love Has Gone* (1964), *Marriage on the Rocks* (1965), *Waco* (1966), *Night of the Lepus* (1972), and all six *Star Trek* movies.

James Doohan

Born: James Montgomery Doohan in Vancouver, British Columbia, Canada, on March 3, 1920.

The command "Beam me up, Scotty!" has become one of the most famous catch-phrases in the annals of popular culture. The "Star Trek" (1966-1969) character of Scotty is none other than the Chief Engineer on the U.S.S. *Enterprise*, Lieutenant Commander Montgomery Scott, who is played by James Doohan.

Doohan began acting as a child in school productions. He dreamed of an opera career, but lack of money forced him to abandon his musical studies. In his native Canada he performed on numerous radio and television shows and in stage productions, as well as making several films for the National Film Board of Canada. He moved to Hollywood in the 1960s and appeared in over 100 roles in film and television, including "Gunsmoke" and "The Man from U.N.C.L.E."

The original "Star Trek" (1966-1991) cast set a new Chinese Theatre record on "Trek's" twenty-fifth anniversary: seven stars, one imprinted square. Left to right: Walter Koenig, William Shatner, Leonard Nimoy, DeForest Kelley, and James Doohan. Nichelle Nichols (center) embraces George Takei.

Doohan's forte was always accents; and when the "Star Trek" opportunity emerged, he wanted the character to have a Scottish accent, perceiving that the Scots are famous for their engineering feats. Doohan himself named the character Montgomery Scott after his maternal grandfather, Captain James Montgomery.

Doohan has been invited to address groups of scientists and engineers and tour scientific laboratories. When traveling, the galaxy's best known engineer prefers to take a train and watch the scenery rather than fly!

His motion picture credits include *The Wheeler Dealers* (1963, U.S. debut), *36 Hours* (1965), *Bus Riley's Back in Town* (1965), *The Satan Bug* (1965), *Jigsaw* (1968), *Pretty Maids All in a Row* (1971), *Man in the Wilderness* (1971), and all six *Star Trek* movies.

Walter Koenig

Born: in Chicago, Illinois, on September 14, 1936.

As the Russian Ensign Pavel Chekov, Navigator of the U.S.S. *Enterprise*, Walter Koenig joined the cast of the original "Star Trek" (1966-1969) television series in 1967, after the first season had been produced. A reporter for the Soviet newspaper *Pravda* had bemoaned the absence of a Russian character in the show since, after all, the Soviets were the first to successfully launch a satellite into space. Producer Gene Roddenberry had already conceived of the Chekov character to appeal to eight-to-fourteen-year-olds and decided to make him a Russian as an acknowledgement to the Soviet Union's contributions to space exploration.

Koenig was raised in New York City and became interested in dramatics while in high school. At both Iowa's Grinnell College and UCLA he studied toward a career in psychology but found himself irresistibly drawn toward acting instead. He appeared in summer stock in Vermont and later enrolled at the Neighborhood Playhouse in New York between 1958 and 1960. Koenig guest-starred in several television series, including "Mr. Novak," in which his role as a Russian defector led to his casting in "Star Trek." He later branched out into writing teleplays and novels, as well as directing and producing.

His writing credits include an animated "Star Trek" episode ("The Infinite Vulcan" [1973]), one of the "Star Trek" comics ("Chekov's Choice" [1985]), and *Chekov's Enterprise: A Personal Journal of the Making of "Star Trek - The Motion Picture"* (1980).

His motion picture credits as an actor include *Strange Lovers* (1963, debut), *Moontrap* (1988), and all six *Star Trek* movies.

Nichelle Nichols

Born: in Robbins, Illinois, on December 28, 1936

As Lieutenant Uhura, Communications Officer on the U.S.S. *Enterprise*, Nichelle Nichols became one of the first black performers in a major non-stereotypical role on a television network series when she was cast in "Star Trek" (1966-1969). When she met with civil rights activist Dr. Martin Luther King, Jr. in 1967, he said, "You're one of the most important people on the planet today....For the first time [white people] see us as we should be."

Nichols studied ballet, and when she was sixteen Duke Ellington asked her to choreograph and perform one of his musical compositions. She went on the road singing with his orchestra. In the 1960s Nichols appeared on the Chicago stage in productions of *Kicks and Company* and *The Blacks*. Her television work included an appearance on "The Lieutenant" which was produced by Gene Roddenberry, who later cast her in "Star Trek." She came to the "Trek" audition with a book on the history of Africa entitled *Uhura*, which is Swahili for "freedom." In 1968 Nichols and William Shatner shared network television's first interracial kiss in the episode "Plato's Stepchildren."

Nichols, who is seriously interested in the subject of man in space, worked with NASA through her own consultant firm and has played a key role in bringing women and minorities into the astronaut corps.

Her motion picture credits include *Porgy and Bess* (1959, debut), *Made in Paris* (1966), *Mister Buddwing* (1966), *Doctor, You've Got To Be Kidding* (1967), *Tarzan's Deadly Silence* (1970), *Truck Turner* (1974), *The Supernaturals* (1986), and all six *Star Trek* movies.

George Takei

Born: Hosato Takei in Los Angeles, California, on April 20, 1937.

George Takei became an international favorite when he created the role of Mr. Sulu, Chief Helmsman and Weapons Officer of the U.S.S. *Enterprise* in the original "Star Trek" (1966-1969) television series. Takei's casting in the show, like that of Nichelle Nichols, represented an important breakthrough for ethnic minorities in network television.

As a boy, Takei and his family were among the many Japanese-Americans confined to relocation centers in the U.S. during World War II. While studying architecture and city planning at the University of California at Berkeley, Takei began his acting career by dubbing English dialogue for several Japanese science fiction films, including *Rodan!* (1957). He attended UCLA, where he earned an M.A. degree in Theatre Arts. His TV work includes appearances on "Hawaiian Eye," "Perry Mason," and "Playhouse 90." Active in politics, Takei was a delegate to the Democratic presidential convention in 1972. In a bid for a seat on the Los Angeles City Council in 1973, he came in second, only three percentage points behind the victor. He subsequently became a member of the boards of both the Southern California Rapid Transit District (1973-1984) and the Los Angeles Theatre Center.

His motion picture credits as an actor in front of the camera include *Ice Palace* (1960, debut), *Hell to Eternity* (1960), *A Majority of One* (1962), *PT 109* (1963), *Red Line 7000* (1965), *Walk, Don't Run* (1966), *An American Dream* (1966), *The Green Berets* (1968), *Which Way to the Front?* (1970), *Prisoners of the Sun* (1991), and all six *Star Trek* movies.

The "Star Trek" square is tinted brown and contains the date ("12-5-91"). Also included are Shatner's right handprint and signature, Nimoy's right handprint and signature, Kelley's handprints and signature, Doohan's right handprint and signature, Koenig's handprints (the right faces south, and the left faces north) and signature, Nichols' handprints and signature, and Takei's handprints and signature. Also in the center of the square is a plaque which contains the inscription:

1966 25th Anniversary 1991
[illustration of the U.S.S. *Enterprise*]
Star Trek® Created by
Gene Roddenberry
©1991 Paramount Pictures

Nimoy's handprint is the splayed finger Vulcan salute, originally conceived by the actor for the 1967 episode "Amok Time" in which Spock returned to Vulcan, his home planet. It opened the television series' second season. Doohan's handprint shows the absence of his right middle finger, which he lost when wounded at Juno Beach on D-Day (June 6, 1944) while serving in the Royal Canadian Artillery during World War II. The legend "NCC-1701," the identifying number on the exterior of the starship *Enterprise*, was conceived by the series' art director Matt Jeffries, who designed the starship, and Gene Roddenberry.

Although a temporary metal plaque was placed in the square the day of the ceremony, it was immediately removed by the theatre management. The spot remained empty until the following March 17 when it was filled by a pink and white tile plaque with gold etching. It is the first non-metal plaque in the forecourt.

December 3 had been suggested as the date for the "Star Trek" ceremony, but all of the cast members were not able to be present; so it was moved to December 5. A crowd of over 3,500 attended the event.

The authors spoke on the telephone with Kelley, Koenig, Nichols, and Takei on separate occasions. Kelley expressed delight when recalling the ceremony, admitting, "The seven of us are there only through the grace of 'Star Trek.'" He added the day also has sentimental meaning for him, as it was his mother's birthday. (She died in 1956.)

During his first years in southern California, Kelley often went to Hollywood, visiting the Chinese Theatre on several occasions. He told us, "I looked at it with all the wonderment of any tourist, never dreaming I'd be part of it one day. I had not been there to walk around since I became active in motion pictures."

On the day of the ceremony the "Star Trek" cast was informed of some of the local lore of the theatre regarding how the footprints originated, how some persons had become so nervous they misspelled their names, etc. When it was Kelley's turn to write his signature, the photographers covering the event kept calling out to him to look up at their cameras. He became distracted from the task at hand and was surprised when it was pointed out to him after he had finished that he left the "s" out of his first name. Luckily, he left enough space to insert it without the cement having to be smoothed over and writing his signature again.

Kelley commented that "it must have taken an engineer to figure out the assigned spaces for everyone to sign, what with seven of us being included in one square." The wet cement had been marked off in advance, and the cast was instructed as to exactly where they were supposed to sign.

Koenig admitted that "I probably had fewer credits than anyone else so enshired. I hadn't done anything like that since I was eleven years old and wrote the name of my local neighborhood gang, the 'Payson Avenue Braves,' in fresh cement."

Nichols said, "It was so meaningful to me on a very personal level, because many years ago, I stood there with my father. He told me then, 'Baby, some day your name will be here!' Consequently, when the officials told us *only* to sign our names, and *not* to imprint our hands, there was never a doubt that I would 'slip' (just like Norma Talmadge) and low and behold, my handprint would be there forever. It was also no surprise that when this happened, the rest of the 'Star Trek' crew quickly 'slipped' and placed their handprints in the wet cement. And just like a 'Star Trek' episode ending, once the deed was done, everyone applauded exuberantly!"

Takei confided a different version of how imprints were added to what was to have been a square of signatures only:

"Before the ceremony Paramount instructed all seven of us that we were strictly forbidden to put down any imprints save our signatures. I am the only Los Angeles native in the group, and I know how this ceremony is supposed to be done! Everyone else had written their signatures, complying with the request; but when my turn came I signed my name and placed a handprint. What were they [Paramount] going to do, after all? Bill Shatner said, 'Look at that! George placed his handprint!' So everyone else got back down and added their hand imprints."

Photographs of the event show Nichols and Takei (who made their signatures last and together) holding on to one another, each waving a cement-laden hand in greeting to the crowd. Interestingly, the signatures of the seven cast members appear on the closing credit roll of *Star Trek VI: The Undiscovered Country*. Perhaps the Paramount management wanted the square to match.

Sid Grauman and Jackie Coogan clown for the camera circa 1925.

The Squares That Almost Were and Those That Vanished

Although the Chinese Theatre's world-famous footprint squares have caught the interest of millions of visitors for more than sixty years, the stories of the personalities who were supposed to imprint a square, but ultimately did not, and rumored removals of large portions of the older squares in the forecourt to make room for latter-day celebrities hold their own fascination. (The stories regarding the removal of the squares of Charles Chaplin, the Dionne Quintuplets and Jean Hersholt, Mickey Rooney, and Edmund Purdom, in addition to the Hardy family wall plaque, have been previously mentioned in the entries chronicling those individual ceremonies.)

Jackie Coogan, one of the greatest child stars of the movies, claimed to have had his imprints recorded in the forecourt. In a 1969 Los Angeles *Times* article entitled "Coogan Reflects On His 50 Years in Show Biz," Margaret Harford interviewed Jackie and wrote:

"His footprints were among the first implanted in the famous forecourt at Grauman's Chinese.

"'I can't find them anymore. They've built a box-office over them,' said Coogan with a such-is-fame shrug."

If they had actually been there and if the box-office was on top of them, they probably would have been relocated at the same time the Wallace Beery/Marie Dressler square was moved (probably in the 1940s). No documentation has ever been found which confirms Coogan's claim that he placed his prints at the theatre. Since his career as a child star had already begun its decline by the time the theatre opened in 1927, it is highly unlikely that he ever did so.

Raquel Torres.

Ceremonies for the imprinting of several celebrities have been contemplated and even scheduled over the years but for various reasons have not come off:

Metro-Goldwyn-Mayer's first sound picture (synchronized sound effects and music with fragmentary non-synchronized dialogue), *White Shadows in the South Seas*, premiered at the theatre on August 3, 1928. Sid Grauman wanted to have the film's female star, Mexican actress Raquel Torres, place her prints. She had been an usher at the 1927 opening of the Chinese and had achieved stardom slightly over a year later. Sid wanted to publicize this Cinderella-like success story, but MGM pointed out to him that they had just issued a fictitious press release stating that Torres came directly from some remote Mexican convent to appear in their film, having been recommended to director W.S. Van Dyke II by a high official in the Mexican government. To have Sid giving out stories about Torres being an usher at

Greta Garbo.

Douglas Fairbanks, Jr. He served in the U.S. Navy during World War II and then resumed his film career in 1946.

the Chinese the previous year would have made MGM look ridiculous; so the studio refused to allow her to make her imprints.

For the premiere of *Grand Hotel* in 1932, Grauman pleadingly invited Greta Garbo to place her prints; but as was expected, the reclusive Swedish actress declined his offer. Grauman decided to turn the situation into a practical joke which fell sadly flat. According to MGM veteran Samuel Marx, Sid came on stage before the film began and announced to the audience that he had miraculously persuaded Garbo to make an appearance after the film. This, Marx wrote:

"...caused a wave of expectation, and the prospect of seeing the elusive star seemed to hang over the screening.

"When the picture ended, the houselights went up. Grauman reappeared to announce, 'Miss Greta Garbo!' and then one of the film's stars, Wallace Beery, in a messy evening gown and unkempt blonde wig, pranced into view. The audience was stunned with disappointment.

"On stage, Grauman shouted repeatedly that it was all a joke. His words were ignored as the audience headed silently for the exits."

A story about a proposed but unrealized footprint ceremony that was originally to have taken place in 1939, and then again suggested in 1945, came to light in a letter to the authors from Douglas Fairbanks, Jr. He was present at the 1929 ceremony for his then wife Joan Crawford and wrote:

"I was invited to add my own prints ten years later, but I was then busy working for our State Department in Washington and abroad, and then when I was asked again six years after that, I was at sea with the Navy. When I returned after the War they apparently forgot to ask me again."

During the 1940s the comedy team of Ole Olsen and Chic Johnson was scheduled to make their imprints. The cement was poured, but they inexplicably failed to appear. The only surviving record of this

mishap is a photograph of the square that had been prepared for their inscriptions, in which a frustrated Grauman scrawled, "Dear Chick [sic] and Ole—This slab was prepared for you but you didn't show—I am disappointed. [Signed] Sid Grauman."

Actress Lauren Bacall was asked to make her prints to coincide with the November 4, 1953 premiere of *How To Marry a Millionaire* (at the Fox Wilshire Theatre, not the Chinese). Her husband, Humphrey Bogart, told writer Joe Hyams, "It used to be an honor—it was at least back in 1946 when I did it." Bogart asked his wife, "Why don't you refuse?" Bacall, who later recalled her husband as "loving a chance to puncture Hollywood's ego," politely declined the theatre's offer, and the studio (20th Century-Fox) that had scheduled the ceremony for October 30 had to cancel the event. At the time (1953), Bacall said, "Perhaps in the flourish of my first picture, *To Have and Have Not* [1944], being part of this legend would have made more sense. It doesn't seem to make sense now." Bacall recounts the incident in her memoirs:

" ...Joe [Hyams] said he'd print my statement in the [New York *Herald*] *Tribune*, and I wrote, 'Before I came to Hollywood, Grauman's Chinese was something very special to me—it meant not only achievement—it was the Hall of Fame of the motion picture industry and the people in it were unforgettables and irreplaceables. I don't think of myself as either—I feel that my career is undergoing a change and I want to feel I've earned my place with the best my business has produced.' That statement made newspapers across the country and, along with all the other news stories, was forgotten the next day. Time went by, I wasn't asked again, and so twenty-five years later, a tourist or aspiring actor going to Grauman's Chinese to see the legendary stars' footprints will not see mine—or miss them."

Lauren Bacall. After refusing to participate, she commented, "I guess I've blown my chance at immortality."

Hedda Hopper at home. Perhaps the reason her ceremony never took place was that she may not have been able to decide which hat to imprint in the cement.

Ole Olsen (top) and Chic Johnson.

Sid Grauman inscribed the square that had been readied for no-show comedians Ole Olsen and Chic Johnson.

A Fox West Coast inter-office memorandum of 1957, discussing preparations for an elaborate week-long celebration of the theatre's thirtieth anniversary, makes detailed mention of culminating the festivities with specific plans to have columnist (and one-time actress) Hedda Hopper place her prints during the

stars away in front of and to the left of the box-office. No reason for the cancellation was disclosed; but a Chamber spokesman stated that, despite the fact that a city permit for the event had been issued and a supposedly official announcement made, the December 16 date had never been conclusively confirmed

The Chinese Theatre during the run of Barbra Streisand's A Star Is Born *(1976).*

event, along with an imprint of one of her famous trademark hats. "We already have Louella O. Parsons and we should have Miss Hopper to keep the record complete," the memo stated. Also, an as-yet unchosen "important actor or actress" of the time was suggested to be footprinted as well. Both events would have tied in with the August 1957 premiere of *The Sun Also Rises*. Hopper never made her imprints, nor did any one else in connection with the picture, and why the ceremony did not occur cannot be documented.

A December 21, 1976 *Daily Variety* article mentioned that the scheduled December 16 footprint ceremony for actress/singer Barbra Streisand, in conjunction with the December 19 premiere of *A Star Is Born*, had been mysteriously cancelled. The plans also included placement of a star for Streisand on the Hollywood Chamber of Commerce's Walk of Fame at a spot in front of the theatre on the same day. For a while, it looked as though actress Marion Martin's Walk of Fame star facing the forecourt would be relocated to the west driveway of the theatre parking lot so that Streisand could be installed in the favored position. The Chamber of Commerce refused the suggestion, and Streisand was to be honored four

with Streisand. A mid-January 1977 rescheduling was anticipated, but Barbra Streisand has yet to place her prints at the Chinese Theatre, although she does have a star on the boulevard in said location.

The sidewalk along the forecourt of the Chinese Theatre is considered the most prestigious position on the Hollywood Walk of Fame. As of this writing it is full, although there are several available spaces along the block on which the theatre is located. For many years, there was only one spot left in front of the forecourt. "They're holding onto it," said Johnny Grant, Los Angeles radio and television personality and the Honorary Mayor of Hollywood, in 1989. "People call me up and say 'I know Ted Mann. We'll put this in front of the Chinese Theatre.' I say, 'Good luck.' Then they call me back and say, 'What's the next-best spot?'"

On July 7, 1977 *Daily Variety* printed an article entitled "Beep! Beep! Herbie's Auto-Nomous Honor," announcing that Herbie, the Love Bug, the celebrated 1963 Volkswagen Beetle that shifted for itself, would be placing his tire prints in the forecourt in connection with his third feature for Walt Disney Productions' "Love Bug" series, *Herbie Goes to Monte Carlo* (1977), on July 11. The film's stars—Dean

July 11, 1977: Herbie, the Love Bug, places his tire prints for promotional purposes. Assisting Herbie are Don Knotts (left) and Dean Jones (right). Julie Sommars (mostly obscured) is at right.

This promotional square of the tire prints of Herbie, the Love Bug, was removed from the forecourt shortly after it was made (see text).

Jones, Don Knotts, and Julie Sommars—were on hand for Herbie's ceremony, which was to be "preceded by a parade and motorcade down Hollywood Blvd. Herbie will lead the motorcade, presumably cleaning his tires of the residue before enshrining them forever."

However, Herbie's imprints were made for promotional purposes only. A special, easily removable cement was used; and, since the square was never meant to be a permanent part of the forecourt, it was taken out shortly thereafter. Herbie's square contained the inscription "The love Bug." Also included were the date ("July 11 1977"), his two front tire prints, his name ("Herbie"), and a silhouette drawing of his left profile. The picture opened—not at the Chinese—at several theatres on August 10.

The most recently known details surrounding a proposed ceremony was the result of an announcement in the March 20, 1991 *Daily Variety*, which stated that Leonardo, the leader of the four Teenage Mutant Ninja Turtles, would be placing his imprints at the theatre on March 22 at 11:00 a.m. in connection with *Teenage Mutant Ninja Turtles II: The Secret of the Ooze* (1991). The picture was scheduled to open at various theatres—not the Chinese—that day. The Turtle characters were introduced in a 1984 comic

Cowabunga! A crime-fighting, surfer-speaking, pizza-eating, man-sized Turtle named after a Renaissance artist in the forecourt? (See text.) Leonardo with his creators Peter Laird and Kevin Eastman during the filming of New Line Cinema's Teenage Mutant Ninja Turtles *(1990).*

book created by Kevin Eastman and Peter Laird. Its success launched Turtle merchandising, a syndicated animated television series, and an amazingly popular feature film in 1990. However, the possibility of footprinting one of the Turtles never passed the initial suggestion stage; so the announcement of an actual ceremony was premature, to say the least.

Over the years, rumors have persisted of theatre officials moving quietly into the forecourt under the dark of night to take away older squares and place them in storage, thereby making room for the inclusion of current celebrities. In his *The Movie Lovers Guide to Hollywood*, Richard Alleman alludes to the rumors of the many stars supposedly banished from the forecourt and into the theatre's basement: "...[a] fate, according to insiders, that a number of the prints of lesser legends is said to have met. According to these same sources, the basement of the Chinese is literally loaded with concrete slabs of long-forgotten stars." These stories are absolutely untrue, although there are at least three incidents regarding the removal—or suggested removal—of portions of the forecourt:

At one time it was suggested that the squares be used as evidence in a court of law shortly after the death of Sid Grauman in 1950. Grauman left no will.

Forty-eight-year-old Mrs. Carrie J. Adair came forward to claim his $750,000 estate, alleging to have been Grauman's common-law wife. A purported Grauman will, dated October 4, 1949, crudely hand-printed in blue crayon, and bequeathing $32,000 to Adair, was anonymously mailed to the court.

The court directed that a handwriting expert be brought in to attempt to establish authenticity of the so-called will, and for a time it appeared that the blocks in the forecourt containing Grauman's printing might have to be brought into court as evidence. Before such drastic measures came about, the writing analyst established that the "will" was an obvious forgery perpetrated by Adair. The case was thrown out of court, and the squares remained safely in the forecourt.

According to Troxey Kemper in his October 10, 1986 Milwaukee *Journal* article entitled "Lasting Impressions: Stars Left Their Marks in Chinese Theatre's Cement," a square dated February 8, 1965 bore the following inscription: "Lots of luck from [Chinese Theatre] assistant managers Hal and Gary. Thanks." Kemper says it was located at the edge of the forecourt at what is now a doorway to the Chinese II Theatre. It is no longer there and obviously was not meant to be an official inclusion in the forecourt.

In the early 1970s, old water pipes under the forecourt had rusted away and had to be replaced. This renovation process required some twenty-odd blocks on the east side of the theatre to be carefully cut out of the forecourt, lifted with block and cable, and safely stored until the damaged pipes could be replaced and a new foundation poured. The squares were carefully relaid in their original positions—smooth, machine-cut edges being the only visible evidence of their temporary removal. Sid Grauman would have approved.

THE END. Made in Hollywood, U.S.A. (Jack Benny [left] and Sid Grauman.)

Select Bibliography

Books, articles, pamphlets, programs, recordings, and clipping sources that were of particular importance in tracing the history of Sid Grauman and the Chinese Theatre, anecdotes regarding the ceremonies, and the Academy Award nominations and wins are listed below:

Books:

Alleman, Richard. *The Movie Lover's Guide to Hollywood*. New York: Harper & Row, 1985.

Andrews, Bart. *Lucy & Ricky & Fred & Ethel: The Story of "I Love Lucy"*. New York: E.P. Dutton, 1976.

Bacall, Lauren. *By Myself*. New York: Alfred A. Knopf, 1978.

Bacon, James. *Made in Hollywood*. Chicago: Contemporary Books, 1977.

Beardsley, Charles. *Hollywood's Master Showman: The Legendary Sid Grauman*. New York: Cornwall Books, 1983.

Behlmer, Rudy, and Tony Thomas. *Hollywood's Hollywood: The Movies about the Movies*. Secaucus, N.J.: Citadel Press, 1975.

Bell, Mary Hayley. *What Shall We Do Tomorrow?*. London: Cassell, 1968.

Benny, Mary Livingstone, and Hilliard Marks with Marcia Borie. *Jack Benny*. Garden City, N.Y.: Doubleday, 1978.

Bergen, Candice. *Knock Wood*. New York: Linden Press/Simon & Schuster, 1984.

Black, Shirley Temple. *Child Star*. New York: McGraw-Hill, 1988.

Brown, Joe E., as told to Ralph Hancock. *Laughter Is a Wonderful Thing*. New York: A.S. Barnes, 1956.

Cannom, Robert C. *Van Dyke and the Mythical City Hollywood*. Culver City, Calif.: Murray & Gee, 1948.

Carey, Gary. *Doug & Mary: A Biography of Douglas Fairbanks & Mary Pickford*. New York: E.P. Dutton, 1977.

Chaplin, Charles. *My Autobiography*. New York: Simon & Schuster, 1964.

Christeson, H.M., and F.M. Christeson. *Tony and His Pals*. Chicago: Albert Whitman, 1934.

Clymer, Floyd. *Cars of the Stars and Movie Memories*. Los Angeles: Floyd Clymer, 1954.

Cooper, Jackie, with Dick Kleiner. *Please Don't Shoot My Dog*. New York: William Morrow, 1981.

Crawford, Joan, with Jane Kesner Ardmore. *A Portrait of Joan*. Garden City, N.Y.: Doubleday, 1962.

Daniels, Bebe, and Ben Lyon. *Life with the Lyons*. Long Acre, London: Odhams Press, 1953.

Davis, Elise Miller. *The Answer Is God: The Inspiring Personal Story of Dale Evans and Roy Rogers*. New York: McGraw-Hill, 1955.

DeMille, Cecil B. *The Autobiography of Cecil B. DeMille*. Edited by Donald Hayne. Englewood Cliffs, N.J.: Prentice-Hall, 1959.

Edwards, Anne. *Judy Garland: A Biography*. New York: Simon & Schuster, 1974.

Fairbanks, Douglas Jr. *The Salad Days*. New York: Doubleday, 1988.

Finch, Christopher, and Linda Rosenkrantz. *Gone Hollywood*. Garden City, N.Y.: Doubleday, 1979.

Freedland, Michael. *Jolson*. New York: Stein & Day, 1972.

Gardner, Ava. *Ava: My Story*. New York: Bantam Books, 1990.

Godfrey, Lionel. *Cary Grant: The Light Touch*. New York: St. Martin's Press, 1981.

Goldstein, Norm. *Frank Sinatra: Ol' Blue Eyes*. New York: Holt, Rinehart & Winston, 1982.

Hall, Ben M. *The Best Remaining Seats: The Story of the Golden Age of the Movie Palace*. New York: Clarkson N. Potter, 1961.

Haver, Ronald. *David O. Selznick's Hollywood*. New York: Alfred A. Knopf, 1980.

Helgesen, H. Terry. "An Annotated Index of the H. Terry Helgesen Collection of Theatre Photographs and Illustrations." (unpublished) Los Angeles: 1978.

Heston, Charlton. *The Actor's Life: Journals 1956-1976*. Edited by Hollis Alpert. New York: E.P. Dutton, 1976.

Hudson, Rock, and Sara Davidson. *Rock Hudson: His Story*. New York: William Morrow, 1986.

Hyams, Joe. *Bogie: The Biography of Humphrey Bogart*. New York: New American Library, 1966.

Jablonski, Edward. *Harold Arlen: Happy with the Blues*. Garden City, N.Y.: Doubleday, 1961.

Knight, Arthur, and Eliot Elisofon. *The Hollywood Style*. London: Macmillan, 1969.

Kotsilibas-Davis, James, and Myrna Loy. *Myrna Loy: Being and Becoming*. New York: Alfred A. Knopf, 1987.

Loos, Anita. *A Girl Like I*. New York: Viking Press, 1966.

Luijters, Guus, ed. and comp. *Marilyn Monroe: A Never-Ending Dream*. New York: St. Martin's Press, 1986.

Marilyn Monroe and the Camera. Boston: Little, Brown, 1989.

Martin, Tony, and Cyd Charisse as told to Dick Kleiner. *The Two of Us*. New York: Mason/Charter, 1976.

Marx, Arthur. *Life with Groucho*. New York: Simon & Schuster, 1954.

Marx, Groucho. *The Groucho Phile*. Indianapolis: Bobbs-Merrill, 1976.

Marx, Samuel. *A Gaudy Spree: The Literary Life of Hollywood in the 1930s When the West Was Fun.* New York: Franklin Watts, 1987.

Mason, James. *Before I Forget.* London: Hamish Hamilton, 1981.

Moore, Colleen. *Silent Star.* Garden City, N.Y.: Doubleday, 1968.

Morino, Marianne. *The Hollywood Walk of Fame.* Berkeley: Ten Speed Press, 1987.

Murphy, George, with Victor Lasky. *"Say...Didn't You Used To Be George Murphy?".* N.p.: Bartholomew House, 1970.

Nickens, Christopher. *Natalie Wood: A Biography in Photographs.* Garden City, N.Y.: Doubleday, 1986.

Nolan, William F. *McQueen.* New York: Congdon & Weed, 1984.

Oakie, Jack. *Jack Oakie's Double Takes.* San Francisco: Strawberry Hill Press, 1980.

O'Brien, Margaret. *My Diary.* Philadelphia: J.B. Lippincott, 1947.

Osborne, Robert. *60 Years of the Oscar: The Official History of the Academy Awards.* New York: Abbeville Press, 1989.

Parrish, Robert. *Growing Up in Hollywood.* New York: Harcourt Brace Jovanovich, 1976.

Pickford, Mary. *Sunshine and Shadow.* Garden City, N.Y.: Doubleday, 1955.

Reynolds, Debbie, with David Patrick Columbia. *Debbie—My Life.* New York: William Morrow, 1988.

Riese, Randall, and Neal Hitchens. *The Unabridged Marilyn: Her Life from A to Z.* New York: Congdon & Weed, 1987.

Robbins, Jhan. *Everybody's Man: A Biography of Jimmy Stewart.* New York: G. P. Putnam's Sons, 1985.

Russell, Jane. *Jane Russell: My Path & My Detours.* New York: Franklin Watts, 1985.

Russell, Rosalind, and Chris Chase. *Life Is a Banquet.* New York: Random House, 1977.

St. Johns, Adela Rogers. *Love, Laughter and Tears: My Hollywood Story.* Garden City, N.Y.: Doubleday, 1978.

Smith, H. Allen. *The Compleat Practical Joker.* Garden City, N.Y.: Doubleday, 1953.

Spada, James, with George Zeno. *Monroe: Her Life in Pictures.* Garden City, N.Y.: Doubleday, 1982.

Stack, Robert, with Mark Evans. *Straight Shooting.* New York: Macmillan, 1980.

Swanson, Gloria. *Swanson on Swanson.* New York: Random House, 1980.

Toffel, Neile McQueen. *My Husband, My Friend.* New York: Atheneum, 1986.

Torrence, Bruce T. *Hollywood: The First 100 Years.* Hollywood: Hollywood Chamber of Commerce and Fiske Enterprises, 1979.

von Ulm, Gerith. *Charlie Chaplin: King of Tragedy.* Caldwell, Idaho: Caxton Printers, 1940.

Walker, Joseph B., and Juanita Walker. *The Light on Her Face.* Hollywood: ASC Press, 1984.

Wiley, Mason, and Damien Bona. *Inside Oscar: The Unofficial History of the Academy Awards.* Edited by Gail MacColl. New York: Ballantine Books, 1986.

Zolotow, Maurice. *Shooting Star: A Biography of John Wayne.* New York: Simon & Schuster, 1974.

Zukor, Adolph, with Dale Kramer. *The Public Is Never Wrong.* New York: G.P. Putnam's Sons, 1953.

Pamphlets:

Grauman's Chinese Theatre Souvenir Brochure. 1953.

Helgesen, Terry. *Grauman's Chinese Theatre.* Circa 1969.

Mann's Chinese Theatre Souvenir Brochure. Circa 1979.

Mann's Chinese Theatre Souvenir Brochure. Boston, Mass: circa 1982.

A Shrine To Art: Grauman's Chinese Theatre Souvenir Brochure. 1938.

Periodicals:

Edmonds, I.G. "Prince of the Picture Palaces." *Westways,* March 1983.

"Filmland's Quaintest Custom—Immortalizing Stars in Cement!" *Screen Guide,* May 1938.

Programs:

Grauman's Chinese Theatre: Premiere of Cecil B. DeMille's "The King of Kings." Los Angeles: 1927.

Haver, Ronald. "Out of the Past: Mr. Grauman's Chinese Theatre." The First Los Angeles International Film Exposition. 1971.

Sound Recordings:

Lux Radio Theatre. "A Star Is Born." September 13, 1937. Transcription.

Clippings:

The newspapers, magazines, press releases, and studio house organs containing information came from:

The American Weekly, Box-Office, Buena Vista Distribution Co., Ltd. press releases, *Columbia News* (house organ), *Daily Variety, The Film Daily,* Hollywood Chamber of Commerce press releases, Hollywood *Citizen News, The Hollywood Reporter,* Indianapolis *Star* magazine, *Life, The Lion's Roar* (Metro-Goldwyn-Mayer house organ), Los Angeles *Daily News,* Los Angeles *Examiner,* Los Angeles *Herald-Express,* Los Angeles *Record,* Los Angeles *Times,* Milwaukee *Journal, Movie Star Parade,* National General Corp. press releases, *Newsweek,* Paramount Pictures, Inc. press releases, Pittsburgh *Post-Gazette,* Rogers & Cowan, Inc. press releases, San Francisco *Examiner, Showmanship, Sky: Delta Air Lines Magazine, Time,* 20th Century-Fox Film Corp. press releases, *20th Century-Fox News* (house organ), Universal Pictures press releases, *Variety,* Warner Bros. Pictures, Inc. press releases, Wichita *Eagle-Beacon,* and miscellaneous photograph captions.

Index

The Authors

Stacey Endres.

Robert Cushman.

Stacey Endres

Stacey Endres was born in Santa Monica, California. She was graduated from Santa Ana College in 1975 with an Associate Arts Degree in Library Technology. She then joined the staff of the Academy of Motion Picture Arts and Sciences' Margaret Herrick Library as a Library Assistant in charge of the Biography files.

During her career at the Academy, she has been acknowledged for her assistance in the researching and production of numerous books, articles, and events that deal with the subject of motion picture history. In 1989 she was made the Coordinator of Special Projects and Research Assistance, a newly-created position.

She lives in Studio City, California, with her husband, writer/producer/director Rudy Behlmer, and their Golden Retriever, Elsa.

Robert Cushman

Robert Cushman was born in Indianapolis, Indiana. He arrived in Los Angeles in 1965 to attend UCLA, where he majored in film, specializing in history, writing, and critical studies. He was graduated Magna Cum Laude in 1969 and was elected to Phi Beta Kappa.

He joined the staff of the Academy of Motion Picture Arts and Sciences' Margaret Herrick Library in 1972, in the then newly-created position of Coordinator of Photographic Services, which over the years evolved to that of Photograph Curator/Photographic Services Administrator. He is responsible for all aspects of the Library's photographic holdings of approximately 6,000,000 individual items.

He lives in the Angeleno Heights section of Los Angeles in an 1895 Queen Anne/Greek Revival style Victorian house.

HOLLYWOOD AT YOUR FEET

The Story of the World Famous Chinese Theatre
by
Stacey Endres and Robert Cushman

For Pomegranate Press, Ltd.

Kathryn Leigh Scott, Publisher/Editor
Benjamin R. Martin, Creative Director/Book Design
Heidi Frieder, Book Cover Design
Leroy Chen, Typography Consultant
Pamela C. White, Karena Kim, Production Assistants

This book was printed and bound in
The United States of America
by
McNaughton & Gunn, Inc.
960 Woodland Drive
Saline, Michigan 48176

The color separations for the cover
by
Southwest Color, Inc.
6720 Valjean Avenue
Van Nuys, California 91406

Forecourt of the Stars
Map Legend

75 - Abbott, Bud, and Lou Costello
103 - Ameche, Don
27 - Andrews, Julie
155 - Arnold, Edward
174 - Artoo-Detoo
106 - Astaire, Fred
7 - Autry, Gene
62 - Barrymore, John
73 - Bartholomew, Freddie
14 - Baxter, Anne
151 - Beery, Wallace
70 - Benny, Jack
113 - Bergen, Edgar
51 - Blondell, Joan
98 - Bogart, Humphrey
60 - Boyer, Charles
29 - Bradley, Tom (Mayor)
129 - Brain, Joe (Private)
96 - Brown, Joe E.
56 - Brynner, Yul
69 - Burns, George
161 - Bushman, Francis X.
132 - Cantinflas
89 - Cantor, Eddie
7 - Champion
113 - Charlie McCarthy
143 - Chevalier, Maurice
29 - Chinese Theatre's 50th Anniversary
133 - CinemaScope
74 - Cooper, Gary
100 - Cooper, Jackie
75 - Costello, Lou
134 - Crain, Jeanne
61 - Crawford, Joan
71 - Crosby, Bing
174 - Daniels, Anthony
91 - Daniels, Bebe
93 - Darnell, Linda
66 - Davies, Marion
154 - Davis, Bette
85 - Day, Doris
160 - de Havilland, Olivia
47 - DeMille, Cecil B.
169 - Donald Duck
168 - Doohan, James
3 - Douglas, Kirk
151 - Dressler, Marie
137 - Dunne, Irene
114 - Durante, Jimmy
111 - Durbin, Deanna

158 - Eastwood, Clint
127 - Eddy, Nelson
68 - Fairbanks, Douglas
54 - Faye, Alice
28 - Fleming, Rhonda
102 - Fonda, Henry
124 - Fontaine, Joan
167 - Ford, Harrison
49 - Gable, Clark
157 - Gardner, Ava
120 - Garland, Judy
170 - Garson, Greer
42 - Gaynor, Janet
165 - Grable, Betty
135 - Grant, Cary
121 - Grauman, Rosa
25 - Grauman, Sid
87 - Harding, Ann
149 - Harlow, Jean
136 - Harrison, Rex
40 - Hart, William S.
156 - Hayward, Susan
83 - Hayworth, Rita
2 - Heflin, Van
90 - Henie, Sonja
152 - Hersholt, Jean
9 - Heston, Charlton
12 - Hollywood's 100th Anniversary
139 - Hope, Bob
162 - Hudson, Rock
34 - Jessel, George
131 - Johnson, Van
109 - Jolson, Al
1 - Kaye, Danny
172 - Keaton, Michael
168 - Kelley, DeForest
123 - Kelly, Gene
57 - Kerr, Deborah
168 - Koenig, Walter
8 - Ladd, Alan
138 - Lamour, Dorothy
84 - Laughton, Charles
78 - Lemmon, Jack
44 - LeRoy, Mervyn
43 - Lloyd, Harold
174 - Lord Darth Vader
10 - Loren, Sophia
146 - Loy, Myrna
166 - Lucas, George
147 - Lundigan, William
144 - MacDonald, Jeanette

30 - MacGraw, Ali
16 - McLaglen, Victor
79 - MacLaine, Shirley
4 - McQueen, Steve
29 - Mann, Ted
53 - March, Fredric
19 - Martin, Dean
55 - Martin, Tony
140 - Marx Brothers
128 - Mason, James
11 - Mastroianni, Marcello
35 - Melchior, Lauritz
112 - Milland, Ray
99 - Mills, Hayley
41 - Miranda, Carmen
170 - Mrs. Miniver
171 - Mrs. Miniver
126 - Mix, Tom
23 - Monroe, Marilyn
39 - Moore, Colleen
173 - Murphy, Eddie
88 - Murphy, George
169 - Nash, Clarence "Ducky"
58 - Neff, Hildegarde
63 - Negri, Pola
81 - Nelson, Charles
148 - Newman, Paul
168 - Nichols, Nichelle
101 - Nicholson, Jack
168 - Nimoy, Leonard
86 - Oakie, Jack
20 - O'Brien, Margaret
77 - O'Connor, Donald
77 - O'Connor, Effie
32 - Parsons, Louella O.
15 - Peck, Gregory
67 - Pickford, Mary
33 - Pinza, Ezio
80 - Poitier, Sidney
52 - Powell, Dick
110 - Powell, Eleanor
145 - Powell, William
65 - Power, Tyrone
5 - Quinn, Anthony
122 - Raft, George
92 - Reynolds, Burt
13 - Reynolds, Debbie
94 - Rhoden, Elmer C.
118 - Ritz Brothers
133 - The Robe (1953)
59 - Robinson, Edward G.
130 - Robson, May

168 - Roddenberry, Gene
107 - Rogers, Ginger
115 - Rogers, Roy
104 - Rooney, Mickey
22 - Russell, Jane
31 - Russell, Rosalind
174 - See-Threepio
6 - Sellers, Peter
168 - Shatner, William
105 - Shearer, Norma
133 - Simmons, Jean
26 - Sinatra, Frank
150 - Skelton, Red
166 - Spielberg, Steven
159 - Stallone, Sylvester
48 - Stanwyck, Barbara
168 - "Star Trek's" 25th Anniversary (1966-1991)
174 - Star Wars (1977) characters
164 - Stevens, George
36 - Stewart, James
141 - Swanson, Gloria
168 - Takei, George
142 - Talmadge, Constance
46 - Talmadge, Norma
163 - Taylor, Elizabeth
48 - Taylor, Robert
95 - Temple, Shirley
24 - Thomas, Danny
38 - Tierney, Gene
126 - Tony
18 - Travolta, John
115 - Trigger
153 - Turner, Lana
125 - Vallée, Rudy
108 - Van Dyke, Dick
50 - Van Dyke, W.S.
37 - Walsh, Raoul
17 - Wayne, John
21 - Webb, Clifton
82 - Werner, Oskar
76 - Widmark, Richard
129 - Williams, Esther
72 - Withers, Jane
116 - Wood, Natalie
148 - Woodward, Joanne
97 - Woolley, Monty
117 - Wyman, Jane
119 - Wynyard, Diana
64 - Young, Loretta
45 - Zukor, Adolph

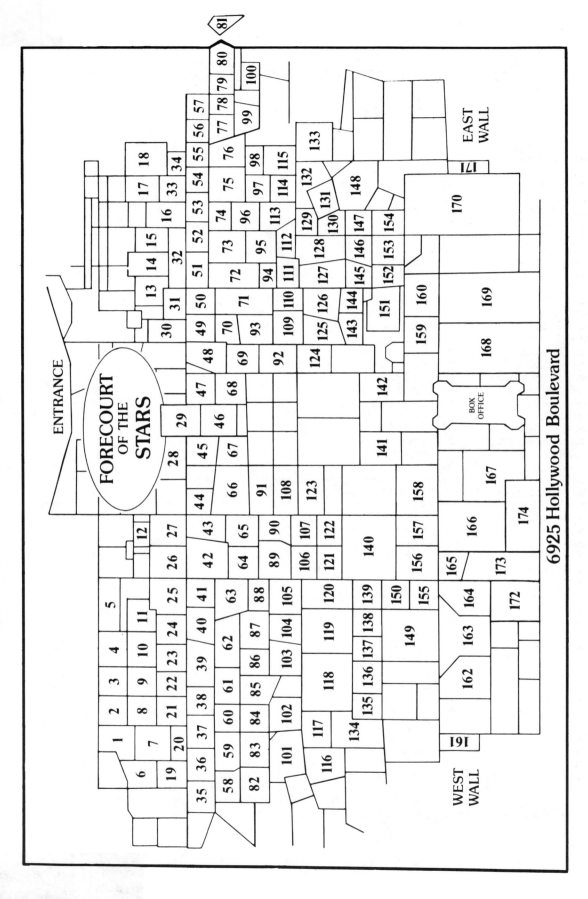

HOLLYWOOD'S CHINESE THEATRE

6925 Hollywood Boulevard